Fodor's

E X P L O R I N G

CARIBBEAN

FODOR'S TRAVEL PUBLICATIONS, INC.

NEW YORK • TORONTO • LONDON • SYDNEY • AUCKLAND

Copyright © 1994 by The Automobile Association.
Maps copyright © 1994 by The Automobile Association.

Published in the United States by Fodor's Travel Publications, Inc.
Published in the United Kingdom by AA Publishing.

Fodor's and Fodor's Exploring Guides are registered trademarks of Fodor's Travel Publications, Inc.

ISBN 0-679-02667-3
First Edition

Fodor's Exploring The Caribbean

Author: **James Hamlyn**
Series Adviser: **Ingrid Morgan**
Joint Series Editor: **Susi Bailey**
Cartography: **The Automobile Association**
Cover Design: **Louise Fili, Fabrizio La Rocca**
Front Cover Silhouette: **Catherine Karnow/Woodfin Camp**

Special Sales

Manufactured in Italy by LEGO SpA, Vicenza
10 9 8 7 6 5 4 3 2 1

James Hamlyn has traveled the islands of the Caribbean for the past five years. When not on the beach—or checking out the bars and restaurants—he takes photographs and writes travel features for the major British newspapers. This is his second travel guide devoted to the Caribbean.

Beach at Prickly Bay, Grenada

How to use this book

This book is divided into five main sections:

❏ Section 1:
The Caribbean Is
Discusses aspects of life and living today, from landscapes to religion

❏ Section 2:
The Caribbean Was
Places the region in its historical context and explores those past events whose influences are felt to this day

❏ Section 3: **A to Z Section**
Is broken down into regional chapters, and covers places to visit, including walks. Within this section fall the Focus-on articles, which consider a variety of subjects in greater detail

❏ Section 4: **Travel Facts**
Contains the strictly practical information vital for a successful trip

❏ Section 5:
Hotels and Restaurants
Lists recommended establishments throughout the Caribbean, giving a brief summary of their attractions

How to use the star ratings
Most of the places described in this book have been given a separate rating:

▶▶▶ **Do not miss**

▶▶ **Highly recommended**

▶ **Worth seeing**

Not essential to see

Some of the maps in this book use internationally agreed symbols to denote nation states:

BS	Bahamas
C	Cuba
CO	Colombia
CR	Costa Rica
DOM	Dominican Republic
HN	Honduras
NIC	Nicaragua
RH	Haiti
YV	Venezuela

Contents

Quick reference

This quick-reference guide highlights the features of the book you will use most often: the maps; the introductory features; the Focus-on articles; and the walks.

Sir Garfield Sobers
Best known as the captain of the West Indies cricket team for over 20 years, Gary was born and educated in Barbados. On his retirement from Test cricket in 1974 he held many of the longest-standing records in the sport. The author of several books, he now works for the Barbados Board of Tourism. He is shown above holding a new variety of heliconia, named after him.

My Barbados

by Sir Garfield Sobers

Although I have traveled extensively and lived happily in other countries, none compares to these 166 square miles in the Caribbean Sea. My heart lifts as soon as I pass through the airport, and hear the "slamming" of dominoes in the taxi area. (I am still proud to have been once ranked in the country's top three or four players!)

Barbados's combination of spectacular sightseeing, sporting activities and sizzling nightlife makes it unique. My favourite area is the east coast, where the Atlantic waves crash upon huge boulders and where clay-streaked hills complete a memorable scene. In the centre of the island is dazzling Harrison's Cave—don't miss it.

In terms of sporting facilities, I am thrilled with our state-of-the-art gymnasium, and Aquatic Centre with Olympic pool. But, Test cricket will always be my love, of course, and I would urge anyone of whatever nationality to see a match in Barbados.

In the evening, you can discover the exciting nightlife centred around St. Lawrence Gap. There, restaurants and clubs with live entertainment are all within easy reach. You may spot me in a bar, mingling with friends. You and I can then toast your visit to my beloved country.

My Jamaica

by Wilton Dyer

Mention Jamaica and I am sure the world's worst-kept secret springs to mind: a visitor's paradise, captivating land of beauty, and landscapes bathed in perennial sunshine are all conjured up.

Begin your enjoyment of this most special of places with a leisurely two-hour rafting journey along the majestic Rio Grande River, which meanders between lush vegetation and breath-taking scenery on the east of the island.

For the more adventurous and less sedentary, there is a range of exhilarating activities to be experienced, from water-sports to climbing Jamaica's daunting Blue Mountains.

My Jamaica, however, is very much that—and so much more, too: its multi-racial population of almost two-and-a-half million people of African, European, East Indian and Chinese origin is a model of racial harmony. A perfect example of an evolving democracy, Jamaica's proven political stability belies its 30-odd years of independence.

My Jamaica is a country with great sporting traditions and a cultural heritage (disproportionate to its size of 4,411 square miles) that casts a long shadow on the global stage.

Our music is one such world famous art form. Casual reference to the late Bob Marley brings instant, pleasant recognition and announces your nationality to almost any stranger you might run into in any corner of the world.

But the essence of my Jamaica is the oft-repeated warmth, friendliness, courteousness, helpfulness and resilience of its people.

Wilton Dyer
Currently working for the Jamaica High Commission in London, England, Wilton Dyer was born and grew up in Jamaica.

Swimmers off the south coast of Barbados

THE CARIBBEAN IS

■ .With its endless beaches, swaying palm trees and a warm turquoise sea, the Caribbean does, surprisingly, live up to its idyllic image. But the landscapes extend far beyond the travel agent's clichés—from sheer volcanic mountains and lush rainforests to inhospitable deserts; and Caribbean life has been changed beyond recognition within a relatively short space of time. .....■

Top: St. Vincent. Above: Shaw Park Gardens, Ocho Rios, Jamaica

Stretching in an arc from the bottom of Florida to the top of South America, the Caribbean archipelago is as varied as it is beautiful. Islands range in size from Cuba (4,124 sq. miles) to tiny Saba (3 sq. miles); mountains soar to over 2 miles in the Dominican Republic, and flat sandspits barely reach sea level. There are extensive rainforests in Puerto Rico and Dominica and barren cactus-filled wildernesses in Haiti. Even on one island, the landscape may change around each corner, as mangrove swamp gives way to pasture land and pine forests replace palm trees. Intensive agriculture and tourist development are gradually altering the Caribbean's contours and climate. Blessed with warm weather all the year round and cooled by the Trade Winds, the region is also occasionally cursed by violent rainstorms and hurricanes.

Known for its coral reefs and its beaches (every island naturally claims the best), the Caribbean also boasts waterfalls, hot springs, and caves. Two of the more bizarre geological attractions are Trinidad's Pitch Lake, a seemingly inexhaustible pool of hot black tar (see page 232), and Jamaica's Cockpit Country, an inhospitable area of limestone hills and hollows, still populated by descendants of runaway slaves (see page 149).

Changing nature Man has left an indelible impression on the Caribbean landscape. Once covered in virgin rainforest, most of the islands are scarred by deforestation and erosion. In Haiti, the island described by Columbus as the most beautiful he had ever seen, tree-felling and over-farming have created virtual deserts where drought and famine are constant threats.

Strangely, little of the flora and fauna that makes up the typical Caribbean landscape is indigenous to the region. Sugar cane, which still flourishes on many islands, was introduced from the Mediterranean by Spanish colonists. Other crops (bananas, citrus fruits) and animals (cattle, dogs, horses) came to the Caribbean from Asia and Europe.

Different worlds The past has shaped the look of the Caribbean through a variety of influences. Cities, towns, and villages bear the unmistakable imprint of former colonial powers. Spanish-built Havana, with its colonnades and plazas, seems a different world from British-built Bridgetown, where a statue of Nelson watches over a "tropical Anglican" cathedral.

Differing histories have also molded the countryside itself. In the formerly Spanish colonies of Cuba, Puerto Rico, and the Dominican Republic, sugar plantations stretch to

❏ The Caribbean is one of the world's last bastions of colonialism. Martinique and Guadeloupe are technically French departments; Aruba, Bonaire and Curaçao remain tied to the Netherlands; Britain still maintains Montserrat, Anguilla and the Cayman Islands as dependent territories. Puerto Rico is a "free and associated state" of the U.S.A., but may soon vote to become the 51st state of the union. ❏

the horizon as they have for 500 years. In Haiti, however, where a slave revolution expelled the French at the beginning of the 19th century, precarious smallholdings have replaced the hated plantations.

Despite the proximity of the U.S., European influence is still keenly felt. In the French *départements d'out-remer* of Martinique and Guadeloupe you can buy baguettes, drink *pastis* and see policemen in *képis*. There is no mistaking the Dutch style of Curaçao or Aruba, where pastel-painted gabled warehouses line the canal and port like a tropical Amsterdam. And Britain has left much of the paraphernalia of colonial rule in its former possessions: red mailboxes, English place names and, of course, cricket fields.

11

A dramatic Caribbean sunset over the shores of Tobago

THE CARIBBEAN IS *People*

■ **"Out of many one people"** is Jamaica's national motto, and it applies just as well to the rest of the Caribbean. The region's population is a rich mixture of African, European, American, and Asian, a "melting pot" legacy of slavery, colonialism, and migration. This ethnic mix has created a unique Creole culture, but a strict racial hierarchy still exists. .....■

The Caribbean's people are all strangers in paradise. The original indigenous population disappeared within half a century of European conquest. Subsequently, people have come, willingly or not, from every corner of the earth. This process included one of history's biggest forced migrations—the importation of some five million Africans into the Caribbean's plantation economy.

Arawaks and Caribs
Little remains of the people who predated the Caribbean's "discovery" 500 years ago. Certain Amerindian words have entered our vocabulary—barbecue, hammock, manioc, for instance—but none of the placid Arawaks survived the cultural devastation of the

Top: children in Montego Bay, Jamaica
Right: a flower-seller in Jamaica gracefully balancing her load

conquest. Today, only a handful of Carib descendants are still to be found in Dominica and St. Vincent, scraping a living by selling their handicrafts to visiting tourists.

Europeans Europe conquered, colonized and re-created the Caribbean in its own image. The first European settlers named cities, villages, and rivers after more familiar places at home. But with few exceptions, the physical legacy of European domination is confined to the Spanish-speaking islands of Cuba, the Dominican Republic, and Puerto Rico, which received influxes of European immigration well into the present century. Each island has its paler-skinned elite, but Europeans as such make up a tiny minority in Caribbean societies. The exceptions to the rule are the "poor whites" of Barbados, a community descended from indentured British laborers

that has so far refused to intermix at all with other Barbadian communities.

Africans The great majority of Caribbean people are at least in part descended from the millions of Africans who crossed the notorious "middle passage." Africa is alive in all dimensions of local life: music, language, religion, and cooking. "Jamaica Talk," for instance, the island's patois, is largely based on West African Ashanti dialect, while African speech and customs are commonplace in Haiti and around the eastern tip of Cuba.

Indians No visitor to Trinidad could fail to notice that 40 percent of the island's population is East Indian in origin. The shops and restaurants of Port of Spain are filled with the sounds, sights, and scents of the Indian subcontinent, while in the countryside Hindu prayer flags surround peasant homes. In Guyana, slightly more than half the population is Indian, descended from the indentured laborers of the 19th century.

Inequalities This rich diversity of race and color conceals massive inequalities, within and between individual countries. In Haiti, for instance, the one percent of lighter-skinned mulattos dominates the black majority. In most other countries, a so-called "pigmentocracy" exists, equating light skin with economic and political power. After more than 30 years of independent government, Jamaica's P. J. Patterson is the first black politician to hold the post of Prime Minister.

Even more striking is the disparity between Caribbean countries. Some, notably Haiti and the Dominican Republic, are among the world's poorest, while others, including Puerto Rico, the Bahamas and the Virgin Islands enjoy relatively high levels of prosperity. Economic hardship has prompted many to leave the Caribbean's poorer countries to live and work in North America and Europe. Perhaps one in seven Dominicans lives in the U.S., and almost as many Puerto Ricans live on the U.S. mainland as in Puerto Rico. In the 1950s, nearly 10 percent of all Jamaicans emigrated to Britain. These exile communities provide a lifeline to the Caribbean islanders.

A Trinidad palm-weaver

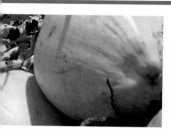

■ **Mangoes, soursops, papaya, yams, breadfruit, callaloo...the list of Caribbean fruit and vegetables is never-ending. Drop a seed in the soil, and you'll have a tree inside a week, say local farmers. But despite extraordinary fertility, Caribbean agriculture faces critical problems: what to do with crops that nobody wants, and what to put in their place. .....■**

The market is the center of Caribbean social and economic life. By bus or on foot, the marketwomen arrive before dawn to set up their displays of fresh fruit and vegetables. Whether in the town square or simply at a rural crossroads, the market and its mostly female workforce display the vibrancy of the region's tropical agriculture. Vast piles of mysterious tubers (widely known as "ground provisions") sit side by side with bunches of green bananas and plantains, the Caribbean's starchy staples. Red-hot peppers, tangy limes, and enormous avocados are some of the other marketplace offerings. Beyond the market, most people seem to have a small piece of land, if only enough to grow a few fruit trees. While there is widespread poverty in the Caribbean, few people actually go hungry.

The Caribbean is still a largely agricultural region, but important changes are taking place in what is grown and where it goes. From the earliest colonial days, the region was an exporter of agricultural commodities, most importantly sugar. In its 18th-century heyday, Saint-Domingue (now Haiti) exported more raw sugar and created more wealth than the whole of the vast British empire. Sugar, the fabled "white gold," made fortunes, provoked wars and brought millions of Africans across the Atlantic in slave-ships.

❏ In 1975 a pound of sugar fetched 76 cents on the world market; in 1982 it was worth only 5 cents. ❏

The discovery of European sugar-beet, global overproduction, and changing dietary tastes have long since undermined the Caribbean sugar industry. Only Cuba is still heavily dependent on sugar exports, while other islands have moved away into other agro-industries. Bananas are the modern-day boom crop, especially in Dominica and St. Lucia, where they represent up to 70 percent of export earnings. Bananas grow everywhere in these small volcanic islands: up steep slopes, around every house, by the roadside. They are mostly cultivated on small-holdings by individual farmers, who pack them into boxes and drive them down pot-holed roads to port. After a long period of special access into the British market, Caribbean bananas are now under fire from the big plantation-based producers of Latin America who grow cheaper, if not better fruit. If local fears that Latin America can outproduce and under-sell the Caribbean are realized, the region will lose yet another essential agricultural market.

Fragile fruit Worries about the future of the banana industry reveal the vulnerability of Caribbean agriculture. Worse even than hurricanes are unstable world commodity markets, over which small producers have no control. Every crop—sugar, coffee, cocoa, tobacco—has seen its ups and downs, and an uncertain future awaits the new "exotic non-traditionals" which farmers are now trying to export to Europe and the U.S. The current generation of export crops includes ginger, mangoes, passion fruit, and cut flowers, much of it des-

tined for the so-called "ethnic niche market" in large U.S. cities.

Fishing Lobster, red snapper, and flying fish are to be found on restaurant menus throughout the Caribbean. But despite extensive coastlines and local demand, most Caribbean coun-

Fish for sale on Aruba

tries have to import fish. Partly because of inadequate marine nutrients and partly through poor storage and marketing, the islands depend on salted and canned fish from Canada. Attempts to upgrade the fishing industry, largely funded by Japan, are under way, but experts warn that the Caribbean sea cannot withstand high-tech, intensive fishing.

■ High in the hills of Haiti, rhythmic drumbeats in the night, animal sacrifices, and entranced dancers swirling around a crackling bonfire are all part of the island's most famous and mysterious religion: voodoo. It is just one of the many religious faiths in a region which claims more churches per capita than anywhere else in the world. .....■

A Baptist worshipper on Tobago. The Caribbean islands accommodate a vast range of religious sects and denominations

Religion is part and parcel of the Caribbean, from continuous radio and TV broadcasts to tiny ramshackle churches on every street corner. There are mosques in Trinidad, Hindu temples in Guyana, and pilgrimage sites in the Dominican Republic. With significant communities of Jews, Muslims, and Hindus, the region is influenced by most major faiths. It is also a prime target for U.S.-based evangelical sects.

Christians Most Caribbean people would describe themselves as Christians. European colonizers brought differing Christian beliefs, a fact reflected in the islands' many churches. Catholicism is officially the main faith of Haiti and the Dominican Republic, is widely practiced in the eastern Caribbean and is now tolerated in Cuba. Anglicanism holds sway in the former British colonies of Jamaica and Barbados. The influence of U.S. Protestant groups is increasingly powerful throughout the Caribbean, and these sects have joined the myriad existing churches. In Barbados, for example, it is estimated that no fewer than 140 different denominations are active, one for every 2,000 Barbadians.

African religions Christianity was the religion of the masters; the slaves had their own faiths, brought with them from Africa. Religious beliefs and practices survived the horrors of slavery, preserving the slaves' identity and memories of their homelands. Over time, these beliefs merged with Christian religion to create new forms of faith and ceremony. These have different names on different islands (santería

in Cuba, pocomania in Jamaica), but the best known is voodoo in Haiti, where religious activity is evident in all walks of life. Each tiny village has its quota of churches—Catholic, Methodist, Baptist, and hundreds more—and every church has its faithful congregation. But there are no open signs of Haiti's other religious phenomenon. As an old joke has it, Haitians are 99 percent Christian and 100 percent voodooist. Even so, voodoo remains largely invisible to foreigners, although visitors have ample opportunity to see suitably arranged versions of the authentic ceremonies (see pages 178–9).

Rastafarianism Popularized in the 1970s and '80s by reggae stars, Rastafarianism has its roots in Jamaica and followers on many other islands. The cult expresses many people's longing for an African identity by invoking Ethiopia as the holy land and the late Emperor Haile Selassie as a god, and promotes the smoking of ganja (marijuana) as a religious sacrament (see page 161).

Radicals in religion Many priests in the Caribbean have long since left the pulpit to get involved in social and political issues. The churches have traditionally been active in health and education, and since "liberation theology" spread from Latin America in the 1970s, they have become more politically outspoken. In Haiti, a radical Salesian priest, Jean-Bertrand Aristide, was elected president in 1991, only to be overthrown by the army nine months later. In many Caribbean countries, religion and politics are becoming increasingly intertwined.

THE CARIBBEAN IS *Politics*

■ **Caribbean politics are anything but dull. Most people love a political argument, and insults can often fly thick and fast. Elections are usually a pretext for a party, while parliamentary procedure is guaranteed to be good entertainment. The Caribbean has had—and still has—its share of unrest, but most islands enjoy healthy democracies and lively debate. .....■**

The region's differing political systems are an integral part of its mixed cultural heritage. The British bequeathed the "Westminster model" of parliamentary democracy, and all English-speaking islands hold regular elections. The British Queen is still nominally head of state in most Commonwealth countries, represented by a Governor General. The Spanish islands, meanwhile, have tended to adopt a presidential system, with a greater tradition of "strong man" leadership.

Party games Most independent Caribbean territories have a multi-party electoral system of government. Elections are normally peaceful, albeit fiercely contested events. On small islands, personalities are often as important as policies, especially when most electors know the candidates personally! Rivalry occasionally leads to violence, especially in Jamaica, where "political tribalism" caused around 800 deaths in the 1980 election campaign. But political violence is not common, and most states are proud of their constitutional credentials.

Hot spots Of all the Caribbean territories, only two are generally agreed to have undemocratic governments. Cuba has been dominated by Fidel Castro and the Communist Party since the 1959 revolution and has ever since alienated the U.S. by refusing to hold free elections. Once the scene of a near-nuclear confrontation between the U.S. and the former U.S.S.R. in 1962, Cuba has become increasingly isolated. Economically strangled by the U.S.

boycott, the island is currently suffering its worst spate of shortages since 1958.

Haiti has had the most turbulent political history of all the Caribbean nations. Wracked by instability and dictatorship since a slave revolution won independence from France in 1804, the country was ruled by the ruthless Duvaliers until 1986. When "Baby Doc" was finally forced to flee the country, a movement for democracy evolved, culminating in the overwhelming election triumph of a radical Roman Catholic priest, Jean-Bertrand Aristide, in 1991. After nine months he was ousted by the military, who were intent on preserving their power despite international opposition. In 1993 the United Nations imposed sanctions in an attempt to restore Aristide to the presidency.

Backyard politics With the end of the Cold War, the Caribbean has lost much of its geopolitical importance in the eyes of U.S. policy-makers. The U.S. invasion of Grenada in October 1983 was an indication of how seriously the White House viewed the rise of radicalism in its "backyard." Since then, left-wing movements have lost much of their support and conservatives are in power on most English-speaking islands.

Trading places Current political controversy tends to concern the region's position in the world economy. With the imminent arrival of the North American Free Trade Agreement between the U.S., Canada, and Mexico, Caribbean states fear that they will be marginal-

QUIEN SE ATRE...QUEDA

ized in terms of trade and influence. As a result, there is now more talk of Caribbean integration and cooperation than ever before, as politicians recognize that only a united front will help weather economic storms.

Government House, St. Thomas

■ **They come in their millions every year. Twelve million arrived by plane in 1992, nine million by cruise ship. Tourists are the new lifeblood of the Caribbean, bringing vital dollars and jobs into the region. The locals may shudder at the complexions, laugh at the poolside limbo lessons, but they know that, for better or worse, tourism represents economic survival. .....■**

With the advent of charter flights and purpose-built hotels, Caribbean tourism is no longer the preserve of the wealthy. In the 1950s only the rich and famous could afford to go to the Caribbean, normally island-hopping by yacht. Now a few hundred dollars or pounds will buy an all-inclusive package deal to Antigua, Barbados, or Jamaica. All the islands are chasing the tourist jackpot; the Caribbean's fastest-growing vacation destination is Cuba.

A modern-day "pirate ship" caters for tourists

Tourism brings an estimated $10 billion into the Caribbean economies. In the Dominican Republic, tourist earnings in 1992 exceeded all exports put together. The industry is the biggest earner in Jamaica, Barbados, and several smaller islands. Overall, economists believe that it has created 300,000 direct jobs throughout the region. Add to this the thousands more who sell agricultural produce to hotels, who make handcrafted goods and who act as "guides," and the figure may be nearer a million.

Cruising Twice a week, the sleepy port of St. George's, Grenada, springs into frenetic action as the cruise ship arrives. As the tourists gingerly step onto *terra firma*, they are greeted by a horde of taxi-drivers, guides, vendors, and scalpers. Few of the hopeful locals will make a fortune. On average, each tourist spends a paltry $20 before returning to the safety of the cruise ship. A cruise tour may cost thousands, but little of that money reaches the islands themselves.

Spending Understandably, Caribbean governments and businesses prefer "stay-over" tourists, who spend time and money in their destinations. The multitude of restaurants, shopping malls, and souvenir stands that line the tourist resorts are proof of this single-minded pursuit of foreign currency. But foreign ownership of airlines and hotels often means that bills are paid outside the Caribbean, reducing the hoped-for "trickle down" effect. More worrying still is the growing popularity of all-inclusive club vacations, where guests pay a single price that covers every drink or surfboard lesson. This, the local restaurateurs will tell you, is not a major incentive to go out and spread the money around.

The Golden Lemon Hotel on St. Kitts, in the Leeward Islands

Blessing or curse? Tourism has brought welcome employment and investment to otherwise stagnant economies. For many young locals, work as a waiter or cleaner is a much better prospect than traditional farming. But tourism's impact is not all positive. Many older people complain that hustling, drugs, and petty crime have become a way of life for the young. Others feel that jealousy and resentment are inevitable consequences of the First World–Third World divide. More seriously, tourism is a shaky bet for sustainable development, as it is notoriously vulnerable to economic instability in the sender countries. The recent recession in North America and Europe sent Caribbean tourism revenues plummeting.

Beyond the beach Eco-tourism is the new buzzword in the local industry. Realizing that people can become bored with sand and sea, operators are now offering vacations which appeal to the adventurous and environmentally aware. You can dive among coral reefs in Belize, explore rainforests in Dominica or hike through mountains in Jamaica. Advocates of eco-tourism praise it as an intelligent use of natural resources; critics point out that it actually destroys the very nature that it sets out to market.

■ **Caribbean food can be as bland or as exciting as you choose it to be. McDonalds, Kentucky Fried Chicken and all the other familiar names are in evidence. But step outside the tourist circuit and there is food to daunt the most adventurous gastronome. Some iguana, perhaps? Or goat's offal? And don't forget the rum—the world's best. .....■**

Real Caribbean food reflects the many diverse influences, historical and cultural, which have shaped the region. The hearty breakfast lives on in Jamaica, but you may be offered mackerel and banana along with your bacon and eggs. In Trinidad and Guyana, the spicy *roti*, a chapati pancake filled with curry, is an unmistakable taste of India. Meanwhile, the French territories of Martinique and Guadeloupe claim the Caribbean's most sophisticated cuisine. A classic dish is red snapper cooked with white wine, garlic, and limes. The hamburger may have made serious inroads into regional tastes, but the lingering imprints of Europe, Africa, and India are still very much in evidence. Local supermarkets are inevitably stocked with North American brands, but don't be surprised to see Camembert in Martinique, Gouda in Curaçao or pudding mix in Barbados.

Variety Most of the Caribbean islands share a few basic dishes. Rice 'n' peas (or red beans) is a staple everywhere and especially good when cooked in coconut water. Root vegetables are a cheap filler, boiled or fried, and go by literally hundreds of different names across the region. Bananas and plantains are ubiquitous, as are the common fruits such as guava, pineapple, and mango. But on top of these staples, each island has developed its own often idiosyncratic recipes. In Jamaica the national favorites are curry goat (often beef) and saltfish and ackees. The latter dish harks back to the era of slavery when salted fish was imported from Canada to feed the island's slave population. The small island of Dominica specializes in "mountain chicken," which on closer inspection turns out to be a local frog. In the Dominican Republic, *mondongo*, a tripe stew, is considered a miracle cure for a hangover.

Rum There is, of course, ample opportunity to acquire a hangover. Every Caribbean island produces rum, ranging from mass-market brands to local firewater. Some of the so-called overproof rum (140 proof) is a serious risk to health, especially when mixed into apparently innocuous cocktails. Perhaps the best way to sample the better rums is with ice and lime juice, the basis of the classic Planter's Punch. Although each island predictably claims to make the best, the better quality rums are generally those from Cuba, Haiti, Jamaica, and Barbados.

Beer The Caribbean is not a wine-producing area, but every island, however small, has its own brewery. Some international brands such as Budweiser and Guinness are widely available, but locals swear—often correctly—that their beer is better. Perhaps the best known is Jamaica's Red Stripe, but other superior brews are Barbados' Banks, Trinidad's Carib and St. Vincent's Hairoun. Less known and arguably the best is Presidente from the Dominican Republic, which often comes served in iced glasses.

Hunger For the tourist, hunger is less of a risk than a gradually expanding waistline. Nor are many people in the main tourist islands likely to go hungry. Hardship is largely restricted to Cuba, where rationing and embargo have drastically reduced dietary intakes, and Haiti, the hemisphere's poorest nation. Equally worrying is the growing dependency of Caribbean countries on importing basic foods in order to feed their own populations. While most countries are now desperate to export their "exotic non-traditionals," they are forced to import basic ingredients such as rice, beans, and sugar for local consumption. This means that the Caribbean is now increasingly consuming what it does not produce and producing what it does not consume.

One of the Caribbean's national dishes: ackees

Recommended specialties

Antigua Goat water (hot goat stew) and fungi (cornmeal dumplings).

Barbados Flying fish, dolphin (dorado, not the mammal), pickled breadfruit and blood sausage.

Cuba *Moros y cristianos*—the local name for rice'n'peas. Otherwise food is hard to come by and often rather unpalatable.

Curaçao *Rijsttafel* ("rice table," a collection of up to 40 different meat and vegetable dishes, originally from Indonesia).

Dominican Republic *Mondongo*, *sancoche* (a stew of six different meats and vegetables), *casabe* (cassava bread).

Grenada *Soue* (pig's feet stew), armadillo, iguana. Grenada is also famous for its spices, nutmeg, and mace.

Haiti *Griot* (deep-fried pork) and most French-influenced sauces.

Jamaica Saltfish and ackees, curry goat and jerk chicken, barbecued and sold from roadside stalls. Jamaica also produces the world-famous Blue Mountain coffee.

Martinique and Guadeloupe *Tiboudin* (spicy sausage), *poulet au coco* (chicken with coconut).

Puerto Rico *Pastillas* (pork and yucca wrapped in a banana leaf and boiled). Puerto Rico is also a center for U.S. fast food, including *servicarro* (drive-in service).

Trinidad *Roti*, *pelau* (rice and curry).

Cooling drinks are a treat and often a necessity in the Caribbean heat

THE CARIBBEAN WAS

■ **Long before Columbus "discovered" the Caribbean islands, Native Americans had started clearing the ground to build their villages and plant their crops. Tribes of Arawaks and Caribs had been living on the Caribbean shores of South America since about 5000 B.C., but by 1000 B.C. the Arawaks were fleeing their aggressive neighbors and driving out Jamaica's earliest settlers, the Ciboneys. .....■**

Three groups of Arawak settlers established villages on the islands: the Tainos, on Jamaica, Cuba, and Haiti; the Lucayanos, in the Bahamas; and the Borequinos, on Puerto Rico. For a few hundred years they enjoyed a gentle, peaceful life, left alone by Carib warriors. But the Caribs eventually caught up and by the late 15th century, when Columbus arrived, their canoe raids and violent attacks were a constant threat to the islanders.

Amerindian life While the Arawaks learned skills such as basket-weaving and traded their crops—cassava, maize, sweet potatoes, cotton, and pepper—from island to island, the Caribs sent raiding parties to loot villages for slaves and supplies. Their expertise in making and using weapons was formidable; Caribs were fast and accurate bowmen, shooting fire- or poison-tipped arrows, and they used a variety of clubs and spears with gruesome added extras such as sharpened flints. Nevertheless, they did develop some talents other than maiming and killing. Caribs were fine potters; each settlement had its own "trademark," often in the form of an animal, which was carved onto its pots.

Arawak communities were based on the family, with a *cacique* (clan chief) ruling each group of villages, helped by a committee of elders or *nitayanos*. They were also religious leaders, in touch with the ancestral and natural spirits and sometimes acting as their mouthpiece, inhaling tobacco fumes to induce a trance and conveying advice or predictions

Amerindians sowing maize

from the spirit world. *Zemis*, wooden or bone figures representing the gods of nature, were housed in special huts, set apart from the ordinary round, thatched homes of the villagers. Religious worship involved dancing, games, and tobacco-smoking; the powdered leaf was lit inside a forked tube (*tabaco*), which was wedged up the nostrils. Caves were used as burial sites by some clans (bones, canoe paddles, and *zemis* have been excavated); carvings of symbols and mask-like faces can still be seen covering cave walls and rocks on several Caribbean islands.

Fighters and killers were the respected members of Carib society. Chief warriors were elected on the basis of their performance in battle, and religious activities revolved around appeasing a vengeful god.

❑ Gold was one of the commodities traded by Arawaks, but it was prized only as an ornament. Carib warriors decorated their bodies with paint, petals, coral bracelets, and anklets, and shells or bones were worn in pierced ears, lips, and noses. Arawaks used dyed clay and grease to cover their bodies, and would bind their babies' heads to give them long, tough skulls. ❑

When European settlers arrived in the Caribbean they painted a grim picture of the Caribs as vicious cannibals who were liable to make a meal out of anyone straying onto their territory. In fact, any cannibalism which did take place is likely to have been ceremonial; fat from the body of a brave captive would be rubbed over Carib boys to give them courage. Even so, Carib society was undeniably brutal, and prisoners were starved and tortured before eventually being killed and served up, as a test of their endurance.

Both Arawaks and Caribs relied to a great extent on the Caribbean's abundant marine life for much of their food, but any edible creature was regarded as fair game. Lizards, snails, and turtle eggs were all snapped up; birds were caught in nets strung between branches, and fish were hooked, speared, or even stunned by poison bark thrown into the water. Each day's catch would be added to a pepperpot, a seasoned stew that was left to simmer for weeks. Pepperpots—now with different ingredients—can still be sampled on Grenada (see page 52).

Symbols from a vanished world: Arawak rock carvings in Puerto Rico

■ After five weeks of sailing the uncharted Atlantic, Christopher Columbus and his unhappy crew were within hours of giving up their voyage of exploration when land was sighted on October 12, 1492. The sailors who believed they had found Japan were actually heading for the Bahamas, and were about to begin an unprecedented era of wealth, war, and oppression. .....■

28

Columbus was born in Genoa in the late 1440s. He became an avid sea-voyager and a collector of maps and charts and by the 1480s, convinced that Japan and the riches of the "East Indies" could be reached by sailing west, he set about searching for the finances to back an expedition. Portugal and Britain turned him down—they had their own ideas for finding new trade routes. The Spanish monarchs, Ferdinand and Isabella, made Columbus wait five years while they drove the last of the Moors from the country; then they agreed to take up his plan, eager to spread the influence of Spain and of the Catholic church, and to break the long-established Arab monopoly of trading routes to the Indies.

Columbus set out with his fleet of three ships—the *Nina*, the *Pinta* and his flagship, the *Santa Maria*—on August 3, 1492. By the time land was sighted he was having trouble preventing mutiny; the worried crew was threatening to throw Columbus overboard and head back home. After naming his first "discovery" San Salvador, the explorer persuaded some of its Arawak inhabitants—who welcomed the newcomers as protection against the Caribs—to come aboard and direct him towards Hispaniola. Here, the *Santa Maria* ran aground, leaving 40 Spaniards to build the first European fort in the Caribbean. Columbus was disappointed at the scarcity of pure gold and spices on the islands, but

Columbus is greeted by Arawak islanders on San Salvador

returned to Spain in triumph with a few "Indians," plants and tobacco leaves as promise of wonders yet to emerge.

A second voyage followed in 1493, with a much larger fleet, bringing builders and farmers to create new settlements and priests to convert the unsuspecting natives. Many of the settlers were convicted criminals, pardoned on condition that they join the fleet. Before long the colonists—who had no prospect of returning home—had started to abuse the Arawaks, demanding food and taxes of gold and cotton, stealing the women and forcing the men into slavery. War soon broke out, and within three years, most of the 200,000 or so "Amerindians" were dead, overwhelmed by Spanish guns

Explorer and treasure-seeker: a 16th-century Spanish portrayal of Christopher Columbus

and swords or by the smallpox that the settlers had brought with them. The Europeans established a capital in Santo Domingo and a row of forts to protect their new colony.

Columbus himself returned to Spain after charting a course to Jamaica and Cuba; five years later he was back again, determined to find the mainland—which he did, after visiting Trinidad and quelling a rebellion among the Hispaniola colonists. The ambitious admiral was intensely disliked, however, and a commissioner sent by Queen Isabella to investigate complaints promptly had him arrested and shipped back to Spain. A fourth voyage also ended in disaster: after sailing along the Central American coast, Columbus's ships were wrecked off the shores of Jamaica, and the explorer and his stranded sailors had to wait for a year before a ship could be sent to rescue them.

Columbus died in 1506, having failed to supply the unlimited riches which had been promised. But a new world had been opened to Spain, with gold reserves to be mined, crops to be farmed and souls to be saved—at the expense of many hundreds of thousands of lives.

❏ Columbus was eager to exploit the native Americans as free labor, and many were set to work mining for gold. The Spanish monarchy, however, disapproved of enslaving potential converts to Christianity, and would only sanction slavery for criminals or captured warriors. European accounts of Amerindian atrocities and cannibalism were often invented to justify the taking of slaves. ❏

■ **Anxious to reap the benefits of Columbus's voyages, Ferdinand and Isabella persuaded Pope Alexander VI to give them legal possession of the Americas. Under the Treaty of Tordesillas (1494), a boundary was drawn up dividing the "New World" between Spain and Portugal, and excluding the rest of Europe from claims to its territories. .....■**

The Caribbean was to be a stepping stone for further exploration, and Spain was to have a strict monopoly over trade with the new colonies; but naturally developments did not go according to plan. In the years after Columbus's last voyage, thousands

30

Pirates attack a Spanish ship

of settlers arrived from Spain, eager to find gold, to own land and to be given power over a workforce of Amerindians under the royal grants known as *encomiendas*. Their vicious treatment of the Arawaks was bitterly condemned by Antionio de

Montesions, a Dominican friar, and by an ex-*encomendero*, Bartolomé de las Casas. Eventually their outspoken attacks on the abuse of Amerindians led to two sets of laws, passed by two successive kings. In 1512 Ferdinand assented to the Laws of Burgos, dictating limited working hours and the provision of food rations for Arawak laborers; and in 1542 Charles V put an end to new grants of *encomiendas* under the New Laws. But Spain had little control over the actions of its Caribbean colonists, and by the 1520s so many Amerindians had been killed off by overwork and hunger that the settlers were already beginning to ship in African slaves to take their place.

In the meantime, the search continued for richer lands, and groups of armed *conquistadores* set out to stake new claims. Ponce de Léon led a party of men to conquer Puerto Rico, massacring the Borequino inhabitants and clearing the land for plantations and ranches. Diego Velasquez took three years to wipe out the Amerindians on Cuba, and by 1520 the *conquistadores* had reached Mexico and the rich prizes of the Aztec Empire.

When word got out that the Spanish had struck gold on the mainland, hordes of settlers left the Caribbean islands and made for wider, wealthier territories. At the same time, sailors from other European countries saw an opportunity for easy money. Spanish claims to exclusive rights over the spoils of their settlements were ignored, as pirates attacked their ships and ports. Their cargoes were also looted

by privateers, sea captains who were authorized by their governments to plunder enemy ships in time of war, and the European powers were in an almost constant state of warfare during the 17th and 18th centuries.

Spain's monopoly on trade with the colonies could not be maintained. Apart from pirate attacks, the system was unwieldy and inefficient. Caribbean settlers would be kept

waiting for months on end, while fleets of Spanish ships loaded up with goods underwent rigorous checks at the Customs Office in Seville. Impatient with restrictions imposed by a distant state, colonists were soon doing a brisk illegal trade with ships from Britain, France, and the Netherlands, and there was little that Spain could do to stop them. Unofficial trade has continued to be part of Caribbean life from the 16th century to the present day.

A buccaneer pictured in 1905

■ Looting Spanish ships was a quick and risky business, and by the early 17th century the rival European powers were considering ways of earning long-term profits from Caribbean lands. While Spanish island colonies dwindled, forgotten by their home country, British and French adventurers were trying their luck at building settlements of their own. .....■

Early experiments in tobacco-growing on the Guyana coast had been dismal failures; the small groups of British and French planters were soon defeated by fever and Carib attacks. In 1622 one of the Guyana colonists, Thomas Warner, decided to try the fresher climate and fertile soil of the Lesser Antilles and set up

take up their own plots of land. In the meantime, France was turning its attention to the Caribbean, and in 1635 Cardinal Richelieu formed a company to colonize Guadeloupe, Martinique, St. Lucia, and Grenada. For the following 10 years or so, settlers made the best living they could, fending off Carib or Spanish attacks

Slaves being shipped from Africa were forced to dance to keep "fit"

a modest plantation on St. Christopher (St. Kitts). Britain, at war with Spain, was quick to see the advantages of a foothold in the "New World" and within three years the Earl of Carlisle was charged with colonizing St. Kitts, Nevis, Barbados, and Montserrat. To cultivate the land, indentured laborers were shipped from Britain, bonded to work for five years, after which they were free to

and sending home their harvests of tobacco and cotton.

Relations between the colonies and their mother countries were uneasy: British settlers resented the imposition of rents and taxes; the French state neglected its Caribbean territories when their profits failed to live up to expectations. Colonists relied heavily on Dutch ships for their supplies and, in turn, the Dutch took every opportunity to benefit from the colonists' resentment and to extend their own empire, colonizing Aruba,

Curaçao, and Bonaire, which lay near Spanish mainland ports, and Saba, Sint Eustatius, and Sint Maarten, conveniently placed on their trade routes with Spain's island colonies.

Sugar and slavery In the course of war against Spain and Portugal, the Dutch had captured several sugar plantations in Brazil, and their ships brought news of the vast profits to be made from the crop. They also seized Portugal's West African slavery centers and established a monopoly of slave provision for the labor-intensive plantations. African men, women, and children, kidnapped from their villages during midnight raids or captured and sold by rival chiefs, were shackled to each other by their necks and marched to coastal slave markets, where dealers picked the healthiest and branded them with irons. Eager for the biggest possible profit margins, captains would fill every available space on their ships, forcing the chained captives to lie shoulder to shoulder beneath the decks for their eight-week voyage. When the ships docked, the surviving slaves were auctioned off to planters, having been oiled and rubbed to cover the effects of their wretched journey.

In an attempt to break the Dutch hold on the slave trade, Britain attacked Dutch strongholds, triggering one of many conflicts between the colonial empires. France, Holland, Britain, and Spain were all anxious to strengthen their economies and expand their influence, and colonized islands switched hands several times, stormed by one navy after another. British Lord Protector Oliver

I would not have a Slave to till my ground
To carry me, to fan me while I sleep,
And tremble when I wake, for all the wealth
That sinews bought and sold, have ever earn'd.
We have no Slaves at home—why then abroad?

COWPER.

An 1827 condemnation of slavery

Cromwell sent a small army to Jamaica in the 1650s; in 1664 the French Minister of Finance, Jean-Baptiste Colbert, bought back Martinique, Guadeloupe, and other colonies from the private companies which had taken them over 20 years earlier. By 1678 Holland was forced to use ships registered in neutral Denmark to break through trade barriers imposed by the other powers, encouraging Danish settlement of the Virgin Islands of St. John and St. Thomas.

At the end of the 17th century most of the Caribbean islands were divided between the French and British empires, which proceeded to exploit the new-found wealth of their sugar industry and the thousands of slaves who produced it.

33

■ **During the early years of conquest and settlement, Europeans had hoped to find unlimited supplies of gold in the West Indies. In the 18th century their dreams of immense wealth were realized as the demand for "white gold" soared and the sugar islands became the Caribbean's richest exporters, supplying over 160,000 tons during the late 1760s. .....■**

Slaves working on a treadmill in Jamaica, 1830

The rewards of this trade were restricted to a very few plantation owners—many of whom lived in Europe and left the management of their estates to agents. Even those who lived in the Caribbean tended to build their great houses at a considerable distance from the plantation fields, partly for comfort but also for security: by the 1770s slaves outnumbered whites by about 10 to one on the main sugar islands and their harsh conditions had already prompted several revolts. Strict laws were passed restricting the movements and rights of slaves: they were forbidden from gathering in large groups, from owning land, and from giving evidence in court; slaves from the same areas of Africa or with similar cultures were parted, in an attempt to dampen feelings of solidarity and close relationships.

Nevertheless, African culture did survive in the traditions of story-telling (see page 61), dance and music (see pages 80–1) and spirit-worship (see pages 178–9). Many slaves risked imprisonment and whipping by running away from the plantations, and over the years runaways established strong communities in inaccessible parts of the islands.

For most slaves, however, life was a constant grind for 16 to 18 hours every day, digging the fields, gathering the sugar cane, feeding it into the crushing mills or pouring boiling sugar extract into coppers. Freedom was a rare reward, granted to long-serving slaves or to the offspring of white men and slave women. Even freemen had to carry passes guaranteeing their status for seven years, and were often forbidden from owning property above a certain value.

Boom and decline For 100 years the white minority managed to suppress slave rebellions while they kept up a steady flow of raw sugar (trade laws allowed the refining industry to operate only in the home countries). Wars continued to break out at regular intervals between the European powers, each one ending in the inevitable shuffling around of territories. By 1763, when the Seven Years War between the British and French came to an end, Britain owned five of the 10 most profitable sugar islands—Jamaica alone produced over 30,000 tons a year—and their planters were some of the empire's most prosperous and influential men.

The rot soon set in. Plantations cost a lot of money to run, and by the late 18th century many had been overused, exhausting the soil. At the same time the French planters, who paid lower export duties, were selling cheaper sugar to more European

A Caribbean sugar mill, 1816

markets, and Saint-Domingue, the French-owned part of Hispaniola, lay claim to the Caribbean's biggest sugar producer. When the colonies in North America rebelled against "taxation without representation," sparking off the Revolutionary War, Britain forbade the Caribbean planters from trading with the mainland, cutting off a valuable source of their income. The Americans turned to French and Spanish sugar islands instead, and British islands were forced to look for ways to cut costs and provide their own supplies. New crops were planted, such as mangoes and breadfruit trees (brought by Captain Bligh of the *Bounty* in 1793), and botanical gardens were opened to cultivate the plants; coffee, cotton, and spices were grown to supplement the main sugar crop. But by the end of the 18th century most of the sugar islands were in decline, and the West Indies were on the verge of radical changes in their social and economic life.

■ **Anti-slavery movements were gathering force in late 18th-century Europe. In France the issue was brought to a head with the Revolution in 1789. The National Assembly resisted the demands of abolitionists such as the Paris-based Société des Amis des Noirs, and in Saint-Domingue the free "coloreds" lost patience with its failure to grant them full legal rights, and armed their own slaves. .....■**

Thousands of whites were killed in the ensuing uprising and 300 plantations were set alight. A French army sent to restore order promised emancipation; the new Jacobin Assembly fulfilled the promise and freed slaves on Guadeloupe in 1794. British and Spanish troops, sent to support Saint-Domingue's planters, were driven out by ex-slave Toussaint l'Ouverture and his army. In 1802 Napoleon had l'Ouverture imprisoned and restored slavery on Guadeloupe; in response, 55,000 blacks took up arms and declared Saint-Domingue the independent state of Haiti.

In Britain, the "West India interest" was losing ground with the decline of sugar profits, and slavery was abolished in 1834. Ex-slaves were obliged to serve six years of unpaid "apprenticeship," but many fled from the cane fields and set up their own plots of land; on Jamaica sugar production slumped by 50 percent. To make up the labor shortage planters took on immigrants as indentured laborers; by 1917 about 280,000 East Indian indentured workers had moved to Jamaica and Trinidad. On islands with little spare land, ex-slaves lacked the option of cultivating their own plots, and Barbados, Antigua, and St. Kitts continued to prosper as sugar islands for many years. Emancipation alarmed the old plantocracy, who feared the loss of political dominance. In 1865, after an episode of violent racial conflict in Morant Bay, Jamaica's assembly asked to be replaced with direct rule, and by 1898 Britain had imposed the status of Crown Colony on all its Caribbean islands.

The French finally abolished slavery on its remaining islands in 1848; as on the British islands, sugar produc-

Emancipation portrayed by François Auguste Biard, 1848

Edmund Burke speaks out against slavery in the British Parliament

tion plummeted and the planters encouraged thousands of Indian laborers to take up indentures. France pursued a policy of integrating its colonies, allowing each island to send three representatives to the National Assembly and granting the vote to all adult men in 1871.

Prosperity was late coming to the Spanish possessions, Puerto Rico and Cuba, and only when trade restrictions had been lifted in the late 18th century did Cuba's sugar industry flourish. As a result, slavery was not abolished until 1886. Resentment against Spanish rule and taxes led to fierce civil war in the 1860s and '70s, and again in the 1890s, by which time a separatist movement had won strong U.S. support. In 1898 U.S. warships destroyed two Spanish fleets off Cuba and under the Treaty of Paris in that year the island gained independence, while Puerto Rico was ceded to America. By 1917, when Denmark sold its Virgin Islands to the Americans, the U.S. was the Caribbean's main political and economic power, funding successful sugar, banana, and coffee industries. To defend this commerce the U.S. intervened in the political life of Cuba, Haiti, and the Dominican Republic (western Hispaniola) during the 20th century.

The Caribbean suffered badly during the 1930s Depression. Corrupt and repressive governments exacerbated the harsh conditions on Haiti and on Cuba, where Fidel Castro's revolutionary forces took control in 1959. On the British islands economic hardship gave rise to powerful labor movements as well as to riots and strikes. An attempt to form a federation of British Caribbean islands failed in the late 1950s, and in the '60s Jamaica and Trinidad were the first of the colonies to gain independence, to be followed by nearly all the other British islands.

The late 20th century has been a time of re-evaluation in the Caribbean. Some islands have found new roles as luxury tourist destinations; many are struggling with severe economic problems and with political instability. This fascinating region is still coming to terms with its complex historical legacy of conflict and conquest.

Caribbean nightlife

The Windward Islands Crowned by sheer volcanic peaks and fringed with beautiful white beaches, the islands of Grenada, St. Lucia, Dominica and St. Vincent are among the loveliest in the Caribbean region. The advent of eco-tourism has added another, adventurous dimension to the more traditional appeal of beaches, river swimming, and yachting. All of these islands have their enthusiasts, and each has a range of hotels and guest-houses to suit all tastes and budgets.

The four Windward Islands lie facing the Trade Winds head on, in a line of jagged, volcanic protrusions—still active and liable to erupt about once every 100 years—regularly spaced on the tectonic fault-line between the Atlantic and Caribbean oceans. Similar to each other in

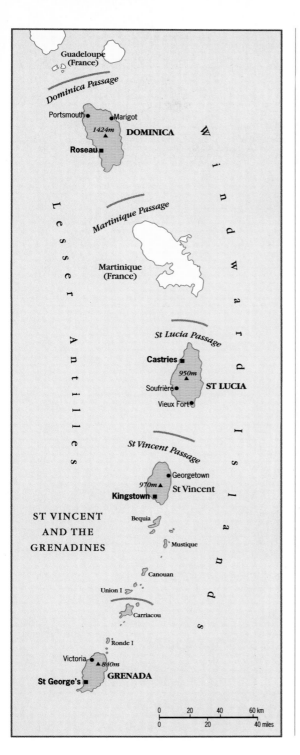

Guadeloupe
(France)

Dominica Passage

Portsmouth ● ● Marigot
▲ 1424m **DOMINICA**

Roseau ■

Windward

Lesser Antilles

Martinique Passage

Martinique
(France)

St Lucia Passage

Castries ■
950m
▲
Soufrière ● **ST LUCIA**

Vieux Fort ●

St Vincent Passage

● Georgetown
970m ▲
Kingstown ■ St Vincent

**ST VINCENT
AND THE
GRENADINES**

Bequia

Mustique

Canouan

Union I

Carriacou

Ronde I

Victoria ● ▲ 840m

St George's ■ **GRENADA**

Islands

| 0 | 20 | 40 | 60 km |
| 0 | | 20 | 40 miles |

A to Z
THE WINDWARD ISLANDS

appearance, and all very small (not more than 19 miles by 9 miles), they are nonetheless physically dramatic, with clouds hanging over the mountain peaks, and thick rainforest and bamboo covering the fertile land.

The islands no longer grow sugar, but their fertility is still the source of some wealth; fruit and vegetables are shipped as far as Trinidad and Anguilla, and the banana is an important export to Europe.

Windward travel
Travel between the Windward Islands is a realistic option if you have money or time. The quickest way to do it is by the "island bus service," the island-hopping planes that run up and down the island chain at least twice a day. LIAT is the biggest operator, but there are others, including Air Martinique. Alternatively you can try traveling by boat (easy in the Grenadines, more difficult elsewhere). This takes time; you may wait several days for a ride on a yacht.

History Peaceful Arawak islanders were decimated by invading Caribs in about A.D. 1000; six centuries later the Caribs were defending themselves against European colonists. As late as 1748, Dominica was left to the Caribs in the Treaty of Aix-la-Chappelle. After swapping hands several times between the European powers during the 18th century, the Windward Islands were finally passed into British hands, and became a Crown Colony in 1874, administered from Grenada. The islands all gained their independence from Britain in the 1970s, though they remain within the Commonwealth and still use the British judicial system.

Island life At one time during the to-and-fro of colonial control, all the Windwards were owned by France, and the French heritage is still strong. Names such as Beausejour Bay and Snug Corner can be seen side by side in Grenada, and French patois is spoken by the country people in Dominica, St. Lucia and Grenada. The strongest influence, however, is African; most Windward Islanders are the descendants of African slaves, freed in 1834 and able to survive by working their own plots of land.

These are lively islands, both as tourist destinations— with all the sun, sea, sand, sex, dancing, and rum punches that implies—and in the local life.

The Windwards offer a remarkable breadth of tourism, from secluded mountain retreats to busy yachting marinas, and from fun-packed, all-inclusive hotels to the most sophisticated elegance. St. Lucia is the most developed island and is becoming increasingly crowded by tourists attracted to its good restaurants and hotels; Grenada, on the other hand, is just beginning to develop. St. Vincent is still practically untouched, but the Grenadines offer the finest in easy island life and island-hopping by yacht (or by mail-boat). Dominica, which joined the group in 1939, is much less developed and therefore more natural.

Calabash Hotel, L'Anse aux Epines Bay, Grenada

Jean Rhys

The novelist Jean Rhys was born on Dominica in 1894 and lived there until 1907, when she left to continue her education in the U.K. After traveling to Paris in the 1920s, Rhys began her long writing career, and set her most famous work, *Wide Sargasso Sea* (1966) in the Caribbean. This formidably depressing book describes the degenerate and stultifying atmosphere of colonial Caribbean life, as seen through the eyes of a Creole heiress, destined to become Rochester's mad wife from *Jane Eyre*.

Castle Bruce Bay, Dominica

Dominica

Dominica claims to have a river for every day of the year. A lush, green, volcanic island, it is full of spectacular scenery and pretty coastal villages. Not an obvious choice for beach-lovers, this is a must for naturalists and those who want to experience the simple, small-island rural life.

At 18 miles by 11 miles, Dominica is the largest of the Windwards—but it is also the poorest and least developed. Many islanders scrape a living on the land or by fishing, and access to much of the country is difficult, despite a number of new roads. For hundreds of years this was a Carib stronghold; the descendants of those who survived French invasion in the 18th century still live here. Developed as a free port, Dominica made its money from coffee, sugar, and slaves—many of whom escaped into the jungle to live as maroons, occasionally taking up arms against the authorities. British and French colonies were established here in turn; positioned between the French islands of Martinique and Guadeloupe, Dominica had strategic value for France, and it has retained a strong French heritage. Many of the 70,000 Dominicans are Catholics and Créole-speakers.

Lime juice
Dominica was at one time the biggest producer of limes in the world. One of the major buyers was Rose's, the company which supplied the British Navy with fruit juice. British sailors took a daily ration of lime in order to prevent scurvy—hence their nickname "Limeys."

The Catholic cathedral at Roseau, completed in 1848 despite a thorough lack of support from the Anglican government

Dominica's capital, **Roseau►►**, lies in the southwest of the island; it's a small, working town of about 20,000 people, with a mixture of modern buildings and pretty stone and wooden Victorian townhouses. In the oldest area of town is Dawbiney Market Square, now the site of a craft market and tourist information center; the new market is at the other end of the Bay Front. The Catholic cathedral, north of the old market site, was built under cover of darkness, after the government refused to support its construction. Not far from here is Fort Young, now a hotel, with bedrooms on its battlements.

The real beauty of Dominica becomes apparent on the outskirts of town. Beneath the huge white crucifix on Morne Bruce are the **Botanical Gardens►►**, with about 150 species on display in its 39½ acres, despite the havoc caused by Hurricane David in 1979, when most of the trees and flowers were uprooted. Directly inland, the Roseau Valley is a fantastically fertile gorge with tiny Dominican houses clinging to the slopes. At its head are the **Papillote Wilderness Retreat►►►**, and three waterfalls called the **Trafalgar Falls►►** (see panel on page 44).

Reached along another fork in the road, the village of Laudat is an entry point to the **Morne Trois Pitons National Park►►►**. This 6,900-hectare park, which takes its name from a mountain peak, gives the best view of Dominica's forests, and has walks to the Freshwater Lake, the site of hydro-electric work, and the Boeri Lake. The adventurous might consider walking to the Valley of Desolation, an area of bubbling pools and mudponds where nothing can grow, and the Boiling Lake, the largest of its kind in the world, a volcanic crater of steaming water that can boil an egg in only three minutes.

South of the capital, the road passes a small strip of hotels in Castle Comfort and crosses lime-growing country (Dominica was once a major lime producer—see panel) to reach the village of Soufrière, which is named after a sulphur spring near by. The best sites for Dominica's much admired scuba diving are in this area; the island attracts a band of dedicated divers every year. Near the pinnacles, caves, and drop-offs, a freshwater hot spring with the exotic name of Champagne fizzes at scalding temperatures. Canefield, to the north of the capital, is the site of the island's more convenient airstrip (the other, Melville Hall, is on the northeastern shore) and the **La Vie Dominik Museum►►** at the Old Mill Cultural Centre. Exhibits here cover Carib, colonial, and independent island life.

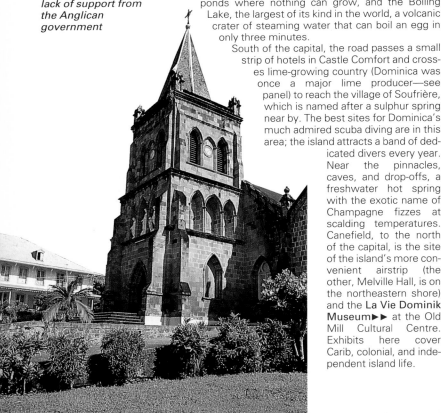

■ **Some of the last survivors of the Carib race, which gave its name to the Caribbean, live on the east coast of Dominica. Once these proud and warlike people held sway over the Eastern Caribbean, but by the late 18th century, after a war of attrition with the expansionist Europeans, the few hundred remaining Caribs had been forced to the remotest part of Dominica and forgotten. Only in 1903 were they officially granted their own territory. ......■**

The Caribs first appeared on the Caribbean islands around A.D. 1000. They came from South America (where there are still tribes of Carib Indians) and island-hopped their way north along the chain, supplanting the peaceful Arawak Indians. Although they grew a few crops, the Caribs were mainly hunters and fishermen, who would stun parrots (for their feathers) by burning pepper beneath them, and could fire arrows with astonishing speed and accuracy.

Caribs were said to be cannibals, but this may well have been a lie put about by Europeans to justify their acts of genocide. One early traveler tells of being presented with a pickled human arm, but there is little archeological evidence of systematic cannibalism.

On the beach at Castle Bruce you can watch canoes being made by traditional Carib methods (see panel). Six miles north of Castle Bruce lies the 3,700-acre Carib Indian Reservation, which was established in 1903. (Don't expect much in the way of ancient culture and costume; the people who gave the Caribbean its name live pretty much as other West Indians.) Although there are no "pure" Caribs left, and their language has died out, their descendants still have the characteristic silky blue-black hair. In addition to canoe-building, they have maintained their woodcarving and basket weaving skills. Carib wares are displayed and can be purchased in little thatched huts along the road. Of interest on the reservation are the Roman Catholic church, whose altar was once a canoe, and L'Escalier Tete Chien ("trail of the snake staircase")— a hardened lava flow that juts down to the ocean.

Canoes
Caribs still build their canoes in the traditional way, hollowing them out from gommier trees. In the past, a large Carib canoe could carry over 100 people. Builders would select a suitable tree and fell it, then hollow it out with tools made from conch shells. Rocks and fire were used to widen the sides, which were then built up with planks before the canoe was finally launched. A war canoe could be paddled at the same speed as a European warship in full sail.

43

Spaniards get a hostile reception from Caribs in 1525

A marketeer guards her stall in Roseau

Wilderness and waterfalls
At the head of the Roseau
Valley, a half-hour's journey from the capital, are
the Papillote Wilderness
Retreat and the Trafalgar
Falls. It is possible to climb
into the waterfalls, which
are harnessed for hydro
power as they crash onto
sulphur-dyed black and
orange rocks. The Papillote
Wilderness Retreat is a 12-
acre garden fed by a small
stream from a 98-ft. waterfall. Paths wind among
bamboo trees, begonias,
bromeliads, and orchids,
and visitors can bathe in
warm springs.

The road inland climbs into the mountains and rainforest,
touching the northern limits of the National Park and giving access to the **Middleham Falls▶▶** and the **Emerald
Pool▶** and waterfall—pleasant but tame. From here the
road descends to Castle Bruce on the Atlantic coast and
turns north to **Carib Territory ▶▶** (see page 43).

Back on the calmer Caribbean coast, the Layou River
Gorge has good spots for swimming; beyond it, the road
passes beneath Morne Diablotin (the island's highest) in
the Northern Forest Reserve. Here you can arrange to
walk through the rainforest to a hideout, where there is a
slim chance of seeing one of Dominica's two indigenous
parrots, the Sisserou and the Jacko.

Portsmouth, set on a huge bay in the northwest, is the
island's second town and is even quieter than Roseau.
Canoe trips arranged here take passengers through the
Indian River mangroves; the area's malarial swamps
drove British settlers to Roseau, ruining Portsmouth's
chances of becoming the capital. The excellently restored
Cabrits National Park▶▶ is an old military garrison set
on the nearby promontory (cruise ships dock on the
peninsula itself). Many of the barrack buildings have been
repaired and there is a museum in Fort Shirley. The Park
also includes a marine section, with scuba diving sites.
Portsmouth's black sand beaches are passable, but
Dominica's best beaches are to the east, in the hidden
north coast coves; try Hampstead or Calibishie.

■ **Caribbean islands are best known for their picture-postcard beaches, where silken sands are lapped by gentle waves. But there are other treats for waterlovers: the mountainous interiors of many islands are laced with rivers, where cool rainwater crashes and tumbles through thick forests, and waterfalls pour into clear rockpools, making ideal spots for secluded and refreshing dips after hiking through the rainforest. ......** ■

Rivers were once gathering places on the Caribbean islands. Before piped water was introduced, the population would go there to collect water and do the Monday washing, and washerwomen (*blanchisseuses* in the French Caribbean) can still occasionally be seen sudsing the clothes up at the riverside and then laying them out on the rocks to dry. Another long-standing practice was (and remains) taking a bath in the river. Although West Indians never go nude on their beaches, they do often take off their clothes in order to wash in the rivers.

Rivers have an important part in Caribbean folklore and legend; many islands share the legend of a beautiful girl sitting by a rockpool, combing her hair with a golden comb and perhaps granting a wish. The story goes that anyone who steals her comb and takes it down to the sea before being caught can keep it. The rockpools of Trinidad are said to be the home of the unpleasant Mama Dlo, the spirit of the water, who is half woman and half anaconda.

The Windward Islands are so well watered that they actually sell water to some of the drier islands; but the best islands for river bathing are the Eastern Caribbean islands from Guadeloupe down to Trinidad. There are also large rivers in the Greater Antilles. Many of the rockpools and rivers are off the beaten track and so bathers should be careful of their personal security. Rivers of slow-moving water might best be avoided—cases of bilharzia (a parasitic flat-worm that enters the blood and bladder), though rare, have been known to occur.

River hunts
On Dominica, hunting parties search the rivers by night for frogs and crabs. Hunters once used flaming torches—they are more likely to be electric flashlights nowadays—to attract the animals, which are so startled by the light that they do not even hide, and are simply picked up.

Rivers in religion
In Haiti waterfalls have religious significance. On saints' days the Catholic and voodoo faithful gather at the riverside for ceremonies that include baptism in the waters of the cascades.

Swimmers can enjoy the pools at Dunn's River Falls in Ocho Rios, Jamaica

Tanga Langua (David Pt) Sauteurs Bay Sugar Loaf Green I
Caribs' Leap Sandy I
Duquesne Bay Prospect Sauteurs
Celeste Levera Pond Bathway Beach
Duquesne Rose Hill Grenada Bay
Union Morne Fendue
St Mark Bay Castle Hill Rivière Sallée
Victoria Lake Antoine Antoine Bay
St Marks St Patrick Black Rock
Maran Bay Maran Antoine River Antoine Rum Distillery Conference Bay
Gouyave Saumache Tivoli Pearls Rock
Florida 840m Mt St Catherine Paraclete Pearls
Palmiste Bay Dougaldston Estate Grand Bras Paradise Great River Bay
Clozier Bylands Telescope Rock
Grand Ray Great Grenville Telescope Pt
Marigot 764m Fedons Camp Birch Grove La Digue Grenville Bay
Black Bay Pt Concord Black Bay Grand Étang Marquis Plaisance Marquis I
Brizan Grand Étang St Andrews Bay
Beauséjour Mango 715m Mount Fann
Flamingo Bay Annandale Waterfall Mt Lebanon Munich Gt Bacolet Pt
Molinière Point Forest Reserve 702m Great Bacolet Bay
Grand Mal Snug Corner Vendôme Mt Sinai Bacolet I
Grand Mal Bay Beaulieu Crochu Mahot
Fortenoy Tempé Windsor Forest Pomme Rose
D'Arbeau Richmond Hill Providence Thebaide
St George's Bay Parade Perdmontemps St David's Galby Bay
St George's Port Frederick Corbeau Town Requin Point
Fort George Belmont Corinth
Grand Anse Bay The Cliff Chemin La Sagesse Nature Centre
Quarantine Pt Ruth Howard La Sagesse Bay
Morne Rouge Bay Woburn Calivigny Westerhall Point
Point Salines St David's Point
International Airport L'Anse aux Épines Chemin Bay
Pt Salines Fort Jeudy
Hog I Pt of Fort Jeudy
Glover I Prickly Pt Calivigny I

0 2 4 6 km
0 2 4 miles

46

Grenada

Now recovered from the political traumas of the 1980s, Grenada is a sleepy island with the Caribbean's most picturesque port, St. George's. A warm, friendly place of small villages and mountain walks, this is an ideal island for either an active or a completely lazy break.

It was on Grenada that the Caribbean rum punch was perfected. In his book, *Touch the Happy Isles*, Quentin Crewe re-tells the story of a planter who sprinkled a mystery ingredient into his guests' glasses at a party in 1813. The addition was nutmeg and it was such a success that West Indians have used it in their rum punches ever since. The nutmeg fruit, which now appears on the Grenadian flag, was for a while one of the country's largest exports; nutmeg trees still grow all over the island. This and the many other spices grown in the hills—cinnamon, cocoa, cloves, pimento, and bay leaves—have given Grenada its title of the Caribbean's Spice Island.

Grenada is the most southerly in the chain of the Windward Islands, and is not as mountainous as the others. Of its string of offshore islets surrounded by coral reefs, the Grenadines, only two are inhabited—Carriacou and Petit Martinique. Grenada itself is only now joining the tourist race and package tourism is confined to the southwestern corner of the island, around Grand Anse and L'Anse aux Epines, where the best restaurants and bars can be found.

Nowadays Grenada's atmosphere is calm and relaxed, but the island has a history of conflict and violence. In the recent past, the 1983 invasion by the U.S. and its Caribbean allies provoked strong reactions, of both outrage and approval. The troops moved in after Maurice Bishop, leader of the increasingly repressive People's Revolutionary Government, had been killed by a rival faction, along with nine of his colleagues. A return to the 1974 constitution, established when Grenada gained independence from Britain, paved the way for parliamentary elections and the island returned to a state of comparative stability. Most Grenadians still remember Maurice Bishop favorably—he had taken power in a bloodless coup, replacing the corrupt administration of Premier Eric Gairy, in 1979—but only the occasional outburst of graffiti remains as a reminder of turbulent times.

St. George's The capital of Grenada, St. George's►►►, is a very pretty town on a natural harbor. Its Georgian stone houses and more recent concrete Caribbean homes are neatly ranged in curved lines on the crumbled slopes of a volcanic crater (long since inactive), their red tiled and tin roofs offset by the tropical greens of the surrounding forest. On the heights above town stands a protective ring of churches and fortresses.

Before the Revolution
When Eric Gairy was elected Grenada's first leader after Independence, he had already built up a large following as a member of the colonial administration, promoting the cause of the workers. However, Gairy's government grew increasingly corrupt and repressive, its policies enforced by the secret Mongoose Gang, and soon an underground anti-government movement gathered strength. The New Jewel Movement united Gairy's socialist opponents; in March 1979 it took advantage of the leader's absence from Grenada to stage a coup, and Maurice Bishop's new administration began to implement its socialist policies.

47

St. George's Saturday market

■ A century ago, the cocoa estates of Grenada would ring to the sound of fiddlers, who played for the workers as they "danced" the cocoa beans. The beans were laid out on huge boucans, or drying trays, and the workers would shuffle through them, turning them so that they dried evenly. Spices grow throughout the Caribbean, but Grenada's mild climate and fertile volcanic soil have earned it the title of "Spice Isle." ......■

Cocoa walks

Cocoa trees need to be shaded from the tropical sun if they are to flourish, so planters imported the tall and bushy *bois immortelle* or *madre de cacao* trees for that purpose. Shaded by their leaves, the "cocoa walks" are cool even in the middle of the day. In January and February the *bois immortelle* flowers bright orange, and whole hillsides in Grenada, Trinidad, and Tobago are patched with flaming orange blooms.

Nutmeg and mace The nutmeg tree (*myristica fragrans*) actually yields two spices: nutmeg and mace. This bushy tree grows to 65 ft. and produces a yellow fruit like an apricot, which splits open when ripe. Its flesh, used to make preserves, protects the nut itself, which is covered with a scarlet waxy netting. This is stripped off and sold as mace, for use as a food flavoring and in cosmetics. The kernel of the nutmeg is extracted from the shell and used to flavor foods (and to treat rheumatism).

Cocoa The Aztecs used cocoa beans for barter and made their national drink, chocolada, with them. The cocoa tree (*theobroma*, "food of the gods") grows to about 50 ft. and sprouts yellow, brown, and purple oval-shaped pods, in which the beans lie in a sweet, white, sticky pulp. These must be fermented, to strip the pulp, and then dried in the sun for several days.

Allspice "Jamaica pepper" and "pimento," as allspice is also known, is native to the Caribbean and has a flavor like a combination of clove, cinnamon, and nutmeg. It is used mainly as a flavoring for foods.

Other herbs and spices

Bay leaves are a well-known cooking ingredient, but they have several other uses: oil of bay can be extracted from both the leaves and twigs of the bay tree, to be used in perfumes and in the preparation of bay rum (a drink and an antiseptic). Ginger originates in the Far East and was brought to the Americas by the Spaniards. Oil of ginger is used as a pain-reliever in the Windward Islands. The sweet-smelling bark of the cinnamon tree is often used in confectionery and in cooking.

Spice Isle produce

48

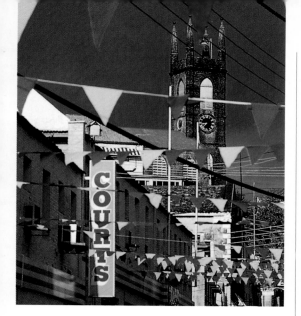

Flags strung over the streets of St. George's

The *Bianca C*
On the shore of the Carenage, in St. George's harbor, a statue of Christ of the Deep and a plaque commemorate those who died when a cruise ship, the *Bianca C*, caught fire in 1961. Its remains were towed out of the harbor to the southwest and sunk, and it is now the largest upright underwater wreck in the world; the stern section alone measures about 115 ft.

The heart of the town is the **Carenage▶▶▶**, the inner harbor, where the traditional island sloops still tie up. Old warehouses have been converted into restaurants and bars on the waterfront, and water-taxis pick up passengers for the bay crossing or the return to Grand Anse.

On Young Street, the Grenada National Museum is set in a French stone barrack-building, and shows memorabilia including Josephine Bonaparte's childhood bath-tub from Martinique. Dominating the harbor from the point is Fort George, also the island police headquarters, where Maurice Bishop and his supporters were killed.

Over the hill (or through the Sendall Tunnel) the other half of St. George's, the Esplanade, is on the Caribbean seafront. Once the site of the public executions, the **Market Square▶▶▶** was not easy to reach before the tunnel was built between the town's two halves in the late 19th century. Today it also serves as the bus station for the west coast, and Saturday mornings are a time of particular chaos, as vendors and busmen exchange shouts and jokes. Vendors hardly ever use the market buildings; they prefer to lay out their wares on tables under golfing umbrellas on the square. Close by is the Minor Spices Society, where Grenada's home-grown spices are on sale; and the **Yellow Poui Art Gallery▶▶** on Cross Street exhibits work by Caribbean artists.

St. George's botanical gardens, on the Lagoon, are a little run down; the Bay Gardens on Richmond Hill are a better bet, showing a range of flora from forest walkways.

Outside St. George's Not far along the coast to the south of St. George's is **Grand Anse▶▶**, Grenada's best beach. There are four or five hotels on the beach itself (others are ranged behind it) and beach bars on the sand. Grand Anse is also the best area for watersports. Other good, secluded beaches, including **Morne Rouge Bay▶▶**, nestle in the coves towards the southwestern

Mamma's Restaurant
On the road south from St. George's, excellent local meals are served at Mamma's Restaurant. Mamma herself is no longer alive, but her children continue the tradition of exotic Grenadian cuisine. About 20 dishes are offered in all, including green figs, christophene, rice in coconut milk, turtle, and even animals such as monkey, opossum, and armadillo.

■   The daily market is one of the liveliest and most accessible features of Caribbean life. Whether it be the overwhelming press of a large city market or a series of small stalls under a tree, the market is a vital focus of community and business. An amazing variety of goods is sold, from tropical fruit and vegetables to pots and pans, from candy and soap to human hair for braiding—all to the accompaniment of the shouts and patter of the marketeers. .....■

The floating market
Curaçao's floating market is made up of 15 or so moored boats. Vendors store their goods on board overnight and lay them out on the quayside stalls during market hours, shading them with flysheets (which are attached to the masts and rise and fall with the movement of the boats). The vendors are resupplied every few days with produce from Venezuela.

Crowds at St. George's market

Cassava
Cassava is a familiar item on most Caribbean vegetable stalls. Most of its 160 species contain a poisonous, cyanide-like juice that must be extracted before the vegetable can be consumed. Carib methods included grating the tuber on a sea fan coral and then squeezing the pulp in a woven bag that tightened as it was stretched. Dried cassava can be used like flour to make cassava bread and cakes (called "bammy" in Jamaica).

Caribbean markets have always been more than just a place for buying and selling. In the days before emancipation in the 19th century slaves would be allowed to make a little money by selling the fruit and vegetables they had grown. After slavery had been abolished, markets became gathering places where people would meet and swap stories. Colonial market buildings are usually made of red corrugated tin (the finest and the busiest is the Marché de Fer in Port-au-Prince in Haiti, which covers about one acre), but vendors often spread their goods out on blankets on the ground outside, rather than on the tables provided. Most stallholders are women, who sit on low boxes or benches with their skirts rolled up over their knees, shaded by two-tone golfing umbrellas. They arrive from the country in the early morning, often leaving by mid-afternoon, when the goods are sold.

Tropical vegetables are an essential feature of most Caribbean markets, and include cassava (see panel), sweet potato, which can be oval or pointed with white, purple or orange flesh; eddoe, also called dasheen, whose spherical tubers have slender stems and heart-shaped leaves; and yam, long, thin and hairy.

Children at the Grand Anse Roman Catholic School

On Grenada's south coast, L'Anse aux Epines has a number of hotels and bars, as well as a sailing marina, and further east, beyond the offshore island of Calivigny (where Grenadians often go for picnics), there is a charming dark sand beach with a restaurant at La Sagesse Bay. The **La Sagesse Nature Centre▶▶** is set in a 98-acre plantation, where guided trails offer interesting glimpses of varied birdlife.

A visit to the **Grand Etang National Park and Forest Reserve▶▶** is worth the tortuous drive into the mountain peaks. From the trails, the profusion of the rainforest can be fully appreciated: ferns that explode in the upper branches of the tall trees, and the mosses and ghostly trees of the elfin forest. The Forest Centre contains a museum, and there is a short walking trail laid out around the Grand Etang itself.

From here the road descends into Grenada's most fertile valleys on the way to the Atlantic coast. In Grenville, which is not much more than a fishing village, one of Grenada's two large **nutmeg processing stations▶▶** is based. The **River Antoine Rum Distillery▶▶** shows a water-driven cane-crusher in action, and follows the long process of boiling and distilling in order to make rum; visitors can taste the extremely strong result. The cane-crusher is one of the last of its kind operating in the Caribbean region.

The road north from St. George's follows the switchbacks of the western coastline and soon reaches Molinière Point, where there is good snorkeling. At the **Dougaldston Estate▶▶**, just south of Gouyave, Grenadian spices are prepared for sale. The preparation for cocoa is especially interesting; in Gouyave itself there is a **nutmeg co-operative▶▶**, where nutmeg and mace are prepared (see panel).

Nutmeg processing plants
It is well worth visiting either of Grenada's two main nutmeg co-operatives; one is in Gouyave, north of St. George's, and the other in Grenville on the Atlantic coast. Each factory is filled with the pungent aroma of the spice and groaning hessian sacks waiting for export. Once the mace has been stripped and graded (according to color), the nut of the nutmeg is put through a crusher and the kernel extracted from the shells. It is then put through a water test: the finest nutmegs sink and are used in food flavoring; those that float are sent to be used by the pharmaceutical industry.

Mr. Canute Caliste
Mr. Canute Caliste, as he calls himself, is Carriacou's resident artist. He has been painting for many years in his own unique, naive style, using the bright colors of the Carriacou sea and sky to express local life. If you are on the island it is well worth visiting his studio in L'Esterre, where his works are on sale. Another Carriacouan, Frankie Franks, has also begun to exhibit paintings.

The village of Sauteurs, on the northern coast, is a reminder of the last Carib Indians in Grenada, who jumped to their deaths off a cliff here (Caribs' Leap) rather than be taken prisoner by French colonists in 1651. Inland, to the southwest of Sauteurs, is the delightful **Morne Fendue▶▶▶**, the plantation house of Betty Mascoll, where rum punch is served on the veranda and the famous lunch consists of pepperpot, a dish that can last for 60 years if replenished and boiled daily. The last pepperpot had to be abandoned during the revolution, when there was a curfew; the current pot is therefore only about a decade old. Beaches in the northern area include Bathway, where there is a protective reef against the Atlantic waves.

Carriacou and Petit Martinique Carriacou▶▶▶ is the biggest of the two inhabited islands politically attached to Grenada. Attractive, welcoming, and laid-back, it measures only 5 miles by 8 miles and has 6,000 inhabitants, who earn their living by selling vegetables and livestock in Grenada, and pursuing "unofficial" trade with other islands. Boat-building is a major island trade, and the colorful sloops constructed by hand in Windward, on the eastern coast, are launched with great pomp and circumstance. Boats to Carriacou sail from the Carenage in St. George's several times a week, and flights land at Lauriston airport. The island is graced with magnificent beaches and its southern shore has a wonderful view stretching 25 miles to Grenada, and taking in a number of uninhabited islands and cays.

Petit Martinique▶, 3 miles to the east of Carriacou, has about 600 fiercely independent islanders, said to be deeply involved with smuggling. There is only one place to stay here; the island is basically untouched by tourism. Only a stone's throw from Petit St. Vincent (see page 55), Petit Martinique takes care of the schooling of the PSV hotel managers' children, who travel across by daily speedboat.

Maurice Bishop, leader of Grenada's People's Revolutionary Government in the 1980s

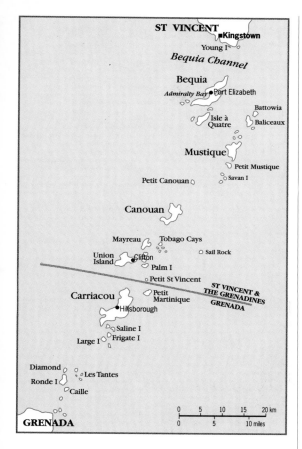

Fair exchange

Young Island is said to have been swapped for a horse. Governor Young had brought a black charger with him to St. Vincent from Britain, and it was greatly admired by the local Carib chief, so he presented the creature to him as a gift. Some time later the two men were together on the veranda of St. Vincent's Government House, looking out towards the idyllic, forested islet just offshore. When Governor Young admired the island, the Carib chief returned the favor and made him a present of the land.

The Grenadines

The Grenadines appeal to adventurous singles and couples who prefer active sports to glitz and gambling. Those looking for five-star amenities or designer shopping should go elsewhere. Hotels are small, the food is simple, and the residents' hospitality provides a peaceful, laid-back atmosphere. The 32 islands and cays that make up the lush and mountainous Grenadines offer numerous unspoiled white bays and coves, and superb snorkeling, hiking, sailing, and swimming. Island-hopping by ferry is a practical alternative to flying. **Young Island►** is a cast-off from the St. Vincent mainland, a private island resort with only about 20 cottages lost among the shrubbery.

Bequia►►► is 8½ miles south of St. Vincent. This is an island of fishermen, seafarers, boat-builders, and whalers, where tourists rub shoulders with, rather than shelter from, the locals. The best places to stay include Frangipani, the Prime Minister's boyhood home in Belmont, and the Plantation House on Admiralty Bay. There are many rooms for rent in private houses, whose owners come down to the jetty to meet the mail boat.

Admiralty Bay, Bequia

When the boat comes in

■ The graceful profiles of locally built boats are a familiar sight on the Grenadines. Brightly painted sloops still ply their trade from island to island as they have for centuries. Life in the Caribbean has always been dependent on boats and even now the smaller islands only really seem to come alive when crowds gather to greet the weekly boat. .....■

Before island-hopping planes became the quickest form of service, Caribbean communities were linked by frequent boat services. Unfortunately, the use of small boats has died off on the larger islands, but part of the fun of visiting the Grenadines, the Virgin Islands, and the French islands off Guadeloupe is to hop from one island to the next by mailboat or ferry.

There is a long tradition of boat-building and sea-faring around the Caribbean islands. Caymanians and Sabians were particularly renowned as sailors and they crewed and captained vessels all over the world for the big shipping lines. Closer to home, inter-island trading was established as a necessary way of life—Anguillians would sail west to Jamaica and south to Trinidad to sell their products. Captains would fund the boat-building by traveling abroad to earn money first for the hull, then for the planking and the deck, then finally for the mast and fittings. Nowadays Grenadine sloops travel regularly to Trinidad, taking fruit and vegetables for sale and returning with goods such as potato chips and canned food. They also go as far north as Sint Maarten in the Leeward Islands, to buy supplies including export liquor and manufactured goods from Europe.

Today's master boat-builders are the Bequians and Carriacouans; although their trade is now dying, it is still possible to see hulls taking shape on the beach and being painted bright red and orange—essential for clear visibility against a turquoise sea.

Smuggling has always been part and parcel of Caribbean life. Although some drugs do make their way to the islands for onward shipment, island smuggling is usually confined to liquor, cigarettes, and white goods, primarily for the avoidance of island duty. Buyers are told in advance when a boat will be putting in at a particular cove—usually in the dead of night.

54

Making sure everything is ship-shape

Boat-launching
A boat launch is an excuse for a big party. First the boat is christened and blessed by a priest with holy water (and sometimes with the blood of a goat). It is even given godparents, whose duty it is to raise the boat if it sinks. As the boat is launched, as many people clamber on board as possible, all dressed in their Sunday best, before finally returning to the shore to eat and drink.

A scrubby outcrop 30 years ago, **Mustique**▶▶ now has 75 of the Caribbean's most luxurious villas, 45 of which are for rent, for a small fortune (gardener, maids, cooks, and mini-moke (donkey) thrown in). Just 1½ miles by 3 miles, Mustique has one hotel, the Cotton House, set in a restored plantation house. Guests including Mick Jagger and Princess Margaret emerge from the seclusion of their villas every Wednesday, jump-up night at Basil's stilted beach bar. The Caribbean seems as incidental to Mustique as it is essential to Bequia.

On **Canouan**▶▶, 1,000 people eke out a poor living. This quiet island (3 miles by 1 mile) of gentle green peaks is rimmed with white sand. Offshore reefs protect the windward bays, and Grand Bay, on the leeward side, is a favorite yacht anchorage.

Mayreau▶▶ is even smaller and quieter, and does not even have a jetty. Loading and unloading is a precarious business; cattle are simply tossed into the sea and told to swim ashore. There are only 150 inhabitants and a couple of cars, but the beaches are wonderful.

Although its towering mountains make **Union Island**▶ the most beautiful of the Grenadines, this is a working island; its marina and airstrip are used by a constant stream of people traveling to the quieter islands near by. Most of the 2,000 islanders are employed in the resorts or fish and trade by sea.

The five **Tobago Cays**▶▶▶—Petit Rameau, Petit Bateau, Barabal, Jamesby, and Petit Tobac—rise gently from the water, protected by a reef 1km offshore. They are uninhabited and maintained as a marine park.

Close by are two tiny cays, each of which is entirely devoted to a single luxurious hotel. **Palm Island**▶▶ has 24 villas set on the beach or scattered among the hundreds of palms planted by the island's owner. **Petit St. Vincent**▶▶▶, known as PSV, specializes in low-key super-luxury, where residents communicate with room service by raising a yellow flag.

Young Island, seen from St. Vincent

Beaches
Beaches with bright white sand can be found throughout the Grenadines, many of them sheltered in coves formed by the irregularly shaped, mountainous islands. On the northern shore of Admiralty Bay on Bequia are the golden sands of Princess Margaret Beach and Lower Bay, a short water-taxi ride from the town; Endeavour Bay is the best beach on Mustique, though the whole island is rimmed with ankle-deep, soft sand. Canouan has a number of pretty beaches and isolated coves, including Maho, Corbay, and Rameau Bay. On Mayreau the best beaches are Salt Whistle Bay and Saline Bay. One of the finest beaches in the West Indies is on Carriacou, at Anse la Roche. None of the beaches has formal facilities.

55

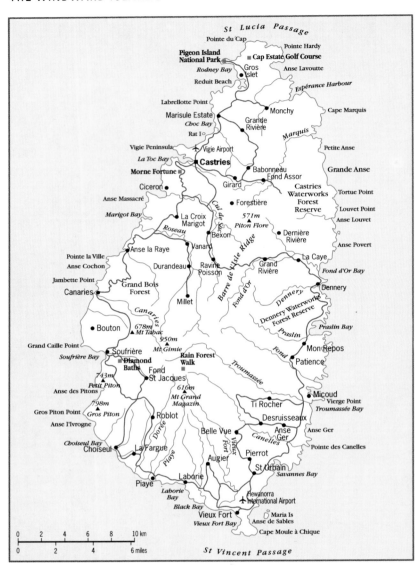

St Lucia Passage

Pointe du Cap

Pointe Hardy

Pigeon Island National Park
■ Cap Estate Golf Course

Rodney Bay Gros Islet

Anse Lavoutte

Reduit Beach

Espérance Harbour

Labrellotte Point

Marisule Estate

● Monchy

Cape Marquis

Choc Bay Grande Rivière

Rat I ○

Marquis

Vigie Peninsula ✈ Vigie Airport

Petite Anse

La Toc Bay ■ **Castries**

● Babonneau

Grande Anse

Morne Fortune ■

Girard Fond Assor

Ciceron

Castries Waterworks Forest Reserve

Anse Massacré

● Forestière

Tortue Point

Marigot Bay La Croix Marigot

Cul de Sac ▲ *571m* Piton Flore

Louvet Point

Anse Louvet

Roseau ● Bexon

● Dernière Rivière

Anse Povert

Pointe la Ville ● Anse la Raye

Vanard

La Caye

Anse Cochon

Durandeau Ravine Poisson

Grand Rivière

Fond d'Or Bay

Jambette Point

Barre de l'Isle Ridge *Fond d'Or*

Canaries

Grand Bois Forest

Millet

Dennery

Dennery

Canaries

Dennery Waterworks Forest Reserve

● Bouton

678m ▲ *Mt Tabac*

Praslin

Praslin Bay

Grand Caille Point

950m ▲ *Mt Gimie*

Fond

Mon Repos

Soufrière

Rain Forest Walk ■

Patience

Soufrière Bay

■ **Diamond Baths** Fond St Jacques

Troumassée

743m ▲ *Petit Piton*

616m ▲ *Mt Grand Magazin*

Micoud

Vierge Point

Anse des Pitons

Troumassée Bay

798m ▲ *Gros Piton*

Ti Rocher

Gros Piton Point

Roblot

Desruisseaux

Anse I'Ivrogne

Dorée

Belle Vue

Anse Ger

Anse Ger

Canelles

Choiseul Bay Choiseul

La Fargue

Augier

Pierrot

Pointe des Canelles

Piaye

Fond Vieux

St Urbain

Laborie

Savannes Bay

Piaye

Laborie Bay

Black Bay

✈ Hewanorra International Airport

Vieux Fort

Vieux Fort Bay

○ Maria Is
Anse de Sables

Cape Moule à Chique

| 0 | 2 | 4 | 6 | 8 | 10 km |
| 0 | 2 | 4 | | 6 miles | |

St Vincent Passage

Left: harbor view from Castries

St. Lucia

On Friday nights crowds gather at Gros Islet, a village on St. Lucia's Rodney Bay, in the north. This Caribbean jump-up transforms the settlement of wooden houses into one big street party: the thumping pulse of local soca, Martiniquan zouk, and Jamaican reggae can be heard from afar, and dancers spill onto the road, wining and grinding beneath banks of flashing lights and stacks of speakers, while vendors sell grilled fish and chilled beer.

The heady mix of tourists and locals at Gros Islet is typical of St. Lucia. Lying between the French island of Martinique and St. Vincent to the south, this is one of the most welcoming of the Caribbean islands and has recently become a popular tourist destination, bringing in over 200,000 visitors a year. The rapid development of a tourist industry, with beach hotels and restaurants sprouting all over the island, threatens to swamp the quiet agricultural life that has characterized St. Lucia for many years, but as yet tourism is concentrated in the northwest, between the capital Castries and the northern tip of the island, where the best beaches are to be found. Venture into the city and beyond and there is still a beautiful island to explore, with inland rainforests and secluded coves accessible only by boat.

Island life St. Lucians are chatty and forthcoming, as will soon become apparent to anyone taking a walk on the streets of Castries or in the country villages. Most speak patois, a Creole language derived mainly from French, but English is the official language. This was a British colony for a century and a half, until Independence on December 22, 1979, but before that the island had a history of struggle and conquest. Its strategic importance sparked off several battles for its possession between the British and French in the 17th century. Britain finally established its possession in 1814, but the French legacy remains, in the names of many towns, the predominant religion (Catholicism) and the Creole food, which includes such delights as *soupe germou* (pumpkin soup with garlic) and *pouile dudon* (chicken in coconut and sugar).

St. Lucia is the most populous (there are around 150,000 islanders) and the most developed of the Windward Islands. Besides tourism, there is some light manufacturing and an extensive agricultural sector which, until recently, consisted mainly of bananas grown for export to Britain under special trade arrangements, but is now coming under threat from cheaper producers in Central America (see page 58).

57

Castries St. Lucia's capital, Castries▶▶, was named after a French Minister of the Marine, the Maréchal de Castries, and laid out on a natural harbor in the 1760s. It soon filled the available flat ground and crept over the heights which surround the bay. Now a sprawling town of 70,000, Castries has burned down many times (most recently in 1948), and only a few colonial buildings remain among its concrete and glass-fronted offices. However, traditional Caribbean architecture survives on the hills around town, on Vigie Point and Morne Fortune.

In Columbus Square, the center of town, Rain Restaurant is a green and white Creole timber-frame house—one of a line of surviving townhouses. This is the main focus of island gossip, and its upstairs veranda is an excellent stop for an afternoon

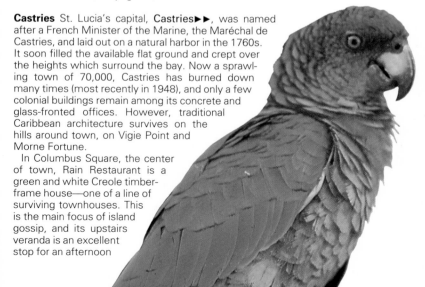

■ **The edible banana's botanical name is** *Musa sapientum,* **or "muse of wise man." It is said that Southeast Asian sages would sit in the shade of banana trees, enjoy the fruit and have wise thoughts. Since the banana made its way to the Caribbean, via the Canary Islands, this pastime has been readily adopted by Caribbeans. .....■**

The Banana Boat Song

Harry Belafonte's Banana Boat Song was originally a Jamaican working song, sung by women banana packers as they raced up and down the gangplanks, loading bunches of bananas onto the United Fruit Company ships. After working through the night, they would sing "Day-oh, day-oh" as day was dawning; the "tallyman" referred to in the song would give the workers tokens each time they came past with a load, tallying up the tokens at the end of the night and paying the women accordingly.

Claims to fame

Bananas are highly valued by sportsmen and women, particularly tennis players and marathon runners, because they have a wide and complex range of sugars that are digested at different rates, thereby releasing energy over a longer period than other sugar foods, such as chocolate. The fruit has a rather less creditable reputation in Sri Lanka, where the story of Adam and Eve features the serpent tempting Eve not with an apple but with a banana.

Banana plants grow singly and in groves all over the Caribbean, their leaves exploding in graceful, green curves to heights of up to 20 ft. Each plant gives fruit only once before it dies, when another plant sprouts from the same root system. As they grow, they throw off drooping stems, on which the 150 or so individual bananas sprout, coming to maturity over nine months. While growing, the plants are protected by blue plastic bags from insects and some are tied in a cat's cradle of string to prevent them from falling over under the weight of the fruit. Bananas grow in clusters of about 12, called "hands"; a collection of 10 or so hands on a single stem is known as a "bunch."

The popular yellow cavendish is the type of banana seen most in Europe and America, because it travels well, but Caribbean markets sell smaller, fatter and sweeter canary bananas (about 4 in. long) and green vegetable-bananas called plantains. Names and species vary according to each island. In the Windward Islands bananas range from big yellow *gros michels* to small "rock figs," and plantains called "green fig," "bluggo," and "buggoman."

Since the 1950s the export of bananas has improved life dramatically for many small farmers in Jamaica, the French Caribbean, and particularly in the Windward Islands. Instead of seasonal work in the cane fields, they now have a reliable year-round income. In the Windwards, three-quarters of export earnings come from bananas. But free market agreements such as G.A.T.T. are bringing Caribbean bananas under threat, especially from "dollar bananas," which are backed by U.S. companies and grown more cheaply on larger Central American farms.

A head for bananas

drink or a cocktail. Diagonally opposite is the 100-year-old brick Catholic Cathedral of the Immaculate Conception (1897). A short walk away, Castries life is at its most ebullient in the market all along Jeremie Street, far beyond the original confines of the market building.

Cruise ships dock on the north side of Castries harbor, and passengers head straight into the shopping complex at Pointe Seraphine, where the St. Lucia Tourist Board provides current information on hotels and events.

Outside Castries Many of the island's hotels are set in coves north of the capital, an easy taxi or bus ride from Castries. The most popular area is **Rodney Bay►►**, with a marina, restaurants, hotels, and the island's liveliest beach. Reduit Beach is a long strip of white coral sand with watersports facilities, particularly busy on weekends late in May when Aqua Action is held, a program of serious and fun watersports. Across the lagoon entrance is Gros Islet, the place to be on Friday nights.

Rodney Bay has long been a center for sailing craft; before the gin-joints came Carib canoes, Spanish galleons, pirate sloops, and naval gunships. Two centuries ago Admiral Rodney himself fortified **Pigeon Island►**, across the bay from Reduit beach. It was desig-

Roadside refreshment
In hot weather it is essential to have a ready supply of liquid and among Windward islanders there is a tradition of selling soft drinks at the roadside. A snow cone of ice scratched from a block by the vendor and heaped into a plastic cup, topped with water, sweet fruit concentrate and a straw, is a great way to keep cool. Sometimes the vendor offers a topping of condensed milk or even crushed nuts. Street snacks include locally grown peanuts, plantain chips made from fried bananas, or coconut chips, cut from the dried copra in the center of the coconut.

59

Castries market

nated a National Park in 1979, and its marked walkways pass military barrack rooms and gun-pits, with a museum and restaurant at the end of the trail. A nine-hole golf course has been laid out among the chic villas of the Cap Estate at the very north of the island; there is another nine-hole course at La Toc, south of Castries.

THE WINDWARDS

Spa fit for soldiers
Louis XVI of France provided the funds to build the Diamond Baths after hearing of the volcanic water's healing powers, as described by the Governor, Baron de Laborie. According to reports at the time, the water was believed to cure rheumatism, among other ailments, and Louis was eager for his troops to feel the benefit. Water flows from the volcano at temperatures of about 105° F.

Islanders gather at Rain Restaurant, Castries

South of Castries, over Morne Fortune (pronounced "Fortunay"), there is a less feverish, less developed St. Lucia of valleys and coastal villages, where banana farmers and fishermen go about their business unaffected by tourism. Beyond Cul de Sac on the west coast is **Marigot Bay►►►**, a steep-sided inlet lined with palm trees, which served as a hideout for pirates and navies in centuries past; a couple of cafés are set on the road down to the bay, and there are bars on the beach itself. At Canaries the coast road turns inland and climbs into rainforest beneath Morne Gimie (3,117 ft.), the highest peak on the island. The descent into the town of Soufrière offers magnificent views of the **Pitons►►►**, two pyramid-shaped volcanic mountains that soar from the sea to heights of 2,439 ft. and 2,620 ft.

Soufrière itself is a town of clapboard houses with wooden balconies, some of which have been restored; the first settlement on the island, it now suffers desperate unemployment and poverty. Its name is taken from the nearby **Soufrière►**, the world's only drive-in volcano, a simmering cauldron of mud which can be tracked down by its foul smell. This is a solfatara—a volcanic vent that steams steadily rather than blowing cataclysmically like others in the area. Inland from Soufrière, the **Diamond Baths►** were built as a spa for the French army in the 1780s, following reports of the water's curative effects; it is still possible to bathe in the naturally heated pools. The **Central Forest Reserve►►** is a protected area of rainforest laid with walking trails, where St. Lucia's own parrot makes its home—though its numbers have unfortunately now declined to near extinction.

The road from Castries down the east coast is an easier run, used to meet flights into Hewanorra international airport, near the southern tip. After passing over the rainforested Barre de l'Isle mountain range, it descends into banana plantations at Dennery before reaching the more remote villages strung out along the coast.

■ **Before the age of cable TV, whole villages would gather under a tree to enjoy an evening of story-telling. Many of the tales, often mixed with song, centered around Anancy the rogue and a cast of other characters—Dog, Goat, Jackass, Kisander the Cat, and Tiger—all of whom had human characteristics. Islanders still tell stories about them all over the Caribbean. ....■**

Anancy is the best loved character in Caribbean folklore. Sometimes a man, sometimes a spider, he is a sweet-talking trickster who, as a man, is considered rather laughable because he speaks with a lisp, but who can turn into a spider and hide when the need arises. Anancy is lazy and greedy, and far happier tricking a slow neighbor out of his meal than working honestly. But he is also fully capable of outwitting his opponents—particularly Tiger, his traditional enemy. Even in his greed, Anancy wins the listener's sympathy, and is often used to deliver home truths—though story-tellers may dissociate themselves from his actions by ending their tales with the words: "Jack Mantora me no choose any."

Above all, Anancy is good entertainment. When he wants a meal of crabs he dresses up as a priest and persuades them to be baptized (promptly throwing them into boiling water); having taken a bet that he cannot catch Snake, he taunts him into bragging about his length, and while measuring him against a log, ties Snake to it and captures him.

The island of Trinidad has a strong tradition of folklore, illustrated in Port of Spain's National Museum. Papa Bois, the guardian of the forest, warns animals of the hunter's presence (see panel). La Diablesse, the devil woman, appears as an old crone whose petticoats clank with chains or as an attractive girl who can drive men mad with desire for her, and the soucouyant is an old woman, who turns into a ball of fire at night and sucks human blood. Mama Dlo, the mother of the water, is half woman, half anaconda, and sometimes sings at the water's edge, but vanishes whenever she is disturbed.

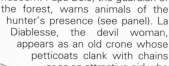

Forest guardian—Papa Bois

Papa Bois
Papa Bois will usually let hunters keep their kills from the forest, but if any become too greedy he will appear as a deer and lure them deep into the forest before turning back into an old man and issuing a stern warning, sometimes sentencing the offending hunter to be married to Mama Dlo.

Duennes
Never shout the name of your child in the Trinidadian forest; it will be stolen by the Duennes. These infant tricksters, who roam among the trees, are the ghosts of children who died before they were christened, and if they hear a child's name, they will call for it and lead it away into mischief.

Top: the soucouyant
Below: Mama Dlo

Winds and eruptions

■ **The Caribbean climate is virtually ideal. Surrounded by sea, the islands enjoy an almost constantly warm temperature, even at night, and during the day the sun is tempered by the Trade Winds, cooling breezes that rise on the Atlantic. But from time to time, the benevolent ocean will deliver disaster in the form of a hurricane. These whirlwinds, accompanied by torrential rain, are immensely destructive. The land will cause chaos in the Eastern Caribbean, an area of tectonic activity where volcanoes occasionally blow and earthquakes strike. ...■**

Hurricane season
A traditional rhyme serves as a reminder of when hurricanes are most likely to strike: "June, too soon; July, stand by; September, remember; October, all over." Most hurricanes do, in fact, occur in the middle of September.

62

Trade by name
Although they were useful to merchant ships and used by sailors from the very first days of trans-Atlantic travel, the Trade Winds are not named after their commercial value. The term was coined in the 16th century as "tread winds"—meaning directional winds.

Trade Winds These equatorial winds flow from a high pressure area in the mid-Atlantic to low pressure regions nearer the equator. They hit the Caribbean islands from the northeast, at an angle that varies through the year because of the earth's tilting. The Trade Winds reduce humidity, while bringing plenty of rain to the tall, mountainous islands. Known as *Les Alizes* on the French islands, the *Passaatwinden* on Dutch land and *Brisas Aliseas* in the Spanish territories, they are at their strongest in the winter months, bringing with them the most pleasant temperatures.

Hurricanes Terrible damage can be inflicted by hurricanes, whose name is derived from the Carib language. They rise in the Atlantic, at the meeting point of the Trade Winds from both hemispheres (north of the equator in the summer); in a phenomenon known as the "coriolis effect," the warm, moist air rises and then condenses, releasing heat, falls and then rises again, strengthening the updraught, until eventually it begins to spiral. Immature hurricanes set off west-northwest, moving at around 12 mph and steadily building up size and power. The winds spiral inwards around a vortex known as the "eye" (which is about 12 miles across), and can reach

After the hurricane: a wrecked boat floats offshore

sustained speeds of up to 105 mph, with bursts of around 185 mph. Extending up to 500 miles across, hurricanes are immensely powerful; their effect is measured in atom bombs per second, and they can stir life at depths of 200 ft. below sea level. Hurricanes are officially labeled once they have attained sustained surface winds of 75 miles; they are then identified according to the established sequence of alternately male and female names.

All the Caribbean islands from Grenada northwards are in the hurricane zone, and in recent years some have been badly hit. Hurricane Gilbert swept through Jamaica and the Cayman Islands in 1988 and in 1989 Hurricane Hugo, the worst this century, laid waste to Guadeloupe, St. Croix, and Montserrat (where over 90 percent of the houses were destroyed).

Volcanoes The Eastern Caribbean is an area of active volcanoes. This line of islands stretches in a curve from Saba to Grenada in the south, on the meeting point of the Atlantic and Caribbean tectonic plates. As the plates move slowly against each other, the magma (a hot, viscous liquid) contained beneath them occasionally escapes in the form of volcanic eruptions.

Volcanoes in the Eastern Caribbean all go by the name Soufrière, taken from the French word for sulphur, because of the foul smell that they give out. The most active volcanoes are on St. Vincent, Guadeloupe, and Martinique; these erupt about once every 100 years with cataclysmic lava flows and 16,400-ft. plumes of smoke.

St. Lucia and Dominica have less devastating "fumarolles," where the pressure is let off constantly and much more steadily—though the heat and pressure in Dominica is enough to make a lake boil. There is also an active volcano in the Grenadines: Kick 'em Jenny is underwater at the moment, but it is growing steadily with lava outflows and is expected to reach the surface some time before the end of the 20th century.

Earthquakes Another dramatic effect of living on the bridge of two tectonic plates is occasional earthquakes, which can frequently accompany the major movements of volcanoes, and cause major land slippages.

The Soufrière "drive-in" volcano, St. Lucia

63

Home safe home
Traditional Caribbean architecture was well designed to cope with rare but severe climatic problems. Stone foundations gave a solid base during earthquakes, while a wooden upper story could wobble in the windblasts of a hurricane. St. John's Cathedral in Antigua has been lined with wood in order to preserve it from the effects of hurricanes and earthquakes.

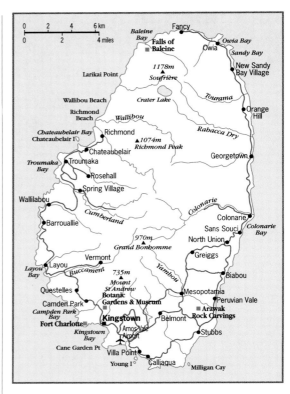

St. Vincent

St. Vincent is a fertile and beautiful island, from its cultivated valleys to the rainforested slopes of its active volcano, the Soufrière. Linked to Grenada by the 60-mile string of the Grenadines, it is usually considered only as a starting point for yachting trips; however, its rugged east coast and fascinating Arawak settlement are well worth seeing. There's also first-rate diving and snorkeling, and hiking on trails as verdant as any in Hawaii.

The 107,000 Vincentians are mainly of African origin, the descendants of plantation slaves, but this was not always a plantation island. Like Dominica, St. Vincent was one of the last strongholds of the Carib Indians. Here, local Indians, known as Yellow Caribs, and escaped African slaves produced a race of Black Caribs, who held out against the colonists. In 1797 they were eventually defeated and their survivors were deported to Roatan, an island off Honduras. The British took over St. Vincent and

built up a trade of sugar, cotton, and arrowroot. Independence was gained in 1979, though St. Vincent remained within the British Commonwealth.

Agriculture still provides much of the island's living; exports include arrowroot starch, bananas, and coconuts. St. Vincent is relatively undeveloped, with a small area of hotels in the southeast and a few other isolated spots.

The capital of St. Vincent and the Grenadines is Kingstown►►, a few streets of Georgian townhouses with cobbled arched walkways set on a wide south-western bay. The town is fairly quiet, except around the Grenadines pier when ships come in, and at the market on Halifax Street, the center of all island gossip. Close by are the Law Courts, where the St. Vincent Parliament sits, and the unusual gothic and romanesque Roman Catholic church, which was built in 1823.

Away from the waterfront, the ground rises through out-lying suburbs to the range of hills surrounding the town. In the northwest of the town are the 20 acres of the St. Vincent Botanic Gardens►►►, opened in 1763. Here, species include the sealing wax palm, red hot cat tail, and roucou, used as body-paint by the Carib Indians, and the St. Vincent Museum, set in the gardens, shows Amerindian relics and colonial exhibits. On the heights to the southwest of the town is Fort Charlotte where, on a clear day, the view extends 65 miles south to Grenada.

Past the airport in the southeast is Villa Point, where restaurants and bars are set among the pretty tin-roofed villas on the waterfront, looking across a small stretch of water to Young Island. Inland are the fertile valleys where St. Vincent's market produce is grown, and at Yambou, off the road to the town of Mesopotamia, Arawak rock carvings►► date from before A.D. 1000.

A journey up the west coast on the Leeward Highway reveals the West Indies at its most natural: small and simple villages filled with hordes of shouting school-children. There are rainforest walking trails in the Buccament Valley►►, and the hike up the Soufrière (3,865 ft.) is a full day's trip, best started from the Rabacca Dry River, north of Georgetown, or alternatively from Richmond, north of Chateaubelair. Boats sail from Kingstown to the popular Falls of Baleine, a 60-ft. cascade into a rockpool at the northern tip of the island, past the coastal villages that line St. Vincent's leeward shore.

Kingstown

Fort Duvernette
Young Island is the nearest of the Grenadines to St. Vincent's shore and beyond it, perched on its 60m over-grown rock, is the defen-sive bastion that once protected the larger island's southern waters. Cannons dating from the 18th century are still at the ready, but these days only tourists are likely to invade the fort (reached via steps in the rockface), to enjoy the impressive views.

THE LEEWARD ISLANDS

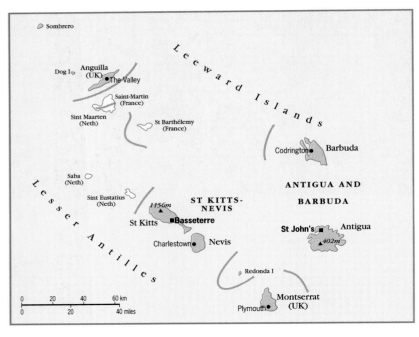

Sombrero

Dog I.
Anguilla
(UK)
The Valley

Leeward Islands

Saint-Martin
(France)

Sint Maarten
(Neth)

St Barthélemy
(France)

Codrington • Barbuda

Saba
(Neth)

ANTIGUA AND
BARBUDA

Lesser Antilles

Sint Eustatius
(Neth)

ST KITTS-
NEVIS
1156m
St Kitts ■ Basseterre

St John's ■ Antigua
▲ 402m

Charlestown • Nevis

Redonda I.

Montserrat
(UK)

Plymouth •

0   20   40   60 km
0   20   40 miles

One of the Leeward islanders: a resident of Antigua

THE LEEWARD ISLANDS

![Darkwood Beach, Antigua]

Darkwood Beach, Antigua

The Leeward Islands The English-speaking Leewards have maintained much of their small-island charm in the face of growing tourism. With a vast choice of beaches, friendly small towns, and varied local customs, they stand in refreshing contrast to the bigger tourist destinations. Antigua is the most developed vacation island, while Montserrat is only slowly adapting to the potential of tourism; Anguilla, on the other hand, is possibly the fastest developing island in the Caribbean. Two centuries ago, when the fortresses along the island chain would send messages back to base in Antigua by mirror flash, the islands were isolated outposts and fast communications were essential. Now their remoteness is a selling point, and many visitors pay a lot of money to enjoy it.

The six Leeward Islands (they were to the lee side of ships arriving from Europe) lie in two lines. In the west, Montserrat, Nevis, and St. Kitts are the rainforested peaks of a relatively young volcano chain (about 15 million years old). To their east are the protrusions of a much older range: Antigua, Barbuda, and, beyond the French islands of St. Barts and Saint-Martin, Anguilla, the most northerly island in the Lesser Antilles. Capped with coral limestone, the latter have some of the finest sand in the Caribbean.

THE LEEWARD ISLANDS

Remissions
The economies of the Leeward Islands have traditionally depended on "remissions" from abroad. Since the sugar industry foundered, people have either cultivated small plots of land or traveled in search of work, sending their earnings home to their families. Many islanders worked on the digging of the "Ditch"—the Panama Canal—and in the Dominican Republic's cane fields at the turn of the century. Later there was a rush to the oil refineries of Aruba and Curaçao, and in the 1950s and '60s there were large influxes to Britain. Most emigration is now to the U.S. or Canada.

History The islands are connected by a common history, having been British colonies for many years, but most have now gone their own way. The island states of Antigua and Barbuda negotiated their full independence in the early 1980s and were soon followed by St. Kitts and Nevis, but they remain in the British Commonwealth. Montserrat and Anguilla are still Crown Colonies of Britain.

British settlers first arrived at St. Kitts in 1623, but disputes over the island's possession raged between Britain and France until 1783. Using an army of slave labor, the colonizers planted sugar cane furiously and became immensely wealthy. But with the abolition of slavery in the British Empire in 1834, the Leeward Islands quickly went into decline. The freed slaves took to the land, dividing it into small individual plots, and scraped a poor living from subsistence farming. Today you will

Sunset over Antigua

still see subsistence farmers living on the Leeward Islands; their lifestyle has not really changed much in over a hundred years.

Island life The Leeward Islands' economies are precarious and, despite the success of a few small industries, all depend to some extent on tourism. This has developed steadily over the past 20 years and in places it seems to have swamped local Caribbean life and traditions, which have all but disappeared in some parts. The more developed islands, Antigua and Anguilla, tend to have better restaurants, but a stroll around Nevis or Montserrat, or a visit to one of their rum shops, is more likely to give a taste of local life. Each island has its special points, whether it is rum-soaked rumbustiousness during Sailing Week (usually the last week of April) on Antigua, a glimpse of the planter's leisurely way of life and historic surroundings on St. Kitts and Nevis, or the deserted beaches of Anguilla.

The islanders are English-speakers (as they are on the nearby Dutch Windward Islands), but accents vary from island to island, as do the characteristics of their people. Distinct traces of Irish can be heard in the inflexions and pronunciations of Anguillan and Montserratian islanders, which are not present in the accents of St. Kitts, Nevis, and Antigua. While there is a certain reserve and politeness on Montserrat and Nevis, the people of Anguilla and Barbuda are known for a proud and independent outlook. Nevertheless, all Leeward Islanders are known for a cool, easy-going attitude which is well expressed in the favorite Caribbean expression "No problem."

Redonda
The island of Redonda lies between Montserrat and Nevis. It is uninhabited (the only people to have lived there were guano miners in the last century and a couple of rastafarians a few years ago), but it is nevertheless the domain of a "royal line" of self-proclaimed kings, mainly poets and writers. Famous courtiers have included Rebecca West and J. B. Priestley; the present king, a certain Jon Wynne Tyson, last visited his kingdom in 1979, planting a flag made out of old pajamas.

Anguilla

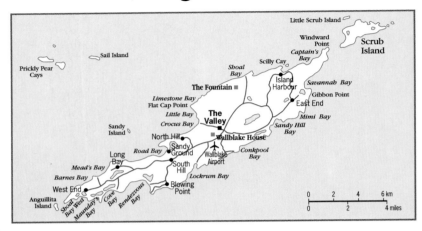

Rebel Marine
You will soon come to know the sleek contours of boats made by Rebel Marine, an Anguillan boatyard. The gull-winged ferries that make the run from Blowing Point to Saint-Martin are made by them (as is the North Sound Express boat in the British Virgin Islands), and many others lie at anchor in Sandy Ground and around the island. The designs take traditional Anguillan lines (from a long tradition of boat-building) and adapt them to modern materials.

Only 20 minutes by ferry from Saint-Martin/Sint Maarten, Anguilla has little except beaches—but they are some of the Caribbean's best. There are about 30 tiny, secluded coves, snorkeling beaches, and walking strands, all with fine sand washed by a clear, turquoise sea. Anguilla's image is of an expensive and exclusive resort island. It has a string of luxurious hotels, though it is possible to find cheaper options: the Anguilla Tourist Office, The Valley (tel: 497 2759) can offer advice, and a leaflet called *Inns of Anguilla* lists mid-range guesthouses. There are no buses on the island and few cars; taxis can be picked up at the airport, from Blowing Point, or from hotels. Just 16 miles long, the island is made entirely of coral limestone. Its flat land is covered in thick scrub, steadily being cleared for building. Anguilla is a rapidly developing island, but it is still a quiet place, with little visual history or "sights"; many tourists use it as a peaceful retreat after spending the day shopping or gambling on nearby Sint Maarten.

It comes as a surprise to learn that this peaceful island once had a revolution (albeit bloodless). In the 1960s Anguilla became part of the Associated State of St. Kitts-Nevis-Anguilla, but its inhabitants objected to St. Kitts'

Lobster-fishing off the Anguilla coast

prominent role (see panel). Anguilla was separated from the three-island state in 1971 and regained its status as a UK-dependent territory.

In the middle of the island, close to the airport, is the capital, The Valley, where the administrative offices, banks, shops, and the only hospital are all based. The other main settlements are Sandy Ground, the main port, and Island Harbour, a fishing village in the northeast, near which is the **Fountain►►**, a cave used by the indigenous Arawak Indians, where carved faces are arranged to be lit by the sun in turn. Blowing Point, on the south coast, is the ferry terminal (linked to French Saint-Martin).

Beaches ring the island, and it is impossible to single out one area as the best. Snorkelers will find shoals of fish loitering at the rocks and reefs, and most hotels have watersports facilities. On the north coast, near the western tip, **Barnes Bay►►** is a strip of sand backed with rocks and broad-leaved sea grape trees, bearing bitter, grape-like fruit. Heading east, **Mead's Bay►** is a curve of deep sand with a lovely sunset view from the Malliouhana end. Calm and protected **Road Bay►►** is a port harboring local boats and some larger ships, and has a string of restaurants and bars. Just beyond Crocus Bay are two excellent suntraps: **Little Bay►►►**, access to which is by boat or by climbing down the cliff, and **Limestone Bay►►**. Shoal **Bay►►** is one of the Caribbean's prettiest beaches, with fine sand and snorkeling offshore. On the north coast, and very difficult to find, is **Captain's Bay►►►**, a half-moon of secluded sand (ask for directions, and follow the coastline). On the south coast, past Blowing Point, is the 1.8-mile **Rendezvous Bay►►**, a mangrove and dune-backed walking strand with a clear view of Saint-Martin. The moorish domes of the Cap Juluca Hotel dominate the crescent-shaped **Maunday's Bay►►** and beyond here, **Shoal Bay West►►►** is overlooked by the tall, white curves of the Cove Castles hotel villas. Two offshore islands, Sandy Island and Prickly Pear Cays, have good beaches and are convenient for a day's sailing trip.

The revolution
Few small Caribbean islands have managed to sever the convenient connections made by colonial administrators, but when faced with independence from Britain in company with St. Kitts and Nevis, the Anguillans rebelled. A few shots were fired and St. Kitts policemen were expelled from the island. As tension grew, the British sent a detachment of paratroopers in 1969—an "invasion" (welcomed by the Anguillans) that was later dubbed the "Bay of Piglets." Anguilla's rebels got their way and the link with St. Kitts was cut forever, but a satisfactory political solution was found only in 1982, when the island was eventually granted its own constitution, headed by a Council of Ministers and an 11-member House of Assembly.

Map of Antigua showing: Boon Point, Soldiers Bay, Dickenson Bay, Beggars Point, Cedar Grove, Long Island, Runaway Bay, New Winthorpes, Barnes Hill, Maiden Island, Great Bird Island, North Sound, St John's Harbour, Cedar Valley Golf Club, Fort Barrington, Hawksbill Bay, VC Bird Int Airport, Parham Harbour, Guiana Island, St Johnstone, St John's, Five Islands, Potters, Parham, Crump Island, Pelican Island, Indian Town Point, Fullerton Point, Five Islands Harbour, Golden Grove, Antiguan Pottery, Seatons, Pares, Willikies, Devil's Bridge, Pearns Point, Jennings, Green Castle Hill 172m, Freemans, Betty's Hope, Glanvilles, Nonsuch Bay, Green Island, Lignumvitae Bay, Bolans, Suckleys, All Saints, Collins Dam, Harmony Hall, Great Deep Bay, Ffryes Point, Sweets, Potsworks Dam, Newfield, Freetown, York Island, Dark Wood Beach, Boggy Peak 402m, Fig Tree Drive, Liberta, Bethesda, St Philips, Half Moon Bay, Crab Hill, Shekerley Mts, Rain Forest 368m, Monks Hill Fort, Soldier Point, Johnson's Point, Urlings, Signal Hill, Falmouth, Willoughby Bay, Cades Bay, Old Road, Falmouth Harbour, English Harbour Town, Carlisle Bay, Rendezvous Bay, Clarence House, Old Road Bluff, English Harbour, Nelson's Dockyard, Shirley Heights, Nanton Point, All Saints Road

Scale: 0 2 4 6 km / 0 1 2 3 4 miles

Antigua and Barbuda

The territory of Antigua and Barbuda actually consists of three islands: Antigua, the main island at 108 sq miles; Barbuda, a smaller, wooded island to the north; and Redonda, only ⅜ of a mile in area, an uninhabited rocky islet lying 25 miles southwest of Antigua.

Contentment on an island cruise

73

Antigua The "365 beaches" of PR literature are an exaggeration, but Antigua does have miles of superb sand. The largest, the most popular and the most developed of the Leewards, it has a mostly dry and flat landscape. Its foremost attractions are the beaches and sailing facilities; English Harbour is a hive of sailing activity during Race Week at the end of April every year.

Antigua is made of limestone coral, covered in grassy flatlands that rise steadily to the southwest. Two centuries ago the island was blanketed with sugar cane, and ruins of the windmills in which the cane was crushed are dotted all over the island. The two main centers are the capital, St. John's, in the northwest, and English Harbour.

St. John's is a busy harbor town, particularly when a cruise ship is in dock. Founded in the early 18th century, it has expanded eastwards in a gridiron pattern, and has attractive 19th-century buildings, with wooden gingerbread balconies. Some of the finest are in **Redcliffe Quay►►**—restored warehouses and townhouses now occupied by shops and cafés. Near the Tourist Information Office (Thames Street) is the Old Court House, where the **Antigua and Barbuda Museum►►** has displays on Amerindian Antigua and the colonial past. Towering above the town is **St. John's Cathedral►►** (1848), and close by is the Antigua Recreation Ground; international cricket Test Matches have been hosted here since Antigua and Barbuda became independent on November 1, 1981. **St. John's Public Market►**, in the south of the town, is at its liveliest on Saturday mornings.

Antigua's main tourist area is to the north of the capital on **Dickenson Bay►►**, where there are half-a-dozen hotels, beach bars, and watersports shops. From here, the road follows the coastline north through chic, residential areas and past secluded coves to VC Bird International Airport (named after Vere Bird, the first Prime Minister after Independence) and the Cedar Valley Golf Club.

In the dry, eastern area of the island the coastline and sea are spectacular (though not suitable for swimming except in well protected bays) and at Indian Town you can see the Devil's Bridge, an archway of rock carved out by the Atlantic waves. The 200-year-old plantation estate of **Betty's Hope►**, to the west, is being restored, and has a visitor center, a renovated windmill, and a shop. In another windmill on the southeast coast is the **Harmony Hall►►** gallery, with works by West Indian artists.

Viv Richards
Antigua's greatest hero was, for most of the 1980s, captain of perhaps the strongest West Indies cricket team ever to have played. Considered the world's finest batsman, he regularly destroyed the bowling of English, Australian, Indian, and Pakistani teams. Born in 1952, Richards played for Antigua and Leeward Islands teams soon after leaving school. He moved to Britain in 1974 to play for Somerset and in the same year played for the West Indies for the first time. He became captain in 1984 and retired from international cricket in 1991.

■ **An extraordinarily fertile and colorful marine life exists under the Caribbean waters. Corals grow like forests on the reefs and underwater slopes, and hiding among them are weird and wonderful shellfish and crabs, while schools of tropical fish with exotic names and colors cruise by. .....■**

Corals, sponges, and shellfish Corals are animals that grow in salt water shallow enough to be within the range of the sunlight. Of the 75 or so species in the Caribbean Sea, about 10 account for nine-tenths of the growth. Perhaps the most familiar is the white brain coral, with a surface that resembles a human brain; other hard corals include staghorn, which grows like crusty deer antlers, elkhorn, with huge sloping branches, starlet coral, with polyps like teeth, and orange clump coral, which has a mass of tentacles. Gorgonians consist of sea fans, which face the tidal flow, sifting nutrients, and sea whips, which blow like feathers in the tide.

Sponges and anemones add their own color and variety to the marine world. Tube sponges can grow to 7 ft., in shades of pink,

Aquariums
Several aquariums in the Caribbean provide alternatives to glass-bottom boats for non-divers. The Guadeloupe Aquarium is between Bas du Fort and Gosier, and on Martinique there is an aquarium on the road to Schoelcher from central Fort de France. Both have well-marked displays of tropical fish from the Caribbean and elsewhere. On Curaçao the Seaquarium is in the Underwater Park, east of Willemstad. A spiral-shaped aquarium operates in the Parque Lenin, south of Havana, in Cuba, and on St. Thomas, Coral World has tanks with over a hundred species of fish on view. Perhaps the most interesting display is at the small aquarium on the waterfront in Frederiksted, St. Croix, where the underwater world is explained in fascinating detail by a guide. All aquariums charge an entry fee; prices vary, but they can be pretty expensive.

orange, purple and yellow, and the white cryptic sponge hides in the crevices of the reef. Anemones look like intricate flowers, with many only at night; those which emerge during the day will often snap back into the rock if the water around them is disturbed. Shrimps (visible in daylight) often live in conjunction with anemones—the banded coral shrimp has a striking red and white striped body.

Night-diving reveals another, self-contained submarine society. Crabs and lobsters come out to hunt for food, and starfish, some of which look like underwater plants, open up to feed in the dark. An octopus, squid, or a tiny sea-

horse might be spotted—though their camouflage is excellent; the sea cucumber, by contrast, is easy to make out, resembling a mobile underwater hot dog. The biggest and best known of the mollusks (shell animals), which are also best seen at night, is the conch, known as the *lambi* in the French-speaking Caribbean.

There are a number of species to avoid when underwater: a touch from the fire coral can give a nasty sting, as can some jellyfish. Avoid the spiny black sea urchin at all costs—its spines cause agonizing wounds if they break off in your flesh.

Fish Around a thousand species of fish live in the Caribbean, many of them on the reefs, where there is plenty of food. Schools of angel fish and butterfly fish can be seen waving in the current; the four-eye butterfly fish has an imitation pair of eyes on its tail to confuse predators. Other species are dazzlingly beautiful—such as the queen angel fish, which is a luxurious shade of velvet-like blue and gold, and the yellow and black rock beauty. Many fish have been graced with names that describe vividly their forms and habits. Damsel fish hide and lay their eggs in the reefs, grazing on algae, and striped sergeant majors defend their eggs aggressively. Grunts are named for the noise they make when alarmed, and surgeon fish are so-called because of the scalpel-sharp fins in their tails.

Wrasses are scavengers that school in a harem, with one male. If the male is eaten, the biggest female simply switches sex and takes over his job. Parrotfish eat off the reef, biting the polyps and their rocky coral base, spitting out crunched-up coral and producing a considerable amount of sand in the process.

Predatory fish include groupers as well as snappers, one of the most numerous species. They school facing into the current, all moving in time and snapping at any food that passes by. Barracuda patrol in small groups or singly, often around a chosen rock. Larger fish than these tend to live in deeper waters off the reef, some under threat from the big-game fishing boats (see page 202).

Above left: a beautiful queen angel fish

Top: orange clown fish

Eating habits
The dentist or cleaner shrimp cleans the teeth of other, larger fish, thereby getting food for itself. The sponge crab takes small lumps of sponge to use as camouflage, and when it fails to find food, it takes the sponge off its back and eats it. The remora, or sucker fish, is a long, thin fish that attaches itself to a larger fish, such as a shark, and feeds off the remains of its meal.

Coral claims
In 1726 the French naturalist Jean André Peyssonnel declared to the Paris Academy of Sciences that coral reefs were made up of living animals, not marine shrubs, as was generally thought. He was ridiculed and had to live out his life as a scientist in exile in Guadeloupe—and though proved right during his lifetime, Peyssonnel received no credit.

Barbuda

The frigatebird colony
The crooked wingspan and forked tail of the huge, black frigatebird is easy to recognize. Its most surprising feature is the male's gullet, a bright red balloon blown to the size of a basketball during display. Although it can be seen on Barbuda, it also flies to the other islands to feed, traveling at up to 93 miles per hour. It even attacks other birds on the wing for food, swooping in from above, grabbing the tail or leg and shaking the victim until it drops its meal. Barbuda's frigatebird sanctuary is well worth a visit; the birds soar high above it, returning to the mangroves to nest in large colonies.

The hilly southwest of Antigua has fine views from Green Castle Hill and a ring of stones thought by some to be ancient megaliths. Beneath Boggy Peak (at 1,319 ft. the highest point of the island), Old Road, now a small village, was the site of Antigua's first European settlement in 1632. Nearby Fig Tree Hill is a lush valley covered with large, shiny "elephant ear" leaves and bananas.

In the southeast are the fortifications erected by British colonists when Antigua was at the height of its strategic and economic importance. Opposite Falmouth Harbour towers Monks Hill Fort, a refuge for women, children, and animals in case of attack. Beyond it are the tourist and sailing areas of English Harbour and **Nelson's Dockyard►►** (see page 77). A short water-taxi ride across the bay brings you to **Clarence House►►**, built in 1787 for the future King William IV and now the Antiguan Governor General's official residence (open to visitors when the Governor General is not in residence). Above it are **Shirley Heights►►**, a series of Georgian barrack buildings and gun emplacements constructed in the 1780s as a defense against the French. The **Dow's Hill Interpretation Centre►►** is set among the battlements and shows an excellent video of Antiguan history, from Indian settlement to the present day.

Barbuda Lying 30 miles to the north of Antigua, Barbuda is one of the few truly undeveloped Caribbean islands. Like Antigua, with which it was politically merged in 1860, it is all coral limestone, and has glorious beaches. Otherwise, its 60 sq. miles are covered in scrub, where goats, donkeys, and wild boar roam. The only town is Codrington, named after the family who owned the island and used it as a private ranch for 200 years before its incorporation into Antiguan territory. (When Antigua began negotiations for independence from Britain in 1980, it was the proud Barbudans who objected, calling for more governing powers of their own.)

Sights on Barbuda include caves in the northeast, where Indian rock carvings have survived, the **frigatebird sanctuary►►►** (see panel), and River Fort, a martello tower on the south coast.

Inventive headgear on one of the streets in Codrington, Barbuda's only town

Nelson's Dockyard

■ **Nelson's Dockyard is as active today as it was 200 years ago, when English Harbour was the most important naval base in the area. But in place of urgent whistles and cannon blasts, there is now a peaceful atmosphere. Preparations may occasionally be as feverish as they were during the 18th-century wars, but today's sailors are more likely to be doing battle in yacht races. ....■**

The pillars of the old Boat House and Sail Loft

Nelson's Dockyard is the best preserved colonial shipyard in the Caribbean, restored over the past 40 years into one of its top sailing destinations. Covered in bougainvillea and hibiscus, the beautiful old stone warehouses contain hotels, bars, galleries, and a museum—but life is still centered on the harbor, where sailing craft line the wharves.

Set on Antigua in a deep and sinuous bay, the dockyard was first developed in 1725 as a victualing and repair station. Ships sheltered here during hurricanes and could be careened (cleaned) when their bottoms were covered with barnacles and weeds. Eventually the dockyard became one of the most important stations in the British Caribbean, and the massive fortifications of Shirley Heights were built in order to defend it.

From the parking lot, the dockyard's first building is the old Pitch and Tar Store (pitch from Trinidad was used to waterproof ships' hulls, now housing the Admiral's Inn, a small hotel. Next door are the pillars of the old Boat House and Sail Loft (the building has lost its upper story), where ships' sails were winched up for repair. A museum in the Naval Officer's House, across the way, has exhibits of maps and model ships from the dockyard's heyday. Next door is the Old Copper and Lumber Store, where sheet metal and wood were kept, and able seamen slept in upstairs dormitories; nowadays the rooms are used as somewhat more comfortable hotel accommodation. In the old Officers' Quarters are galleries, shops, and a balcony snack bar with a superb view of the harbor. The Galley Bar, once the cookhouse, now caters to hungry visitors as a bar and restaurant.

Nelson
It is unlikely that Horatio Nelson would ever have consented to give his name to the dockyard. The famous British admiral served here between 1784 and 1787 while he was captain of HMS *Boreas*—and he hated it, considering the dockyard itself a "vile spot." He was lonely and had the unpleasant job of putting a stop to unofficial trading between the Leeward Islanders and ships from the young American nation. At one point Nelson was confined on board for eight weeks, knowing that if he set foot ashore he would be arrested by the resentful planters. He returned to the Caribbean only once, for 24 hours in 1805, when he was chasing the French Admiral Villeneuve.

Hibiscus in bloom

A restored building in Plymouth

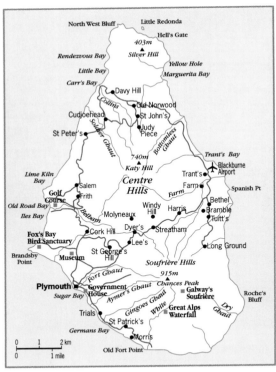

Montserrat

Montserrat is a small, friendly, and relaxed island; still recovering from 1989's devastating Hurricane Hugo, it is blessed with lovely scenery and an unusually pretty main town. As its name might suggest, Montserrat is a mountainous island, whose volcanic peaks have a jagged, almost serrated profile. Columbus named it on his second voyage, in honor of a monastery near Barcelona, and Montserrat still maintains an almost monastic serenity. Its irregular form, just 10½ miles by 7 miles, lies about 25 miles southwest of Antigua. There are 12,000 islanders, plus some expatriate residents and medical students at the American University of the Caribbean. Only a few beaches can be found on the island, and just a couple of them, in the northwest, have light-colored sand.

Plymouth►►, the small capital, lies on the southwest coast. Many of the houses, especially in the area of Wapping, are built in a classic West Indian style, with stone foundations and painted wooden upper floors. **Government House►►**, the Governor's residence (Montserrat is a UK-dependent territory), stands on the hillside above Wapping in attractive lawned gardens, and is open to visitors.

Beyond the town, Montserrat is a typical volcanic Caribbean island with fertile countryside, where "ghauts" (a local name for river ravines) run down from the mountains. Most villages are scattered along the protected lee-

ward (Caribbean) coastline, but there are also settlements near the airport and up in the central hills. Their names—St. Peter's, St. John's, Salem, Bethel, Parsons—recall the fact that the island was a haven for 17th-century Catholics (see panel). In the country, farmers still live a simple life, cultivating their crops and selling them at the market much as they did 50 years ago, when the island was one of the poorest in the Caribbean.

Chances Peak is Montserrat's highest point, at 3,000 ft., and is reached after a two-hour walk through the lush rainforest off the road to Parsons. To the south of Plymouth, on the coast road beneath Government House, is Galway's Estate▶▶, a collection of restored 17th- and 18th-century sugar plantation buildings, complete with windmill and boiling house. A 45-minute walk above the village of St. Patrick's leads to the Great Alps Waterfall▶▶, a 69-ft. cascade with a swimmable rockpool. Galway's Soufrière, Montserrat's main volcanic outlet, is beyond the falls. The sulphur referred to in its name soon becomes evident in the powerful smell of its steaming pools.

North of Plymouth, the Montserrat Museum▶▶ is set in an old windmill, and has exhibits from pre-Columbian settlements on Alliouagana (the name given to the island by indigenous Indians), and displays relating to colonial life. Coots, kingfishers, and herons can be seen at the Fox's Bay bird sanctuary, in the coastal swamp around Bransby Point. Belham Valley is the site of the island's 11-hole golf course and home to a number of comfortable vacation villas, and north of here are Montserrat's best beaches: Carr's Bay, Little Bay (which is reached by climbing down the hillside), and Rendezvous Bay.

Government House, the Governor's residence in Plymouth—a typically Caribbean building

79

■ **Music is played everywhere in the Caribbean: on buses, on vast personal stereos, in bars and clubs, and at Carnival, when whole islands stop work to dance in the streets. West Indians will tune almost anything to make music: wheel hubs, bamboo poles and even cheese graters, but the most famous instrument of all is the steel drum, or "pan," invented in Trinidad about 50 years ago. .....■**

Almost every Caribbean island has its own unique musical style; all of them have a strong rhythm that irresistibly inspires dancing. Particular styles of dancing vary from island to island, but the movement always centers around the hips and pelvis.

Caribbean music also incorporates a tradition of social comment. The Calypsonians of Trinidad are the most famous satirists, and many other styles have carried messages of protest: ska was a shout from the poor ghettos of Kingston in Jamaica in the 1950s, and even in Cuba, where political dissent is not tolerated, "trova" songs have been known to question the integrity of party members.

Reggae and soca The British Caribbean has two main rhythms: reggae, which has recently developed an offshoot from Jamaica called ragga (see page 152), and soca, which originated in Trinidad and is played in the southeastern Caribbean. Soca (a contraction of "soul-calypso") consists of a fast and hard rhythm with a double beat.

Salsa and merengue
Salsa comes from Puerto Rico and Cuba (other Cuban rhythms include the rumba and the cha-cha). This is a bustling, distinctly Latin rhythm; dancing partners face one another as if they were waltzing, but their

Festivals
A biennial World Steel Band Festival takes place in Trinidad in November, and Pan Jazz, a mix of steel band music and jazz, is held on Tobago every March. Other music festivals include Cuba's February Jazz Festival, Jamaica's Reggae Sunsplash in July, and, in the same month, the Merengue Festival in Santo Domingo, in the Dominican Republic.

Transforming a steel drum into a musical instrument

legs move elastically in a subtly sensual movement. Merengue is another hip-swinging, Latin rhythm, from the Dominican Republic.

Zouk and compas The French islands of Martinique and Guadeloupe have produced their own rhythm with a double beat and a very quick tempo, zouk, whose songs have French Creole lyrics. In Haiti, compas is another French-inspired, raw rhythm.

Steel pans The steel band, whose sound has come to represent the whole Caribbean, was invented in Trinidad during World War II. It started in the back streets of Port of Spain, where the discarded oil drums of Trinidad's oil industry were beaten, tuned and turned into instruments. Initially pan was regarded suspiciously by the authorities, partly because the yards where the music developed were the hangouts of ghetto gangs. But its popularity grew and soon pan replaced "tamboo bamboo" (musical bamboo poles) as the music of Carnival.

Steel pan lids are bashed out in a bowl and given a number of flat surfaces to produce different notes. There are five different ranges in the pan orchestra. Bass pan players have five full-size drums (each one can only give four notes). Cello pan players have three pans which are cut down to three-quarter size, each having seven notes. Guitar pans and double second pans both come in pairs, playing notes in the middle range (the guitar pan plays chords, while the double second takes the melody). Tenor pans, or "ping pongs," are the lead instruments in the orchestra and the highest in the range. They have 30 notes, covering a two-and-a-half octave range, and are about 1 ft. deep.

As many as 60 players can play in a steel band and it is well worth visiting a "pan yard' to see them play. Not only is the noise impressive—a symphony of pings, clangs and bongs that combine into a coherent sound—but the energetic drummers moving in unison are an entertainment in themselves.

Pan yards play all year round, but the easiest time to see them at work is during the run-up to Carnival at the beginning of the year. Steel bands with colourful names—"Desperadoes," "Renegades" and "Invaders"—have nowadays been superseded by soca as the main music of Carnival, but they still play at Jouvert, the parade which takes place on the Monday morning of Carnival week.

A musician from the Dominican Republic

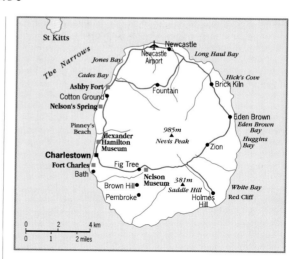

Nevis

Alexander Hamilton
Nevis's most famous son is Alexander Hamilton, who is commemorated in the museum set in his former home in Charlestown. Born in 1755, he lived in the house for the first five years of his life, until his mother moved to St. Croix (now one of the U.S. Virgin Islands). Impressed by the wealth of merchants on St. Thomas, he described them as "wheeling their gold through the streets in wheelbarrows." Hamilton moved to North America, where he fought in the Revolutionary War as George Washington's aide and was instrumental in founding the American Constitution, becoming the first Secretary of the Treasury. Known as the Little Lion, because he was a short man with a fierce temper, Hamilton died in a duel in 1804. He is pictured on $10 bills.

The small volcanic island of Nevis lies between St. Kitts and Montserrat, across a strait called the Narrows. It is almost circular—just 5½ miles by 8 miles—and rises to a central peak of 3,232 ft. A semi-permanent wreath of clouds on the summit reminded early travelers of snow and inspired the name Nuestra Señora de la Nieves—Our Lady of the Snows. Nowadays, life for the 9,000 Nevisians is pretty slow, and the grandeur of the island's prosperous past—when it was known as the "Queen of the Caribbees"—is disappearing into the undergrowth; but the island is proud of its beautifully restored plantation houses, where many visitors stay. The atmosphere of the island has changed with the arrival of a large beach hotel—but it still has a certain regal calm, and an evening stroll along its lit walkways, while the air rings to the singing of tree frogs and flashes with fireflies, is an unforgettable experience.

Nevis is politically attached to St. Kitts, but its personality is very different. Visitors to Nevis enjoy the peace and quiet, the hammocks for snoozing, and lobster-bakes on palm-fringed beaches. The island's capital is **Charlestown►►**, a small collection of stone and timber-frame houses laid out irregularly on the leeward coast. Except on market days (Tuesday, Thursday, and Saturday morning) and when the ferry arrives from St. Kitts, the town can best be described as comatose. Inland from the jetty (the ferry docks at Memorial Square, a triangular park overlooked by banks and stores) are the Court House and Library; here there is a small tourist office. At the northern end of the town is the **Alexander Hamilton Museum►►** (see panel), set in a stone townhouse, in which the Nevis Assembly sits (upstairs) to conduct its business.

North of Charlestown, **Pinney's Beach►►►** is the island's best beach—a 3-mile strip of dark golden sand backed with tall palms, with magnificent views across the Narrows to St. Kitts. The island's first settlement of 80 planters, who arrived from St. Kitts in 1628, was situated

Beach life is still a quiet affair on Nevis

on this beach, until it was tipped into the sea by an earthquake. The Four Seasons Hotel now stands here, with an 18-hole golf course. The circular road passes other good beaches en route to Nevis's airport and the island's only other town, Newcastle.

To the south of Charlestown are the ruins of **Fort Charles►**, the island's primary defense in colonial times; nearby are the old **Bath Hotel and Spring►**, built in 1778 and now reduced to a shell. In its heyday as a spa hotel, the Bath welcomed thousands of aristocratic visitors, who came to take the curative waters.

At **Fig Tree Church►►**, on the road east of Charlestown, you can see the register of Horatio Nelson's marriage to Nevisian Fanny Nisbet on March 11, 1787, during a moment off from his lonely duties around the Leeward Islands. The **Nelson Museum►►**, in the Morning Star Estate Great House, a little further on, has mementos and artifacts from the Admiral's life, including letters and pictures. From here you pass into the less populous eastern parts of the island, where abandoned plantations, which were once the focus of the island's wealth, are now mouldering ruins.

While touring the island it is worth stopping at one of Nevis's 18th-century plantation house hotels, where lunch or dinner can be taken on the veranda. Montpelier Plantation Inn (tel: 469 1932), in the south, has cottages with 16 rooms in its grounds; and the Hermitage Plantation (tel: 460 5477), in St. John's in the south, offers upscale accommodation and still has traces of sugar-processing equipment in its gardens. Details of other plantation houses can be obtained at the tourist office in Charlestown (Main Street, tel: 469 5521) or from the Tourist Boards (see **Travel Facts**).

A deserted windmill stands as a reminder of colonial wealth

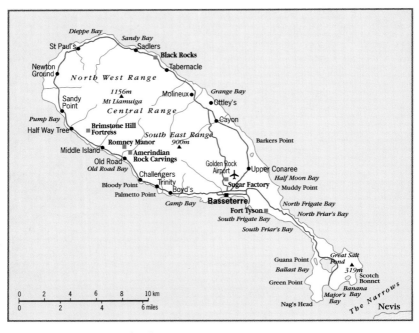

St. Kitts (St. Christopher)

Looking towards Nevis from Timothy Hill, St. Kitts

Two centuries ago, most of the West Indies looked like St. Kitts, with vast tracts of bright green sugar cane swaying in the breeze, and estate houses standing aloof in colonial elegance. Many of these houses have been preserved, along with an atmosphere so English that it seems natural to play croquet and take afternoon tea. But the modern age is catching up with St. Kitts, in the form of beach tourism. The island's southeastern peninsula, which has the best white sand beaches, has been set aside for development, and the tourist race is beginning— though it remains relatively low key for the time being.

St. Kitts is larger and livelier than its sister Nevis, appealing to a more active crowd. Nevis is just a few miles to the south and the Dutch island of St. Eustatius 5 miles to the north. Measuring around 68 sq. miles, the island is shaped vaguely like a paddle, with forest-clad mountains and an old volcanic crater occupying its blade. In the northwest the highest peak, the 3,793-ft. Mount Liamuiga, is believed to take its name from the indigenous Indian name for the island.

St. Kitts is an informal version of the island's original European name, St. Christopher, given by Columbus on his second voyage in 1493. Historically, this was the "Mother Colony" of the West Indies—the first island in the Eastern Caribbean to be settled successfully by Europeans, in 1623. British and French colonists helped each other to establish a foothold in hostile Indian and Spanish territory, before sending colonizers to other islands. Using indentured workers and slaves, they turned St. Kitts into a rich plantation island. They also began to fight over it, as they were to do for centuries afterwards. For proof of the bitterness of their battle, you need only visit Brimstone Hill, one of the biggest forts in the Caribbean (see page 87). An early French Governor of the island was de Poincy, whose name is remembered in the poinciana, a tree that grows all over the Caribbean islands. Together with Nevis, St. Kitts became independent in September 1983. There are 37,000 Kittitians, many working in agriculture or tourism.

Basseterre►► is the island's capital, situated on the protected Caribbean coast. Its name is one of the few remaining vestiges of the island's French heritage—unfortunately, its French buildings were all destroyed in fires. However, there are attractive British colonial timber-frame and stone buildings around the town center, some of which house cafés and restaurants. Just behind the waterfront is the **Circus►►**, an open traffic circle overlooked by townhouses with elegant upper-story balconies. In the center is a colonial clocktower, the Berkeley Memorial, and the nearby **Independence Square►►** is an open park with a fountain, poincianas and palm trees. The square is surrounded by elegant townhouses, one of which contains the **Spencer Cameron Gallery►►**, displaying local and expatriate Caribbean work, and the Catholic Cathedral of the Immaculate Conception, with its twin spires and a fine rose window. On Cayon Street is the Anglican St. George's Church, built of brown stone in traditional English parish church style. The St. Kitts Tourist Board has its office on Church Street, next door to the government buildings.

85

Rawlins Plantation Hotel, St. Kitts

The volcanic Black Rocks

Intriguing trees
The poinciana is sometimes jokingly referred to as the "tourist tree" because it turns a startingly bright shade of red in July and August. Its pods, which look like long wooden string beans, are used by children to make music—as they make a "shack-a-shack-a-shack" noise when shaken. Another brightly flowering tree is the African tulip tree, which has red blooms all year round. It is also known as the "flame of the forest" or the "fountain tree" because its unopened buds squirt water when they are squeezed.

The main tourist area on St. Kitts is southeast of Basseterre. There are hotels, villas, a golf course, and a popular beach in **Frigate Bay►►**, and **Friar's Bay►►►**, over the next hill, has a marvelous beach of soft golden sand, which gets busy when cruise ships arrive. The new peninsular road leads past salt ponds, which formed common ground in the days of joint English and French occupation, to the southern beaches, where there are superb views of the channel and of Nevis.

Northwest of the capital, the road runs past the island's light industry and emerges into sugar cane country, planted on the coastal flats beneath the central mountain range. A circular road (accompanied by a railroad to transport harvested cane) follows the coast, touching all the small Kittitian villages; it can be driven comfortably in a day. A walk into the rainforest on the mountain can be arranged by tour operators.

Old Road Bay► is the site of the first British settlement and was the capital until 1727. Amerindian **rock carvings►►** can be seen on the Wingfield Estate, near by. Romney Manor, a 17th-century great house set in tropical gardens, is the home of **Caribelle Batik►►**, a store selling silk-screened prints and clothes. At Middle Island is the **grave of Thomas Warner►**, the man who led the successful settlement in 1623. From here the road soon passes under the massive defenses of **Brimstone Hill►►►** (see page 87).

The **Black Rocks►** are a curious formation of volcanic lava on the Atlantic coast; from here the road leads to Basseterre via the airport and the **sugar cane factory►►**, which is best visited while it operates, between the months of January and June.

Forts

■ **Huge forts still tower over many Caribbean settlements, monuments to an era when imperial fleets and armies were sent to defend their valuable territories. Two centuries ago the Caribbean was a hardship posting and these massive bastions recall a time of violence and instability, when loud drum rolls and frantic whistle blasts would herald urgent preparations for war. .....■**

Building and maintaining a fort the size of Brimstone Hill, on St. Kitts, which could hold over 1,000 troops, involved a complex operation. Every stone had to be dragged up to the summit to create the huge structure's bastions and ramparts, inner stronghold, parade ground, barracks, cookhouses, and hospital.

Brimstone Hill (named after the satanic whiffs of sulphur from a nearby volcanic vent) took 100 years to build and was occupied by both British and French during the long 18th-century wars. In 1782 it faced its severest test when it was attacked by 8,000 French troops. The defenders, who held out for a month, were bombarded so heavily that only two rooms in the fort were left undamaged. When they eventually surrendered, the soldiers were allowed to march out with full colors as a tribute to their bravery. A museum in Fort George, the central bastion, has a video show and a description of the siege.

Other forts On Antigua the hills around English Harbour, an important link in the chain of British defences, are cluttered with ramparts and barracks, described at the Dow's Hill Interpretation Centre.

Puerto Rico's two bastions overlook the approaches to San Juan, itself surrounded by walls 33 ft. thick. On the point stands San Felipe del Morro, with 98-ft. ramparts and a maze of tunnels and dungeons; at the other end of Old San Juan is Fuerte San Cristobal, which was built so that each of the outer bastions had to be captured before the inner citadel could be taken.

The most impressive fort in the Caribbean is Haiti's Citadelle, where 10,000 men could hold out for a year without resupply. About 20,000 men are believed to have died building it (see page 181).

Cannons
Cannons litter the Caribbean islands, some abandoned in the forts, others put to good use, buried upright in the ground at the corners of buildings to protect them from passing truck wheels. On the British islands many cannons are printed with the cypher of King George III, a crown superimposed over the letters GR (George Rex). A small arrow can often be seen, stamped into the metal—the symbol used by naval stores.

87

Brimstone Hill's strategic outlook

THE VIRGIN ISLANDS

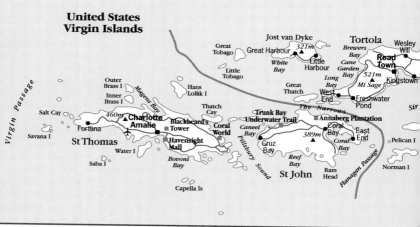

St Croix (USA)

Hams Bluff · Davis Bay · Baron Bluff · Columbus Bay · Buck I · Buck Island Channel · Tague Bay · Point Udall

Butler Bay · 353m ▲ Mt Eagle · Christiansted Harbor · **Christiansted** · Seven Hills · Grapetree Bay

Rain Forest · St George's Botanical Gardens · Kingshill · ▲259m · Robin Bay

Frederiksted · Rum Distillery · Great Pond Bay

Whim Great House · Canegarden Bay

Sandy Point · Long Point Bay · Harvey I

South West Cape

0   5   10 km
0   5 miles

United States Virgin Islands

Virgin Passage

Great Tobago · Jost van Dyke · Great Harbour · 321m · **Tortola** · Brewers Bay · Wesley Will

Outer Brass I · Inner Brass I · Hans Lollik I · White Bay · Little Harbour · Cane Garden Bay · **Road Town** · Kingstown

Salt Cay · Maggens Bay · Thatch Cay · Great Thatch · Long Bay · 521m ▲ Mt Sage

Savana I · Fortuna · 460m ▲ **Charlotte Amalie** · Blackbeard's Tower · Coral World · West End · Freshwater Pond · Sir

Little Tobago

Saba I · Water I · Havensight Mall · Caneel Bay · Trunk Bay Underwater Trail · Annaberg Plantation · Coral Bay · East End · Pelican I

St Thomas · Bovoni Bay · Cruz Bay · 389m ▲ · Coral Bay

Pillsbury Sound · Reef Bay · Ram Head · Flanagan Passage · Norman I

Capella Is · **St John**

Tranquil touring among the Virgin Islands by yacht

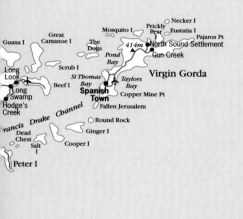

West End Pt · Soldier Pt · Loblolly Bay
Flamingo Pond · Red Pond · The Settlement
Anegada
East Pt

British Virgin Islands

Necker I
Mosquito I · Prickly Pear · Eustatia I
Great Camanoe I · The Dogs · Pajaros Pt
Guana I · 414m · North Sound · Settlement
Pond Bay · Gun Creek
Scrub I · **Virgin Gorda**
Long Look · St Thomas Bay · Taylors Bay
Beef I · **Spanish Town** · Copper Mine Pt
Long Swamp · Fallen Jerusalem
Hodge's Creek
Francis Drake Channel · Round Rock
Dead Chest · Ginger I
Salt I · Cooper I
Peter I

0	5	10	15 km
0		5	10 miles

The Virgin Islands In mood and style, the U.S. and British Virgin Islands are worlds apart. The British islands are quieter and less developed, and islanders have an old-world sense of reserve and courtesy. The U.S. islands, on the other hand, are brash and busy and have a brisk night life. With sailing, diving, and watersports almost a way of life, these prosperous and sophisticated islands are ideal for those who don't intend to stray too far from the beach. Most visitors go to the high-rise St. Thomas or the more laid-back St. Croix (U.S.V.I.), while Tortola (B.V.I.) is less crowded and largely caters to yachts.

Scattered over miles of incomparably blue sea, the Virgin Islands are, with the exception of Anegada, steep and green, the peaks of a submerged chain of volcanoes. Just under half the 90 or so islands are a British Crown Colony; the rest are "an unincorporated territory of the U.S.A." In the west are the three main United States Virgin Islands (U.S.V.I.): St. Thomas, St. John and, to their south, St. Croix, and assorted cays. Sprinkled to the east of the American islands, the British Virgin Islands (B.V.I.) are smaller and more numerous, the largest among them being Tortola and Virgin Gorda.

A deserted sugar mill on St. John

In the U.S.V.I., where people work at resorts on land their forebears once owned, there is great disparity between rich and poor and some resentment towards Americans. In the B.V.I., where people tend to own the land, there is virtually no shopping or nightlife; on Tortola and Virgin Gorda no hotels are taller than a palm tree and most are owned by locals or expatriates. The U.S.V.I. are for visitors who want a bustling environment; the B.V.I. are for sailors and those who want to escape the holiday crowds.

The Danish in the Caribbean
Though they are not known as great colonists, the Danes took part in the race for Empire early on and settled St. Thomas in 1665, encouraging its use as a trading base by declaring it a free port. They moved on to St. John in 1717 and St. Croix in 1733 and planted them entirely with sugar cane, bringing in slaves to work the fields. The Danes were the first to ban the slave trade (the carrying of slaves from Africa), in 1792, but slavery itself continued on the islands until 1848, when the Governor went against his King's orders and declared emancipation. The islands were nearly sold to the U.S. in 1866, but it was not until 1917 that the islanders themselves voted for the transfer of government.

History The Virgin Islands were given their name by Columbus when he sailed among them on his second voyage of exploration; the virgins concerned were the 11,000 beautiful followers of St. Ursula, who according to legend were killed by Huns on a pilgrimage to Cologne. For many years, pirates roamed their shores, waiting for ships to plunder and refitting their vessels in hidden coves. Charlotte Amalie, on St. Thomas, became a busy market place for the pirates' captured goods.

The U.S.V.I. were owned for centuries by Denmark, but not much remains of Danish influence except the names (such as Charlotte Amalie and Christiansted) and the old trading warehouses and townhouses. St. Croix and St. John were at one time carpeted with sugar cane, but during the last century the industry declined, and the islands were eventually bought by the U.S. in 1917 for $25 million.

Meanwhile the B.V.I. remained barren backwaters, planted while the going was good, but soon falling back into obscurity. At one point the British Government considered selling these islands to America as well. It never happened, but the pull to the U.S. is still strong. The B.V.I. have adopted the U.S. dollar as their currency and many islanders move to find work on St. Thomas.

Island life Today, the U.S.V.I. offer the American experience in a tropical setting. The banks are American, as are the fast food joints, the Grand Union supermarkets, the currency and the baseball. St. Thomas and St. John are geographically close, but in character they could not be further apart. St. Thomas is overdeveloped and crowded (particularly when the cruise ships put in), and offers some of the Caribbean's best shopping in Charlotte Amalie, as well as good bars and restaurants. St. John, just a 20-minute ferry ride away, is quiet and undeveloped. About two-thirds of it is undisturbed jungle, protected by its National Park status. There are, nevertheless, a number of places to stay in Cruz Bay and at the East End. The third island, St. Croix, offers a variety of beach hotels, restaurants, and interesting town buildings.

By comparison, the pace of life on the British islands is slow and peaceful. For every 15 people who travel to the U.S.V.I. on vacation, the B.V.I. get one. Of the B.V.I.'s 150,000 or so visitors a year, three-quarters come from the U.S.—and most come to sail, without even booking into a hotel. The B.V.I. are not about discos, high-rise hotels, fast food, and casinos. They are about superb beaches, many only accessible from the sea. While the U.S.V.I. have gone for numbers, the B.V.I. have gone for bank rolls. Tortola is the hub of B.V.I. yachting, and from here there is access by ferry to many of the other islands, including Virgin Gorda, with its top-rank hotels, secluded beaches, and offshore cays, or tranquil Jost van Dyke. Like the pirates of yore, you can sail among the Virgins by day and put in to an isolated cove for the night; but nowadays conditions are rather less harsh for sailors, who can even order dinner over the V.H.F. radio and have a barbecue waiting when they arrive.

A British touch on Virgin Gorda

Surf culture, Tortola style

Tortola

A century ago, when even St. Thomas was a backwater, Tortola was written off as "forsaken." Today the island is enjoying something of a boom, which has led to growing development, as the 12,000 islanders and expatriates build on the towering heights. A dock for cruise ships is also being constructed, which may well tip the balance away from the island's present peace.

Tortola is 12 miles by 3 miles and has a scrubby and meandering spine of steep mountains, rising to 1,709 ft. at Mount Sage. The main settlement is Road Town, a ramshackle, sprawling capital made up of a few streets collected around a deep bight in the southern coastline. Features include yachting marinas, a small museum, a botanical garden, bars and restaurants, and a couple of stores. Tortolans live in small settlements around the coast; transportation is usually by taxi or rental car.

The best bays and beaches are on the island's north side. At the West End, where most of the hotels are, you will find the Pirate's Pub and the Pusser's Pub immediately after clearing customs; to the north is a perfect, isolated curve of sand called Smuggler's Cove►►►. Heading east you come to Long Bay, a superb run of white sand, and Apple Bay, where surfers enjoy the big waves (look for Bomba's Surfside Shack, a beach bar made of driftwood). The long and lovely Cane Garden Bay►► has small places to stay and a string of beach bars; Quito's Gazebo has live music every night except Mondays. From here, it is an almost impossibly steep climb to the mountain's spine, which eventually descends into Road Town.

East of Road Town, the road follows the coastline to Long Look, where there is a small town. A toll bridge leads to Beef Island, the site of Tortola's airport. There are good beaches here, including Josiah's Bay and Long Bay►► on Beef Island. The Last Resort is a lively restaurant and bar on an island in Trellis Bay.

A bar sign at Frenchman's Cay, western Tortola

92

New marina developments are springing up in Tortola; this one is at Frenchman's Cay near West End

Guana
Guana is a naturalists' island off the northeastern tip of Tortola, maintained as a wildlife sanctuary. Its 847 acres are said to harbor the richest fauna seen on any island of its size in the world—from flamingos to hawks, from bats to cats, and from wild donkeys to sea turtles.

Virgin Gorda

Virgin Gorda is even quieter than Tortola, but it has some of the Virgin Islands' most chic resorts hidden in its coves and offshore cays. Lying east of Tortola (and reached by ferry), it was discovered, like St. John in the U.S.V.I., by Rockefeller, who built the Little Dix Bay hotel here. Virgin Gorda means "the fat Virgin"—the island supposedly looks like a reclining woman. Its 8-sq.-mile area is divided into three mounds and covered in scrub and cactus, rising to a 1,358-ft. peak in the north. The most distinctive scenery is in the south, where massive granite boulders, the Baths, form a maze of water-filled, smooth-faced caves.

Boats from Tortola dock at the southern settlement of Spanish Town, where many of the 1,500 or so islanders live. The town is really little more than its marina, with bars and an easy-going atmosphere. Virgin Gorda's best beaches—including the Baths—are south of Spanish Town. In the southeast of the island are the ruins of an old copper mine, active during the last century.

The road to the north of the island passes isolated coves such as Savannah Bay and Pond Bay before reaching Virgin Gorda's second town, Gun Creek. This overlooks the North Sound, a stretch of water almost completely surrounded by tall peaks, cays, and small islands with fine beaches. Two splendid hotels lie at this end of the island, accessible only by boat from Gun Creek. Biras Creek is a place of understated wealth overlooking a calm sound, a bay (with the main beach), and wild Atlantic surf; and the Bitter End Yacht Club prints a newspaper showing the wide range of watersports on offer. Gathering places on the islands around the sound include a bright pink Pusser's Bar in Leverick Bay; an elegant restaurant, Drake's Anchorage, on Mosquito Island; a beach bar on Prickly Pear Cay, and the tiny Saba Rock, which is just a bar that wakes up in the evenings.

The Baths

The Baths
The Baths form a series of coves to the south of Spanish Town. Best approached by sea, the boulders are stacked in jumbled piles and backed by coconut palms. From the land you can reach them through the scrub from the Mad Dog Bar. Made of granite, a stone that does not normally appear in the Caribbean, they may have been carried here by glacial movement during the Ice Age.

■ **Watersports are an integral part of a Caribbean vacation. The warm seas and constant Trade Winds make its islands excellent places for windsurfers, scuba-divers, jet-skiers, and parasailors. But there is nothing to beat the freedom of sailing, and the calmer stretches of sea are flecked with white as yachts of all shapes and sizes ride the ocean breezes, dolphins dipping and darting beneath their prows. ......■**

Regattas

The biggest annual sailing event in the Caribbean is Race Week in Antigua, which includes five days of races followed by parties in the evenings. A major regatta is held in the British Virgin Islands every April, and in June and July Martiniquans race the *yoles rondes*, which have distinctive square sails and crews of 12 leaning out over the water on booms; in August Anguilla has a race week for elegant, locally built boats; and also in August Carriacou, in the Grenadines, stages its own small regatta.

Parasailing

Parasailing is an unusual sport to try while in the Caribbean, and can be arranged on most islands, usually on the most developed beaches. The sport is something like water-skiing in the sky: as a motor boat speeds along, the "skier," attached by a long line and wearing a parachute, rises into the air—without getting wet and with the advantage of tremendous views.

With such a variety of islands lying within easy reach of one another, island-hopping by yacht is an effective way of seeing the Caribbean. Yachts are easily arranged for four to eight people or more, and can be rented as bare-boats (no crew) or crewed (with captain and hands to order the supplies and do the sailing and cooking). All yachts have fridges, kitchenware, and bedding, most provide masks and snorkels, and some carry windsurfing and diving equipment. Day sails are available from several islands, but if you find the idea of taking a yacht out on the ocean waves a little daunting, most hotels have small sailboats (hobie cats and sunfish) which can be sailed near the shore.

The best sailing destinations are the Virgin Islands and the Grenadines. Both regions are spectacularly beautiful, with convenient sailing distances separating the islands. The Virgins have good marina facilities, but this means crowds during the high season. The Grenadines have a wilder beauty, but restaurants and bars have found their way even to many of the quieter bays.

Reliable year-round winds make windsurfing a popular Caribbean sport. The best windsurfing areas are: the Dominican Republic, particularly around Cabarete on the northern shore, where World Championships are occasionally held; Barbados's southern shore around Maxwell and Silver Sands, and Aruba. The sport is well catered for in the French Caribbean and is also becoming more popular on the Cayman Islands.

Scuba diving

■ Divers acknowledge the Caribbean as an ideal setting for one of the world's most exotic sports, with its vast areas of colorful coral, and its strange and beautiful tropical fish. Snorkelers, too, can enjoy access to offshore reefs from most islands; and glass-bottom boat trips provide views of underwater wonders without even the need to get wet. .....■

Although it does not have the abundance of the Indo-Pacific area, the Caribbean can boast around 75 species of corals, which include brain corals, sea fans, and whips, hydra-headed anemones, gorgonians, and sponges. More mobile sea creatures include crabs, lobsters, starfish, rays, eels, and even turtles or sharks. Diving at night reveals a completely different world, as some corals close and others open, while fish emerge to feed on them, crunching away at the polyps, or sleep tucked away in sleeping bags of mucus so that their scent cannot be picked up by predators.

Diving sites
The best diving sites are off the Cayman Islands, with sheer drops to limitless depths, and Bonaire, where the coral-clad slopes are at gentler angles. Saba, a steep-sided volcanic cone, has an abundance of corals and the Grenadines' waters are not as crowded.

95

As well as the natural beauties of the sea, shipwrecks are a source of endless fascination, and near some islands ships have been sunk deliberately in order to provide artificial reefs for underwater explorers. Off the shores of Anguilla, divers can swim over a 197-ft. hulk sitting upright on the seabed.

Scuba (Self Contained Underwater Breathing Apparatus) diving was invented in the early 1940s and developed rapidly as a sport, popularized by divers such as Jacques Cousteau. There are several suppliers in the Caribbean and it is easily arranged on most islands. Many hotels offer qualifying courses with the affiliated dive organizations (PADI and NAUI); there are also non-qualifying resort courses that enable novices to dive almost immediately. (Remember to arrange personal insurance before leaving home.)

Marine parks
Most islands have instituted marine parks around their shores in order to protect their corals and fish. Divers are forbidden from picking coral or hunting fish with spear-guns within these areas. Do not buy coral jewelry on the islands—it is made from live coral, which is culled from the reef.

Smaller British Virgin Islands

Ferries around the B.V.I.
Regular ferries criss-cross the waters of the Virgin Islands. There are frequent services between Road Town on Tortola and The Valley in Virgin Gorda. The sleek North Sound Express runs between Beef Island (the airport at the eastern end of Tortola) and the expensive hotels of the North Sound (the east end of Virgin Gorda), and a daily service links The Valley and Beef Island. Several daily sailings carry passengers to Jost van Dyke, from West End on Tortola. Some offshore islands have their own water ferries: Peter Island, for example, from the C.S.Y. Marina just out of Road Town, and Guana Island (from Beef Island).

Anegada▶ is not a typical Virgin Island. It stands alone, 19 miles out in the ocean, and whereas the other Virgins are tall and volcanic islands, Anegada is a 7-mile curve of coral. The island is scrubby and flat (only 30 ft. at its highest point) and culminates in a submerged tail called Horseshoe Reef, a magnificent living coral expanse, which has claimed more than 300 unwary ships over the centuries. The name Anegada means "inundated"— which it occasionally is, by passing waves. Only 250 people live here, sharing the island with goats and iguanas; their sole collection of houses is called The Settlement. The island is not much visited, but there are a couple of places to eat and stay, including a chic diving hotel, and Loblolly Bay is the best of many beaches.

Jost van Dyke▶▶▶ is almost devoid of tourism, other than visiting yachts. It lies north of Tortola and takes its name from a Dutch pirate. Just a few hilly square miles in area, the island is reached by ferry from West End on Tortola. Great Harbour, the main port, is a port of entry to

Jost van Dyke

the Virgin Islands, and has a church, a police station, and a few beach bars (one of whose owners welcomes visitors with a personalized calypso). There is an excellent beach at White Bay, and yachts put in at Sandy Cay, one of a couple of sheltered cays off the island. The best time to visit is on New Year's Eve, when 2,000 or so revelers sail in for a night's drinking and dancing on the sand.

Necker Island▶▶▶ is an idyllic green speck rimmed with blinding white sand and translucent blue water. Set off the northeastern tip of Virgin Gorda, it is owned by the founder of Virgin Airlines, Richard Branson, who has built a Balinese house and rents the island to groups, families, or companies—at a high cost.

Sir Francis Drake Channel

Sir Francis Drake Channel is the sailing heartland of the Virgin Islands—a magnificent stretch of water off Tortola, where the white triangles of the yacht sails beat back and forth over an unbelievably blue sea. On its southern side the channel is bounded by a necklace of small, irregularly shaped islands, which run southeast in a graceful curve from Virgin Gorda to St. John in the U.S.V.I. In their isolated coves are some superb stretches of sand, ideal places for tropical seclusion.

Starting in the northeast, **Fallen Jerusalem** and **Round Rock** lie off Virgin Gorda. Designated a National Park, Fallen Jerusalem has rocky terrain that gives it the appearance of an ancient city in decay. **Ginger Island** is uninhabited, but the next in line, **Cooper Island►►►**, has about 10 inhabitants—the staff of the Cooper Island Beach Club on Manchioneel Bay, which often attracts a lively crowd of "yachties" during the evenings. Scuba diving facilities are available, and there is a beautiful beach.

Salt Island►► takes its name from a salt pond that is still farmed. Rent, payable to the Queen of England, is set at a sack of salt a year, but apparently it has not been collected recently. This is one of the Virgin Island's most popular dive sites, with the wreck of the R.M.S. *Rhone*, which sank in the 19th century, lying offshore. Next in line is **Peter Island►►**, where there is just one very chic island resort with rooms scattered along Deadman's Bay (a charming place, despite its name). Offshore is a small outcrop called Dead Chest, where Bluebeard, a.k.a. Long John Silver, put his mutinous crew ashore with one bottle of rum. **Norman Island►**, the last island in the chain before St. John, is also uninhabited, but is worth visiting for the eerie, waterbound caves at Treasure Point.

Sailing—the only way to travel between the many beautiful Virgin Islands

B.V.I. diving
The Virgin Islands have some excellent diving sites. In Sir Francis Drake Channel there are caves, pinnacles, and submerged rocks, smothered in corals and teeming with fish, some of which have become tame enough to feed. Blonde Rock, off Dea Chest, and the Dogs, off Virgin Gorda, are good examples. Anegada has many wrecks, some of them still poking above the waves where they foundered, but the most famous is that of the *Rhone*, which sank off Salt Island in 1867. This wreck was used in the filming of *The Deep* and it is possible to dive inside its bow section, which lies in 79 ft. of water. The broken pieces of its stern, including the propeller gear, are at about half this depth.

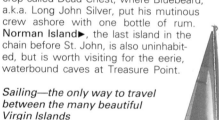

St. Croix

St. Croix (pronounced "St. Croy") is the largest of the Virgin Islands and lies alone, 31 miles to the south of the main U.S.V.I. group. This was the senior island in Danish colonial days because of its successful plantation economy, but whereas St. Thomas has been overtaken by the hustle of modern America, St. Croix has retained a quieter, historic feel. Roughly twice the size of St. Thomas, it is a far more sparsely populated island, with varied scenery including mountains, forest, and beaches, and much land devoted to dairy and cattle-breeding farms.

St. Croix's main town is **Christiansted▶▶▶**, which sits on the waterfront in the east. The pretty bay is full of yachts now, but the Danish influence can still be seen in the town's architecture, with its terraces, patios, and arched yellow colonnades. Fort Christiansvaern was the town's old defense, and the commercial center was around the Old Customs House and the Scale House (now a tourist information office) near the wharf, where merchants would weigh their goods on landing. The Steeple Building contains a museum of Indian artifacts, and on King Street is Government House, still housing government offices. The dry east has most of the island's hotels tucked into its coves and there are golf courses at Buccaneer Bay and Teague Bay. One of the best beaches is on Buck Island, a National Park to which trips can be arranged by tour operators (see **Travel Facts**).

Centerline Road heads west towards Frederiksted through the agricultural land that made St. Croix so wealthy during the 19th century. The **St. George Botanical Garden▶** is a peaceful retreat on an old plantation estate, growing Amerindian and other Cruzian plants. Also off the main road is the Cruzian Rum Distillery, where you can view the production and buy the rum itself, and beyond this is the moated **Whim Great House▶▶**, an unusual rounded estate building that has been restored using 19th-century colonial-style antiques; in the kitchen, old Caribbean utensils and sugar machinery are displayed.

In **Frederiksted▶▶**, on the west coast, there are more colonnaded trading buildings (including the restored Fort Frederik), one of which now houses an impressive **aquarium▶▶**. North of the town, Mahogany Road leads through spectacular forest.

Hurricane Hugo
In 1989 St. Croix suffered badly when it was hit by Hurricane Hugo. About 80 percent of the island's buildings were damaged by the hurricane, and a fifth of the population had to leave and set up home elsewhere. After many years of rebuilding, St. Croix has now restored most of its buldings; only a few roofless eyesores can still be seen.

98

A Frederiksted beach bar

St. John

Trunk Bay

One of the most beautiful islands in the Caribbean, St. John is the smallest and least developed of the U.S.V.I. It lies just a few miles east of St. Thomas, a short ferry-ride across the Pillsbury Sound, but is so tranquil that it seems a world away. Two-thirds of the island are given over to a National Park, so most of its steep, volcanic hills are left to grow as natural jungle.

There are guided trails through the Park (on foot, on horseback, and even underwater through the corals of Trunk Bay), led by well-informed rangers, and there is an information center about the park opposite Mongoose Junction just outside Cruz Bay (tel: 776 6201). On the north coast you can see the ruins of the **Annaberg Plantation►►**, a relic of Danish days, when the island was covered with sugar cane. There are camping facilities on the island, for travelers with or without tents.

Around the fringes of the National Park St. John's coastline has been developed. **Cruz Bay►►**, at the western tip of the island, is the main town and here you will find several good bars and restaurants, as well as the St. John Museum, which traces a slave revolt against Danish planters in 1733, soon after the island was settled; after defending themselves for nearly a year, the rebels were defeated by imported French troops, and many committed suicide rather than return to slavery.

Travel between the islands
Most of the Virgin Islands are linked by ferry: there are regular links between St. Thomas (Red Hook) and St. John (Cruz Bay) and St. Thomas (Charlotte Amalie waterfront) and Tortola (West End and then Road Town). Sometimes the link continues to Virgin Gorda (The Valley). There is also an irregular link between St. John and Tortola (West End). St. Croix is 31 miles south of St. Thomas and is best reached by air (there are plenty of flights each day), but a novel way to make the link is by seaplane (when the service is running), if you can bear the embarrassment of declaring your bodyweight.

■ **Three centuries ago the Caribbean waters were infested with pirates. Bands of seaborne outlaws would lie in wait in hidden coves before taking to the high seas in their fast ships and attacking passing trade. Piracy was a dangerous lifestyle—capture usually meant death—but the rewards were great; a good haul could provide life on Easy Street for months on end. .....■**

Blackbeard the Pirate.

The infamous Blackbeard

Women at sea
Two women joined the macho world of piracy in the 18th century. Anne Bonney was the fiery daughter of an Irish lawyer, and Mary Read was brought up as a boy and served as a soldier and sailor before setting off to the Caribbean. Both women fell in with Jack Rackham and joined his pirate crew. They were all caught off the shores of Jamaica and sentenced to death; both women "pleaded their bellies" (pregnancy) and Bonney escaped execution, but Read died in prison.

Piracy started in the Caribbean soon after the word spread that the Spaniards were taking gold from the Aztecs. The stakes were high from the start—intrusion into Spanish waters was punishable by death—but adventurous interlopers like François le Clerc and Pie de Palo ("pegleg") were willing to take the risks. British pirates arrived in the late 16th century, including Jack Hawkins and Francis Drake, who made their fortunes on slave-trading expeditions and later by ransacking cities on the Spanish Main.

Known variously as freebooters, filibusters, and sea rovers, pirates often started out as privateers, permitted by local Governors to attack enemy shipping in times of war—but the rewards were so good that the practice was extended to include any ships that might bring in a prize, and was continued in peacetime. A single capture could bring vast riches (usually a cargo of goods—silks, arms, animals, and grog). Once these had been sold the pirates would spend their loot on booze and women until the money eventually ran out and they had to go in search of more.

On board ship, however, there was a strict regime. Generally pirates were accomplished sailors, who operated small, fast ships. The crew would sign "articles" stipulating their obedience to the captain and their duties: keeping their weapons clean, dispatching themselves bravely in battle, and refraining from playing cards and bringing women aboard (which carried a death penalty). Punishments included lashes of the whip and "marooning" (being left ashore on an island with water, a pistol, gunpowder, and shot). Each man had a share in any prizes captured on the venture, and injured men were compensated from the loot. There was usually a musician on board, who was expected to play six nights a week but rested on Sundays.

When faced with a pirate attack, a captain knew that he would be killed if he put up a fight. There are some particularly gruesome stories of pirates' cruelty: the Frenchman Montbars was said to cut out men's guts and make the victims dance till they died; and his compatriot l'Ollonios removed the heart of one man and fed it to another.

Gallery of rogues For a century until 1700, no ship was safe in the Caribbean, and pirates were feared and reviled. However, there is no disputing that there were colorful characters among their ranks.

The best known Caribbean pirate was Blackbeard (Edward Thatch). This huge man cultivated a diabolic image, tying ribbons in his long pigtails and beard, and putting slow-burning fuses under his hat so that he appeared to be on fire. A reward of £100 was offered for his capture and he was eventually caught after a chase at sea. Blackbeard died fighting rather than suffer the ignominies of surrendering, and his head was hung from the bowsprit of his ship.

Bartholomew Roberts is thought to have captured 400 ships in two years. He drank only tea (even when his crew was getting drunk on rum) and he always kept the Sabbath. Roberts was a dandy, going to battle in fine dress; he was killed in a skirmish with a British ship.

Stede Bonnet was a Justice of the Peace and a landowner from Barbados, who decided to buy a ship and become a pirate. Known as the "gentleman pirate," Bonnet was eventually captured and hanged.

Treasure is loaded onto a 16th-century ship

Henry Morgan
Henry Morgan was an indentured laborer who became the leader of the Port Royal buccaneers in the 1660s, leading expeditions against Spanish cities and netting 750,000 pieces of eight in an attack on Panama City, which he destroyed in the process. Having made his fortune, Morgan switched sides, becoming the Lieutenant Governor of Jamaica, a position which entailed stamping out piracy.

Putting on the style
As dandies and natty dressers, some pirates wore tricorn hats, coats, and cordoba boots—but looting was hot work in the Caribbean, and most wore baggy shirts and pants with no shoes. Hats included Jacobin caps and turbans, and hair was often braided and then stiffened with water and flour. Earrings were believed to improve the eyesight—and the person who sighted a prize gained an extra share.

St. Thomas

Cruise ships in port, Charlotte Amalie

St. Thomas is the U.S.V.I. capital island and the most developed of all the Virgins. It is a mountainous 12 miles by 3 miles and has a population of over 50,000, so this is hardly a secluded tropical retreat; it does, however, offer excellent bars, restaurants, and clubs, many of which are concentrated around its main town, Charlotte Amalie.

Charlotte Amalie owes its birth and its still thriving life to a fine harbor. One of the Caribbean's best waterfronts, it has always been a busy port, sheltered by hills and protected by islands. Pirate ships and ocean traders once brought the business here; now it comes on cruise ships and yachts. For every visitor who comes to stay, three come on cruises, primarily to shop—for gold, French perfume, Colombian emeralds and Balinese wood carvings. The town has another side, however: the arched façades of its stone trading buildings downtown and the elegant hillside mansions retain an atmosphere of centuries past.

The cooler slopes above Charlotte Amalie are dotted with grand mansions, built by rich traders and linked by stepped alleyways and sinuous roads. Government House (1867), once the seat of the Danish council and now the Governor's official residence, stands above the town center; inside, murals depict Columbus's arrival on St. Croix in 1493 and the handover of the U.S.V.I. from the Danes to the U.S. Just above it is Blackbeard's Tower (where the pirate was supposed to have lived), reached by the 99 Steps.

Even beyond Charlotte Amalie, the hillsides are covered with houses. On the spine of the hills above the town is Drake's Seat, where the mariner and pirate was reputed to have watched for Spanish ships; the view is magnificent. In the east of the island, Coral World has an underwater observation tower and aquariums.

Most of the beaches on St. Thomas are heavily developed (except the short strip of Magens Bay), so it is easy to find watersports equipment, but not seclusion. Coki Beach, next to Coral World, is particularly lively.

Fact or fiction?
Herman Wouk's *Don't Stop the Carnival,* one of the finest books to have come out of the West Indies, was inspired by life on the Virgin Islands. His Gull Reef Club is supposed to have been modeled on a hotel on Hassel Island, in Charlotte Amalie harbor, and on the Hotel on the Cay off Christiansted in St. Croix. The book tells of the succession of disasters that befall a hotelier, and rumor has it that Wouk didn't dare return to the island because the story was so painfully accurate, and because so many of the hoteliers thought they recognized themselves in the main character, Norman Paperman.

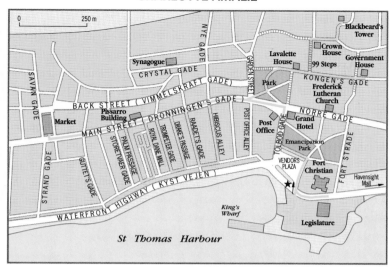

CHARLOTTE AMALIE

0   250 m

Blackbeard's Tower

NYE GADE

Synagogue

CRYSTAL GADE

Lavalette House

Crown House

99 Steps

Government House

GARDEN STREET

Park

KONGEN'S GADE

Frederick Lutheran Church

SAVAN GADE

BACK STREET (VIMMELSKRAFT GADE)

NORRE GADE

Pissarro Building

DRONNINGEN'S GADE

Grand Hotel

Market

MAIN STREET

TROMPETER GADE

DRAKE'S PASSAGE

RAADET'S GADE

HIBISCUS ALLEY

POST OFFICE ALLEY

TOLBOD GADE

Post Office

Emancipation Park

FORT STRADE

ROYAL DANE MALL

PALM PASSAGE

STORETVAER GADE

GUTTET'S GADE

VENDORS PLAZA

Fort Christian

Havensight Mall

STRAND GADE

WATERFRONT HIGHWAY (KYST VEJEN)

King's Wharf

Legislature

St Thomas Harbour

103

 Charlotte Amalie

Ferries arrive at Charlotte Amalie's waterfront downtown, as will the planned seaplane service, but many visitors disembark at the yacht marina or cruise-ship dock across the harbor, and stumble straight into Havensight Mall, the first of the island's shopping centers, which was converted from a series of warehouses. Safari buses and taxis provide transportation for passengers from here into town.

Charlotte Amalie's old trading streets are laid out on the waterfront. As you arrive, you will pass the light green **Virgin Islands Legislature Building►**, which was built by the Danes as a police barracks in 1874 and now houses the U.S.V.I. Senate. Across the road is the dark red and gold **Fort Christian►►**, which dates from the Danes' arrival in the 1660s, and is now the setting for the Virgin Islands Museum, which displays exhibits tracing early and colonial life on St. Thomas; these are set out to great effect in the dungeons.

Beyond the two grand colonial buildings at the head of Main Street, the old Grand Hotel and the Post Office, is the main shopping area. Here, the

brick and stone buildings bear well-known international names—Ralph Lauren and Benetton among them—but there is also room to accommodate local names such as A. H. Riise (selling perfumes, jewelry, crystal and watches).

It is well worth wandering through the small alleys and passages that wind between Main Street and the waterfront, where there are yet more stores and pleasant cafés and salad bars. A plaque on Main Street, between A. H. Riise and the town's fruit and vegetables market, marks the birthplace of the Impressionist painter Camille Pissaro.

The 19th-century Virgin Islands Legislature Building, on the waterfront, is now the headquarters of the U.S.V.I. Senate

THE FRENCH ANTILLES

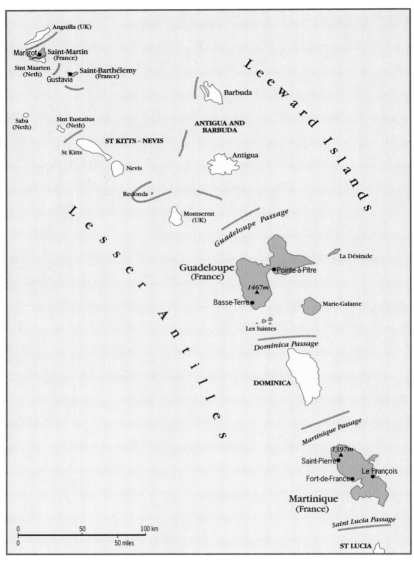

Leeward Islands

Anguilla (UK)

Marigot
Saint-Martin (France)

Sint Maarten (Neth)
Saint-Barthélemy (France)
Gustavia

Barbuda

Saba (Neth)

Sint Eustatius (Neth)

ANTIGUA AND BARBUDA

ST KITTS - NEVIS

St Kitts

Antigua

Nevis

Redonda

Montserrat (UK)

Guadeloupe Passage

Lesser Antilles

La Désirade

Guadeloupe (France)

Pointe-à-Pitre

1467m

Basse-Terre

Marie-Galante

Les Saintes

Dominica Passage

DOMINICA

Martinique Passage

1397m

Saint-Pierre

Le François

Fort-de-France

Martinique (France)

Saint Lucia Passage

ST LUCIA

0   50   100 km

0   50 miles

Fêtes patronales
Fêtes patronales take place on the French- and Spanish-speaking islands to celebrate the saint's day of each town's patron saint. There is often a parade in the town, and on the French islands a gastronomic blow-out is enjoyed in the streets. Check for dates with each island's tourist board.

The French Antilles Unmistakably French in their food, culture and general outlook, the "overseas departments" of Martinique and Guadeloupe combine tropical scenery with a sophisticated European lifestyle. Visitors can explore Guadeloupe's rainforests, Martinique's historic towns and villages, and the chic beach resorts of Saint-Barthélemy; Pointe-à-Pitre and Fort-de-France provide bustling town life, while the tiny isles of Les Saintes, La Désiderade, and Marie-Galante offer white sand beaches and quiet island life. Variety and beauty are the hallmarks of the French West Indies, made up of the single island of Martinique and the six islands which comprise the *Région* of Guadeloupe. The main island, Guadeloupe, is actually

The Chutes de Carbet, Guadeloupe

two islets of contrasting landscapes, linked by a small land bridge. The administrative *Région* of Guadeloupe is an archipelago, consisting of the islands of Les Saintes, La Désirade, Marie-Galante, and Saint-Barthélemy, as well as the half-French, half-Dutch island of Saint-Martin/Sint Maarten. As the French islands are in the northern and center sector of the Antilles, they enjoy similar climates and vegetation. Only one of the islands (Martinique) is in the region defined by the Windward group.

Lying between the Caribbean Sea and the Atlantic Ocean, the French Antilles, spread across 350 miles of sea, include

French stores in Guadeloupe

Victor Schoelcher
Victor Schoelcher was the champion of emancipation in the French Caribbean islands. He traveled to the Caribbean while on business in the 1820s and was so appalled by the conditions of the slaves that he made abolition his lifetime's work. In France he raised public consciousness by publishing pamphlets against slavery, and when the Second Republic arrived in 1848 and slavery was finally outlawed, Schoelcher himself was given the job of dismantling it, becoming the deputy of Guadeloupe for many years.

two of the region's three volcanically active islands. Apart from the inner, Caribbean side of Guadeloupe and central/northern Martinique (which are covered in tropical mountain forest), the islands are green and humid, with excellent beaches and deep coves and bays. The eastern section of Guadeloupe remains part of an arc of limestone isles, and the western parts are a continuation of the volcanic link. Also in this chain, Martinique, the largest volcanic connection of the Windward islands, has three major peaks. Guadeloupe's volcano, Soufrière, is at 4,813 ft. the highest peak to be found in the Eastern Caribbean.

The names given to the main islands in the Carib language—*Karukera* ("Island of Beautiful Waters") for Guadeloupe and *Madinia* or *Madinina* ("Island of Flowers") for Martinique—illustrate the mystical appeal of these islands. Even the half-island of Saint-Martin has a relatively fertile, forest-clad, hilly terrain compared with its southern, Dutch counterpart. The smaller islands off Guadeloupe and the most northerly island of the French Antilles, Saint-Barthélemy, are arid, rocky, and with sparse, drought-loving vegetation; Guadeloupe's limestone islands and the volcanic Les Saintes feature coral reefs and beautiful, sandy beaches. Karst landscape on Marie Galante and Saint-Barthélemy (and on some parts of Guadeloupe), together with poor soil, generally restrict arable cultivation, unlike the rich, watered lands of most of Guadeloupe, Martinique, and Saint-Martin.

Although situated in and among staunchly British or Dutch islands, the French Antilles have maintained their unmistakable French air. Rather than negotiating a political break with her colonies, France has taken the view that they should be a full part of the republic, and since 1974 Guadeloupe and Martinique have had the right, as French *Régions*, to elect their own representatives to the National Assembly. A small independence movement has emerged in Guadeloupe, and the detention of one of its followers led to a general strike in 1985.

History French settlers first colonized Guadeloupe and Martinique in 1635, and African slaves were shipped in to work the new sugar plantations. By 1669, Martinique was such a successful colony that the French moved their administrative base there from St. Kitts. In the wake of the French Revolution, Guadeloupe's slaves were freed, their colonial masters were killed and their plantations

wiped out. Martinique reacted differently, calling on the British to maintain the status quo. Slavery was re-introduced in 1802 and the British occupied Guadeloupe, but France confirmed her hold on the island in 1815—which was unfortunate for the slaves, for although slavery was abolished in the British colonies in the 1830s, emancipation did not come to the French territories until 1848. To fill the labor gap, the French Antilles encouraged the immigration of thousands of East Indians, who moved in as indentured laborers. In the 1930s, Martinique became a center for the black consciousness movement known as *Négritude* and led by Aimé Césaire and Etienne Lero. Guadeloupe and Martinique were granted departmental status in 1946, giving them equal rights to every *Département* in France.

Island life The French Antilles have capitalized on their greatest assets: the vivacious mingling of races from many lands, and the enchanting surroundings. Tourism has brought an unprecedented influx of revenue and has transformed the lot of the islands without undermining their natural beauty or affecting the local way of life. The people of Martinique and Guadeloupe are known for their physical beauty and Gallic style. Although French is the official language and French influence permeates island life, from the food and buildings to the designer stores and the *boules* games, there is also a distinctively Caribbean side to the culture. The air pulses to zouk, a classic Caribbean beat; the countryside is laden with rainforest, sugar cane, and tropical fruit; and the people speak a unique Creole, heard everywhere although its exclusion from official life has made it something of a poor relation.

With the mingled attributes of a robust culture, fertile soil, and abundant seas, a climate combining aridity with high rainfall, and all the requisites of the voracious tourist trade, the French Antilles seem to have arrived at a fairly happy balance of nature. Certainly they are among the most attractive and peaceful islands to be found in the entire Caribbean region.

Creole cuisine
The French Caribbean has a strong tradition of Creole cooking, turning the techniques of French cuisine to Caribbean ingredients, including seafood and tropical fruits. Many restaurants serve classic and *nouvelle* French cuisine and some also offer the Caribbean equivalent, *nouvelle cuisine créole*. *Blaff* is a traditional manner of frying fish in spices; for *court bouillon*, fish is poached in a special liquid of lime, wine, and onion and tomatoes. *Touffe* uses a casserole and *colombo* is a sort of Caribbean curry. You may come across *z'habitants*, a local dish of crayfish. *Accras* are batter balls, usually made with fish, and *souskai* is a way of marinating fruit.

107

Hobie cats on a Saint-Martin beach

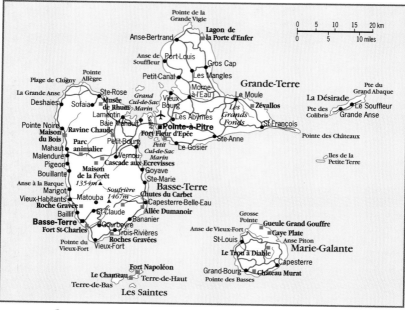

Pointe de la
Grande Vigie

Anse-Bertrand   **Lagon de
la Porte d'Enfer**

Anse de
Souffleur   Port-Louis
Gros Cap

Plage de Cligny   Pointe   Petit-Canal   Les Mangles
Allègre

La Grande Anse   Ste-Rose   *Grand*   Morne-   **Grande-Terre**   Pte du
Deshaies   Sofaia   *Cul-de-Sac*   Vieux   à-l'Eau   Le Moule   Grand Abaque
Musée   *Marin*   Bourg   Zévallos   **La Désirade**   Le Souffleur
de Rhum   Les   *Les*   Pte des   Grande Anse
Lamentin   Les Abymes   *Grands*   Colibris
Pointe Noire   Baie Mahault   *Fonds*   St-François
Maison   **Ravine Chaude**   **Pointe-à-Pitre**   Pointe des Châteaux
du Bois   *Fort Fleur d'Epée*
Mahaut   **Parc**   Petit-Bourg   *Petit*   Ste-Anne
animalier   *Cul-de-Sac*   Le Gosier   Iles de la
Malendure   Vernou   *Marin*   Petite Terre
Pigeon   **Cascade aux Ecrevisses**
Bouillante   **Maison**   Goyave
Anse à la Barque   **de la Forêt**   Ste-Marie
Marigot   *1354m*   *Soufrière*   **Basse-Terre**
Vieux-Habitants   Matouba   *1467m*   **Chutes du Carbet**
Roche Gravée   Capesterre-Belle-Eau
Baillif   St-Claude   **Allée Dumanoir**   Grosse
Basse-Terre   Bananier   Pointe   **Gueule Grand Gouffre**
Fort St-Charles   Gourbeyre   Anse de Vieux-Fort   **Caye Plate**
Trois-Rivières   St-Louis   Anse Piton
Pointe du   **Roches Gravées**   Le Trou à Diable   **Marie-Galante**
Vieux-Fort   Vieux-Fort   Capesterre

Fort Napoléon   Grand-Bourg   **Château Murat**
Le Chameau   Terre-de-Haut   Pointes des Basses
Terre-de-Bas   **Les Saintes**

0   5   10   15   20 km
0   5   10 miles

Guadeloupe

Guadeloupe has two distinct halves, like the wings of a butterfly. In the west is Basse-Terre, a rainforested volcanic monster similar in appearance to Dominica, farther south. The eastern wing, across the narrow Rivière-Salée (Salt River), is Grande-Terre, a relatively flat, coral-based outcrop from a much older range of volcanoes.

Many of Guadeloupe's hotels are located along the southern shore of Grande-Terre, which offers all the usual watersports and a string of good waterfront restaurants and bistros. This "wing" of Guadeloupe is composed of a shattered limestone outcrop with karst hills which are known locally as *montagnes russes*. Low plains, known as *fonds*, reach out to the white, sandy beaches and

French festivals
In keeping with their love of food, the French Antilleans stage Cook's Festival each year (in April on Martinique, May on Saint-Martin, and in August on Guadeloupe). Each island's leading cooks are invited to bring along their finest creations for judging, and there follows a general feast. Carnival in the French Caribbean features the main processions on Mardi Gras (Shrove Tuesday) and Mercredi des Cendres (Ash Wednesday). On the Wednesday the color scheme is black and white, and the day culminates in the burning of the carnival figure, Momo.

Chez Deux Gros, Grande-Terre—see page 279

spectacular rocky cliffs ranged along its coastline.

The terrain on Basse-Terre is for the most part wild, with cascading waterfalls and mountain streams. Its mountain range is the source of the Grande Rivière Goyaves, the island's longest river at nearly 20 miles. Inlets of black, volcanic-sanded beaches lie on the south and southeast coast of the island.

Guadeloupe's climate is tempered by the cooling northeast Trade Winds, generally no more than breezes—*Les Alizes*. Hurricanes occurred in 1928, 1956, 1966, 1979, and 1989, mostly in August or September, but the islands generally enjoy idyllic weather.

Island life About 337,000 people live in the archipelago of Guadeloupe, almost 50 percent of whom are under 20

Crowds in Pointe-à-Pitre

years of age. Most are black or mulatto; some are descendants of early settlers—*Békés*—or of East Indian indentured workers. Tourism and administration provide work for nearly half the population, and agricultural activities occupy more than another quarter. Industry accounts for a large proportion of Guadeloupe's wage-earners.

Officially, the language in Guadeloupe is French. Créole, however, is the language of the people—once banned from educational establishments, but now a proud demonstration of individualism.

Pointe-à-Pitre This large city, sprawling along the coastline in the crook of Guadeloupe's two large islands, has a population of about 100,000. Its heart is the **Place de la Victoire**►►, a large square set with trees and lined with cafés, overlooking the busy harbor, La Darse, where ferries depart for the offshore islands. The tourist information office is near La Darse and behind the square is the cathedral, built mainly of metal in order

Boats on Ste-Anne

Getting around Guadeloupe
As one half of the island is flat, with plantations and beaches, and the other is mountainous (with a 75,000-acre National Park), Guadeloupe is no easy place to view on one excursion. Grande-Terre is criss-crossed with roads that do not give straightforward access to all its attractions and should be divided into at least three journeys. Basse-Terre has few roads crossing its peaks and gorges; one circumnavigates the area, running around the coastline, but sightseeing needs at least three full excursions. The "neck" of the island, between Grande-Terre and Basse-Terre, takes yet another trip.

to withstand the occasional fierce Caribbean hurricanes.

From here the crowded streets stretch in all directions, overlooked by tall houses with intricate balconies and shutters. On the rue Frébault, in the main shopping district, a **covered market►►** provides Caribbean mayhem and every imaginable kind of produce. There are two museums in the town: the **Musée Schoelcher►►**, 24 rue Reynier, shows memorabilia associated with the 19th-century campaigner against slavery, Victor Schoelcher; and the **Musée St-John Perse►**, on rue Nozière, traces the life of the Nobel Prize-winning Guadeloupean poet, Alexis Saint-Léger. East of the town, an **Aquarium►►** in Bas du Fort displays tropical fish, and the Fort Fleur d'Epée, an 18th-century defensive bastion built of coral rock, is under restoration.

Outside Pointe-à-Pitre The towns along Grande-Terre's south coast—Le Gosier, Ste-Anne, and St-François—are the main centers of tourism, with packed beaches and waterfront restaurants. Further east, the beaches are emptier, and at the Pointe des Châteaux there are superb strips of sand where nudism is permitted.

North of this coastal strip the country opens out and cane fields rustle in the breeze; here, the towns are quieter and isolated from the tourist clamor; in Morne-à-l'Eau, the cemetery is full of the distinctive local checkered gravestones, covered with black and white tiles. Some *Blancs Matignons* live in this area, the descendants of impoverished white settlers who have stayed here for centuries, choosing not to mix with black Guadeloupeans.

To the west of Pointe-à-Pitre, across the Rivière-Salée, the scenery suddenly changes and Basse-Terre's mountains tower ahead, their peaks wreathed with clouds. The quickest road to the capital town, also called Basse-Terre, runs south along the island's eastern shore. Past Sainte-Marie, where Columbus is thought to have landed on his second voyage, the route runs through the **Allée du Manoir►►**, an avenue of 98-ft.-high royal palm trees. Inland, on the slopes of the Soufrière, are lakes—the Etang Zombi and the Grand Etang—and three waterfalls known as the **Chutes de Carbet►►**. The coast road continues to the charming town of Trois-Rivières, which is scattered down the steep hillside; near the coast, where ferries depart for the nearby Saintes, Arawak carvings on the rocks, dating from around A.D. 1000, are the star attraction of the **Parc Archéologique des Roches Gravées►►**. From here, the road switchbacks through the mountains on its way to the town of Basse-Terre.

Chengy Hindu temple

■ A trail on maps of Guadeloupe is marked Trace des Contrabandiers (The Smugglers' Trail). It follows the spine of mountains of Basse-Terre and carves its way through the magnificent rainforest. Two centuries ago, this was a long and possibly dangerous hike, but if no ship was available travelers simply had to walk. Routes such as this are now being opened again as beautiful walking trails. ......■

Waterfalls in a Guadeloupe rainforest

Perpetual rain
Rainforests create their own rain. Atlantic winds are laden with water and when they hit the island slopes they are forced upwards, condensing into huge white clouds above the mountain peaks. These clouds drop their loads onto the forest, and when the sun comes out it causes evaporation, putting water from the forest back into the sky, where it joins a never-ending cycle.

The Caribbean's mountainous islands are criss-crossed with paths. Most were cut by armies, but used by rebel maroons who hid out in the hills, and by runaway slaves. In the 19th century, walking traders would carry up to 110 lb. of goods for sale on trays placed on their heads. These *porteuses* were immensely fit, capable of walking up to 25 miles a day across the mountains.

Tropical rainforests grow on all the tall, well-watered islands of the Eastern Caribbean and in the Greater Antilles. At lower elevations gommiers and other hardwood trees such as mahogany tower over fern-covered floors, with canopies at about 80 ft., their trunks grappled by creeping vines. Above 3,200 ft. are the montane or cloud forests, where ferns and orchids form graceful curves from the upper branches of the trees. Higher still, above 5,000 ft., are the elfin forests of stunted trees covered with mosses and lichens.

Most of the Eastern Caribbean islands have instituted National Parks, which are left wild and undeveloped. Well-organized forest trails have been laid on Dominica (for information tel: 448 2401), Martinique (tel: 73 19 30), and Guadeloupe (tel: 80 05 79). In the Greater Antilles Jamaica has excellent walking in the Blue Mountains (contact Maya Lodge, tel: 927 2097) and Puerto Rico has a number of National Parks (contact the Natural Resources Department, tel: 723 0028). Guided tours are the safest; even on small islands it's easy to get lost. Sneakers or light ankle-height boots are usually adequate; a sweater is needed for higher climbs, and a waterproof jacket for protection against downpours.

Maison de la Forêt, Guadeloupe

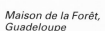

*Morne-à-l'Eau
cemetery*

Introducing the pineapple
Columbus was "astonished
and delighted" with the
pineapple when he was
presented with it on his
arrival in Guadeloupe, during his second voyage to
the Caribbean. After its
introduction to Europe, it
was regarded as a luxury,
and became a symbol of
generous hospitality;
pineapples can still be
seen crafted in stone on
the entrance gates to
several country houses.

Spread over the hillside, Basse-Terre has more style
than Pointe-à-Pitre, with attractive stone and wooden
town buildings. **Fort St-Charles**►► (1650), overlooking
the harbor, is a huge defensive bulwark with a small
museum. Inland from Basse-Terre, on the slopes of the
Soufrière volcano, is the town of Matouba, where a 200-
year-old trail, Trace Victor Hugues, leads eventually to hot
baths fed by volcanic springs (an 18-mile haul, not to be
undertaken lightly!). The **Maison du Volcan**►► has displays explaining volcanic activity, and is near the Bains
Jaunes hot springs, and from here the road leads up to
the crater itself, which still occasionally makes itself
known, spewing out dust and even lava.

Two alternative routes from Pointe-à-Pitre to Basse-
Terre take in the north of the island. On the northern
coastal route, among traditional cane-growing flats, a
working sugar factory complete with steam-driven
crusher operates at the **Domaine des Sévérins**►►, at
Saint-Rose, and the story of sugar production is told at the
Musée de Rhum►►. On the northwestern corner of the
island are some of Guadeloupe's best beaches, particularly the Plage de Cluny and la Grande Anse, a 2-mile
sweep of golden sand and palms. Near the 17th-century
town of Pointe-Noire is the **Maison du Bois**►, which
shows local building techniques and illustrates the wide
range of uses for different Caribbean woods.

La Traversée crosses through the middle of Basse-
Terre, passing a number of falls including the **Cascade
aux Ecrivisses**►►, as well as the **Maison de la Forêt**►►,
which traces the development of the island's natural life.
Past a small zoo, where forest animals are kept in cages,
the road descends to the sea and rejoins the coast road,
turning south towards Basse-Terre. There is a very popular black sand beach at Malendure, with good diving
available on the Ile de Pigeon.

Malendure is a renowned site for diving

La Darse, Pointe-à-Pitre

La Désiderade Virtually unspoiled by tourism (and the English language), La Désiderade offers a quiet get-away and white beaches. The "Desired One" was often the first island spotted by 16th-century sailors longing for land after a tedious Atlantic crossing. Their desire was usually frustrated, however, as ships would sail past this barren, windy island. Only 7 miles by about 1 mile, La Désiderade is a table mountain lying 5 miles east of Grande-Terre in the Atlantic Ocean. It has a population of under 2,000, spread along the southern shore between the main town of Grande Anse and the village of Le Souffleur.

Marie-Galante The beach at Petit Anse is the big draw of Marie-Galante, the largest of Guadeloupe's offshore islands. Almost circular in shape, it measures nearly 60 sq. miles and has a population of 20,000, about half of whom live in the main town of Grand-Bourg. Named by Columbus in 1493 after his flagship, *Santa Maria de Galante*, it—a longtime Carib stronghold—eventually was captured by Europeans and turned into a sugar island (Marie-Galante rum is still renowned). Beyond Grand-Bourg, ruined windmills are forlorn reminders of the sugar trade's peak. The Château Murat, a restored 18th-century plantation estate house east of Grand Bourg, houses a museum of island customs and industry, and farther inland an underground cavern, Le Trou à Diable, can be explored—but sturdy footwear, a flashlight and caution are required.

Les Saintes The lures of Les Saintes include a nude beach, scuba diving, and a beautiful bay that's been called a mini Rio. These volcanic peaks lie to the south of Basse-Terre. Only two are inhabited: Terre-de-Bas and Terre-de-Haut. The population of the former is descended from plantation slaves; **Terre-de-Haut▶▶**, which was newly planted, centers around tourism, with hotels and restaurants on the waterfront of Bourg, its only town. White fishermen—descended from French colonials—wear "salako" hats, similar to Chinese coolie hats. There are good beaches (one nudist) on Terre-de-Haut, and sights include Fort Napoléon, with a museum, and a tower with a magnificent view, Le Chameau, on the island's highest point.

The Battle of the Saints
The Battle of the Saints, so-called because it took place just off Les Saintes in 1782, was a turning point in the fight for European imperial supremacy over the Caribbean islands. It was also a first in naval terms; a captain in the British navy saw a gap between the French ships and managed to "break the line", splitting the French fleet into two parts so that the flagship could not communicate with most of its fleet. The battle ended in victory for the British, who held sway over Caribbean waters for the two following decades.

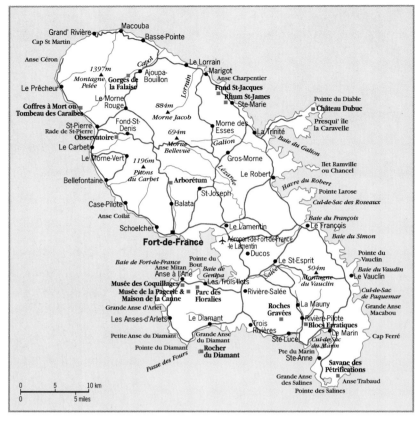

Grand' Rivière Macouba Basse-Pointe
Cap St Martin
Anse Céron
Le Lorrain
1397m *Capol* Le Lorrain
Montagne Ajoupa- Marigot
Pelée Gorges de Bouillon Anse Charpentier
Le Prêcheur la Falaise *Lorrain* Fond St-Jacques
Le Morne Rhum St-James
Coffres à Mort ou Rouge 884m Ste-Marie Pointe du Diable
Tombeau des Caraïbes *Morne Jacob* Château Dubuc
St-Pierre Fond-St- Morne des Presqu' île
Rade de St-Pierre Denis 694m Esses la Caravelle
Observatoire *Morne* La Trinité *Baie du Galion*
Le Carbet *Bellevue* *Galion*
Le Morne-Vert 1196m Gros-Morne Ilet Ramville
Pitons Le Robert ou Chancel
Bellefontaine *du Carbet* Arborétum *Havre du Robert*
Lézarde St-Joseph Pointe Larose
Case-Pilote Balata *Cul-de-Sac des Roseaux*
Anse Coilat
Schoelcher Le Lamentin *Baie du François*
Le François
Fort-de-France Aéroport de Fort-de-France *Baie du Simon*
le Lamentin
Ducos Pointe du
Baie de Fort-de-France Pointe du Le St-Esprit Vauclin
Anse Mitan Bout *Baie de* 504m *Baie du Vaudin*
Anse à l'Ane *Genipa* *Salée* Montagne Le Vauclin
Musée des Coquillages Les-Trois-Ilets *du Vauclin* *Cul-de-Sac*
Musée de la Pagerie & Parc des *de Paquemar*
Maison de la Canne Floralies Rivière-Salée Grande Anse
Grande Anse d'Arlet Roches La Mauny Macabou
Les Anses-d'Arlets Gravées Rivière-Pilote
Le Diamant Blocs Erratiques
Petite Anse du Diamant Grande Anse Trois Le Marin Cap Ferré
du Diamant Rivières *Cul-de-Sac*
Pointe du Diamant Rocher Ste-Luce *du Marin*
du Diamant Pte du Marin
Passe des Fours Ste-Anne Savane des
Pétrifications
Grande Anse Anse Trabaud
des Salines
Pointe des Salines

0 5 10 km
0 5 miles

Petit Punch
This popular French
Caribbean drink is taken
before lunch. A heap of
brown sugar crystals is
dashed with local white
rum and stirred. A quarter
of lime is squeezed in and
the mix is downed in one
gulp. Ice water is then
swilled around to collect
the last of the sugar, and
downed as a chaser.

Martinique pâtisserie

Martinique

Martinique—far more tourist-oriented than Guadeloupe—
has always been the heart of the French Caribbean. St-
Pierre, once its most important town, was known as the
Paris of the Lesser Antilles, and its booming sugar trade
was vitally important to the French, who were even prepared to give up their claims to territories in India and
Canada in return for keeping the island in the 18th century. As its Amerindian name, *Madinina* ("Land of Flowers")
implies, this is a fertile island, and since the French arrived
in 1635 (they have owned it ever since), it has been successfully farmed. Agriculture and fishing are still important and there are vast acres of bananas, pineapple, and
sugar cane. Martinique is mid-way
down the chain of the Lesser
Antilles, between the independent
islands of Dominica and St. Lucia.
Shaped something like a boxing
glove, it measures 50 miles by 20
miles at its widest point. In the
mountainous north, the active volcano Montagne Pelée (4,583 ft.) is
the highest peak; rainforests cover

The library in Fort-de-France

The head code
There is a certain elegance and coquettish air about French Antilleans that mirrors their metropolitan counterparts. A century ago there was even a flirtatious message in the way island women wore their madras headdresses. Tied with checkered silk material, the headdress indicated a code in the number of points protruding. One corner meant that the woman had no lover; two points meant that her heart was taken. Three points meant that officially her heart was taken, but that a man might try his luck.

the Pitons du Carbet, and to the south, the land descends to fertile plains and *mornes* (foothills).

The island's relatively large tourist industry is not immediately visible, as there is a strong local community. The population of 350,000 is descended from a mix of French, African, East Indian, Chinese, and Arab races; French is the official language, and the French influence can be seen in everyday life, from the croissants to the Peugeot 205s. But there is also a lively Creole culture, and good Caribbean restaurants, stores and bars.

Fort-de-France Martinique's capital is a modern town set in a bay on the calm Caribbean shore. It has grown enormously since the eruption of Montagne Pelée devastated St-Pierre, in 1902, and over 100,000 inhabitants now live in the center and in the suburbs that have clambered all over the surrounding hills. Overlooking the waterfront in the Baie des Flammands, where yachts and the occasional cruise ship ride at anchor, the center of the town is **La Savanne►►**, an open park studded with 100-ft. royal palm trees, where the Martiniquans take their evening walks. A statue of Josephine, the French Empress, looks across the bay to her birthplace at Trois-Ilets. There is a helpful tourist information office on the waterfront on Boulevard Alfassa. The **Musée Départementale►** has a well-presented if minimalist display of Amerindian pottery, and the most striking building is the **Bibliothèque Schoelcher►►**, a domed structure of brightly colored metal and glass, built for the 1889 Paris Exhibition and transported here to house a library commemorating Victor Schoelcher's anti-slavery campaign. Fort St-Louis, the original defense on the point, is still a military base.

Driving in Fort-de-France is not a good idea. The streets are crowded, and several are given over to markets—such as the fish market on the Rivière Madame, near the blooms and geological displays of the Parc Floral. Beyond the suburbs, the scenery turns into mountainous rainforest and sugar cane flats. Here, life is calmer and simpler: Catholic churches overlook town squares, and orange and green fishing boats are moored in the bays.

Jardin de Balata

■ **Fans of James Bond will know that 007 was a confirmed bird-watcher. His creator, Ian Fleming, lived on the north coast of Jamaica and took the name for his famous spy from a real ornithologist, the author of *The Birds of the West Indies*. The Caribbean is on migratory routes north and south and, like tourists, many birds from further north like to winter in the Caribbean. With so many habitats (shoreline, mangrove swamp, forests) within a relatively small area, visitors can expect to see a striking variety of different species. .....■**

116

Top: scarlet ibis
Right: Jamaican mountain goats

Zoos
The Caribbean islands have a small number of zoos. In Santo Domingo, the capital of the Dominican Republic, the Parque Zoologico Nacional keeps elephants as well as tropical animals, and in Port of Spain, Trinidad, the Emperor Valley Zoo has tropical animals seen in Trinidad, including the tree porcupine, the crab-eating racoon and monkeys such as the weeping capuchin and the red howler. Animals are free to roam in the Barbados Wildlife Reserve, in the north of the island, and on Guadeloupe the Parc Zoologique et Botanique, on Road D23 in Basse-Terre, has walkways through the rainforest.

Mangrove swamps and coastal lagoons are good places to look out for herons, ducks, and more exotic creatures such as gallinules and jacanas, whose long toes enable them to walk over lilies. Colonies of flamingos nest on the island of Bonaire, and kingfishers can often be spotted flitting along rivers.

Pelicans are a familiar sight on many islands, flying in formation around the shoreline or diving into the sea for food. Tropicbirds occasionally soar near the coast, and the magnificent frigatebird cruises high in the air, waiting for passing meals. Gulls, terns, gannets, and boobies skim along the surface of the sea before rising and plunging to catch fish, and small crowds of oystercatchers and sandpipers walk along the beaches as they feed, dodging the breaking waves.

On open ground, the white cattle egret can be seen wherever there are grazing cows, and thrushes, finches, and larger birds such as cuckoos and crows (called John Crows) are common. Slightly harder to spot are mocking birds and flycatchers, which snatch up insects on the wing, and tanagers, which feed on fruit.

In contrast, some of the most familiar birds are self-assured enough to try stealing the sugar from breakfast tables: the carib grackle, which is also called a blackbird in some areas, has a V-shaped tail and displays by puffing up its feathers; and the bananaquit has distinctive yellow and black plumage.

It takes a lot of luck to see the Caribbean's more exotic birds. Shimmering hummingbirds flit around the flowers on a permanent search for nectar; the purple-throated and green-throated hummingbirds and the Antillean crested hummingbird live in most islands of the Eastern Caribbean. High in the forests there are still Caribbean parrots, though these are now an endangered species, particularly in the Eastern Caribbean, where there are parrots unique to St. Vincent, St. Lucia and Dominica (the imperial and red-necked parrots).

The island of Trinidad is an exception in the Caribbean, both in its animal and its bird life, because it has considerable spill-over from the South American continent. Over 400 bird species make this the best island for bird-watching, but the most spectacular sight is the scarlet ibis, with its vivid red plumage and downward-curving bill. It might just be possible to see a bright blue motmot or maybe a mannikin; the male mannikin, with its white breast and black cap and wings, spends about 70 percent of its time displaying, strutting with its competitors around the female, making noises like a little firecracker and even turning somersaults.

Caribbean animals Most animals on the Caribbean islands—goats, chickens, donkeys, cattle, and even monkeys and mongeese—were imported by settlers. Indigenous survivors, most of which are endangered, include the coney, which is somewhat like a guinea pig and lives in the Jamaican John Crow mountains and in Hispaniola; the agouti, a tail-less rodent the size of a rabbit, living in the Eastern Caribbean; the American racoon, and the tatou, an armadillo that survives in Grenada. Reptiles are more widespread. Tiny geckos and lizards crawl over walls, and tree frogs peep noisily in gardens. Iguanas, which can grow to nearly 4 ft., are found on a number of islands, and the few snakes include small constrictors, the most notorious being the fer de lance, with eyes that glow orange at night.

Perhaps the most curious of a wide range of insects are Hercules beetles, which grow up to 6 in. and have claws protruding from their heads, and Cuban tarantulas, which can grow to the size of a man's hand.

Animal settlers
In the early days of European settlement, sailors would leave animals ashore and plant fruit-bearing trees on remote islands so that there would be a supply of food for anyone who might be shipwrecked. Père Labat, an early French traveler, tells of a sailors' tale that the shipwrecked crew with a pig on board should throw it into the sea and row after it, as it would know innately the direction of the nearest land.

Sandflies
Apart from mosquitoes, the most annoying insects that frequent beaches are sandflies. So small that they are virtually invisible, sandflies are known on some islands as "no-see-ums," and their bite causes an infuriating itch.

117

Iguanas live on many Caribbean islands

THE FRENCH ANTILLES

Diamond Rock
The sheer-sided Diamond Rock stands a mile or so off the south coast of Martinique and is rarely visited, but for 18 months in 1805 it was occupied by 100 British sailors, who built a fort there in order to deny the channel to French ships. All the supplies, building materials, and food had to be winched up from ships below. Eventually the French made a serious effort to take it back and bombarded the Rock for three days before the commander surrendered.

St.-Pierre, once a bustling city

Outside Fort-de-France Martinique is a large island, and although the roads are good, a leisurely circuit can take a couple of days. Buses run from the waterfront at Fort-de-France, and *taxis collectifs*, shared taxis, follow regular routes. Car rental companies operate in Fort-de-France and the main tourist areas, and at the airport.

The closest tourist resort to Fort-de-France is Pointe du Bout and its beach, Anse Mitan, south across the bay, to which there are ferries from the waterfront downtown. This is a lively area with good restaurants and cafés, though the beaches are not the best. To the south, beyond the town of Trois-Ilets, is the **Musée de la Pagerie►►**, dedicated to Josephine Bonaparte and set in the farm where she was born. There is a golf course near La Pagerie and, close by, a museum of sugar, the **Maison de la Canne►►**.

West along the coast, the **Musée des Coquillages►** in Anse à l'Ane has exhibits of shells; further along, the three attractive coves at **Les Anses-d'Arlets►►**, isolated on the southwestern shore, are worth a detour. As the coast road winds its way to Le Diamant, it passes the solitary Diamond Rock, a few miles offshore (see panel). Working **rum distilleries►►** can be visited at Trois Rivières and La Mauny near Rivière-Pilote, inland from the seaside town of Sainte-Luce.

Le Marin, which has a large marina, and Ste.-Anne, further south, are the two principal tourist towns in the southeast. The area's most popular beach is the Pointe du Marin, between the two, but the best beaches in Martinique are at the very southern tip of the island: **Grande Anse des Salines►►**, a 2-mile sweep of palm-backed sand, and nearby Anse Trabaud. The **Savane des Pétrifications►**, near the Grande Anse des Salines salt flats, is a desolate field of petrified trees and branches.

The east coast of Martinique is mainly agricultural and the sea can be quite rough here, whipped up by Atlantic winds, though there are beaches tucked into the folds of the coastline. At the town of Morne des Esses, locally woven baskets and mats are sold in a number of workshops, and at Sainte-Marie the **Rhum St. James Rum Distillery►►** can be visited.

Balata's version of the Sacré Coeur

St.-Pierre's survivor
At one time, St.-Pierre was the most chic and stylish town in the Eastern Caribbean. It boasted a theater and a cathedral and "Pierrotins" followed Paris fashion to the letter. Although the town was almost totally destroyed by the volcanic eruption of 1902, one man was saved because he had been put in a police cell overnight after a drinking spree. The walls of the cell protected him from the heat and gases of the explosion. He later joined a circus, exhibiting himself in a reproduction of his cell.

119

Two spectacular roads lead north from Fort-de-France to the town of St.-Pierre, one climbing into the rainforested mountains and the other following the coves and headlands along the coast. The Route de la Trace, an old forest road cut by the Jesuits three centuries ago, climbs up through the suburb of Didier and passes through Balata, where a replica of the Sacré Coeur in Paris was built in 1923 as a World War I memorial. The road continues to the **Jardin de Balata▶▶**, where walkways lead past hundreds of species of tropical plants. From here, La Trace forges into the peaks of the Pitons du Carbet, where many of the same species grow in the wild.

The coast road passes through fishing villages such as Case-Pilote, named after a Carib chief, and Le Carbet, where Paul Gauguin lived for two years in the 19th century; the **Musée Gauguin▶▶** exhibits some of the works which he painted at the time.

Though it was never the official capital, St.-Pierre was the business and social center of Martinique—until May 8, 1902, when the whole town was engulfed by a cloud of volcanic lava and nearly all the 26,000 inhabitants were killed. The town is still inhabited and many of its old buildings, including the theater and some waterfront warehouses, still exist, though as ruins. There are a couple of museums on the rue Victor Hugo— the **Musée Historique▶**, with displays about town life before 1902, and the **Musée Volcanique▶▶**, which has grim exhibits from the day of its destruction, including clocks that stopped at the moment of eruption. Montagne Pelée itself looms quietly over the remains of the town.

St.-Pierre souvenir

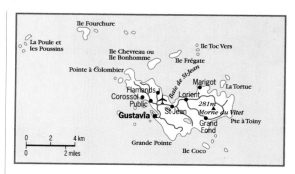

Breton heritage
St. Barts was first colonized by Bretons and Normans, and there is still a community of white Barthéleminois, whose language has retained remnants of 17th-century Breton. Another curious hangover of their ancient heritage, still occasionally seen, is their *calèche* hats, cotton bonnets fitted with wooden slats that stick out above the face like a visor. Apart from shading the wearer from the sun, they keep away other intrusions, earning them the nickname *quichenotte*—supposedly a corruption of "kiss-me-not."

Offshore islands near Saint-Barthélemy

Saint-Barthélemy

Saint-Barthélemy, a tiny tropical speck set in an aquamarine sea, has seen the full ebb and flow of Caribbean fortune. From a backwater visited occasionally by pirates it became a thriving trading post for 50 years before slipping back into obscurity. Today, the island is once more on the crest of a wave, having become one of the Caribbean's most luxurious and desirable destinations.

St. Barts, as this most French of the French Caribbean islands is affectionately known, has a rarified and exclusive air. It is the favored retreat of a chic clientele of stars and the seriously rich, who zip around the island's boutiques and beaches in mini-mokes and on *mobylettes* (mopeds). Tropical sophistication is taken to perfection here—at a very high price.

Although St. Barts is just under 8 sq. miles in size, with no hill rising above 920 ft. (Morne Vitet), the scrub-covered scenery is surprisingly rough and dramatic, and six large lagoons are scattered across the landscape. The island lies 15.5 miles to the southeast of Saint-Martin, on the same coral geological shelf, and this gives it similarly magnificent white sand beaches. More than 20 tiny islets and islet groups lie in St. Barts' waters, of which the largest is Ile

Fourchue; others include the Ile Frégate twin islands, Les Balines, La Baline ("The Whales" and "The Whale"), Pain de Sucre ("Sugar Loaf"), Boulanger ("Baker") and La Poule et Les Poussins ("The Hen and Chickens").

Flying down to St. Barts

Like Saint-Martin, St. Barts is a *commune* of Guadeloupe, 155 miles to the south, administered by a *sous-préfet* from Paris, but it has not always been French. After 100 or so years of trading with smugglers and pirates, the 1,000 French settlers learned in 1785 that the island had been leased to the Swedes in return for trading rights in the Baltic. Sweden made St. Barts a free port and for half a century the island prospered. When it was handed back to the French in 1878, its duty-free status was retained, and has been kept to this day.

The capital of St. Barts is **Gustavia►►**, named after Gustaf III, the Swedish King who made the 1785 exchange. It has just a few pretty streets, some with Swedish names, set on three sides of an excellent natural harbor. In its heyday the town was defended by four fortresses, of which two, Fort Gustav and Fort Karl, can be visited. The St. Barts **museum►►** is set in the restored Wall House on the seaward arm of the bay. Unfortunately, not much of the original town survives today—it was destroyed by fire in the 1850s—but some of the old stone warehouses have been carefully restored and now provide atmospheric settings for bars and restaurants.

St. Barts can easily be explored in a day. A drive around the steep, switchback roads takes in the occasional old church or traditional country house with plastered walls and tin roofs dotted among the modern villas. You might even hear a bit of local dialect or see an islander dressed in the traditional costume of a long white skirt and bonnet or *calèche*.

North of Gustavia, the road runs through Public to Corossol, an old fishing village where there is a shell collection at the **Inter Oceans Museum►►**. The village is also the best place to find St. Barts weaving, made from the latanier palm, which grows all over the island.

To the northeast of the capital, the Plaine de la Tourmente is the site of the island's airstrip and of a graveyard. St.-Jean, to the east, is one of the centers of the tourist industry, with boutiques, restaurants, sporting goods stores and mini-moke rental outlets. At Lorient, further east again, local fishermen work as they have for centuries; beyond this point, the country opens out, though there are hotels tucked away in the bays. When the winds are up, the windsurfing is excellent in the east.

The Club la Banane— a tourist's-eye view of St. Barts

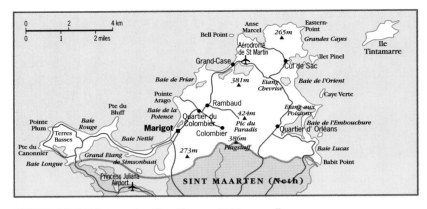

122

Saint-Martin

The border that divides the island of Saint-Martin between France and Holland (see pages 140 and 142) is barely noticeable. The countryside is much the same on both sides. Only an obelisk and a bilingual sign mark the fact that this is the smallest island in the world to be divided between two sovereign states. France, which owns the northern half of the island, looking towards Anguilla, marginally got the better of the division (see panel), with 21 of the total 37 sq. miles.

This is a physically beautiful island with tall, green and yellow concave slopes (the tallest is Pic du Paradis, at 4,564 ft.), and a tortuous coastline indented with coves and superb white sand beaches. The main landmass is pierced with lagoons and salt ponds, and one "wing" is almost entirely occupied by a vast lake—one of the largest natural lakes in the Antilles, divided between the Dutch and French; the French part is attended by two low islands, Ilet Pinel ("Penal Island") and Caye Verte.

Saint-Martin is a *commune* of Guadeloupe, and has a distinctly French air—policemen wear *képis*, and French restaurants, bistros, and clothing stores line the main resorts. But the atmosphere of the island is basically international and modern, having boomed, like the Dutch side, from a lazy backwater to a large tourist destination 20 years ago. The population has exploded to 11,000 to cope with the influx of tourists; this is not a place for getting away from the crowds.

Marigot►► is the capital town on the French side, a small nexus of streets set between

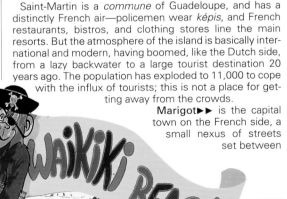

the Baie de Marigot and the Simpson Bay Lagoon. The few old townhouses with wrought-iron balconies and the waterfront warehouses have been restored and now buzz with shoppers and drinkers taking time out from the beach. On the Boulevard de France, overlooking the bay, is the **market square**▶▶, which is busy most of the day, and the tourist office. The **Musée Saint- Martin**▶, near by, traces the indigenous and colonial history of the island. The ruined Fort St. Louis, the town's defense in the days of imperial wars, still has a magnificent view over Anguilla and the town's approaches, and overlooking the lagoon on the other side of town, the **Port la Royale**▶▶ marina is lined with cafés and restaurants.

Marigot: the town and harbor...

Past the marina, to the west, some of the island's best beaches can be found in Baie Rouge and Baie Longue. The road south out of Marigot leads past the obelisk marking the border and to the main airport.

North of Marigot is a more natural Saint-Martin, although the hills are dotted everywhere with modern villas. There is a lookout near the summit of the Pic du Paradis that gives marvelous views of the nearby islands.

Beyond the local settlement of Colombier and an excellent, often uncrowded beach at Friar's Bay is the appealing town of Grand-Case, set along the sandy waterfront. Known as the gastronomic capital of the island, it has a row of excellent restaurants and bars set above the sea.

Past the airstrip to the east the countryside becomes surprisingly sparse, although most bays have hotels. Orléans is a 17th-century settlement, once the capital but now no more than a few villas and a couple of sores. Of the east coast beaches, the best for windsurfing are Baie de l'Embouchure (for beginners) and Baie de l'Orient, which is a nudist beach.

...and café society

THE NETHERLANDS ANTILLES

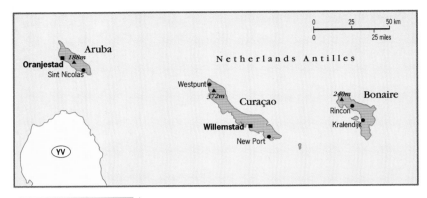

Aruba is renowned for its white sand beaches

The Netherlands Antilles The six Dutch-speaking islands of the Caribbean carry the clear imprint of their colonial history; on Curaçao, even canals, gabled warehouses, and windmills can be seen. Their appeal is not only historical; the dry island of Aruba has superb beaches and Bonaire has some of the region's best preserved reefs. Aruba, Bonaire, Curaçao, and especially Sint Maarten all have developed tourist infrastructures, while the tiny outcrops of Saba and Sint Eustatius see far fewer visitors. The islands lie in two groups, separated by 497 miles of sea: the volcanic Dutch Windwards, Sint Maarten, Saba, and Statia (the SSS islands), near the northern end of the Lesser Antilles; and the Dutch Leewards, Bonaire and Curaçao, off the coast of Venezuela. Aruba was politically part of this group until it separated from the Netherlands Antilles in 1986, but many still refer to these as the ABC islands. The two groups represent some of the more beautiful—and most inhospitable—of the West Indies islands.

A Dutch heritage spanning 350 years has formed much of the character of each island. Red-bricked, pastel-painted, and gabled houses recall the heyday of the Dutch Empire, contrasting with the modern buildings erected since the oil

Bola Tabla, Curaçao

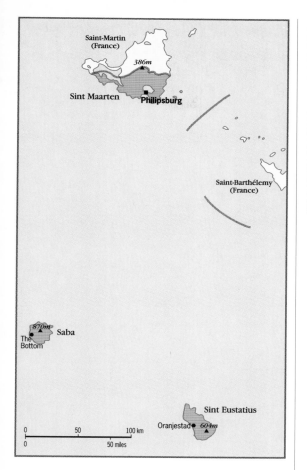

Saint-Martin
(France)

386m

Sint Maarten

Philipsburg

Saint-Barthélemy
(France)

870m Saba

The
Bottom

Sint Eustatius

Oranjestad 604m

0	50	100 km

0   50 miles

boom of the 20th century, all set incongruously among golden beaches, coconut palms, and limpid waters.

History The Dutch West India Company first spotted the strategic and economic significance of the Lesser Antilles in the 1620s; Sint Maarten was a neat stepping stone to Dutch colonies in Brazil, and Aruba, Bonaire, and Curaçao (colonized on a small scale by the Spanish in 1511) provided salt for the profitable herring industry. As trade increased—Curaçao became a center for the slave trade—so did the interest of rival empires, and during the 18th century the islands were seized by one European power after another. In 1816 the Dutch regained their hold, but the era of booming trade was over, and the islands fell into decline until the arrival of the oil companies, Royal Dutch Shell and Exxon, in the early 20th century. Oil refineries were set up on Aruba and Curaçao, bringing an influx of workers from neighboring islands and new prosperity. In the 1980s the oil industry, faced with falling profits, shut down its Antilles operations and islanders were thrown back on the tourist trade as a major income-earner, supplemented with grants from the Netherlands.

THE NETHERLANDS ANTILLES

A view of Saba from Sint Maarten

Path to independence?
The Dutch islands were in step with the rest of the Caribbean in their growing desire for political self-government in the early part of the 20th century. Labor union movements in the oilfields increased the political awareness of the islands and a *Staten*, or Parliament, was formed in 1936. During World War II, while Holland was occupied by the Germans, the Dutch islands were left to fend for themselves and gained experience of self-government. There was not the headlong rush for independence after the war that was seen among the British islands, but autonomy was granted in 1954. Holland has stated that it will allow the islands to become fully independent when their economies are reliably stable, but many islanders prefer to remain with the Kingdom of the Netherlands for the foreseeable future.

Red roofs on Saba

Today the Netherlands Antilles are divided into three territories: Curaçao (the administrative capital), Bonaire, and the three Windward islands, Sint Maarten, Sint Eustatius and Saba. Each has its own representative body (the Island Council), elected every four years, which selects commissioners. Together they form the Executive Council for each island or island group. The Queen of the Netherlands appoints the Lieutenant-General and the island Governor, who serves a term of six years and appoints Antillian ministers. Aruba was deemed a state apart (*Status Aparte*) from the other administrations in 1986, and is now an autonomous part of the Netherlands, in theory preparing for full independence in 1996.

Aruba craft stall

Cudarebe — California Lighthouse
Malmok
West Punt
Hadikurari
Palm Beach — Chapel of Alto Vista
Pos di Noord
Eagle Beach — Noord
Wariruri
Gold Mine Ruins
Boca Mabos
Bushiribana
Paradera — Andicuri Natural Bridge
Casibari — Ayo
Fort Zoutman — Diorite
165m Boulders
Oranjestad — Hooiberg — Santa Cruz
Paardenbaai — Queen Beatrix Airport — Boton — Miralamar Pass — Dos Playa
188m — Boca Prins
Jamanota — Fontein Cave — Guadirikiri Cave
Tunnel of Love
Rincon
Spaans Lagoon — Savaneta — Sint Nicolas — Boca Grandi
Commandeursbaai
Seroe Colorado — Punta Basora

0 — 5 km
0 — 3 miles

Status Aparte
Status Aparte was the eventual solution reached by the Arubians to give them autonomy from Curaçao, the capital island and traditionally the center of the Netherlands Antilles. Arubians felt it unjust that wealth generated by their own oil business should have to be channeled via Curaçao before being returned to them. It took over 50 years to change the island's status; the act had to be passed on Curaçao, where the Curaçaoans themselves had a majority of the seats, but Aruba eventually severed the link in 1986 and the island now has its own Parliament, as well as its own currency and flag.

Oranjestad roofscape

Aruba

From the air, Aruba seems small and flat, with a ribbon of blinding white sand running down its western side. In fact, although the island is only 19 miles by 6 miles, its hills rise to over 490 ft., and the combined stretch of Palm Beach and Eagle Beach is one of the Caribbean's finest strips of sand. The island's distinctive beauty lies in its countryside—an almost extraterrestrial landscape full of rocky deserts, cactus jungles, and secluded coves. With its low humidity and average temperature of 82 degrees F., Aruba has the climate of paradise; rain comes mostly during November.

The 70,000 Arubians have a wide range of origins, including Spanish, Portuguese, East Indian, and Caribbean Indian, as well as Dutch. The official language is Dutch, and English is widely spoken, but most Arubians speak Papiamento, a dialect drawing from Spanish, French, Portuguese, Dutch, African, and English.

Colonization came relatively late to Aruba, which was virtually ignored by

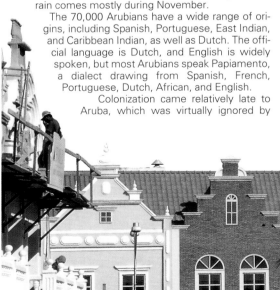

European powers until the 20th century, and its people have retained a strong sense of independence (see panel opposite).

The capital, **Oranjestad▶▶**, lies on the protected south-western shore of the island; the town and its outlying suburbs are the center of Aruban life. Named after the Dutch Royal House of Orange, this is Aruba's main port; some of the older buildings around the main street, Nassaustraat, date from the oil boom earlier this century, but most are modern imitations with traditional flourishes, containing the banks and shopping malls of the modern town. A line of fishing boats forms the quayside Schooner Market, selling produce from Venezuela.

Fort Zoutman (1796) is the oldest building on the island, and contains the **Museo Arubano▶**, tracing Aruba's history, and the **Museo Archeologico▶**, depicting indigenous Indian life. The **Museo Numismatico▶▶**, on Irausquin Plein, has a collection of 30,000 bills and coins, and there are 700 species of shell on display at the **De Man shell collection▶▶**, in a private house at 18 Morgenster Street (by appointment, tel: 24246).

To the west of Oranjestad, the coastal road runs past the cruise ship dock to Aruba's magnificent beaches: **Eagle Beach▶▶▶** (known as the "low rise strip") and **Palm Beach▶▶▶** (the "high rise strip"). There is no shortage of watersports or bars here—nor is there any lack of crowds.

East of the town, the road passes through suburbs into the scrub. Sprinkled among the growing number of new houses are traditional buildings, with talismanic symbols painted on the clay walls and roofs made of cactus wood and grass.

Aruba's highest hill is Jamanota (617 ft.), but its most distinctive is the **Hooiberg▶**, standing over 540 ft. high, with stairs to ease the climb. To its north are the huge, gray, and rounded **diorite boulders▶▶** at Casibari and Ayo, and on the north coast, east of Oranjestad, are the ruins of the Bushiribana gold mines, whose discovery in 1825 led to a brief gold rush (a smelting site at Balashi produced over 2 million pounds of gold). Also in this area are the ruins of a 16th-century fortress, and at **Andicouri▶▶**, the sea has carved a bridge from the coral rock. San Nicolas, in the southeast, is the island's second town and the site of the old oil refinery.

Aruba's Dutch legacy is still apparent...

...while tourism is taking over on its inviting beaches

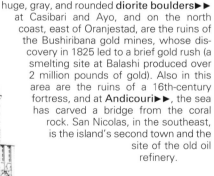

Above and far right:
Bonaire's salt stacks

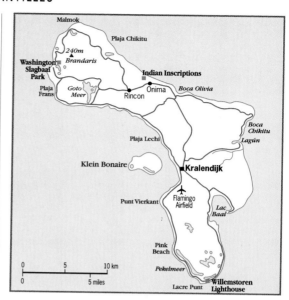

The salt industry
As you drive south on Bonaire you will come to the vast white stacks of Bonaire's salt, beneath which several cranes bustle about. Salt production has recently been revived for industrial purposes; sea water is let into shallow "pans" and the sun and the wind then do their work, evaporating the water. The resulting brine is channeled into other pans to increase the evaporation effect and eventually a bed of white crystals appears. These are harvested and cleaned before being stacked by a crane on rails in mounds ready for shipping.

Bonaire

Bonaire is a stark desert island, perfect for the rugged individualist who is turned off by the over-commercialized high life of the other Antillean islands. A mecca for divers, the island offers one of the most unspoiled reef systems in the world. The water is so clear that you can lean over the dock and look the fish straight in the eye. The Bonaire Marine Park—a model of ecological conservation—includes roughly the entire coastline, from the high-water tidemark to a depth of nearly 200 ft. This is not the island for connoisseurs of fine cuisine, shopping maniacs, beachcombers, or those who prefer hobnobbing with society; but what lies off its shores is guaranteed to keep divers enthralled.

Shaped somewhat like a foot, Bonaire is a crooked 23.6 miles long. In the bight of the protected coast is the football-shaped Klein Bonaire, about to be kicked towards Curaçao; many dive-sites are based here. Like its neighbors, Bonaire is dry and windswept, covered in scrubby vegetation and dotted here and there with tall cacti. From the salt flats in the south, the land rises to the 787-ft. Mount Brandaris in the northwest. Much of the coastline is limestone coral shelf, but there are breaks in the wall where the sand collects to form decent beaches. Two colonies of flamingos nest on the island and can be seen feeding in the lagoons during the day. A circuit of the island can be completed in a day; cars can be rented from the hotels or from rental companies.

Industries on Bonaire include oil bunkering (storing oil for shipping), salt harvesting, and radio transmitting stations, but tourism (mainly diving) is the most important economic sector and it has changed the island radically in the last 10 years. From a lazy backwater (which the island had remained from the moment the Dutch arrived in

1636) it has suddenly geared up for large numbers of visitors, but a certain funky sleepiness has survived. Bonaireans speak Papiamento, though Dutch is the official language and English is widely understood.

The capital, **Kralendijk**►►, lies in the protected bight of the western shore, on the coral (*kralen*) wall (*dijk*). A few traditional Bonaire houses, painted gold with white stucco, stand among the mostly modern buildings; bars and restaurants line the waterfront, and hotels are spread along the shores on either side of the town. Fort Oranje, the town's old defense, now contains the island museum, displaying indigenous Indian and colonial Bonairean artifacts. The whole town comes to life for Carnival and for parades and festivals during late June.

Beyond the hotel strip, going north, the road passes the tanks of the oil storage depot and continues to the Goto Meer, one of the flamingos' favored nesting spots. The island's northwestern tip is made up of the 13,489-acre **Washington Slagbaai Park**►►, where marked roads give views of Bonaire's semi-arid flora, as well as possible glimpses of the iguana and some of the estimated 130 species of Bonaire birdlife (including pelicans, bananaquits, and sandpipers). Another road heads back to Kralendijk via Rincon, the island's second town, and Indian inscriptions at **Onima**►.

A circular road runs around the southern toe of the island beyond the airport to **Pink Beach**►►, named after the striking color of its sand, and then to the vast white stacks of harvested salt at the **salt works**►► (see panel opposite). Another flamingo colony nests in this area. Colored obelisks stand on the coast; these were originally used as shipping guides on an otherwise indistinguishable coastline. Two groups of small huts huddled on the shore were built as two-man dormitories in 1850 for slaves who worked the salt pans. Lac Baai has two good beaches; nudism is permitted on one.

Kralendijk

131

Nature and wildlife
The divi-divi tree, which grows in the Dutch Leewards, has a gnarled but basically vertical trunk about 6 ft. high, but its branches are forced to grow at 90° to the trunk by the strong Caribbean wind. The ABC islands are mainly dry and covered with cactus and scrub, or *cunucu*. Birds that live there include the orange and black troupial, Curaçao's national bird, and the oriole, which lays its eggs in a hanging nest 3 ft. high.

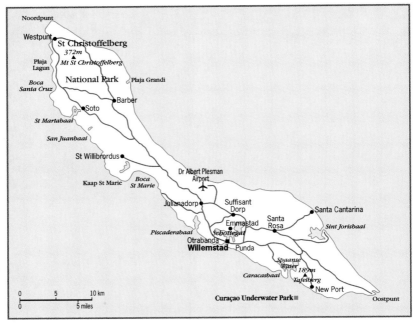

Curaçao

In Willemstad, Curaçao's capital, spiffy rows of pastel-colored townhouses look as though they were transplanted from Holland. The doll's-house look of the island's Dutch architecture makes a cheerful contrast to a terrain that is dotted with stark cacti. Curaçao has neither great beaches nor enchanting scenery. But watersports attract enthusiasts from all over the world, the shopping is first-rate, and some of the best reef diving is here. The sun smiles down on Curaçao, but thanks to the gentle trade winds it never gets stiflingly hot.

The largest of the Netherlands Antilles, the island lies between Aruba and Bonaire, 34 miles from the coast of Venezuela. It is a long, thin island—37 miles by 9 miles—made from lava emissions encrusted with coral limestone.

History Curaçao is the traditional heart of the Dutch Caribbean, and has been the administrative capital since the Dutch arrived in 1634. Dubbed the "Land of Giants" by explorer Amerigo Vespucci, who felt dwarfed by the indigenous Caiquetios tribe, Curaçao was left alone by early colonizers, though many of its inhabitants were taken as slaves to the Hispaniola gold mines. By the early 17th century, there was a handful of Spanish settlers, but these were chased out by Dutch invaders. Slave-trading was the island's prime source of wealth, and emancipation signaled its decline. In 1915 a new source of prosperity was introduced with the building of an oil refinery, and the population soared as workers moved in. During the 1960s and 1980s the oil industry was dealt two blows: "automation," which reduced the number of employees,

Dutch cuisine
Food in the Dutch Leewards is very different from dishes elsewhere in the Caribbean. A number of restaurants specialize in local cuisine, made even more exotic by its Papiamento names. Dishes include *sopi* (soup) and *stoba* (stews), made with *galina* (chicken), *bestia* (lamb), *carco* (conch) and *kreeft* (lobster) or even *juwana* (iguana). Side dishes include *snijboonchi* (stringbeans), *giambo* (cactus fruit), *funchi* (maize meal) or *toetoe* (cornmeal mixed with beans and bacon, topped with Edam cheese). *Kesho yena* is spicy chicken, also covered with Dutch cheese.

and the effects of rising prices. Eventually the business was wound down and there are now plans to expand the tourist industry. Duty-free shopping already attracts regular cruise ships, but there are only a few mid-range hotels on the southern shore, mainly around Willemstad, the capital. Curaçao's beaches are not the Caribbean's best, but the island does have some excellent restaurants.

Island life With 150,000 inhabitants, Curaçao is the most populous of the Netherlands Antilles, and its life as a trading port has given it an extremely varied mix of people. Though Dutch is the official language, Curaçaoans generally speak Papiamento as a first tongue; most also speak English and Spanish. Of all the Dutch Caribbean islands, Curaçao shows the strongest Dutch influence, in its buildings, its food, and its faces.

Willemstad Lying on the protected southern shore, Willemstad has developed around the Schottegat, a huge natural harbor, which attracted the first Dutch colonizers. The oldest part of the town is Punda▶▶ ("the Point"), of which the main quay, the Handelskade▶▶ is one of the most striking sights in the Caribbean; its buildings (such as the 1708 Penha House) combine the curly gables of Amsterdam with the bright colors of the West Indies. Like the streets behind it, the Handelskade still works as a trading area, now serving cruise-ship passengers rather than merchants. Perpendicular to it is the Floating Market▶▶▶, a line of wooden boats docked at the quayside, where you can buy fruits and vegetables shipped in from Venezuela and displayed on slab tables shaded by awnings attached to the masts, which rise and fall along with the rocking of the boats.

The Mikve Israel Synagogue▶▶, located on Columbusstraat, dates from 1732; the Jewish Historical Museum, in its courtyard, displays among other artifacts a 250-year-old ceremonial bath. Fort Amsterdam▶ is the town's original defense, and it was built in 1634. It is now the residence of the Governor of the Netherlands

Curaçao's Dutch-influenced architecture

133

Willemstad's main quay, Handelskade

Antilles and the seat of their Parliament. Four other 17th-century forts surround the port, two of which are now restaurants. There is a tourist information booth under the arches of the Waterfort, and the **Plaza Biejo**►► is an excellent stop for lunch; customers sit at long tables, watching the pots boil before them, and choose from such popular Curaçao dishes as *stoba* (stew) and *toetoe*

Above and left: the floating market at Willemstad

(a combination of maize meal, beans, bacon, sugar and cheese—see panel on page 132).

Otrabanda, on the other side of the main harbor channel, is reached by the **Konigin Emmabrug**►►►, a pedestrian pontoon bridge formed by about 15 barges that move constantly on the waves, making for a bouncy walk across. Occasionally the bridge opens to let ocean-going tankers through; ferries operate at these times. In Otrabanda there are more excellent examples of the distinctive Dutch Creole architecture: colonial houses, with their orange tiles and curly gables, many painted with Curaçao gold. **The Curaçao Museum**►► is in an old townhouse, once used as the naval hospital; exhibits include part of the first airplane to fly from the Netherlands to the island. South of Brion Plein is the Coney Island Amusement Park; northwest of here, the Beth Haim Cemetery has some of the oldest European tombs in the Americas.

Outside Willemstad The suburbs of Willemstad creep around all sides of the Schottegat harbor, where container ports and dockyards line the shore. The autonomy monument, on the eastern side, is a 1954 sculpture of six birds, commemorating the year when the six Netherlands Antilles were granted self-rule. Further along is the **Curaçao Liqueur Distillery►►**, in the Landhuis Chobolobo, where Curaçao liqueur is produced from the peel of small, green oranges in a few vats (distillery open to visitors Monday to Friday). The massive oil refinery, built by Shell on the northwest shore of the harbor, was once the largest in the world. The best view of its tangled pipes and chimneys is from the hills around Fort Nassau, behind Punda. Near the sports stadium is the restored 18th-century **Landhuis Brievengat►►**, a cochineal plantation house with gently sloping tiled roof, white stucco, and flagstone interior, which is open to visitors.

East of Willemstad is the **Curaçao Seaquarium►►**, with recreated reefs and tropical fish. Glass-bottom boat trips and scuba diving are available in the nearby Curaçao Underwater Park, a restricted marine area, beyond which is the Spanish Water lagoon, a popular weekend spot.

West of Willemstad is the *cunucu* countryside, where isolated plantation houses (*landhuisen*) stand among the scrub and dramatic cacti. Near the western tip of Curaçao is the **Christoffel National Park►►**, 4,593 acres on the slopes of the 1,220-ft. Mount St. Christoffelberg, where there are marked driving and walking trails and a museum of natural history. Curaçao's best beaches are towards the western end, on the south shore of the island.

135

Simon Bolivar
Simon Bolivar (El Libertador) was forced to spend a period of exile on Curaçao after a failed South American uprising in 1811. His revolutionary campaigns in the northern part of South America eventually helped liberate the countries that became Venezuela, Bolivia, Peru, Ecuador, and Panama from Spanish rule during the early 19th century.

Fishing off Curaçao

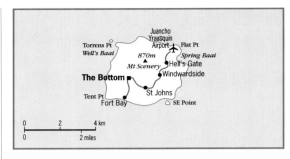

Flat Point and The Road
Flat Point is, in fact, on a
gentle slope, but it is the
only area of Saba large
enough to have an airstrip
(1,300 ft. long). The Road is
a feat of engineering which
it was said would be
impossible to build.
Between Windwardside
and The Bottom there is a
plaque to Joseph
Lambertus Hassell, who
followed a correspon-
dence course in engineer-
ing and then designed and
built The Road, starting at
Fort Bay and heading up to
The Bottom and on to
Windwardside and eventu-
ally via 19 hairpin bends
down to Flat Point. The
Road is still in good condition, after nearly 50 years.

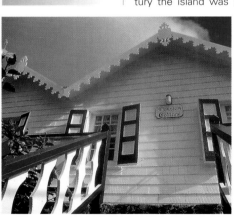

*One of Saba's pretty
white cottages*

Saba

Saba has recently passed a law decreeing that all the
roofs shall be painted red. Draconian, perhaps—but red
roofs have long been a tradition on Saba. They go well
with the white cottage walls, the picket fences and the
striking greens of this remarkably fertile island.

Another draconian aspect of Saba is its geography. It is
small, extremely rugged, and difficult to reach. Mount
Scenery, the waterborne peak of an extinct volcano, soars
to 2,854 ft., on an island only 3 miles by 1.8 miles. The
1,200 hardy Sabians have their island neatly tamed; they
must, in order to survive here.

Dutch colonists from Sint Eustatius were the first
Europeans to settle on the island, in 1640. Twenty-five
years later, Saba was taken by a British privateer, and all
non-English-speakers were shipped away. In the 19th century the island was returned to Dutch possession, and
Saba survived on the money sent
home by its menfolk, who earned
a reputation as skilled sailors, and
on the lace-making and thread-
work of the women. The oil boom
on Aruba and Curaçao provided
work for islanders in the 20th century (and depleted Saba's population), but after its collapse the
island turned to its small tourist
industry to add to the funds paid
out by the Netherlands Antilles
government. There are a few
places to stay—which seem more
like friendly mountain guesthouses than Caribbean beach hotels—
and though Saba has no natural
beaches, the diligent islanders
have built an artificial one.

The island's four settlements are all linked by a sinuous
artery, respectfully known as The Road (see panel). Its
capital is a village by the name of **The Bottom**▶▶,
thought to derive from the Dutch *Botte* (bowl). Most of
the houses do, indeed, lie at the bottom of a bowl, but
new buildings are steadily creeping up the towering,
forested peaks that surround it. The Governor's
Residence, in the village, is an attractive balconied
Caribbean house. A number of bars are run from timber-
frame houses, such as Cranston's Antique Inn, where you

frame houses, such as Cranston's Antique Inn, where you can join the Sabians for an afternoon drink.

On the sheltered coast beneath The Bottom are Saba's two harbors: Ladder Bay and Fort Bay. The first is reached by steps; in the days before The Road, Sabians had to carry all their supplies up here on their shoulders. Fort Bay has been the principal port since 1972, when the jetties were built here. It is also the departure point for scuba diving operations. From here there is nowhere to go but back up to the village, from which The Road leads to St. John's, a small collection of houses on an area of relatively flat ground.

Magnificent views of the coast open out 1,200 ft. below as The Road reaches **Windwardside►►**, which rivals The Bottom as Saba's principal village. The tourist office can be found here, as well as banks and hotels. Windwardside is even neater and prettier than The Bottom, its white houses set behind stone walls, with gardens of bougainvillea and hibiscus. The **Saba Museum►**, set in a private home, shows Amerindian artifacts and 19th-century exhibits. Older village women still knit the renowned Saba lace, which can be bought at the Island Craft Shop.

Beyond Windwardside is the village of Hell's Gate, and from here, The Road descends tortuously to the optimistically named Flat Point, site of the island's airstrip (see panel opposite).

Like many of the old trails used by the islanders before The Road was constructed, the steep path to the top of Mount Scenery has carefully laid steps (they start just outside Windwardside) leading through the rainforest and elfin forest; on a clear day the views to be had along this

Windwardside village

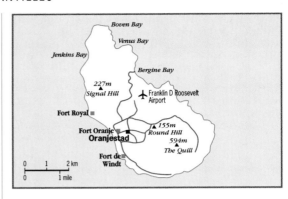

The First Salute

Sint Eustatius was the first place in the world to recognize the U.S. When, in November 1776, a ship flying an unfamiliar flag arrived in harbor, the island gave the customary salute, according it an official welcome. The *Andrew Dorea* was flying the flag of the rebel American colonists and this was the first recognition of their sovereignty. The British were so angry that they persuaded the Dutch to recall the Governor responsible for the incident, de Graaff.

Sint Eustatius

Two hundred years ago, Sint Eustatius was one of the richest and most important islands in the West Indies. As many as a hundred ships would put in to this busy trading port at a time. But the mile of warehouses that once ran along the Lower Town's shore has gone, and only a few walls remain from the island's era as the "Golden Rock."

Almost all of the 18th-century's booming business was breaking the trade laws, as goods which should have been sold to the colonies' governing countries were smuggled to Statia (as the island is usually known) for quick and direct payment. A brisk arms trade developed during the Revolutionary War, and as colonial powers battled over their possessions, the island changed hands

Island philosophy

over 20 times. Statia's golden age came to an end after the British, led by Admiral Rodney, took over the island and sold off all its goods (see panel opposite).

Today Statia is a quiet backwater with only 2,100 inhabitants, mainly of African descent and English-speaking, although the official language is Dutch. The island is undeveloped—there are only a few hotel rooms and no white sand Caribbean strands—though with the help of the EC Statia is renovating its historical buildings.

Lying 30 miles south of Sint Maarten (the main access to

Statia), between the volcanic peaks of Saba and St. Kitts, the island is just 12 sq. miles in size. In the south is a perfectly formed extinct volcanic cone called the Quill; the volcanic sand makes all Statia's beaches dark.

The capital and only town, Oranjestad, sits on a cliff 525 ft. above the island's sheltered Caribbean coast. Its **Upper Town▶▶** has cobbled streets and a few old stone houses with wooden wrap-around balconies among the newer buildings, and from its clifftop courtyard of cobbles, date palms, and cannon, **Fort Oranje▶** has a superb view of the bay. The **Sint Eustatius Historical Museum▶▶▶** is set in de Graaff House, named after the Governor who was responsible for the First Salute (see panel). There are rooms devoted to Arawak and Carib Indian culture, the colonial years (with period furniture) and more recent island history. Some of the Upper Town's historical buildings are no more than shells, but it is worth climbing the tower of the Dutch Reform Church for its fine view. The ruined Honen Dalim synagogue, on the alley Synagoogpad, is one of the oldest in the western hemisphere.

Lower Town▶▶ is where the trading warehouses once stood; as trade expanded, a dyke was built to reclaim more land from the sea. An ancient stone walkway descends from Fort Oranje to the small line of restored buildings recreated with the original bricks. The **Cotton Gin House▶▶▶** is well worth a visit, and has 20 rooms and a restaurant. Its 18th-century atmosphere has been carefully created with brick walls, large shuttered windows and mock-gas lighting.

Beyond the town, Statia's countryside is relatively open, though modern homes are steadily filling the available space. An older Statia is still just visible in the fences of spiky agave and cactus plants and the inevitable goats. It is an easy walk to the lip of **the Quill's crater▶▶**, where lush rainforest grows down in the bowl (it can be a very slippery climb). In the south of the island there is a good view of St. Kitts from the tiny Fort de Windt; in the north, an area of uninhabited hills is the site of Statia's only major industry, an oil bunkerage and a refinery that produces 250 barrels a day.

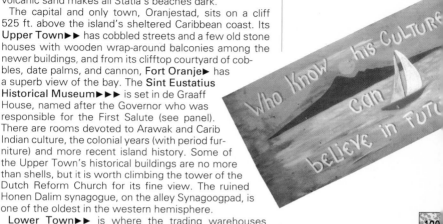

139

Admiral Rodney's revenge
A few years after the First Salute the British had their revenge when Admiral Rodney captured the harbor and kept the flags flying as though the island were open for trade, impounding 150 ships that unwittingly came into harbor. Rodney carried off the merchandise and destroyed the retaining walls. His suspicions aroused by a sudden rise in the number of deaths on the island, Rodney had several coffins dug up, to find that merchants were hiding their gold in them.

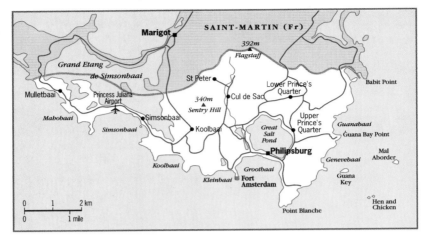

Shopping sprees

Amid the vast cruise ships that dock at Sint Maarten's capital are smaller, wooden craft, whose captains also come to enjoy some of the Caribbean's best shopping. Sint Maarten is where many West Indians go at Christmas, for wine, electrical goods, tobacco, and alcohol. Local yachts make the run as far down as the Grenadines, where many of them were built.

Philipsburg's beach

Sint Maarten

Seen from a distance, Sint Maarten appears serene and tranquil, with land rising from the sea in graceful curves to form steep mountain peaks. But this peaceful air belies the hectic activity of Sint Maarten, one of the busiest and most developed islands in the Caribbean.

Despite being just 37 sq. miles in area, the island is divided between two countries (the smallest island in the world to fly two flags). Since it was first settled in 1648, it has been shared between the Dutch and the French (see pages 122–3 for the French territory, Saint-Martin) and give or take the odd invasion, relations have been pretty amicable. There is even a peak called Mount Concordia as a tribute to their goodwill. The island stands on the same landmass as Anguilla and St. Barts, an ancient volcanic bank, inactive and coral-encrusted, and has superb white sand beaches. Dutch Sint Maarten occupies 16 sq. miles in the southern part of the island.

Given its size, Sint Maarten's tourist industry is huge, and this has changed the island dramatically over the last 20 years. There has been extensive building and the population has increased tenfold, to about 40,000, to service the industry. Though Dutch is the official language, a whole range of spoken languages can be heard here, from Haitian Kreyol to Papiamento (though everyone here can speak English).

The island is crammed to the hilt with hotels, restaurants, bars, clubs, and casinos; the airport at Juliana is a hive of activity, with flights arriving from the main Caribbean islands as well as from Paris, Amsterdam, Frankfurt, and several U.S. cities. Sint Maarten is also popular as a cruise ship stopover, and its status as a duty-free port brings in about half a million tourists a year, as well as locals, to take advantage of the best shopping in the Caribbean.

■ **One of the most attractive features of Caribbean architecture is "gingerbread" design, which embellishes houses with an elaborate latticework of wood carved into squiggles, sweeps, and twirls. The term is supposedly derived from 16th-century German pastry-makers, who were well known for their ornately decorated gingerbread creations. ......■**

The flamboyance of gingerbread appealed to plantation owners and estate managers, who had grand houses built to show off their wealth, with elaborate verandas overlooking their estates. Public buildings were also given the gingerbread treatment, the most fanciful of which are in Haiti. Saba, one of the Dutch Windward Islands, has several well-maintained gingerbread houses with green or red window frames, surrounded by pretty tropical blooms, concentrated in a small area (Windwardside and The Bottom). Gingerbread's popularity spread, and the style was taken up in the U.S. during the prosperous 1860s and 1870s, after the Civil War. Good examples can be seen in the beach resort of Cape May, New Jersey.

Traditionally, Caribbean houses were constructed in wood, there being no need for the warmth provided by stone and brick. Wood was cheaper and buildings could even be dismantled and taken away (in Barbados, farmers' homes were known as "chattel" houses because they could be moved with other goods and chattels). Many of these houses remain, their walls made from strips of clapboard and their roofs tiled with wooden shingles.

Curaçao, Bonaire and Aruba's houses are made with brick and plaster—wood was scarce and at risk from fire, so its use in building was banned. The walls are painted in gold, light brown, purple, and deep green, and the effect is completed with orange "dakpannen," clay roof tiles, and white borders. The story goes that Admiral Kikkert, a Governor of Curaçao, suffered from headaches brought on by the reflection of the sun in Willemstad's whitewashed buildings, so he ordered that they be painted any color other than white.

Old San Juan's city hall, Puerto Rico

Country architecture
Traditional Caribbean country shacks were made with "wattle and daub," a latticework of springy twigs that were covered in mud and allowed to dry in the sun. The roof was then added and topped with thatch, providing a remarkably cool indoor environment. A few wattle and daub houses still exist on the poorer islands.

A restored colonial house in French Saint-Martin

Tourist stores in Philipsburg

The capital and main town on the Dutch side of Sint Maarten is **Philipsburg▶**, set on a narrow spit of land between Great Bay and the Great Salt Pond (the source of salt which originally attracted the Dutch West India Company to the island). It has just four streets and a sprinkling of traditional houses among an otherwise modern town that has sprouted since the tourist boom. The town faces south, towards Saba and Sint Eustatius, the other two Dutch Windward Islands.

Visitors who stream off the cruise ships arrive at de Ruyterplein, a small square which is the setting for the pretty Old Courthouse Building and the tourist information office. Leading through it is Front Street, Philipsburg's mile-long shopping arcade, where the best of the duty-free bargains can be found—European fashion, jewelry, crystal, and porcelain—as well as plenty of cafés and bars. On Front Street, the **Sint Maarten Museum▶▶** has exhibits of pre-Columbian and colonial island life, from Indian pottery to Delft dinner services. Behind the West Indian Tavern are the ruins of a 300-year-old synagogue, the first on the island. The town's founder, John Philips, is buried in an 18th-century cemetery to the west of Philipsburg.

Philipsburg's outlying areas completely encircle the lagoon, and determined shoppers will find yet more arcades around its shores, but generally this is where the islanders live. A **zoo▶** on the Madame Estate keeps animals from South America and the Caribbean area. Further afield, Sint Maarten's eastern side is surprisingly untouched and secluded.

The main route out of Philipsburg is often clogged with traffic; in Koolbaat (Cole Bay), a left turn leads alongside the Simpson Bay Lagoon to the busiest tourist area. Simsonbaat (Simpson Bay) itself has a good beach, and beyond the airport is Mulletbaat (Mullet Bay), with watersports, stores, and a golf course. The road to Marigot crosses the border, which is marked only with an obelisk and a sign saying *Bienvenue à la Partie Française*.

Peter Stuyvesant
Peter Stuyvesant was an early Governor of Curaçao (in 1638) and later of all the Dutch possessions in the Americas, which he governed from Nieuw Amsterdam (New York). An autocratic leader, he lost his right leg in a fight for Sint Maarten in 1644 and wore a silver ornamented false leg as a replacement. Stuyvesant was forced to surrender the North American possessions to the British in 1664, but continued to live in the Great Bouwery in Manhattan until his death in 1672.

■ Almost every brochure for a Caribbean holiday includes a picture of a waiter bearing a tray of exotic, sweet-tasting tropical fruit. Not all will be in season at any one time, but a visit to the market is always worthwhile for the displays of this fertile region's appetizing produce. ......■

The pineapple, used by Amerindians for food and wine-making, grows on a stem in the center of a low bush of about 30 stiff, spiky, cactus-like leaves, and takes about 15 months to mature. Black pineapples are a slightly smaller and sweeter variety.

Pawpaw, or papaya, grows on a tall and slender tree of very light wood. The fruit, which starts off green and matures to yellow and orange, with flesh which is orange when ripe, can grow to 18 inches in length. Papaya is said to be good for high blood pressure, and the seeds are used as a remedy for constipation.

The fruit of the soursop, which is not sour at all, is irregularly shaped, sometimes oval, with small, black hooks protruding from its aromatic, light green skin. Inside, black seeds sit in a white, pulpy flesh that tastes like a combination of mango and pineapple. Although the fruit is delicious, its seeds make it difficult to eat fresh—so it is probably best tasted in ice-cream.

Related to the soursop, the sweetsop looks like a fleshy green pine-cone, about 4 in. tall. It is known locally as the sugar apple or custard apple; its seeds are contained in a sweet, creamy pulp, rather like custard.

Tender fruit
Papain, extracted from the pawpaw, is used as a meat tenderizer; West Indians simply wrap their meat in pawpaw leaf and leave it to stand. Pineapple is also a meat tenderizer, with pretty powerful effects: stranded soldiers on a South Sea island during World War II found that their teeth fell out after they had eaten too much of the fruit.

Hybrid fruit
Jamaica has created two curious fruits as hybrids of other citruses (which grow all over the Caribbean). The ortanique is part orange, part tangerine; the size of the former, but with a skin that peels like the latter; and the ugli fruit, which takes its name from its lumpy appearance, is a cross between a grapefruit, an orange, and a tangerine.

Young breadfruit, usually eaten baked or roasted

Guava fruit is really an outsize berry, which turns from green to yellow when ripening. Inside, its seeds sit in a white or pink pulp. Guava has a bitter-sweet taste and provides five times as much Vitamin C as orange juice.

Mango trees, though not native to the Caribbean, grow throughout the region; their yellow and red fruits have some of the sweetest-tasting flesh of all.

144

Great Corland Bay, Tobago

Other Caribbean states The larger, independent nation states of the Caribbean, separated by physical and cultural obstacles, and often suspicious of each other if not openly hostile, are marked by their diversity. Jamaica's lushness and extensive rainforests are a reminder of what Haiti, 100 miles east, must have been before generations of impoverished peasants cleared the hillsides in search of charcoal. Jamaica has all the attributes of the travel agency clichés—beaches, rivers, mountains—but it also has social and economic problems, as any visitor to downtown Kingston will see. Cuba is cracking and crumbling behind its wall of isolation. The colonial splendor of old Havana is gradually collapsing under the weight of

OTHER CARIBBEAN STATES

neglect; yet this was once the most inviting tropical resort in the world. Haiti and the Dominican Republic share an island, but their border is more often closed than open. For all the Dominican Republic's colonial treasures and natural beauty, thousands of poor islanders risk their lives each year to cross the Mona Passage to Puerto Rico, where rural and U.S.-influenced lifestyles exist side by side. The oil-producing nation of Trinidad and Tobago, famous for its Carnival and calypso, faces an uncertain future after years of wealth; while Barbados is perhaps the most developed of all the islands. No two islands are similar. If you want to know more than a little piece of the Caribbean, explore some of these fascinating states.

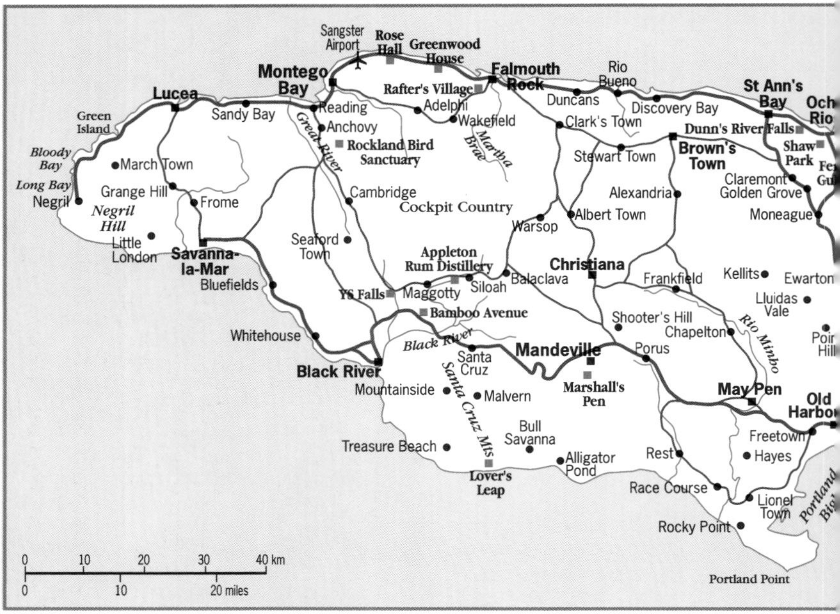
Sangster Airport
Rose Hall
Greenwood House
Montego Bay
Falmouth
Rock
Rio Bueno
St Ann's Bay
Lucea
Rafter's Village
Adelphi
Duncans
Discovery Bay
Green Island
Sandy Bay
Reading
Wakefield
Clark's Town
Dunn's River Falls
Anchovy
Great River
Martha Brae
Bloody Bay
March Town
Rockland Bird Sanctuary
Stewart Town
Brown's Town
Shaw Park
Long Bay
Negril
Grange Hill
Frome
Negril Hill
Cambridge
Cockpit Country
Alexandria
Claremont
Golden Grove
Albert Town
Moneague
Warsop
Little London
Savanna-la-Mar
Seaford Town
Appleton Rum Distillery
Christiana
Bluefields
YS Falls
Maggotty
Siloah
Balaclava
Frankfield
Kellits
Ewarton
Lluidas Vale
Bamboo Avenue
Shooter's Hill
Chapelton
Rio Minbo
Whitehouse
Black River
Santa Cruz
Mandeville
Porus
Black River
Mountainside
Malvern
Santa Cruz Mts
Marshall's Pen
May Pen
Old Harbo
Bull Savanna
Freetown
Treasure Beach
Alligator Pond
Rest
Hayes
Lover's Leap
Race Course
Lionel Town
Portland Bight
Rocky Point
Portland Point
0 10 20 30 40 km
0 10 20 miles

Higglers and hustlers
Higglers are known by similar names all over the Caribbean: hucksters, hackers, Madame Sarahs, traffickers, and suitcase-traders—and they follow the best tradition of West Indian small traders (usually female). They buy up goods in bulk—perhaps in a nearby town, but more recently on other islands and even as far afield as Panama and New York—which they ship home and sell at market, mainly to Jamaicans. Hustlers, by contrast, are opportunists looking for a quick buck, and they often step outside the law. They concentrate on the tourist trade, offering products ranging from T-shirts and African carvings to drugs, and are reluctant to take "no" for an answer—although persistent and polite refusal eventually has its effect.

Jamaica

The third-largest island in the Caribbean (after Cuba and Puerto Rico), the English-speaking nation of Jamaica enjoys a considerable self-sufficiency based on tourism, agriculture, and mining. Its physical attractions include jungle mountaintops, clear waterfalls, and unforgettable beaches, yet the country's greatest resource may very well be the Jamaicans themselves. Although 95 percent of the population trace their bloodlines to Africa, their national origins lie elsewhere: in Great Britain, the Middle East, India, China, Germany, Portugal, South America, and many of the other islands in the Caribbean. Their cultural life is a wealthy one: the music, art, and cuisine of Jamaica are vibrant, with a spirit easy to sense but as hard to describe as the rhythms of reggae or a flourish of the streetwise patois.

History Jamaica was born of strife, as a colonial outpost, first of 16th-century Spanish settlers (who destroyed the Arawak Indian inhabitants) and then of the British, who cut their plantations in the hills. Pirates brawled on the

Jahbah's health food center in Negril

CHICKEN
JAHBAHS

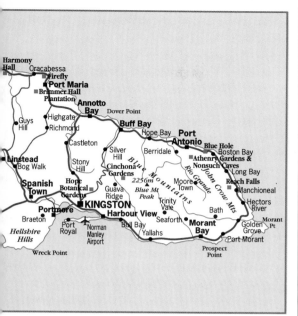

Jamaican jerk
Jerking is a special way of cooking meat that was started by the maroons in their hideaways. Originally it was wild hog, shot in the hills, that was cooked slowly in a barbecue sunk into the ground, but now you can buy jerked chicken, sausages and fish. These days there are "Jerk Centers" all over the island, but the traditional home of jerk pork, a very hot and spicy dish, is Boston Bay, near Port Antonio, where you can choose your meal as it is cooked on pimento wood at a number of roadside shacks.

Maroons
The maroons were a community of runaways who lived high in the inaccessible Jamaican interior, in the John Crow Mountains in the northeast and the Cockpit Country in the northwest. Their name comes from the Spanish word *cimarrón* ("wild"); the earliest maroons were slaves left behind by the Spaniards when they fled from the British in 1655. Maroons were highly successful guerrillas and were never conquered; eventually the colonial authorities were reduced to negotiating with them, agreeing to guarantee their freedom and a considerable measure of self-government (which they still have today), in return for certain conditions, which included returning runaway slaves.

coastline, and the flourishing plantations, worked by slaves, were attacked by runaway maroons (see panel). Uprisings among the slaves led to several serious rebellions and terrible bloodshed, and even after their emancipation in the 19th century the hardship and violence continued. Demonstrations marked the run-up to full enfranchisement in 1944, and preceded complete independence from the U.K. in 1962.

Over the past 30 years the island has built one of the biggest tourist industries in the Caribbean, giving easy access from Europe and the U.S. and a full range of accommodation: beachfront luxury, all-inclusives (offering entertainment and accommodation), guesthouses on the cliffs in Negril, villas, and mountain retreats. The resort towns of Montego Bay, Ocho Rios, and Negril have good restaurants and lively entertainment in bars and nightclubs.

Island life Jamaica is a cultural leader in the Caribbean; its boisterous culture of reggae and rastafarianism attracts visitors from all over the world. Economically, the two and a half million islanders have not had an easy ride recently; rising gas prices and a fall in earnings from the main export, bauxite, led to austerity measures and unrest in the 1980s, and there is still considerable unemployment and inflation. A drop in the number of foreign visitors has also had its effect on islanders, with a weakening currency, soaring prices, and less work available. The government's austerity program was greeted with riots in 1985, and violent outbreaks still occur in Kingston. Riots reach a peak during the fiercely contested elections, but visitors are generally sheltered from this side of life; for them, Jamaica remains primarily a place of peace and beauty, with all the character and vibrancy that have come to characterize the Caribbean.

Swims
On the road between Black River and Bamboo Avenue you will see vendors holding plastic bags of pink "swims"—local shrimps cooked in pepper sauce and well worth trying. Swims are tasty, but the pepper sauce is very hot, so be warned.

Coffee factories
Blue Mountain coffee is renowned as some of the best in the world. At the Mavis Bank and Silver Hill coffee factories, berries are pulped and fermented to reveal the beans, which are then dried and husked before being bagged for export (much of the crop goes to Japan). Though there are no formal tours of the factories, you can ask to be shown around.

Black River safari cruise

►► Black River

Southwest Jamaica, around Black River, is a little-known corner of the island, where a quiet, rural lifestyle still exists, untouched by the development and tourism of the north coast. The fishing town of **Black River►** is somewhat run down, though there is still some charm in its old wooden buildings, set up when logwood exports (the source of the indigo before synthetic dyes were developed) brought prosperity a century ago. On the **Black River Safari►►**, you can cruise along the river itself into Jamaica's largest swamp, where mangroves form a tunnel around you, and you may glimpse herons, egrets, and even crocodiles.

There are a few isolated, usually deserted bays scattered along this coastline. From Crane Beach, just outside the town, the scrubby savannah land extends to the southeast, where lone cows graze attended by white cattle egrets, eventually reaching **Treasure Beach►►**, a lost and lazy settlement set on a superb strip of sand. Another good beach can be found at Bluefields, to the northwest of Black River.

Inland, north of Black River, the main road skirts the swamp and then leads to **Bamboo Avenue►**, a fine sight which is worth a quick detour. For just over 3 miles the huge bamboo plants form an arch over the road, hanging in graceful bushy curves. Just north of here are the **YS Falls►►**, a series of waterfalls and ponds where you can swim. These can sometimes be crowded with tourists, but the falls themselves are stunning.

►►► Blue Mountains

The heavily forested **Blue Mountains►►** tower above Kingston, but the pace of life in the small mountain communities there is very different from the capital. **Ivor Lodge►►►**, a spiffy, three-room guesthouse in Jack's Hill (a steep and winding climb, but accessible) is a traditional wooden house with a magnificent view over the city, ideal for lunch or an early evening cocktail. You can walk the Blue Mountains, including the 7,400-ft. Blue Mountain peak, with guides arranged at the less formal Maya Lodge▶▶, close by. At Castleton, on the road over to Annotto Bay on the north coast, botanical gardens dating from 1862 are laid out beside a river; here, guides will show you a variety of exotic flora, birds, butterflies, and the ingenious trapdoor spider.

Another main road into the Blue Mountains leads up from Papine, passing immediately into gorges and steep-sided valleys, where fruit and vegetables are grown. There are gardens at Cinchona (reached from Clydesdale), where quinine was once extracted from cinchona trees; other places to visit include the World's End Rum Distillery at Guava Ridge and coffee factories at Mavis Bank, near by, and Silver Hill (see panel, opposite). The Pine Grove Hotel is a good stop for refreshment.

▶ Cockpit Country

The Cockpit Country lies in the northwest of Jamaica, to the south of Falmouth. This has always been one of the most inaccessible and remote areas of the island, and for years it provided a hideout for the guerilla-style runaway maroons. Its romance lies in its appearance—shaggy, pointed mountains of karst limestone—and in its names. During the maroons era, it was known as the Land of the Look Behind, and had districts such as "Quick Step" and "Me No Sen, You No Come," which were so dangerous that British soldiers would ride back to back on their horses. Even today the Cockpit Country is rarely visited by outsiders, and the few roads that run around it are rough and little used.

The Appleton Rum Distillery▶▶▶ is a working sugar cane factory and rum distillery that is well worth a visit if you are in the area. (It can be visited on the Appleton Estate Express train from Montego Bay; tel: 952 2887.) Tours show the newly cut cane being carted around and rolled through crushers to release the juice, which is boiled at high temperatures before being crystallized into sugar using massive centrifuges. There is a restaurant and bar at the distillery.

Traditional costumes at Kingston

Manatees
The endangered manatee is a large marine mammal that occasionally appears on the shores around Black River and even in the river estuary. Also known as the sea cow, it can grow to 13 ft. in length and can weigh up to 310 lb. With its small, rounded tail, front flippers, and tiny, underdeveloped eyes, the manatee is believed to have been the source of many sailors' tales of mermaids on distant rocks.

Tree of life
The national flower of Jamaica is the delicate, light blue bloom of the *Lignum vitae* tree. Its name means "wood of life," and it is valued for many things; the wood, which is extremely hard, is used to make axle shafts, bowling balls, and even to replace metal ball-bearings, and the resin is used in the treatment of breathing disorders.

The national heroes
The Jamaican national heroes, whose statues stand in Heroes Park, are Paul Bogle, a preacher, and George William Gordon, who were both blamed and executed for a rebellion in Morant Bay in 1865; Marcus Garvey, the activist and founder of the Universal Negro Improvement Association, which was so influential among black people in the early part of this century; and Independence leaders Alexander Bustamante and Norman Manley. Nanny, a female maroon leader, has recently joined the ranks of the national heroes.

Spanish Town
Kingston did not become Jamaica's capital until 1872. Before that the capital was Spanish Town, where you can still see the grand old Georgian colonial administrative buildings and courthouse in the main square. In the cathedral there are tablets in the floors and walls dating back to the late 17th century. It is worth the half-day's trip from Kingston by bus or taxi to see these reminders of the past.

▶▶ **Kingston**

Kingston, the capital of Jamaica, sits on the southern shore of the island, between a huge natural harbor and the Blue Mountains. It is a far cry from the north coast resort towns; Kingston is very much a Jamaican city, whose character is unaffected, in the main, by tourism. Downtown it is a melee of traffic, people, and streetside trade: noisy buses, neatly dressed schoolchildren, stray goats, and vendors touting their wares. There are not many formal "sights" here, nor much left of architectural interest, but with a population of well over half a million, Kingston is a good place to catch some genuine Jamaican life. Unfortunately, this includes a criminal element, as in most busy cities, and you should be careful when walking around—especially in ghetto areas like Trenchtown.

The heart of downtown Kingston pulses around the Parade▶▶, a bus terminal and market area, where vendors sell every conceivable consumer item from the sidewalks and "busmen"—the good-humored bus ticket collectors—do their utmost to persuade passengers onto their buses, watched over by the stately Ward Theatre and Kingston Parish Church. You might look quickly at the National Gallery of Jamaica▶▶ for a formal view of the island's art and then at National Heroes Park▶▶, which has statues of the leading lights of Jamaican history and Independence (see panel).

Most visitors to the capital stay uptown in New Kingston, a business and residential area with a more relaxed tempo and a number of good restaurants and bars. Devon House▶▶▶ is an historic oasis in the modern town and it is worth spending time in its atmospheric grounds, perhaps taking a meal under the mango tree or trying one of the excellent ice creams on sale here. The main house was constructed in 1881 in classical style adapted to the tropics, and is open to visitors. Its courtyards contain stores, restaurants, and cafés. Further along Hope Road, you pass Kings House, the Governor General's residence, the Tuff Gong Studio▶▶ (with a museum about Bob Marley) and the Hope Botanical Gardens▶▶, with an orchid house and a small zoo.

Devon House, Kingston

Port Royal

■ Rich and debauched Port Royal earned the names "Gilded Hades" and "the wickedest city in Christendom" in the 17th century, when pirates would sail into town laden with loot and binge until their next seaborne escapade. In 1692 the revelry came to an abrupt halt. At about noon on June 7, a massive earthquake struck and the city disappeared under the waves, killing 2,000 people at a stroke. .....■

Port Royal lies on the tip of the Palisadoes Peninsula, at the mouth of Kingston Harbour. It was fortified by the British in 1655, and became a gathering place for English buccaneers. Soon, this was the Caribbean's richest town; merchants shipped their wares here for onward sale, and buccaneers, hounded from their base on Tortuga, off Haiti, brought their own loot. Taverns (there was one for every 10 inhabitants) were crowded with prostitutes and men were killed at the drop of a hat. When the earthquake struck, the townspeople thought it was Judgment Day. Whole streets slipped into the bay and ships were flung into the town's remains on a tidal wave. Of 3,000 houses, only 200 were left standing—but the spirit of Port Royal wasn't immediately extinguished; as the dust settled, some of the survivors simply carried on with their drinking.

After the earthquake, Port Royal was rebuilt, only to be devastated by a fire in 1703. Its remaining residents then moved to Kingston, leaving their town to the navy.

Port Royal today Nowadays Port Royal is a quiet village, reached by ferry from the Kingston waterfront and known for its fried fish and bammy (a flat Jamaican cake made with cassava). Fort Charles, a lumbering stone fortress whose embrasures are still lined with cannons, survived the earthquake, though it sank a few feet. Inside, in quarters where the British Admiral Nelson stayed in 1779, is the Maritime Museum, with models of ships and maritime memorabilia. The nearby Giddy House is a Victorian armory that ended up at its weird angle and received its name in 1907, after another earthquake.

Lucky break
In the graveyard of St. Peter's Church (1725), the story of Lewis Galdy is written on his tombstone: he was "swallowed up in the Great Earthquake," but was disgorged into the sea a few minutes later as another shockwave passed, and kept swimming until he was eventually rescued by a boat.

Cannons at the ready, Port Royal

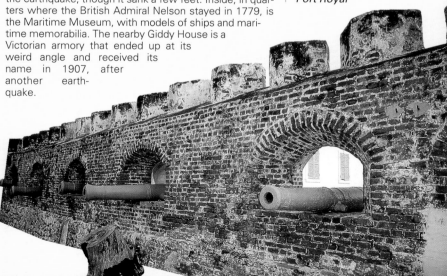

■ **Jamaica is musically the loudest and the most productive of all Caribbean islands. Folk culture and religious traditions have given birth to a wealth of dance rhythms, and music has a strong element of protest, developed by singers ranging from the "rude boys" of the 1960s to the "ragga" singers of today. But this does not restrict the scope of musical life; tune the radio to Irie FM for certain proof that Jamaicans can put just about any song to reggae and make it sound good. .....■**

Marching bands
In the British Caribbean there is still a tradition of marching bands, very much in the British military fashion. Musicians dress in suitably formal and colorful tunics, but when marching, rather than keeping to a formal, disciplined style, they swagger and swing their instruments around.

Until 50 years ago the popular dance rhythm in Jamaica was mento. With its slow, melodic sound and strong lyrics, this was similar to the old calypsos of Trinidad—and, like them, mento had a satirical edge. Ska dance music emerged in the late 1950s, at a time of political upheaval, as Jamaica moved towards independence, and was initially frowned on by the establishment; it introduced "rude boys" and delivered a socially conscious message.

Rocksteady, a slower version of the ska rhythm, incorporating a heavier bass riff and stronger vocals, put in a brief appearance in the mid-1960s, but was soon superseded by reggae. This immensely popular music com-

Above: Maxi Priest and Shabba Ranks; top: Shaggy

Toasting
Toasting was developed in Jamaican clubs, as DJs sang their own quickfire lyrics over current popular tunes while introducing the records. This rapid, off-the-cuff patter is difficult for the uninitiated to understand, but it requires a lightning mind and a good deal of skill, and is hugely popular with club-goers.

bined elements of ska and rocksteady, and its "chaka-chaka" rhythm was given international appeal by bands such as Bob Marley and the Wailers, and Third World.

Reggae has had lasting success, spawning new bands in many other countries, but in Jamaica the music scene has moved on. Most recently it has adapted rap music to produce dancehall, a hard and repetitive rhythm overlaid with a heavy rapping voice; and in ragga (from "ragamuffin"), the strutting rude boys have come to the fore again, with singers such as Shaggy, Shabba Ranks, Mad Cobra, and Yellowman, the king of slack (slightly vulgar songs).

Echoes of an English country town in stately Mandeville, once a colonial retreat

▶▶ Mandeville

The central Jamaican town of Mandeville is 2,000 ft. above sea level, and enjoys a cooler climate than the coast. In imperial days beaches were considered unhealthy and the British colonials would come here for their summer retreat from Kingston. Nowadays the town is the center of a rural (and recently industrialized) area—a far cry from the beach-hustling and commercial resorts of the north coast for which Jamaica is widely known. There are just a few places to stay, and they have a relaxed and stately air.

Mandeville itself was built along the lines of an English country town, with a parish church and a Georgian court-house facing each other across the grassy common, or green. The colonials would have taken their constitutional walks here, but the green now serves as the bus terminal, and is a focus of chaotic Jamaican life.

On the hills around Mandeville is some of Jamaica's most fertile land; the roadsides are lined with stalls selling all the fruits and vegetables in season: mangoes, oranges, bananas, peanuts, and cashews. Just south of town is **Marshall's Pen▶▶▶** (visits by appointment, tel: 962 2260), a classic Jamaican mansion surrounded by gardens on what was once a coffee plantation. Built in the late 18th century, the house is made mostly of wood and is furnished in period style. It is possible to arrange bird-watching trips on the estate (tel: 962 2260). On the coast to the south of Marshall's Pen is Lover's Leap, where there is a spectacular look-out. There are also superb views from Spur Tree Hill, southwest of Mandeville.

The region around Mandeville is Jamaica's bauxite mining country. Used to make aluminum, bauxite is a major export, and open cast mines form orange scars across the landscape. At Shooter's Hill, to the northeast, you can arrange a tour of the Pickapeppa sauce factory (manufacturing a popular spicy sauce); ask when they are likely to be boiling up—this is the best time to visit.

Jamaican birds
Of the 250 or so birds that spend time in Jamaica (the island is on a migratory route and some stop by on their way north and south), there are 25 endemic species. These include the Jamaican owl, with its eartufts and guttural whirring call; the Jamaican woodpecker, black and white except for its red head, and the yellow-bellied cuckoo, which can be seen in the Mandeville area; others include the Jamaican becard, which suspends its nest of vegetable matter from a tree, entering through a hole in the bottom, and the doctor bird (see panel, page 155).

Cashews
The cashew nut, cultivated in the Mandeville area, grows in a shell at the end of the cashew apple on an evergreen tree. Inside the shell is an oil that can blister human skin and is poisonous if burnt; it must be dried in the sun and roasted to remove the oil before an inner shell can be broken off to reveal the nut. This laborious process is the reason why cashews tend to be so expensive.

OTHER CARIBBEAN STATES

Beaches
Many hotels are set on beaches and most of these have watersports facilities. In Montego Bay itself Doctor's Cave Beach is the most popular choice, and tends to get very busy. There is an entry fee, but facilities include changing rooms and bars. Other strips of sand are accessible at Walter Fletcher Beach and Cornwall Beach.

The White Witch of Rose Hall
The most famous mistress of Rose Hall was Annie Palmer, who lived there around 1820. Her story has no doubt been embellished over the years, but she is said to have murdered three husbands, and had many lovers, including some of her terrified slaves, maintaining her power over them through witchcraft and sometimes killing them when she lost interest. Finally she herself was murdered by one of her lovers who realized he was losing favor with her.

▶▶ **Montego Bay**

Montego Bay, in the northwest of the island, is the best known of Jamaica's resorts. Mo Bay, as it is known, is a lively town; there are plenty of bars along Gloucester Avenue and some good restaurants, both international and local, set in the old stone buildings and down on the waterfront. The hotels include some of the Caribbean's snazziest, such as the Half Moon Club and Round Hill: these are not in the town itself, but scattered in coves along the coast to the east and west. There are many package hotels around Montego Bay, but independent travelers will also be able to find cheaper accommodation, particularly on Sunset Boulevard and Queen's Drive, and in the suburbs. Activities available in the area include river rafting trips and visits to a number of great houses, which can be arranged on day trips from the town by tour operators (see **Travel Facts**).

The heart of Montego Bay itself is **Sam Sharpe Square**▶▶, where vendors hype their colored T-shirts, peanuts, and sky-juice (plastic bags of ice crystals with a dash of fruit concentrate) to passers-by. In the corner of the square is the Cage, a lock-up for errant slaves from the days before emancipation, and a statue of Sharpe himself, a slave leader who was executed after his sit-down strike turned into a full-blown uprising in 1831. Towards the sea from here you will find the **Craft Market**▶, where there are souvenirs, wooden carvings, and straw hats on sale for tourists. North along Gloucester Avenue is **Doctor's Cave Beach**▶▶, the most popular beach in the town, and another fine Jamaican institution: the **Pork Pit**▶▶▶, where you can buy jerked chicken and pork.

As you leave the town heading east along the north coast you pass the famous Half Moon Club hotel and its golf course and come eventually to **Rose Hall**▶▶▶, Jamaica's best-known great house. Set in stately gardens overlooking the coast, Rose Hall was built in the 1770s in imitation of British mansions of the period. The grand interior is furnished with antiques, but the guides concentrate on telling you about the house's former mistress, Annie Palmer (see panel). The less pretentious **Greenwood**

Doctor's Cave Beach, Montego Bay

Seller at the straw market, Mo Bay

Jamaican doctor bird
The doctor bird, or the red-billed streamertail, is the Jamaican national bird and one of the prettiest hummingbirds. As its name suggests, it has a red bill; the male's chest is a shimmering fluorescent shade of green. In flight it displays a pair of back tail feathers about three times as long as its body.

Seaford Town
Seaford Town, south of Montego Bay, looks like a normal Jamaican town but has an unusual history. Lord Seaford granted the land to German settlers who came here to farm it in 1835, and their blond descendants can still be seen. A similar experiment involved importing Indian laborers to Little London on the south coast, near Savanna-la-Mar; they, too, were absorbed into the local community and culture.

Great House▶▶ stands on a hill about 5 miles beyond Rose Hall. Built in about the same period, it was owned by the family of the poet Elizabeth Barrett Browning and gives a clear impression of the privileged plantation lifestyle of the time. Inside, there is antique furniture and a fine collection of musical instruments.

Beyond the town of Falmouth is the Martha Brae river, on which rafting trips are available; they start upstream at Rafter's Village and arrive on the coast at Rock, where there is a phosphorescent lagoon that glitters at night when disturbed. The Glistening Waters restaurant takes its name from this strange phenomenon.

Heading west from Montego Bay, the road skirts the bay itself and heads for the area of Reading, passing hillsides dotted with expensive villas. Beneath them is Catherine Hall, where the Bob Marley Performing Centre hosts the annual reggae gathering, Reggae Sunsplash. From here the coast road leads eventually to the western resort town of Negril, passing on its way the mouth of the Great River, where you can arrange to take a river rafting trip (by torchlight at night), and the hotels at Round Hill and Tryall, where there is also a famous golf course.

Turn south at Reading and you will climb immediately into the hills. Near Anchovy is the delightful **Rockland Bird Sanctuary▶▶**, best visited when all the birds come to feed, from 3:30p.m. on. Some of the hummingbirds, including the Jamaican doctor bird, will actually feed from your hand. Set among fields of banana and citrus, **Belvedere Plantation▶▶** has re-created a village from the last century, displaying various trades, such as iron forging and weaving, and the fascinating herb garden. There is also a garden walkway along the river with labeled plants.

■ **Bob Marley shot to international fame in the 1970s, popularizing reggae and rastafarianism across the world. Though he had the toughest Jamaican roots, Marley was awarded Jamaica's highest public honor, the Order of Merit, and his legacy remains in hundreds of songs, which are still played all over Jamaica. .....■**

Tuff Gong
The Tuff Gong Studio was bought by Marley as his home and recording studio in 1976. Set on Hope Road in New Kingston, an uptown area of Kingston, it is a far cry from the shanties of Trenchtown. Tours of the studio show the gold records awarded for Marley's top-selling discs and video recordings of Marley performing his songs.

Robert Nesta Marley was born on February 6, 1945. Deserted by Norval Marley, her white Jamaican husband, Marley's mother, Cedella, raised Nesta in Nine Miles village, in the parish of St. Ann's, on Jamaica's north coast. When he was a youth they moved to the poorest shanty area of Kingston, and he worked as a welder.

Determined to succeed as a musician, Marley formed "The Wailing Wailers" in the early 1960s with Bunny Wailer and Peter Tosh. Together, they typified the "rude boy" image and found popular success with over 30 ska songs; but, having made little money, the band split up and Marley had to turn to welding again to make a living.

The 1970s finally brought financial success and the new Wailers were signed by Island Records. By this time Marley had become a rastafarian and the band began

The Marley mausoleum
Bob Marley's mausoleum, in his home village of Nine Miles, is a site of pilgrimage to many fans and can be toured. Unfortunately it is now overrun by hustlers trying to sell pirated cassettes and "spliffs," and a visit is not a relaxing experience.

playing reggae. The album *Catch a Fire* hit the international charts and was followed by *Natty Dread*, *Exodus* (the best-selling album of all), *Kaya*, and *Uprising*.

By now a world-famous celebrity, Marley emigrated from Jamaica after an attempt on his life, but returned in 1978 to stage the One Love Peace Concert, in which he persuaded Prime Minister Edward Seaga and opposition leader Michael Manley to make a gesture of unity against the gangland wars which were then plaguing the island.

Bob Marley died of cancer at the early age of 36 on May 11, 1981. His body was laid to rest in a mausoleum at Nine Miles in St. Ann's (see panel).

▶▶▶ Negril

The town of Negril lies at the far western tip of Jamaica and, more than any other place on the island, typifies the Jamaican image of a hedonist's hideaway on an idyllic beach. Sunset-watching has been a hallowed pastime here since the 1960s, when the village was adopted as a home by hippies. Since then Negril has been discovered by tourists; there are large hotels on the beach and people are bussed in daily to watch the sunset from Rick's Café. But the old laid-back life still exists, and it is still possible to escape the crowds. There is not much to see in Negril—but then that is hardly the point of the town. You can expect to be hustled there—but then who could resent a vendor who arrives by canoe bearing a briefcase, or who greets you by massaging your leg with aloe?

Negril divides neatly into two halves: the beach and the cliffs. If there is a town center it is at the rotary, from where the road runs inland towards Savanna-la-Mar. The road runs north towards Montego Bay alongside **Long Bay▶▶▶**, one of Jamaica's best beaches—5 miles of superb sand with hotels and beach bars (try Cosmo's at the top end) scattered along it. Beyond Hedonism II, on the point, is the wide stretch of **Bloody Bay▶▶**, which takes its name from the days when whalers used to clean their catch here.

South of the rotary, the coastal road of Negril's West End winds its way along the clifftops, where there are small hideaway hotels, guesthouses and bars (try the LTU bar or Kaiser's). The cliffs are not very high—though they might seem so to people about to jump off into the sea, something of a sporting tradition in some bars. Negril has a number of outdoor music parks where you can sometimes hear big Jamaican bands. At the southern end of Negril is the 100-ft. **lighthouse▶**, which has good views of the surrounding area.

Sunset from Rick's Café

Hedonism II
Hedonism II (there was no Hedonism I) was the first of Jamaica's all-inclusive hotels. Once inside the gates there is no charge for the facilities, which include scuba diving, sailing, trapeze instruction, toga-tying, finger-painting for adults, and even "nudes versus prudes" volleyball.

Calico Jack
The infamous pirate "Calico" Jack Rackham (named after his penchant for calico underwear) was captured in Negril in 1720 and executed. With him were two women pirates, Anne Bonney and Mary Read. Bonney, who was pregnant and escaped execution, said that: "If he had fought like a man he would not be dying like a dog."

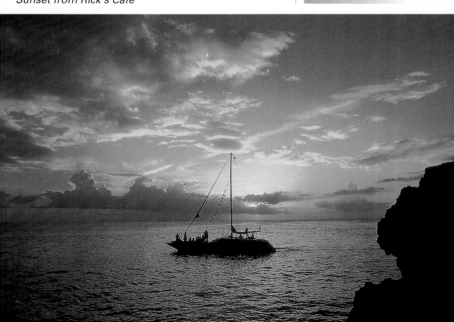

Ackee and saltfish
Ackee and saltfish was once a hardship food, but has now achieved the status of national dish. Ackee is the fruit of a tree that originates in Africa. Its red pods must ripen and open naturally before the lobes of yellow flesh can be taken out and boiled (otherwise it is poisonous). When cooked, ackee looks and even tastes rather like scrambled egg. Saltfish (salted cod) was the cheapest high-protein food available in the 18th century, imported to feed slaves. Since then it has become expensive, but this has not decreased its popularity.

Columbus in trouble
After exploring the coast of Central America on his fourth voyage, Columbus was stranded with his crew when his ships sank in St. Ann's Bay in 1502. The island's inhabitants, the Arawaks, agreed to feed the explorers, but after an altercation withdrew their aid. Columbus managed to change their minds again by calling on God to take away the moon, knowing that a total eclipse of the moon was due. Eventually, as there was no sign of rescue (a ship from the Santo Domingo settlement sailed away leaving the unpopular Columbus behind), two members of the crew took a canoe and braved the seas between Jamaica and Hispaniola to fetch a ship and collect the stranded sailors.

▶▶ **Ocho Rios**

Halfway along the north coast, Ocho Rios is Jamaica's second biggest resort town. As in Montego Bay, the resorts are scattered for several miles on either side of the town, which itself stretches along the seafront and has become a much-frequented vacation spot for Kingstonians. Ochie, as it is affectionately known, is well provided with beaches, watersports, and entertainment; there are expensive resorts and some cheaper hotels, and a clutch of lively bars can be found on James Avenue, near the center of town. The main beaches are Mallard's Beach and Turtle Beach, directly beneath twin skyscrapers on the seafront; and to the west of Ocho Rios there is a good strip of sand at Mammee Bay. Many excursions can be made into the surrounding countryside, making this a popular cruise ship destination.

The heart of the town is around the clocktower, where cars and buses, market vendors, and the occasional goat vie with one another for supremacy. There is nothing much to see in Ocho Rios itself, but Jamaica's best-known tourist attraction, **Dunn's River Falls▶▶**, lies to the west of the town center. The falls are a remarkable sight, as the river cascades over limestone outcrops, dropping steadily nearly 660 ft. Most people start at the bottom and climb through the lips and falls, pausing occasionally to swim in the pools (bathing suits are essential and sneakers are recommended). The falls are popular with tour buses and tend to be crowded with sunburned tourists; souvenirs are sold at the end of the climb.

Farther along the coast road to the west of Dunn's River Falls are a number of small towns and occasional hotels in an isolated bay. **St. Ann's Bay▶** is the birthplace of black

Dunn's River Falls

Relaxation at Ocho Rios

activist Marcus Garvey. There is not much to detain you here, but spare a moment to think of Christopher Columbus, who was forced to spend over a year here waiting for rescue when his ships sank (see panel). Nearby is the site of Jamaica's first Spanish settlement, Seville Nueva, recently restored as an archeological park.

The road south from Ocho Rios climbs immediately into the hills. **Shaw Park Gardens**►► are festooned with flowering bushes and trees set among streams and ponds. The main road to Kingston then passes into **Fern Gully**►►, a deep cleft in the hills. Despite being busy with traffic, the route runs past impressive scenery: huge ferns and trees clamber up the walls and hang over the road, blocking out the light and keeping the gully cool.

Heading east from Ocho Rios along the coast road, you cross the White River, on which there are daytime rafting trips and torchlit night excursions with dinner included; these can be arranged at hotels. **Prospect Plantation**► is a working Jamaican plantation where native fruit and vegetables, including soursop, cocoa, tamarind, and ackee (see panel), are grown, and trees (bearing plaques) were planted by famous visitors including Winston Churchill and Charlie Chaplin. It can be toured either by tractor-drawn carriage or on horseback. **Harmony Hall**►► is an art gallery set in a restored gingerbread house, exhibiting works by Caribbean artists.

About 15 miles farther on—past Goldeneye, the house of James Bond's creator, Ian Fleming (which can be rented as a villa)—is **Firefly**►►►, where Noel Coward lived until his death in 1973. The house itself is simple, the few furnishings and musical scores still as Coward left them, but Firefly's most spectacular feature is its marvelous view: from the drawing room this extends for miles along the north coast and as far as the Blue Mountains. Inland from Port Maria is **Brimmer Hall Plantation**►►, a working estate growing a range of fruit and vegetables, which can be toured in a tractor-drawn trailor.

Marcus Garvey
Marcus Mosiah Garvey was a black activist during the early 20th century. His aim was to help Africans and their descendants improve their situation in a white-dominated, colonial world. Through his Universal Negro Improvement Association he built up a massive following in the Caribbean and the U.S., keeping in touch with the organization's branches throughout the world by means of its newspaper, *Negro World*. Garvey died in relative obscurity in Britain, but in 1964, his bones were brought back to Jamaica, where he was proclaimed the first Jamaican national hero.

OTHER CARIBBEAN STATES

Beaches
Set against the backdrop of the John Crow Mountains, the beaches around Port Antonio tend to be steep-sided coves, but there are pleasant strips of golden sand in the area. Be careful of currents—the sea can become rough when onshore winds are blowing. There are good beaches at San San and at Boston Bay, and Frenchman's Cove is often deserted. Though not a beach, the Blue Hole is a favorite spot: a stunningly blue sea pool with edges fringed by palm trees.

Bananas galore
The banana trade made Port Antonio rich at the turn of the century, reaching its heyday in the 1920s. The fruit was brought down the Rio Grande on bamboo rafts, to be shipped out to the U.S. When Errol Flynn bought Navy Island in Port Antonio harbor in the late 1940s he popularized the use of these rafts for pleasure; it has since become a staple of a Jamaican vacation.

▶▶▶ **Port Antonio**

The northeast is a little-known corner of Jamaica, but one of the most rewarding. Although there are hotels here, the area is distinctly less commercial than the big resort towns on the north coast. Small rural communities are dotted along the steep slopes of the John Crow Mountains, which tumble down to the coast. The scenery is fertile and unspoiled; nature quickly reclaims any human invasion, with fences becoming hedges and telephone wires furring up in no time.

Street scene, Port Antonio

Port Antonio itself is a charming town with an easy, relaxed pace, set between mountains and a magnificent double harbor. The few streets of clapboard houses have become a bit run-down since the decline of the town's prosperity, which flowed from the banana industry early this century, and then from its brief reign as Jamaica's most exclusive resort in the 1950s, when the likes of Errol Flynn and Bette Davis were frequent visitors.

There is a fine panorama of the town from the Bonnie View Hotel. Beneath it, behind the harbor, is the oldest part of town, with official stone buildings such as the courthouse and parish church; beyond this is the Point, with beautiful old wooden town houses. Just off the Point is Navy Island, once owned by Errol Flynn, where his former residence is now a hotel.

East of the town, beyond the Blue Hole (see panel), is **Boston Bay▶▶▶**, the home of jerk, which is freshly cooked at roadside stalls. The **Sam Street African Art Museum▶▶▶**, inland of Long Bay, has fine exhibits; 6 miles farther south are **Reach Falls▶▶**, some of the island's prettiest and normally free of tourist buses.

Inland from Port Antonio, Berridale marks the start of the fairly pricey two-and-a-half-hour river-rafting trip on the Rio Grande (two per raft; transportation is provided to the start of the route from the Rafter's Rest, on the river mouth). The road then climbs further into the John Crow Mountains and leads to **Moore Town▶**, an old maroon settlement, to which visits can be arranged by the Port Antonio tourist office (City Centre Plaza, tel: 993 3051). Not far off the route, southeast of Port Antonio, are Athenry Gardens, with walkways and labeled plants, and Nonsuch Caves, illuminated caverns festooned with stalactites.

■ **The word "rasta" tends to conjure up a picture of musicians dressed in red, gold, and green, and sporting hydra-heads of dreadlocks. But the picture is a misleading one. In Jamaica, most rastafarians live quiet, religious, often reclusive lives and rarely set foot in tourist-dominated towns. .....■**

Rasta beliefs first emerged during the 1930s in the poor ghettos of west Kingston as the religious crystalization of anti-colonial, black consciousness movements. Although it has often been sensationalized and misunderstood, rastafari is still a Judeo-Christian-inspired faith, and many believers carry bibles and go to services.

Rastas have no central church, but there is a system of recognized beliefs common to all followers. According to the rastafarian interpretation of the bible, Ras (prince) Tafari is a divine incarnation, believed to have taken earthly form as the Emperor Haile Selassie of Ethiopia. To rastas, Africans are God's chosen people, and some look ahead to eventual black supremacy. Ethiopia is believed to be Zion, or heaven on earth—a belief linked with the "back to Africa" movement. Other countries, particularly Jamaica (to which blacks were forcibly brought to atone for their ancestors' sins) and white nations, are regarded as Babylon, or hell on earth.

Most believers lead simple, austere lives, rejecting the trappings of modern Western life. They eat "ital" (from "vital" or natural), mostly vegetarian foods, and usually prefer herbal remedies to Western medical treatment. Most rastas wear their hair uncut and uncombed, in long, thick "dreadlocks," and most regard smoking marijuana, or "ganja" (which is illegal in Jamaica) as a sacred activity.

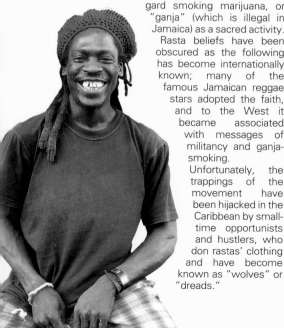

Rasta beliefs have been obscured as the following has become internationally known; many of the famous Jamaican reggae stars adopted the faith, and to the West it became associated with messages of militancy and ganja-smoking.

Unfortunately, the trappings of the movement have been hijacked in the Caribbean by small-time opportunists and hustlers, who don rastas' clothing and have become known as "wolves" or "dreads."

Lion of Zion
Haile Selassie was known as the "Lion of Judah"; as a proud, African animal, the lion is often used in rasta art. The lion's mane is taken to symbolize a full head of dreadlocks, and followers will consciously emulate the lion's slow, proud bearing.

Rasta craft market in Montego Bay

Ganja
Marijuana was introduced into the Caribbean by agricultural workers from India, who arrived as indentured laborers (on contracts to work the canefields) after the abolition of slavery in the 19th century. Smoked in a "chalice," and believed by rastas to bring wisdom, the leaf has several names, including ganja, cully weed, holy herb, and wisdom weed.

Sunrise at Cayman Brac

The Cayman Islands

Thousands of visitors fly down to the Cayman Islands for reliable sun and sand and the finest diving seas so close to the mainland U.S., and the islands are well geared up to receive them. Cayman's successful tourist industry is supplemented by the offshore finance sector; the islands' status as a tax haven and the presence of several millionaires has given the 29,000 Caymanians the highest average per capita income in the Caribbean—although many islanders have menial, low-income jobs.

The Cayman Islands are formed by limestone caps of submerged mountain peaks, rising 25,200 ft. from the valley floor. These three British-dependent islands have distinctly different atmospheres. They lie to the northwest of Jamaica, separated into two groups. Grand Cayman, the senior island and site of the capital, George Town, is 20 miles by 7.5 miles and is busy, commercial and flat. About 85 miles to its northeast are the twin cays of Cayman Brac (population about 1,500), with better beaches and sailing, and Little Cayman (population less than 60), offering some of the region's best fishing. All three are generally dry and scrubby, with areas of swamp, and lie very low in the water, but for all their unattractiveness above the waterline, they have some of the most impressive underwater sites and marine life in the Caribbean. There are a number of scuba operations on the islands, diving mainly off the walls—vertical underwater drops clustered with coral—in the north and west of Grand Cayman; it's also possible to try something more exotic, such as swimming with stingrays. Even if you are not a diver, you can see the corals from the Atlantis Submarine (tel: 949 7700), which dives 120 ft. down on the reefs near George Town.

Tourism has mainly taken hold on Grand Cayman along Seven Mile Beach, where bars and restaurants stand shoulder to shoulder among the many hotels. You can dine extremely well here, mostly on international fare, in chic restaurants, but the large numbers of visitors from the U.S. have brought fast food chains and rib joints in their wake. Nightlife is limited, but there are shows in the hotels and a couple of places to dance. Cayman Brac and Little Cayman are, on the other hand, very peaceful and quiet, and their inhabitants, like those of Grand Cayman, are generally known as being some of the most easy-going people in the Caribbean.

A Cayman Islands totem pole

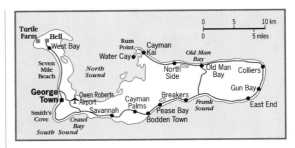

Beaches

Seven Mile Beach is an archetypal Caribbean beach with perfect golden sand that shelves gently away to the west. The water is calm on this protected side of the island, and there are magnificent sunsets. All kinds of watersports are available there, from water-skiing to parasailing; the only problem is that it is sometimes pretty crowded. Caymanians tend to go to Smith's Cove, an inlet between the coral rocks to the south of George Town. Other beaches that are worth exploring include Cayman Kai and Water Cay, on the north coast.

Grand Cayman This is the largest and most developed of the Caymans, and it is here that you will find the capital and the only real town, George Town, a small collection of wooden and concrete buildings on the waterfront in the protected southwest of the island. Its quiet streets come alive with the arrival of cruise ships and during the annual festivities, the Batabano carnival (April) and Pirates' Week (late October), when choreographed hordes of swashbucklers carouse there. The **Cayman Maritime and Treasure Museum▶▶** has exhibits of Cayman life across the ages, from Columbus to piracy and contemporary treasure-hunting. The **Cayman Islands National Museum▶** is run by the National Trust and has displays illustrating the islands' history and natural life.

Life for most visitors is centered on Seven Mile Beach, which is heavily built up with hotels and condominiums along its (strange, given its name) five-and-a-half-mile length. Here you will find the liveliest bars and restaurants. In their prosperity, the Cayman Islands have been swamped with satellite dishes, big cars, and other trappings of North American culture, but as the tourist development thins out to the north and further afield in the east, you will occasionally see the neat, wooden buildings of the old-time Caribbean, white clapboard houses with pink or blue shutters and shingle tiled roofs, set in carefully tended gardens of hibiscus and bougainvillea.

Swimming with stingrays off the Cayman Islands

In West Bay, north of Seven Mile Beach, **Hell▶** is a pitted and scorched terrain of worn coral limestone (postcards mailed here will have the postmark Hell). At the **Turtle Farm▶** you can learn how turtles lay their eggs by crawling up onto the sand and burying them in a hole dug with their back flippers, but this is kind of a sad place, where the animals are cooped up quite severely. About five percent of the turtles bred every year are released into the wild, and turtle products may not be taken into the U.S.

The route to the east of George Town passes Owen Roberts airport on its way to the scrub-covered eastern end of the island. Just before Bodden Town, a coastal settlement *en route*, there is a small 17th-century fort, Pedro's Castle. Beyond here the island is undeveloped except for a few houses and isolated hotels. As you drive around you will see glimpses of an older Caymanian life in the fields, where cattle and goats roam, dragging their tethers.

Straw-weaver, Cayman Brac

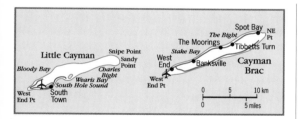

Little Cayman and Cayman Brac The other two Cayman Islands, both long and thin and each about 12 miles long, lie tip to tail some 85 miles to the northeast of Grand Cayman. The channel in between them may not look it but is, in fact, a treacherously deep stretch of water. It is possible to charter plane trips to both Cayman Brac and Little Cayman and return on the same day. Cayman Brac takes its name from the "brac" or cliff at its eastern end, the highest point in the Caymans (a princely 148 ft.). There are just 1,500 Brackers and they have a reputation for their friendly hospitality. Cayman Brac has a **museum▶** (in Stake Bay) and a few stores, but generally it is as sleepy today as it has been for the last 100 years. Apart from the people and the opportunity to do nothing in warm surroundings, the best reason for going to Cayman Brac is the coral; there are superb dive sites and snorkeling grounds around the western tip of the island.

Only about 60 people live on Little Cayman, where three hotels offer diving and fishing facilities (around Bloody Bay, in the northwest, the reef wall drops off at a depth of 20 ft.). The island is home to hundreds of birds, including magnificent frigatebirds, whose males puff up their red throat sacs to massive proportions in display.

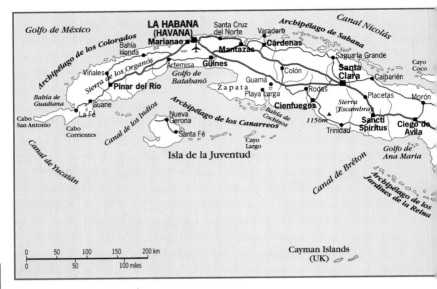

Golfo de México
LA HABANA (HAVANA)
Marianao
Santa Cruz del Norte
Varadero
Cárdenas
Canal Nicolás
Archipiélago de Sabana
Cayo Coco
Bahía Honda
Archipiélago de los Colorados
Viñales
Sierra de los Órganos
Artemisa
Güines
Mantazas
Sagua la Grande
Santa Clara
Caibarién
Pinar del Río
Golfo de Batabanó
Colón
Rodas
Placetas
Morón
Babía de Guadiana
Guane
La Fé
Guamá
Guamá
Z a p a t a
Playa Larga
Cienfuegos
Sierra Escambray
1156m
Sancti Spíritus
Ciego de Ávila
Cabo San Antonio
Cabo Corrientes
Canal de los Indios
Nueva Gerona
Archipiélago de los Canarreos
Babía de Cochinos
Trinidad
Santa Fé
Cayo Largo
Golfo de Ana María
Canal de Yucatán
Isla de la Juventud
Canal de Brёton
Archipiélago de los Jardines de la Reina

0   50   100   150   200 km
0   50   100 miles

Cayman Islands
(UK)

A Cuban passion: 1950s cars

Cuba

An extraordinary, enigmatic country, Cuba is strikingly different from other Caribbean islands—a place of revolution, violence, and hardship; but also a beautiful land where ancient and modern exist side by side.

Havana (La Habana), Cuba's capital, is less than 100 miles from Florida's Key West, but its proximity belies the political gulf between the two countries. Before Fidel Castro's 1959 Revolution, 90 percent of visitors to Cuba were from the U.S. Today, U.S. citizens are forbidden from spending their dollars in Cuba; only excursions for scientific or research purposes are permitted. Heavy fines may be imposed on those flouting the law, and U.S. citizens wishing to travel in Cuba should contact the Dept. of Treasury, Washington, D.C. 20220 (tel: 202 376 0410).

Cuba lies at the gaping mouth of the Gulf of Mexico and is the largest of the Caribbean islands, a snake-like 777 miles long, though never much more than 75 miles wide. Much of the fertile, agricultural land is covered in sugar cane, the most important crop, and there are three mountain ranges: in the west, the karst formations of the Sierra de los Organos, whose red earth is covered with tobacco plants; the Sierra de Escambray, halfway along the island, and in the island's eastern province is the Sierra Maestra, including the 6,580-ft.-high Pico Turquino, where revolutionaries hid in the 1950s.

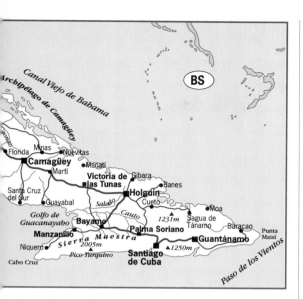

Cuban cocktails
Two of Cuba's best known cocktails were favorites of Ernest Hemingway and he was supposed to have had a saying: 'My mojito in the Bodeguita, my daiquiri in the Floridita' (the Bodeguita del Medio and the El Floridita are long-established Havana restaurants). A mojito is made with rum, sugar, fresh mint leaves and Angostura Bitters (from Trinidad). It is then shaken with ice and strained into a glass. A daiquiri is also based on rum, which is blended with cane sugar and fresh fruit, so that it comes out as an ice-cold, crystalline sludge. A Cuba Libre, named soon after the Revolution, is rum on ice with the juice of a lime, topped with cola (a version of which the Cubans continue to produce).

The entire island is ringed with around 4,000 miles of sandy beaches, coral cays, islands, and large, secluded bays.

Even without American visitors, Cuba lays great emphasis on tourism. It has to, in order to bring in much-needed hard currency—especially now that financial support from the former U.S.S.R. has dried up. Europeans and Canadians flock here for inexpensive vacations; Havana and Santiago de Cuba, the second city, are now linked by air to many European capitals, including London.

History Cuba was Columbus's second landfall in 1492, and for the next five centuries Spanish adventurers arrived here expecting to make their fortunes. They decimated the indigenous population, replacing them with African slaves, who worked the prosperous sugar plantations. Over the years the slaves mingled with Spanish colonists to form today's mixed Cuban race. During the 16th and 17th centuries, "New World" treasure flooded into Spain via Havana, which quickly became the richest city in the Caribbean.

Spanish colonization gave way briefly to British rule; then the U.S. took control of the island until, in 1902, Independence was declared. In the early 1940s, Americans began to exploit Cuba and its cheap labor. The island played host to thousands of visitors from the U.S., and a wide variety of entertainments and diversions became available, ranging from privately organized gaming casinos to explicit shows. Havana's streets were the setting for extortion, illicit alcohol distribution, trade in narcotics, and prostitution. The state, under the dictatorship of Fulgencio Batista, exploited tourism at the expense of the Cuban population and the country.

Embittered Cubans, led by Dr. Fidel Castro, rose up against the Batista regime but were incarcerated on the Isla de Pinos (renamed the Isla de la Juventud after the Revolution) in 1953. On their release, Castro and the revolutionaries undertook military training in Mexico,

*Main square,
Trinidad, Cuba*

joined by the Argentinian doctor, Che Guevara. In 1956 they sailed to Cuba on the *Granma* and hid in the Sierra Maestra, with a band of guerrillas which at one stage numbered only 12. Their following grew, as soldiers deserted Batista to join the rebels. Batista fled Cuba on January 1, 1959, and the revolutionaries took control. Castro defeated a U.S.-sponsored invasion at the Bay of Pigs in 1961, and in 1965 he made the Communist Party of Cuba the island's sole legal political party.

Staying in Cuba Accommodation in Cuba can vary dramatically. The most popular and largest of Cuba's beach resorts is Varadero beach, in Matanzas Province, east of Havana, but there are quieter resorts around the coast, such as the Hotel Colony on Isla de la Juventud, an offshore island in the southwest. Most hotels are mid-range resorts, but luxury resorts such as the Paradiso in Varadero have started to appear. Many resort hotels are joint investment ventures between Cuba and Argentina, Brazil, Canada, Germany, Spain, and France, and are able to meet high standards. Cuba's own hotels and casual accommodation, however, leave a lot to be desired, as Cubans are restricted by a lack of facilities and supplies.

Island sights and entertainment The world-famous Varadero beach, Havana's East Beaches, Santa Lucia beach, and Guardalavaca and Daiquiri beaches are just some of Cuba's many seaside resorts. On the offshore cays, such as Cayo Sabinal and Cayo Coco, facilities are provided for reef snorkeling and diving trips. The most popular cay is Cayo Largo, off Cuba's southern shores, a

Revolutionary art
There are no billboard advertisements in Cuba, but revolutionary posters are an art in themselves—brightly colored and featuring famous Cuban faces or working scenes. Some rail against the "Yankee Imperialists" of the United States; others show Fidel and other state heroes, such as Jose Marti, the poet and journalist who was killed soon after taking arms against the Spanish in 1895, and the Argentinian Che Guevara, encouraging the Cubans to fulfill their social duties.

PLAYA GIRON
PRIMERA DERROTA DEL IMPERIALISMO EN AMERICA LATINA

After the Revolution
For the average Cuban, life improved after the Revolution. Medical care and education became available to all and starvation became a thing of the past. At the same time, Castro established a one-party constitution, and political dissenters were simply locked up. Castro, usually known as Fidel, was a popular figurehead and to some extent he still is, though most of his population cannot now remember what life was like before the Revolution.

coral island resort whose air links from Varadero make it an easy day's excursion.

Beyond the beaches, Cuba offers some of the Caribbean's most historic areas. The Old Town of Havana is 2 sq. miles of cobbles, colonnades, and Spanish colonial palaces, some dating back to the early 16th century. In the south of the island is the "living museum" of 16th-century Trinidad, which recently joined Old Havana as a designated UNESCO World Heritage site.

Although gambling is now forbidden in Cuba, it still has a lively entertainment scene, including renowned shows like Havana's 50-year-old Tropicana and a rival nightclub on the outskirts of Santiago de Cuba city.

A good central highway and a 150-year-old railroad run down the spine of the country, and there are over 18,000 miles of roads. Facilities for car rental and chauffeur-driven cars are good, but expensive; cars available include VWs, Scania, Nissans, and Mercedes Benz. Cubans still drive 1950s American cars—when gas is available—and ox-carts, horses, and bicycles are common alternatives.

Domestic flights link most large towns and the Varadero beach resort, which is also joined by a highway, to Matanzas in the south. Flights within Cuba are not expensive and are generally easily booked. Independent travel is possible anywhere except in restricted areas, though it can be difficult to find meals outside tourist resorts and accommodation can be basic. However, new lodges and camp sites, plus Cubatur's helpful official guides, have made independent touring a realistic option.

Island life The Cuban currency, the peso, is rarely seen by tourists, as the U.S. dollar is the most readily accepted currency. Cuban Tourism Bond Notes, or coupons, are also circulated in resort areas, as well as specially minted coins. Dollar-only stores, off-limits to Cubans, stock everything from bikinis to toothpaste. Seeing the best of the scarce resources reserved for tourists has understandably caused resentment among Cubans, for whom life is very hard. Hustlers are appearing in larger numbers, and visitors should be particularly careful with their belongings in Havana and Varadero. Rationing has now reached a point where many people simply do not get enough food. Electricity is severely restricted and fuel for private vehicles is virtually non-existent. Even the much-vaunted services of health care and education are under threat through lack of resources. Improvement is unlikely while the U.S. embargo continues, and, for its part, the Cuban Communist Party has shown little inclination to change.

For all their difficulties, the 11 million Cubans are a lively nation, whose Latin Caribbean character shines through in their rhythmic music. It is well worth attending an evening at a *casa de la trova*, where professional musicians play in competition with one another; and in July each year the Cubans drop everything for Carnaval, a weekend of dancing through the streets.

Motorized art
The cars driven by Cubans are a curious leftover from pre-Revolution days, when the island was almost an offshore state of the U.S. Dating from the 1950s, these magnificent, fin-tailed beasts are adorned with a great expanse of chrome on their bumpers and fittings, and are cared for lovingly, despite the fact that gas shortages have recently made them a rarer sight on the roads.

169

Trova
The trova is a special Cuban ballad which, like many Caribbean songs, has an element of social comment. Trovas are as likely to celebrate a national hero or take a swing at corruption in the Communist Party as they are to sing of love. The name trova is derived from the Provençal *trobar* (to find, or compose—as is the word troubadour, used to describe the medieval romantic poets of Provence.

A Cuban country house

A street in Old Havana

The baroque 18th-century cathedral

▶▶ Havana (La Habana)

The modern city of Havana, on the north coast of Cuba near the western end of the island, has radiated outwards from the earliest colony, which was settled on the western shore of Havana harbor in 1514, and is now made up of four distinct districts: Old Havana, Central Havana, Vedado, and Miramar.

Even in its dilapidated state, there is a charmed feel about **Old Havana**▶▶▶. Its tight alleys and cobbled squares, colonnades, and colonial palaces built in coral rock are incongruous companions to the present-day city's high-rise hotels. The heart of the town and its finest square is the Plaza de la Catedral; the 18th-century baroque cathedral sits on its northern side, and it is flanked by the Museum of Colonial Art, the El Patio restaurant and the Postal Museum. (Under the arches on the eastern side of the square, the horrorstruck face frozen in carved stone is, in fact, Cuba's oldest mailbox.)

Hemingway's favorite Bodeguita del Medio restaurant is near by, as is the grand Plaza des Armas, originally the parade ground, with its imposing Palace of the Captain Generals, City Museum, Flota House bar, a statue of Manuel Cespedes (a 19th-century Independence leader), and the classical-style El Templete portico, built to celebrate the first mass on Cuban soil. Just off the square, the Castillo de la Fuerza is Cuba's oldest fortress (1544), whose roof is topped by the city's symbol, the tiny golden statue of La Giraldilla. Numerous cannons, which were recently excavated near the ancient city walls, now surround the fortress.

To the west, Old Havana is bounded by the Paseo de Marti, an avenue giving easy access to the Memorial Museum, the National Museum (containing many old masterpieces), the ornate Garcia Lorca Theatre, and the Capitol (a copy of Washington, D.C.'s). Overlooking Old Havana, across the port entrance, is the 16th-century fortress of El Morro, now a museum and restaurant.

Through the keyhole
It is always worth taking a look inside the buildings, both public and private, in Havana, if you can see or find your way through the front door. There may be glimpses of superb inner courtyards, with arched colonnades on each story, constructed so that the sunlight and heat did not penetrate into the rooms themselves. Others have elaborately decorated stairways or beautiful, fan-shaped stained glass windows.

Heading north through the open Parque Central, you emerge into the 19th-century Prado, a broad boulevard with a raised promenade where Habaneros sit and pass the time of day. Close by is the old Presidential Palace, an eclectic building of columns and balustrades, which now houses the Revolutionary Museum, displaying photographs and guerrilla maps; outside, military hardware on display includes tanks, planes, and Castrol's invasion boat, the *Granma*.

From the seafront, the 2-mile Malecon, a promenade where young Habaneros gather on summer evenings (and where *carnaval* is staged), leads west to the modern districts of Havana, including Vedado. At the head of La Rampa, a bustling business street, stands the Havana Libre Hotel, built in the 1950s as the Hilton. The Bar Turquino, on the top floor, has a magnificent view of the city. South of here are the stately buildings of the City University and finally the open Plaza de la Revolucion, where a statue of national hero José Martí stands beside a huge concrete column constructed in the shape of a communist star. Political rallies are held here, and often draw up to as many as half a million people.

To the west of the square is the Cementerio Cristobal Colon (the Columbus Cemetery), an impressive collection of magnificent mausoleums.

Elsewhere, there is a wealth of galleries, museums, and palaces. A visit to the Casa de las Americas gallery, which shows modern Latin American art and craft, and has regular recitals and theatrical events, is particularly worthwhile—and Havana's excellent ice cream should be tasted at La Coppelita park on La Rampa.

Hemingway's island
Ernest Hemingway lived in Cuba during the 1940s and 1950s and he set two of his novels on the island: *Islands in the Stream* and *The Old Man and the Sea*, supposedly set in the village of Cojimar. Two restaurants in Old Havana were particular favorites of his: the riotous Bodeguita del Medio on Calle Empredado, and the more formal and stately Floridita on Calle Obispo, where you can try some of the best lobster in the Caribbean. Hemingway lived in the suburb of San Francisco, in a hillside house called La Vigia, now open to the public. He was a keen deep-sea fisherman, and a marina west of Havana bears his name.

Moncada Garrison
The Moncada Garrison in Santiago, now a school, is honored in revolutionary lore as the place where Castro made his first strike against the Batista regime. On July 26, 1953, 130 young rebels assembled in Siboney Farm to the east of the city and launched an early morning attack, some of them unarmed and arriving in comandeered taxis. Militarily, it was a dismal failure; most were rounded up as they tried to escape, and many were killed. The survivors received long prison sentences.
Moncada is recalled on the black and red party flag in the insignia "M-26-7," and July 26 is celebrated as a national holiday.

■ **An old legend of the West Indies tells of large Cuban women rolling the world's finest cigars on their thighs. Whether or not this was true, the reality nowadays is rather less picturesque, though it is still intriguing to watch Cuban cigars being rolled by hand, cut with large metal blades and pressed in antique wooden vices. .....■**

Early smokers
Columbus was the first European to see Indians smoking tobacco, which is indigenous to the Americas. Twisted leaves would be wrapped in dried palm leaves or maize husk and smoked by Mayan Indians during religious ceremonies. The Mayans believed tobacco to be medicinal, and the word "cigar" is derived from their own term for smoking, *sik'ar*. Tobacco quickly gained popularity in Europe, where, in the 17th century, smoking was a sign of great wealth.

Cigar types
The traditional Cuban cigar is a corona, which measures about 6 in. and has straight sides, with one rounded and one cut end. The corona chica has the same shape, but is about 4 in. in length. Ideales are slender and torpedo-shaped, tapered at the lighting end, as are the smaller bouquets. Panatellas are thin and cut open at both ends; a cheroot is even thinner.

Tobacco, a bright green plant with long, oval leaves, grows on many Caribbean islands for use in cigarettes— but only Cuba and the Dominican Republic have cigar industries. The finest Cuban tobacco, reserved for its cigars, grows in the northwestern province of Pinar del Rio, where the earth is thick and deep red, and the leaves grow with a minimum of starches and sugars. Dotted around the neat tobacco fields are drying houses, with wooden walls and palm-thatch or aluminum roofs, where the leaves are cured for up to three months after picking.

Once dried, the leaves are sorted according to age— older leaves have a stronger flavor but younger leaves are more elastic and better for rolling—and are bundled off to the factories. While one factory worker sits at the head of the room, reading aloud from a newspaper, the others sit at long tables, placing "binder" leaves in their hands, laying tobacco filler (the offcuts of the last rolls) on top and then making the first, skillful roll. Each cigar is then pressed in a vise to give it the correct shape. One half of the strong, evenly colored "wrapper" leaf is then rolled around it, and finally the cigar is trimmed. After the manufacturer's bands have been slipped on, the cigars are packed in boxes, between leaves of aromatic cedar wood, for export.

Some of the most famous cigar manufacturers are based in Cuba, including Monte Cristo, Partagas, Romeo y Julietta, H. Upmann, and Davidoff. Within Cuba, cigars are remarkably cheap and factory tours can be arranged through Intur or Cubatur. Due to sanctions against the Castro regime, Cuban cigars are illegal in the U.S.

Outside Havana West of Havana is Pinar del Rio Province, the home of the finest Cuban tobacco. It takes a good day's drive to see the neatly ranged fields of bright green tobacco plants and thatched drying houses. There is a museum of tobacco in Pinar del Rio itself, as well as a number of cigar factories. Around Viñales the landscape is punctuated with strange karst "haystack" hills, known in Cuba as *mogotes*.

To the east of Havana is Cuba's best resort town, Varadero, where hotels and restaurants stand on the 12 miles of powder-like sand. Windsurfing and parasailing can be arranged here, and there are lively evening bars, including the Cueva del Pirata, a discotheque set in a cave. There are also museums about Cuban history and about the indigenous Indians, the Tainos.

Uneasy lease
Guantanamo, a remote, easterly province, has a curious anomaly, in that there is a U.S. naval base there, on Cuban sovereign land. It was arranged on a lease in 1902, but since the Revolution the Cubans have refused to accept the nominal annual payment of $5,000.

Cienfuegos traffic

173

On the south coast beneath Varadero is the swampy Zapata Peninsula, site of the infamous Bay of Pigs invasion in 1961, and now of the Bay of Pigs Museum and a number of tourist resorts. Further west, through the sugar flats, is the pretty town of Cienfuegos, one of Cuba's major ports, where interesting buildings include the 1870 cathedral, the Thomas Terry Theatre on the Parque Marti, and the Moorish-influenced Valle Palace, a decorative art museum on Punta Gorda.

The southern slopes of the Sierra de Escambray tumble into the sea around the town of **Trinidad**▶▶▶. Founded in 1514, Trinidad was a successful shipping town in the early 19th century and has been restored to its former grandeur. The cobbled central square, Plaza Marti, has beautiful colonial Spanish buildings painted yellow and complemented with bougainvillea blooms, as well as two museums: the Museo de Architectura Colonial and the Museo Romantico. To the east of the town, the ruined Torre de Iznaga is an old watchtower built to oversee slaves in the sugar cane fields.

Cuba's second town, **Santiago de Cuba**▶▶, commands a stunning position on a vast south coast harbor. In the shadow of the great Sierra Maestra mountains, this city's cathedral is the oldest on the island (1514). Conquistadors Hernando Cortez and Diego de Velasquez lived in the 1520 mansion on Cespedes Park, in Santiago's center. In all, the city has 14 museums, of which notable examples are the Bacardi Museum, a reminder of the rum family's origins (they moved to the Bahamas after the Revolution), and the Museum of Carnival.

The Bay of Pigs
The Bay of Pigs (Bahia de Cochinos) was catapulted into the headlines in April 1961 when 1,400 Cuban exiles staged an invasion of the island, partially backed by the U.S., in order to oust Castro and his revolutionaries. It was a military fiasco and most of the exiles were rounded up within a couple of days. In Cuban revolutionary lore it was written up as the first great defeat of imperialism on Latin American soil. Castro declared Cuba communist a couple of days later.

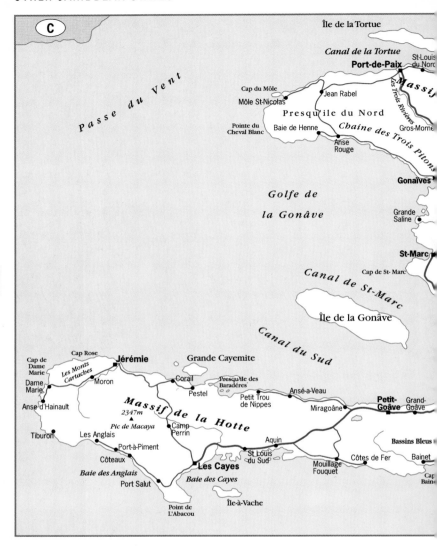

C

Île de la Tortue

Canal de la Tortue

Port-de-Paix

St-Louis du Nord

P a s s e   d u   V e n t

Cap du Môle

Môle St-Nicolas

Jean Rabel

M a s s i f

Les Trois Rivières

Presqu'île du Nord

Pointe du Cheval Blanc

Baie de Henne

Chaîne des Trois Pitons

Gros-Morne

Anse Rouge

Gonaïves

Golfe de la Gonâve

Grande Saline

St-Marc

Cap de St-Marc

Canal de St-Marc

Île de la Gonâve

Canal du Sud

Cap Rose

Jérémie

Grande Cayemite

Cap de Dame Marie

Les Monts Cartaches

Moron

Corail

Pestel

Presqu'île des Baradéres

Petit Trou de Nippes

Ansé-à-Veau

Petit-Goâve

Grand-Goâve

Dame Marie

Anse-d'Hainault

Massif de la Hotte

2347m

Pic de Macaya

Camp-Perrin

Miragoâne

Bassins Bleus

Tiburon

Les Anglais

Aquin

Côtes de Fer

Bainet

Port-à-Piment

St-Louis du Sud

Côteaux

Baie des Anglais

Les Cayes

Baie des Cayes

Mouillage Fouquet

Cap Bain

Port Salut

Île-à-Vache

Point de L'Abacou

Haiti

Only 30 years ago, Haiti's excellent beaches, sophisticated hotels and proximity to the U.S. made it one of the area's top vacation destinations. Today, Haiti is politically unstable and tourists are advised not to visit the country. If and when some semblance of stability returns, the adventurous traveler will be rewarded with a culture of extraordinary color and vitality. Few countries contain such striking contrasts of devastating poverty and luxurious lifestyles, hardship and hope. Travel there is a bombardment of the senses: the primitivist art, adorning buildings, walls, and vehicles; the cramped, brightly painted buses and trucks called tap taps (after the noise made

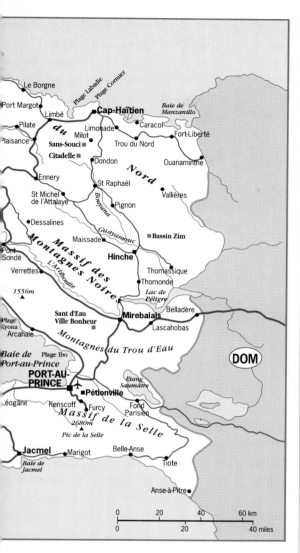

Le Borgne
Plage Labadie
Plage Cormier
Port Margot
Limbé
Cap-Haïtien
Baie de Manzanillo
Pilate
Limonade
Caracol
Plaisance
Milot
Fort-Liberté
Sans-Souci ■
Trou du Nord
Citadelle ■
Dondon
Ouanaminthe
Ennery
St Raphaël
St Michel de l'Attalaye
Vallières
Pignon
Dessalines
Guayamouc
Maissade
■ **Bassin Zim**
Pont Sondé
Hinche
Verrettes
L'Artibonite
Thomassique
1556m ▲
Thomonde
Lac de Péligre
Sant d'Eau
Belladère
Ville Bonheur
Mirebalais
Plage Kyona
Lascahobas
Arcahaie
Montagnes du Trou d'Eau
Baie de Port-au-Prince
Plage Ibo
PORT-AU-PRINCE ✈
Étang Saumâtre
DOM
Léogâne
■ **Pétionville**
Kenscoff
Furcy
Fond Parisien
Massif de la Selle
2680m ▲
Pic de la Selle
Jacmel
Marigot
Belle-Anse
Baie de Jacmel
Tiote
Anse-à-Pitre

0   20   40   60 km
0   20   40 miles

du Nord
Massif des Montagnes Noires

Buccaneers
Buccaneers were runaways from many European nations who crept into the remote west of Hispaniola in the early 17th century. Renowned as riflemen, they survived by wandering the plains killing wild cattle. The meat was smoked over a boucan, this giving us their name. Later, working from a stronghold on the Ile de la Tortue off the north coast of Haiti, they became pirates, known as the Brethren of the Coast.

Crowds in the streets of Port-au-Prince

by the original trucks), with their carved wood and religious maxims displayed along the sides, and scenes from the Bible on the hoods; the strange world of voodoo and the ceaseless hubbub of the markets. Love it or hate it, there is nowhere in the world like Haiti.

This is not an easy island for travelers. White visitors are particularly targeted with constant demands for money, from people who are genuinely in dire need. Haiti's currency is the gourde (five gourdes make a *dollar haïtien*), named after the large, hard-shelled fruit of the calabash tree and introduced by the country's despotic leader, Henry Christophe, in the early 19th century.

Access to Haiti is not easy. Most flights from Europe and the U.S. go to Miami for connections to the main airport at the capital, Port-au-Prince (a few flights land in

Toussaint
Toussaint l'Ouverture is the principal hero of Haitian independence. A former slave, he joined the rebels in 1791 as a doctor, but soon became one of the military leaders because of his skills on the battlefield. After defeating French, British, and Spanish armies, he took over the whole of Hispaniola. His success provoked Napoleon Bonaparte, who sent an army to reclaim the colony. Its commander, Leclerc, lured Toussaint into negotiations and took him captive. Toussaint was shipped to Europe and left by Napoleon to starve and freeze to death in prison. As he was deported, he is reputed to have said: "In overthrowing me, they have cut down in St. Domingue the trunk of the tree of black liberty. It will shoot up again through the roots, for they are numerous and deep.". A couple of years later, the population rebelled and France lost the colony for ever.

A multi-colored tap tap

Cap-Haïtien, on the north coast). Crossing the border from the Dominican Republic (at Jimani or Ouanaminthe) is straightforward, but going back the other way involves a mind-boggling and frustrating amount of red tape, including visits to Immigration, the army, and the border police. There are good places to stay in Pétionville, the prosperous suburb above the capital, well priced now in their faded grandeur, as well as a clutch of good restaurants, mainly patronized by expatriates and rich Haitians.

Haiti occupies the western third (10,715 sq. miles) of the island of Hispaniola, which it shares with the Dominican Republic. "Haiti" or "mountainous land" was the original Amerindian name for the island, and it is an accurate description. Shaped like a crab's claw closing round the Golfe de la Gonâve, it is about 90 miles from north to south and has two long mountainous ranges that stretch west like pincers towards Cuba and Jamaica. The highest peak is the Pic de la Selle (8,795 ft.), in the southeast. The country is generally fertile and there is a rich variety of scenery: good palm-backed beaches (the closest to Port-au-Prince are Ibo beach and Kyona; Cormier and Labadie are found outside Cap-Haïtien); cactus-covered plains, and huge, rainforested mountains. However, in a country of around six million mainly rural inhabitants, deforestation and soil erosion have now become a serious problem, after so many years of ground clearance.

Port-au-Prince

History Haiti has a history of turmoil. The first 40 European settlers, left there in 1492 by Columbus, all died within a year. In 1697 the French were handed control of western Hispaniola (then called Saint Domingue) by the Spanish, and made it an immensely wealthy colony, exporting sugar, coffee, and indigo. At the end of the 18th century, after years of torture and starvation at the hands of their colonial masters, the

HAITI

African slaves finally rebelled, led by Toussaint l'Ouverture. In 1804 Haiti declared itself independent—the world's first black republic. Its political life since then has been troubled: civil war between the mulatto south and the black north was followed by a succession of tyrannical leaders and U.S. invasion in 1915. The Americans left in 1934, and in 1957 François Duvalier, "Papa Doc," became the ruthless dictator, maintaining his grip on power through the notorious secret police, the *tontons macoute*. His son, Jean Claude ("Baby Doc") continued the reign of terror and corruption until in the mid-1980s a movement of revolt known as Operation Deschoukay drove him out of the country. Elections were then held, marked by violence, and there followed several coups and attempted coups; today, Haiti remains a politically unpredictable and unstable country.

Island life Ordinary islanders, most of whom work on the land, have suffered the consequences of corrupt and repressive government, and Haiti is now the poorest country in the western hemisphere. The vast majority of its population is descended from Africans; many of the small and powerful "mulatto élite" emigrated from the island during recent troubles. French is the official language, and its influence can be heard in the everyday spoken language, Kreyol.

Haiti has an amazingly vibrant artistic and religious life. Its primitive-style art, with primary colors and almost cartoon-like forms, has been copied all over the Caribbean. Many of the traditional themes of Haitian life are portrayed, including agricultural, biblical, and voodoo scenes. Voodoo itself is a mix of Catholic and African beliefs, often sensationalized as "black magic," and running deep in the Haitian psyche. Haiti has its own dance rhythm—compas—which fills the streets during Carnival, from January 6 to Mardi Gras, before Lent. This is the best time to witness the extraordinary spirit of the Haitians, which survives despite years of insecurity and hardship.

The Black Jacobins
One of the far-reaching effects of the French Revolution was to bring to a head the tensions of Haitian society in the late 18th century. Political rights, granted in theory to the mulatto population by the French National Assembly, were denied within the colony, and violence erupted. In 1791 the black population, who had suffered appallingly as slaves to the white colonists, themselves rebelled, and the country was split between the southern mulattos and the northern blacks (where Toussaint l'Ouverture rose to prominence). The story of Toussaint l'Ouverture and the Haitian revolution is told in C.L.R. James's powerful book, *The Black Jacobins*. Published in 1938, this was an influential work at a time when British West Indians were re-assessing their history and turning their minds towards Independence.

177

Fishing off Cap-Haïtien

■ **Voodoo calls up sinister and frightening images: candle-lit ceremonies of dancing, chanting, and mesmeric drum rhythms; initiates in trances flailing around, intoning predictions, eating hot coals, or making animal sacrifices. There is an element of truth in these images, but voodoo should not be written off as "black magic." Widely misunderstood outside Haiti, voodoo has a deeply rooted role in everyday island life. .....■**

Duppies
Duppies, also known as jumbies, are the wandering souls of the dead. People who die unhappy or without a proper wake are said to become restless spirits, returning to haunt those who knew them in life. Belief in duppies is widespread, and even educated people who otherwise disregard obeah will acknowledge their existence.

Haiti is not the only island where voodoo is practiced. Other forms of the religion exist elsewhere: santería, across the border in Santo Domingo and in Cuba; pocomania, in Jamaica, and shango, in Trinidad. In these parts of the Caribbean, however, the beliefs are gradually dying out, while in Haiti voodoo continues to touch everyone's life, and was particularly prevalent in the days of Papa Doc, who made himself a high priest of voodoo.

Like a number of the Caribbean systems of belief, voodoo has mixed African and European origins. All have a common theme in their appeals to spirits to intervene in life on earth. Spirits, or lwas, are summoned, in drums and dance, to "mount" a follower, who then falls into a trance, taking on the spirit's characteristics, dancing and speaking in tongues or making predictions. The worship

Zombies
In Caribbean folklore, zombies are "undead" souls, and tales are told in Haiti of people who are turned into zombies while still alive. A poison is believed to make their metabolic rate drop so low that they seem to be dead. After burial, they are supposedly exhumed by the poisoner, revived and used as slaves, never recovering their original mental state.

A voodoo ceremony, painted by Gérard Valcin

of spirits was originally brought by slaves from Africa and merged with Caribbean beliefs and Catholic saints. In Haitian voodoo the snake god Damballa, who makes his followers dance in a writhing motion, is equivalent to St. Patrick, often pictured with snakes at his feet; Ogun, the god of war, whose followers appear to be brandishing swords, is associated with St. James, and Erzulie is equated with the Virgin Mary.

Like the angels of the Christian panoply, lwas can be benevolent or vengeful. They come to give advice, but they must also be appeased. If times are hard it is because the lwa is displeased. "Rada" lwas, such as Erzulie, are known for their wisdom and benevolence; "petro" lwas, like Tijan Petro, are known for their power.

Voodoo ceremonies are conducted according to a calendar, which includes important Catholic events; for example, devotees celebrate the appearance of the Virgin Mary at the Ville Bonheur waterfall near Mirebalais on July 16 each year. The usual setting for a ceremony is a village temple with a mud floor, a hounfort, and the ceremony proceeds under the direction of a houngan (priest) or a mambo (priestess). After recitations from the Catholic liturgy, the drums strike up with the special rhythms of the lwa to be invoked. An initiate then traces on the ground the lwa's *véver*, a complex pattern of lines laid out with cornmeal. Eventually a dancer is mounted by a lwa and exhibits his or her characteristics, either making predictions to the community, giving advice or making demands. The lwa will be presented with its favorite food or drink and eventually there may be an animal sacrifice. Followers who have been mounted apparently remember nothing after the event.

It is almost impossible for visitors to Haiti to attend genuine voodoo ceremonies, but occasional shows are held with commentaries; contact Le Péristyle de Mariani, on the outskirts of Port-au-Prince.

Obeah Another feature shared by all the Caribbean beliefs is the use of magic, known as "obeah" or "myal" in the British Caribbean and "wango" in Haiti. Obeah men ("bocors" in Haiti) act as advisers and intervene in human affairs through the use of incantations and spells. These may be used to heal a sick person, to ensnare a lover or to settle a score; they may also rid a person of a vengeful duppy (ghost). Spells are set with herbal concoctions and other ingredients, such as blood, sweat, eggshells, and broken bottles. Obeah was outlawed in Jamaica as early as 1760, but it is still practiced widely, though secretly, in rural areas all over the Caribbean region.

The drums of voodoo
The driving force behind every voodoo ceremony is the drumming, which engenders a trance and summons a particular lwa. There are three drums of different sizes, each one carved of mahogany; and each lwa has its own particular drum rhythms.

179

Other religions
Besides the revivalist sects of pocomania and Revival Zion, Jamaica has many spirit-based religions. Kumina is a religion with less European influence than most—probably because it arrived relatively recently, brought by free Africans who came willingly to Jamaica after emancipation in 1838. Kumina appeals to its own zombies, the spirits of ancestors, as well as to the gods of the Congo, its followers' original homeland. Convince is a faith that appeals to the African "bongo" gods and to the spirits of the maroon leaders (see panel, page147), as does Kromanti. There are similar sects in Trinidad (the Shouters) and in St. Lucia (the Kele).

A ritual mask, worn by men taken over by female spirits

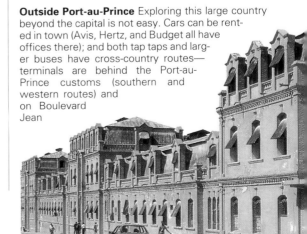

180

The Oloffson
The Oloffson Hotel is a magnificent townhouse on the rue Capois in Port-au-Prince, built by President Guillaume Sam in the 19th century as his summer palace. Standing in a garden of royal palms, the Oloffson has balconies and fanciful turrets, and simply drips with gingerbread fretwork. British novelist Graham Greene stayed here and used the hotel as the setting for his novel, *The Comedians*. The man who inspired the character of the journalist, Petit Pierre, still has his breakfast on the veranda each morning.

Sans-Souci Palace
Sans-Souci Palace was the early 19th-century creation of the megalomaniac Haitian leader Henri Christophe, and even in its present state of ruin, it gives an idea of his mad vision. He wanted Sans-Souci to be the equal of the grandest palaces in Europe, and this four-story palace was designed to rival Versailles. Christophe declared himself "King" and lived there in sumptuous splendor, surrounded by courtiers, while his people languished outside. Eventually his chutzpah caught up with him and when opposition forces were approaching he took his own life, shooting himself with a silver bullet.

Port-au-Prince Haiti's capital lies in the southwest, in the deep bight of the Golfe de la Gonâve. It is a buzzing city of over a million inhabitants, many of whom live in the shanty towns that cluster around the main town. Although there is not much to see in the city, it takes two or three days here to adjust to Haitian life.

The official center of Port-au-Prince is the **Place des Héros▶**, an area of broad, open streets and trees, dominated by the classical white Palais National. Statues of the Haitian national heroes include Toussaint l'Ouverture, Jean Jaques Dessalines, the first leader of the independent republic, and the *marron inconnu* (the unknown rebel slave). The **Musée National▶▶** is set underground in the center of the square and has exhibits illustrating the country's turbulent history.

The heart of Port-au-Prince is around rue Dessalines, downtown towards the waterfront, where a gridiron of tight streets teems with traffic and pedestrians. The busiest area is around the **Marché de Fer▶▶▶**; here, vendors cram the pavements under red corrugated tin roofs, selling every imaginable household product. Near by, the **Cathédrale de la Sainte-Trinité▶▶** has religious scenes depicted by primitivist artists. Works by the country's best artists—Hector Hippolyte, Philome Obin, and Benoit—can be seen at the **Centre d'Art▶▶**, behind the Palais National. Set in an old colonial townhouse near by is the **Musée Defly▶**, offering a glimpse of privileged Haitian life at the turn of the century.

As in many West Indian cities, the most prosperous area is on the hillside overlooking the town. At around 1,650 ft. above sea level, **Pétionville▶▶** has a calmer air than downtown Port-au-Prince and most of the good hotels are there, as well as French and local restaurants (Haitian food has a Gallic style—check out *accras* (fish batter balls), *griot* (fried pork), and *tassot*, a spicy marinaded turkey). There are also a number of galleries there which sell Haitian works of art.

Further uphill is the **Barbancourt Rum Distillery▶**, set in an imitation castle, where exotic rums (including apricot and mango) have been distilled for nearly 250 years. In the next town, Kenscoff, surrounded by steep slopes, there is a **Baptist Mission▶▶** which has a café and craftwork on sale; near by are the ruins of Fort Jacques and Fort Alexandre.

Outside Port-au-Prince Exploring this large country beyond the capital is not easy. Cars can be rented in town (Avis, Hertz, and Budget all have offices there); and both tap taps and larger buses have cross-country routes—terminals are behind the Port-au-Prince customs (southern and western routes) and on Boulevard Jean

Dessalines barracks, Port-au-Prince

Sans-Souci Palace

Downtown Port-au-Prince

Jacques Dessalines (northern routes).

The town of Jacmel, on the south coast, can be reached in half a day. Once prosperous from coffee cultivation, it is now run down, but there is still grandeur in its hillside houses. There is a black sand beach in the town, and in the hills above are the **Bassins Bleus►►**, a series of three dramatic waterfalls. At the other end of the southern peninsula, Jérémie is another dilapidated coffee town, once the home of Alexandre Dumas' family.

Haiti's second town, Cap-Haïtien, lies on the north coast, nearly a day's journey from Port-au-Prince. The route passes the **Ville Bonheur waterfall►** near Mirebalais, where pilgrims gather on July 16 before crossing the cactus-covered Plaine de l'Artibonite to commemorate a vision of the Virgin Mary. Inland from Gonaïves, near the town of Hinche, is a 100-ft. waterfall, the **Bassin Zim►**; on the far side of the 1,640-ft. Massif du Nord is Cap-Haïtien. As Cap Français, this was the French colonial capital and the most cultured place in the Caribbean; today little remains of its past glory except a few elegant buildings. South of town, at Milot, are two of the Caribbean's most extraordinary buildings: **Sans-Souci Palace►** and the **Citadelle►►►** (see panels).

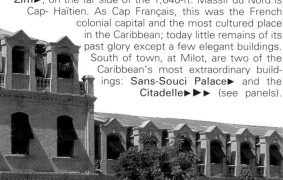

The Citadelle
Standing atop the 2,870-ft. Pic la Ferrière, the Citadelle is by far the largest fortress in the Caribbean. It was built by Christophe as a defense in case the European powers tried to take Haiti back (they did, losing about 100,000 soldiers in the process). With walls 33 ft. thick, it took 14 years to build, and 20,000 of the ex-slaves who were forced to do all the work are supposed to have died completing it. The Citadelle never saw action, but it was large enough to hold out with 10,000 men for a year. If it seems like a strenuous walk to reach the Citadelle, pity the slaves who had to drag every stone and cannon up to the site.

Map labels:

Cabo Isabela
Bahía de la Isabela
Monte Cristi
Luperón
Puerto Plata
Playa Dorada
Cabo Macoris
Villa Vásquez
Los Hidalgos
Sosúa
Cabarete
Boca del Yásia
Pepillo
Pico Isabel de Torres
Salcedo
Guayubin
Cordillera Septentrional
Gaspar Hernández
Rio San Juan
Cabrera
Dajabón
Mao
Yaque del Norte
Sabaneta
Monción
Santiago
Moca
Salcedo
Nagua
Loma de Cabrera
San Jose de las Mantas
Janico
San Francisco de Macoris
Resturacion
Cordillera
La Vega
Pimentel
Villa
Yuna
RH
Pedro Santana
3175m Pico Duarte
Jarabacoa
Salto de Jimenoa
Fantino
Cotui
San Juan
Central
Camu
Las Matas de Farfán
Constanza
Bonao
Maimon
Sabana Grande de Boya
Comendador
San Juan
Bohechío
Villa Altagracia
Yamasá
Monte Plata
Hondo Valle
El Cercado
Sabana Yegua
Peralta
San José de Ocoa
Sierra de Neiba
Parque Nacional Isla Cabritos
Neiba
Yaque del Sur
Vicente Noble
Azua
San Cristóbal
Yaguate
Yabacao
SANTO DOMINGO
Jimaní
Lago Enriquillo
Duvergé
Puerto Viejo
Bahía de Ocoa
Bani
Nizao
Sabana Grande de Palenque
Pedernales
Sierra de Baboruco
2275m
Barahona
Bahía de Neiba
Cabo Rojo
Paraiso
Enriquillo
Sabana del Algodón
Cabo Falso
Oviedo
Isla Beata
Cabo Beata

182

The Dominican Republic

The country Columbus called "the fairest land under heaven" is home to the oldest European settlement in the Western Hemisphere, but the Dominican Republic has two modern faces. Its glorious beaches, fascinating colonial heritage, and mountain-top resorts contrast sharply with the grinding poverty of many of its islanders. With its 3,300-mile shoreline, the Dominican Republic has one of the largest tourist industries in the Caribbean. Most of its hotels are mid-range beach-front resorts, scattered in complexes along the northern and eastern shores, but other options include the luxury Casa de Campo—where polo ponies can be rented—or a hotel in Santo Domingo's historic colonial city. The

Quisqueya
Quisqueya was the name used by the indigenous Taino Indians for their island when Columbus arrived in 1492. It is still used as a poetic name for Hispaniola, but principally survives as the name of a locally brewed beer. (Presidente is a lighter and slightly more bitter but tastier local beer.)

183

island also has quiet, isolated resort towns, such as Cabarete and Las Terrenas, where you can relax in guesthouses under the palm trees.

The Dominican Republic is one of the cheaper and better value package tour destinations in the Caribbean,

Carvings set up for sale at a Dominican Republic market stall

OTHER CARIBBEAN STATES

"Mexican night" at the Playa Dorado restaurant

easily reached from the U.S. and Canada, both by scheduled and charter flights. There are plenty of charter flights from Europe, though independent travelers may have to go via Miami or via Spain, where there are several flight connections.

Despite the million or so annual visitors, the tourist industry is surprisingly unobtrusive once you leave the coastal fringe of hotels. In contrast to many of the other Caribbean islands, which are visibly affected by the industry, the Dominican Republic is large enough to allow independent travel and to maintain a lively local Latin culture. Adventurous travelers might even consider crossing the border into Haiti, the Caribbean's poorest but most flamboyant and fascinating country (see pages 174–81).

One of the best places in the Caribbean to immerse yourself in history is the colonial city in Santo Domingo, the oldest city in the Americas, which enjoyed its heyday in the 16th century, when conquistadors came here to plan their voyages to the American mainland. Nowadays you can relax in the bars and restaurants with no fear of being arm-twisted into an invasion force. The modern city of Santo Domingo is also worth exploring; a quick look at the hundreds of restaurants there offers ample evidence that leisure is one of the largest industries in the Dominican Republic.

This is a Latin American island, full of surprises. Merengue music is heard everywhere; if you get on a

La Isabella
Santo Domingo was not the first of the "New World" towns. La Isabella, named after the Spanish queen, was settled by a thousand willing adventurers in 1493 on the explorer's second voyage. The site is near Luperon on the north coast, but there are only archeological remains now. The colonists moved to Santo Domingo's present site in 1498 because La Isabella, set among malarial swamps, was unhealthy, and riches beckoned after gold mines were found nearer Hispaniola's southern shore.

bus, you might find the passengers singing along. Islanders gather on the plazas in the late evening to take in the cooler air; and they love to dance, so clubs are a popular meeting point.

The Dominican Republic forms the eastern two-thirds of the island of Hispaniola—a contraction of La Isla Española, as Columbus called it when he landed in 1492 (Haiti forms the western third of the island, ceded to French rule by the Spaniards in 1697). At 18,765 sq. miles, it is the second largest country in the Caribbean after Cuba; geographically, it is the most extreme. Topping the massive Cordillera Central, Pico Duarte (10,420 ft.) is the tallest mountain in the West Indies, and in the southwest, Lago Enriquillo is a lake set in the lowest point of land, 98 ft. below sea level. In the north there are rampantly fertile mountains with crashing rivers; in the south, on the Barahona peninsula, there is desert. The greater part of the country has seemingly endless stretches of bright green hillsides and cane fields, spiked with magnificent royal palm trees.

Island life The seven million or so Dominicans are of mixed African and European blood, with a strong Amerindian influence, dating from the early days of colonial settlement and recognizable in many Dominicans' distinctive straight, dark hair. This is a desperately poor nation; its poverty is particularly evident in

Fruit-sellers lay out their wares on the roadside in a Dominican Republic market

Dominican dishes
Comida Criolla, or Creole Food, as local dishes are known, includes a wide range of meats: beef, farmed by *campesinos* (cowboys) in the southeast, pork, goat (*chivo*), and chicken. These are served in rather heavy but tasty dishes such as stew, *sancocho*, which is made with a variety of meats, and *mondongo*, made with tripe. Seafood and fish are popular, as are many tropical vegetables, including plantains and cassava.

185

Fresh fruit milk shakes
Dominicans use their fruit to the best advantage in freshly prepared drinks. *Jugo* is plain squeezed fruit juice served with ice, but the best drinks are *bastidas*, squeezed fruits whisked up with milk and ice. Flavors include *pina* (pineapple), *china* (orange), *lechola* (pawpaw), and *guanabana* (soursop).

Windsurfers at Casa de Campo

Merengue
The national rhythm of the Dominican Republic is the merengue, a strongly Latin and impossibly quick beat. You will hear it played by local string bands and in the clubs, where dancers exercise their elastic legs, racing across the dance floor in a close embrace. There is a merengue festival in Santo Domingo each year, in the third week of July, when bands and dancers fill the streets.

the countryside and on the outskirts of the main towns, where many people live in makeshift shanty flats. The limited public services break down regularly (big hotels have their own power plants). Since there is no social safety net, life can be extremely hard for the islanders, some of whom try to escape to the U.S.—a dangerous journey, often undertaken in inadequate, leaking boats. The Dominican Republic throws the contrasts of Caribbean tourism into the sharpest relief. With so many prosperous tourists passing through, opportunists have inevitably come to regard them as walking dispensers of dollars, and outside the tourist complexes you will probably be hassled for money. There is considerable prostitution—"sex tourism" has now become an established trade in some places—and there is a high incidence of AIDS, so the risks to all parties are clear.

The Dominican Republic has a troubled political tradition, which has hit ordinary Dominicans hard. Throughout the 19th century, the island lurched from one ruling power to another, as Spanish, Haitians, Americans, and Dominican independence fighters battled for its control. Independence came in 1844, but the country soon fell into the hands of despots, and slid into bankruptcy. The U.S. sent troops to administer the country between 1916 and 1924, to a mixed reception from islanders, who longed for stability but resented military rule. In 1930 General Rafael Leonidas Trujillo, the Dominican army's commander, established a ruthless dictatorship, ruling the country for the next 30 years as his personal estate, organizing the "disappearance" of thousands of opponents and rifling through the treasury. He was assassinated in 1961, and there followed a series of coups, civil war, and military intervention by the U.S. Elections were held in 1966 and won by Balaguer, now a blind octogenarian who has been re-instated several times after elections troubled by violence and allegations of fraud.

▶▶▶ Altos de Chavón

Altos de Chavón is near the eastern town of La Romana, attached to the Dominican Republic's premier resort, the huge and luxurious Casa de Campo. The "Heights of Chavón" are a pretty replica of a medieval Spanish hilltop town standing high above the Chavón river. The village has a slightly unreal feel, for the 30 or so coral-rock houses are so obviously imitations. But festooned with colorful bougainvillea blooms, this is a pleasant and satisfying place to spend an afternoon or evening. As well as an informative museum of Amerindian history, there are a number of good restaurants and bars, the attractive church of St. Stanislaus and an amphitheater where concerts are staged. There are also fabulous views of the Chavón river valley, particularly when it is lit up at night. Buses connect Altos de Chavón with Casa de Campo.

▶▶ Cordillera Central

The Cordillera Central is the Dominican Republic's highest and most strikingly beautiful mountain range, which runs through the center of the country from the northwest down towards the capital. It contains the highest mountain in the Caribbean, the Pico Duarte (10,420 ft.). Though the lower mountains are covered in beautiful royal palm trees, the pine-clad heights are tall enough to have frost; the steep and fertile valleys (where distinctly un-Caribbean fruits such as strawberries and apples prosper) are cut by cold waters from the mountains above. The towns of Constanza and Jarabacoa are cool hillside retreats, popular with visitors from the capital, who regard them as an ideal escape from the hotter zones down below. Look for the waterfalls of Aguas Blancas 12 miles from Constanza, and the 100-ft. Jimenoa Falls near Jarabacoa.

New communities
As well as the community of German and Austrian Jewish refugees who were granted sanctuary in Sosua on the north coast in the 1930s (see page 188), Trujillo invited a community of Japanese farmers in the 1950s, offering them land in return for passing on their farming skills. Some of their descendants still live and work around Constanza.

187

Tourist accommodation, Sosua

188

Beaches
There are excellent beaches on the Amber Coast. The resorts are clustered around protected bays, where palm-backed sand shelves gently into the sea, and these are the best places to go for watersports. Sosua is the busiest, and therefore gets very crowded, but further on there are long strips of deserted sand, battered by the Atlantic waves and winds. Cabarete is renowned for windsurfing, and also has a fine beach.

Amber
Amber is the national gem of the Dominican Republic, which has some of the world's largest amber reserves, and a large mining area in the Cordillera Septentrional. Strictly speaking amber is not a stone, but the sap from trees that has solidified over millions of years. The youngest is the lightest in color and can be almost translucent; it is graded by color, through rich yellow to red. The most valuable are pieces with prehistoric insects or leaves preserved within them. Be wary of pieces offered to you on the streets; these may be plastic.

▶▶   **Puerto Plata and the Amber Coast**

The Amber Coast, on the north shore, has the greatest concentration of Dominican tourism. Here, several hotel complexes cater to package tourists who fly into the international airport near Puerto Plata, but the seaside villages of Sosua and Cabarete, which are set on excellent beaches, have guesthouses and bars that are ideal for independent travelers.

Puerto Plata itself has a strong Dominican life. Attractive old Creole houses still stand in the town, and the squares, with shady trees and benches, come alive in the late afternoons with old gents and salesmen selling lottery tickets. There are just a couple of hotels on the rocky seafront, but the town has a number of good restaurants and bars (see **Hotels and Restaurants**). The **Amber Museum▶▶**, in a grand town house with classical balustrades and columns, has exhibits explaining the origin and mining process of the gem. A cable car takes passengers 2,625 ft. to the top of Mount Isabel de Torres, just south of the town; its running times are unpredictable, but hotels will usually arrange seats for visitors. A statue of Christ dominates the magnificent view of the coast and the forested Cordillera Septentrional to the south.

Playa Dorado is a purpose-built resort, a collection of hotels to the east of the town. It is set on a superb beach, where there are watersports and a good beach bar, but this is private and reserved for hotel guests. The resort town of **Sosua▶▶** is split into two parts, set on either side of the lively Sosua beach: Los Charramicos is the westerly, more Dominican half; El Batey has a stronger European influence, a legacy of the wave of Austrian and German Jewish refugees who came here fleeing the holocaust (restaurants here still serve Austrian and German food).

One of the best resorts on the island, **Cabarete▶▶▶** is a lazy seaside town with palm-thatch garden bars and beachside restaurants, patronized by windsurfers; windsurfing World Championships are occasionally held here. Beyond Cabarete, the beaches continue, on and off, for miles along the coast.

Restaurant in Puerto Plata

■ **The Dominican Republic's landscape is graced by many thousands of royal palm trees, soaring up to 165 ft. from the ground and exploding into bushy palm fronds. Dominicans who travel away from home will often say that they miss the royal palm most of all.** ......■

Around 2,600 species of palm trees and shrubs grow in the tropics and subtropics, varying in height from 6 in. to 200 ft. Palms do not have branches, but their fronds, which can be as long as 30 ft., emerge in sequence at the top of each stem, pointing vertically at first and gradually leaning to the side as younger fronds push them aside.

The coconut palm As well as being the quintessential Caribbean palm, the coconut is the most useful and versatile. Almost all of its parts can be used: the fronds in thatch and the trunk in building; in the past, the husk of the coconut was used to weave ropes and mats; coconut flesh is eaten, and copra (dried coconut flesh) can be used to make oil for washing or burning. Coconut milk, a popular drink, has even been used as an intravenous fluid. Take care when sitting under coconut palms, though—falling coconuts can cause nasty injuries.

The palmchat
Native to Hispaniola, the palmchat is the national bird of the Dominican Republic. It has a greenish-brown coat and a white breast with dark streaking, and lives and feeds in flocks. Its communal nest has separate compartments for up to 30 pairs, and is built on the trunk of the royal palm.

189

Palm-fringed sands in the Dominican Republic

The royal palm This most stately and magnificent of palms grows throughout the Caribbean, and is Cuba's national tree. It can stand up to 165 ft. high, with a smooth trunk as much as 3 ft. thick and a bushy crown of fronds. The heart of the royal palm is used in salads, and its fruit is used for animal feed.

Other palms The cabbage palm is similar in appearance to the royal palm, although it grows only to about 130 ft. Known as the *palma cana* in Spanish, the latania palm, with fan-like fronds, is used for weaving, particularly in St. Barts. The ornamental golden palm is a bright green bush that appears in many Caribbean gardens; and the fishtail palm, with fronds shredded into 8-in. fishtail-shaped leaves, bears fruit that can be distilled into alcohol.

Palm avenues
Royal palms and cabbage palms are often planted to form beautiful avenues. Some of the best are the Allée Dumanoir, on Basse-Terre in Guadeloupe, and the driveway that leads to Codrington College in Barbados (see page 220).

Yachts at Las Terrenas

►►► Samaná

The lush Samaná peninsula is in the isolated northeast, but it is worth making the effort to get there to see the town of Las Terrenas, the island's best resort. Set on the northern shore of the peninsula across a ridge of mountains, Las Terrenas has golden sand swept by low-hanging palms. There is an easy-going feel to the place, with its string of thatched restaurants, candle-lit at night, and its few excellent hotels and guesthouses. At the Tropic Banana you can spend the afternoon listening to a Dominican string band (guitar, soul-comb and cheese-grater, and sit-on beat-box).

Set on the huge Samaná Bay (named Golfo de las Flechas, or Gulf of Arrows, by Columbus after the local Carib Indians showered him with arrows), the town of Samaná itself is not very attractive, though it has a few guesthouses and a collection of good restaurants on the waterfront. You can arrange to see the **whales►►►** that collect offshore early in the year (from January to March) and take trips to the **Los Haïtises National Park►►**, where among the limestone caves and mangroves you can see terns, jacanas, and ibises. At Las Galeras, in the northeast, there is a good beach with a couple of quiet hotels.

►   Santiago

You may only pass through Santiago, the Dominican Republic's second city, while traveling on to another destination, but it is a good traveler's stop. It is a working city set on the cliffs above the Yaque river in the Cibao Valley, one of the country's most fertile regions. Hustlers are not as active here as they are in the tourist resorts. The **Museo del Tabaco►►** relates the story of cigars and tobacco, which is grown in the area, and in the **Museo del Arte Folklorico►►** you can see exhibits of local arts and crafts and also the carnival masks worn at religious festivals.

Beaches
On the northern side of the Samaná peninsula strips of golden sand stretch either side of Las Terrenas, and hotels rent out watersports equipment. On Samana Bay itself you can arrange to visit Cayo Levantado, an offshore island, or make your way up to Las Galeras, a small beach resort in the northeast.

Larimar
The Dominican Republic has a unique variety of turquoise, known locally as Larimar. This hard, light-blue stone, sold as jewelry throughout the country, is mined in the Bahoruco mountains on the south-western Barahona peninsula.

Sugar

■ **Sugar was such a valuable commodity during the 17th and 18th centuries that it became known as "white gold." Empires were built on the sugar trade; whole islands were planted with sugar cane, and navies were sent to capture and defend them. Meanwhile, the planters grew rich and their African slaves lived and labored in miserable subjection. ......■**

Sugar cane (*Saccharum officinarum*) is an over-grown grass. It grows to about 12 ft., can be green or deep purple in color and takes 18 months to mature, blooming with a tall, white, wispy ear. Cane fields are sometimes burned to rid the canes of their corn-like leaves, creating enormous columns of smoke that are visible for miles.

Cane-cutting is grueling work. In colonial times, teams of cutters would work in lines, led by singers and drummers as they swung their machetes in rhythm. Once the cane was cut, other gangs carted it off to the mill. The cane-cutting season lasted for about six months, ending in July; the annual Barbados carnival, Cropover, is a survivor of the end-of-season celebrations.

River Antoine Rum Distillery's sugar mill, Grenada

Technology has advanced from mule-driven mills to wind-driven and finally steam-driven crushing machinery, but sugar production has remained basically unchanged for 350 years. Canes are cut to length and passed repeatedly through metal rollers, so that the juice runs away and the pulp, or bagasse, emerges dry. Bagasse burns well and is used to fire the engines that drive the rollers. The cane juice is clarified in the boiling house in huge copper boiling pans (also heated with bagasse). As it cools, the sugar crystallizes into granules. Nowadays the sugar is passed through a centrifuge, separating the crystals from the molasses, which are themselves used as animal feed and for distilling rum.

In the mid-19th century, the development of sugar beet as an alternative to cane sugar cut into the West Indian trade, and now only a few islands cultivate the crop in any substantial quantity. The biggest industries are based in Cuba and the Dominican Republic, each producing about 7 million tons, and in Jamaica, which produces about 2.5 million tons every year.

Sugar loaf
Sugar loaf mountains can be found all over the English-speaking world. They take their name from their steep-sided shape, which resembles the "loaf" of early sugar manufacture. Wet processed sugar would be placed in a mould like an inverted pyramid and allowed to drain, so that the brown molasses would seep to the bottom and white sugar crystals were left at the top. When the mould was broken, a pyramid-shaped "loaf" of sugar was revealed.

191

OTHER CARIBBEAN STATES

▶▶▶ Santo Domingo

Santo Domingo, the island's capital and largest city, is the oldest surviving European settlement in the Americas. Its heart is the colonial city, on the bank of the Ozama river on the island's southern shore, but La Capital, as it is known, has expanded enormously over the centuries and now has around two million inhabitants. It has all the problems of fast-growing cities in poor countries: congestion, inadequate electricity and water supplies, and grinding poverty. But there is also a compelling Latin vibrancy here—best seen on the **Avenida del Puerto▶▶▶**, as crowds gather for their evening promenade.

Hidden by its ancient walls above the Avenida del Puerto, the **colonial city of Santo Domingo▶▶▶** is a calm enclave, with coral-rock alleyways and shady courtyards. Its most impressive building is the **Alcazar de Colon▶▶▶**, Columbus Palace, just inside the city walls. Built in 1514 for Columbus's son Diego as his viceregal palace, the solid stone house is fronted by a double row of arches; its interior has been restored and furnished with tapestries, earthen water-pitchers and leather-bound chests. Ranged before it are the viceroy's administrative buildings, the **Atarazana▶▶**. These once contained the colonial armory and customs houses; they now house the Museum of Marine Archaeology, stores, a gallery, the Fonda restaurant, and a couple of bars, including Drake's Pub (see panel). The city's oldest surviving building is the Casa del Cordon (1503), now a bank, across the street from the post office; look for the Franciscan order's cord motif, which is carved above the door.

From the Alcazar the city walls lead to **Calle de las Damas▶▶**, named after colonial ladies who would promenade here. Set in the former colonial offices, the **Museo de las Casas Reales▶▶** has exhibits from early Spanish colonial times, including suits of armor and wall maps. The imposing **Panteon Nacional▶** guards an eternal flame commemorating the Dominican national heroes, Duarte, Sanchez, and Mella, who formed the underground independence movement La Trinitaria during Haitian occupation in the 1830s, and eventually won independence

The Faro a Colon (Columbus Lighthouse)

for the Republic in 1844. Further along the street are the cool, quiet palace courtyard of the **Casa de Bastidas►►** and the **Fortaleza Ozama►**, a fortress whose cannons are now set in gardens.

The Plaza de Toledo alley leads into the Parque Colon, Columbus Square, where a statue of the explorer overlooks benches and trees. On the southern side of the square is the **Catedral Santa Maria de Menor, Primada de America►►**, the oldest cathedral in the Americas. Completed in 1523, the cathedral, with its pointed battlements, was said to be the burial place of Columbus until his remains were moved to the Faro a Colon in honor of the quincentennial celebrations in 1992—though there are rival claims from Cuba and Spain.

From the Parque Colon, El Conde, one of the city's busiest shopping streets, leads up to the **Parque Independencia►►**, the chaotic hub of the modern city. All distances in the country are measured from here. Behind the old city gates are the imposing memorial and sunken mausoleum dedicated to Duarte, Mella, and Sanchez. Leading off the square, the Avenida Mella is another shopping street, where you will find the Mercado Modelo, the lively market. To the south of Parque Independencia is the **Malecon►►**, the palm-lined seafront boulevard where Dominicans like to take the evening air, sitting in rocking chairs or scooting by in open-top convertibles.

Inland, the **Plaza de Cultura►** houses the National Theatre and Modern Art Gallery and three museums. Despite its rather dull appearance, it is worth visiting the Museum of the Dominican Man, where exhibits trace the history of Caribbean Indians and their customs. Visually more impressive is the **Palacio Nacional►**, a baroque palace built by the dictator Trujillo on Calle Dr. Delgado.

On the city's northwestern outskirts, the **Jardin Botanico Nacional►►** is a calm retreat, with an orchid house and an aquatic plant house of flowering lilies.

In the eastern suburbs, the **Faro a Colon►►** is a 100-ft. lighthouse built in the shape of a cross as a monument to Columbus. More imposing than attractive, it contains six museums and (it is said) the explorer's remains.

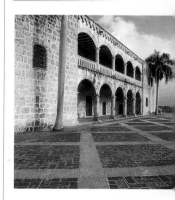

Alcazar de Colon

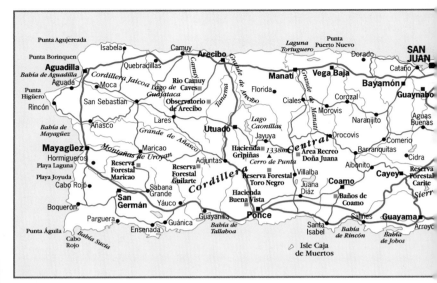

Puerto Rico

With good communications and plenty of hotels, Puerto Rico is an easy and attractive island to explore. San Juan is probably the best preserved Spanish colonial city in the Caribbean and has a lively cultural and artistic life; the southwest offers the best beaches and quieter accommodation. As a semi-autonomous commonwealth territory of the U.S., Puerto Rico is well known by American travelers. It is easy to reach—flights from Miami, New York, and several other U.S. cities land at San Juan's Luis Muñoz Marin airport, as do frequent U.K. flights, and most European airlines connect at New York. It also has a large, well-organized tourist industry; the beaches around San Juan are as developed as those in Miami, and Old San Juan, seven beautifully restored blocks of 18th-century colonial buildings, is one of the Caribbean's foremost cruise ship destinations. But there is far more to Puerto Rico than the tourist circuit. As well as a vibrant culture, the island offers endless exploration in its rainforests, caves,

Signs in San Juan

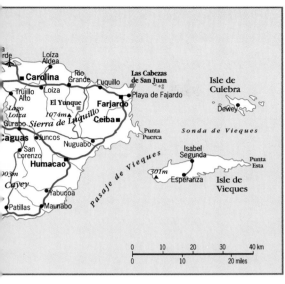

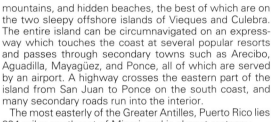

Puerto Rican eating
San Juan offers food from all over the world, but it is worth tasting the local dishes. Many are based on rice, including *arroz con pollo* (spiced chicken and rice) and *asopao*, like a paella. Seafood is often spiced with traditional flavorings: *sofrito* (onion, garlic, and pepper) and *adobo* (lemon, garlic, salt, and spices). Side dishes include *mofongo* (spiced and battered plantain) and *yuca frita* (spiced cassava with cloves and parsley).

mountains, and hidden beaches, the best of which are on the two sleepy offshore islands of Vieques and Culebra. The entire island can be circumnavigated on an expressway which touches the coast at several popular resorts and passes through secondary towns such as Arecibo, Aguadilla, Mayagüez, and Ponce, all of which are served by an airport. A highway crosses the eastern part of the island from San Juan to Ponce on the south coast, and many secondary roads run into the interior.

The most easterly of the Greater Antilles, Puerto Rico lies 994 miles southeast of Miami, and is almost rectangular in shape—110 miles in length and about 37 miles from north to south. A range of mountains runs through the

center of the island from east to west and marks a distinct division of climate: on the north side there is rainforest, and the rain in the northwest has created amazing karst cave systems (see page 200); in the south, the land is mainly dry and cactus-covered.

History Although it was visited by Columbus during his second voyage to the Americas in 1493, Puerto Rico was not settled by Europeans until 1508, when an expedition from Santo Domingo was led by Juan Ponce de Léon, who became the island's first Governor. Having first exploited and then defeated the native Tainos Indians, Ponce de Léon died in Cuba on a search for the Fountain of Youth. His bones were brought to San Juan, and eventually laid in San Juan Cathedral.

For the next 300 years, Puerto Rico's settlers suffered constant invasion—from Caribs, pirates and raiding European armies. After long years of neglect by its mother country, the colony was revived by a Spanish envoy in the 18th century, and trade from its sugar exports began to pick up. A new constitution was granted in 1812 and an independence movement started to emerge, to be ruthlessly put down by a succession of military Spanish Governors. An uprising in 1868 which led to the first declaration of a republic was soon put down by the Spanish,

196

The restored fire station in Ponce

The U.S. connection
Puerto Ricans have formed large communities on the American mainland, particularly in New York, where they are known as Neo Riquenians. The island has special Treasury laws, according to which the islanders do not pay Federal taxes, and therefore have no representation in Congress.

but in 1897 autonomy was finally granted. Before the new government could fulfill its role, the U.S., at war with Spain, invaded the island, and seven months later Puerto Rico was ceded to the Americans. U.S. citizenship was granted to islanders in 1917, but senior government appointments remained in American hands. Initially there was a movement towards independence—a 1937 rally ended in 19 deaths after police shot at the protestors. In 1952 the island became a Commonwealth of the U.S., and recent political debate has revolved around the question of whether Puerto Rico should become the 51st State of the Union. One of the obvious benefits of the American con-

The Spanish-influenced 17th-century Cathedral of Our Lady of Guadeloupe in Ponce

nection is Puerto Rico's prosperity, in comparison with nearby islands.

Island life American and Latin American culture live side by side, and often meet in an incongruous mix. Both English and Spanish are widely used—Spanish is the official language of Parliament; high-rise, air-conditioned office buildings tower over traditional Caribbean markets; cable TV, fast food and American cars are all a way of life, as are roadside stalls and, away from the larger towns, a simple, rural existence. The three million Puerto Ricans are strongly Catholic, and their most important festivals, the *fiestas patronales* (Saint's Day celebrations) combine a devout faith with the compulsion to dance—particularly to the salsa, a racing beat led by brass and African drums. Held by each individual town, the *fiestas* have costume balls, parades, picnics, and fairs; perhaps the most exuberant of them all is the Festival of the Innocents, in which, on December 28, the whole town of Hatillo on the north coast becomes a massive, costumed brawl.

   Apart from American-style fast food, Puerto Rico has a strong culinary tradition. Many dishes are based on rice, but plantains are also used as a staple in *mofongo* and *pinon* (see panel, page 195). Daytime snacks can often be bought at the roadside fruit stalls—try *alcapurria* and *bacalao* (crab and cod-fish batter balls) or *empañadas* and *picadillos* (meat or cheese sandwiches).

   The most popular island pastimes are baseball and (particularly in the country) cock-fighting, a brutal sport that regularly attracts bets of large sums of money. The contrast between a cheering mass of fans at a baseball game and a group of islanders exchanging their wagers around a cockpit illustrates neatly the dual character that has become part and parcel of Puerto Rican life.

The *guayabera*
Recently, American fashions have come to Puerto Rico in a big way, but the traditional dress for men on the island is the *guayabera*. Shaped rather like a jacket or an extended shirt, this is worn as the outer garment over an undershirt or T-shirt. Most are made of cotton and are worn during the day, but there is a more formal version for evening wear, made with pineapple fiber. The *guayabera* is usually embellished with patterned embroidery, running in stripes down the chest.

Festival of the Innocents at Hatillo, on the north coast near Arecibo

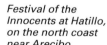

Arecibo Observatory
The Arecibo Observatory is an impressive sight: a bright white dish, 1,300 ft. across, neatly cupped in a karst sinkhole. It listens to waves across the spectrum and bounces them back to the massive recording gear that hangs 650 ft. above the dish itself (there is a two-story building up there, too). The information is then relayed to the offices before being sent to Cornell University for analysis.

Hacienda Gripiñas—colonial-style accommodation

▶▶▶ Cordillera Central

The Cordillera Central, the major mountain range in Puerto Rico's interior, runs parallel to the coast, splayed east and west on either side of the island's highest peak, Cerro de Punta. Running through them is the *ruta panoramica*▶▶▶, a scenic road over 120 miles among the peaks from coast to coast, taking in forest reserves and waterfalls. It's a long trip (two or three days), particularly if you stop off to explore, but there are charming mountain hotels en route and good roadside cafés, and the journey reveals a little-known side of Puerto Rico.

The *ruta panoramica* sets off from Maunabo, in the southeast of the island, beyond the tourist resort of Palmas del Mar. From here it rises into the Cayey mountains and the **Carite Forest Reserve**▶, inhabited by 50 species of bird, and then Cayey itself, where it crosses the main San Juan-to-Ponce road. It then continues to Aibonito and Barranquitas, two modern towns in steep-sided valleys. Close by is the **San Cristobal Canyon**▶▶, an impressive cleft over 650 ft. deep, where there is a 100-ft. waterfall. To the south, Coamo is an old colonial town, founded in 1579; the medicinal springs to its south were used by the indigenous Indians and later by Ponce de Léon. In the 19th century, they became fashionable as baths; restored as a modern *parador* (a government-run inn-cum-hotel), they still retain a period dining room.

Ascending steadily, with magnificent views, the route continues to Doña Juana Recreational Center, where there are 200-ft. falls, and on to the Toro Negro Forest Reserve, where there are trails to the island's highest point, Cerro de Punta (4,390 ft.). Just a few miles from here as the crow flies is one of the island's most charming retreats, the **Hacienda Gripiñas**▶▶▶. This *parador* is set in the wooden estate house of a former coffee plantation, overlooking the valley, and represents the best of old colonial Puerto Rico.

Though the *ruta panoramica* itself continues westwards, it is worth making a detour to the north at the town of Utuado. Beyond another

attractive *parador*, lost in greenery on the shores of Lago Caonillas, the **Caguana Indian Ceremonial Park►►** is set in a valley floor surrounded by massive peaks. It has a small museum and about 10 *bateyes*—sports and ceremonial grounds of beaten earth which were used by the indigenous Amerindians. Surrounded by carved stones, they are believed to date from the 9th century and possibly even earlier.

Just to the north of the park, in karst country, is the largest radio telescope in the world, the **Arecibo Observatory►►** (see panel). This 20-acre dish, owned by Cornell University, fills a whole valley and first discovered quasars. Not far off is the **Rio Camuy Cave Park►►**, a cave system where an introductory lecture is followed by a cable-car-ride and walks through the caves. Thousands of years of dripping rainwater has created a host of impressive stalactites and stalagmites in caverns 165 ft. high. The hillside town of Lares, on the southern boundary of karst country, was the setting for a rebellion against Spanish authorities in 1868, revered in Puerto Rican history as the *Gito de Lares* (the Cry of Lares).

Rejoining the *ruta panoramica* itself at Adjuntas, you climb into higher hills, with superb views. The road passes through the Guilarte Forest Reserve (where there are walking trails) and near the Maricao Forest Reserve, with a fish farm and a viewing tower overlooking the entire west coast. From here, the route descends to sea level, arriving at the coast at Mayagüez, the island's third largest town, mostly rebuilt after a disastrous earthquake in 1917. The **Mayagüez Zoo►►**, north of the town, exhibits animals in open compounds, and tropical plants are on view in the University of Puerto Rico's Tropical Agricultural Research Station, nearer the town.

Tourist bus logo

The Cordillera Central's lush scenery

■ The Caribbean archipelago runs southeast from the Tropic of Cancer, near the tip of Florida, down to the coast of South America, and has an impressive variety of terrains. The islands lie on the join of the Atlantic and Caribbean tectonic plates, where massive ructions have produced a string of volcanoes in the Eastern Caribbean. At the same time, the warm tropical sea has given rise to coral reefs, which have gradually clustered the islands with limestone as they age and die. ......■

200

Cave visits

All coral-based islands have caves, carved out by rain over the millenia. The best organized cave tours include the Rio Camuy park (tel: 765 5555) in Puerto Rico and Harrison's Cave (tel: 438 6640) in Barbados. Both tours have introductory explanations and a trip on a cable car to view the stalactites and stalagmites. The Cueva del Indio in the Viñales region of Cuba are also worth visiting, as is Anguilla's Fountain Cave, thought to have been an Arawak religious site.

Names and uses

In the British Caribbean old limestone shelves (dead coral reefs) on the seafront are known as "ironshore" and in the Spanish Caribbean as "black teeth." Many early Caribbean buildings were constructed with the bright, pitted coral rock, quarried on the islands themselves.

Over the millenia corals have created whole islands. When a hard coral dies it leaves a limestone skeleton, on which the next generation of corals can fix itself. Eventually a reef is formed and, as the level of the sea rises and falls, the growing reef can be left exposed as land. Wave action breaks down the dead reefs, carving natural bridges, blowholes and coastal caves, as well as creating bright, white sand. The islands which form a line from Anguilla through Antigua to Grande-Terre in Guadeloupe are all coral limestone, as are the Caymans, encrusted around a string of old volcanoes that died off 100 million years ago.

In the Greater Antilles, age-old coral limestone has been pushed up into the mountains by seismic activity. There it has been eroded into areas of cone and tower karst mountains, named after a region of shaggy-topped limestone outcrops in the former Yugoslavia. Karst peaks are distinctive, steep-sided mountains between 330 ft. and 660 ft. tall (they once had roofs suspended between them, but these were undermined by heavy rain and collapsed long ago). From above they look like shaggy egg cartons; beneath them, the rocky earth is laced with sinkholes, caverns, and underground rivers. In Jamaica karst mountains are known as "cockpits" (referring to cockerel fight venues, rather than to airplanes). Karst peaks can also be seen around Viñales in Cuba (where they are called *mogotes*), in the Dominican Republic's Los Haïtises National Park, and in the northwest of Puerto Rico.

►► Ponce and surrounds

Isolated from San Juan by the central mountain range, Ponce has a radically different feel from the island's capital; the area is hotter and has less rain, so its pace of life is rather more leisurely. The 200,000 Ponceños are renowned for their independence, and for their pride in a heritage dating from the 17th century, when Ponce de Léon's great-grandson founded the city.

Ponce's tree-lined central plaza and a number of streets surrounding it have recently been restored. Most striking is the striped red-and-black **Parque de Bombas►►** (fire station), erected for an agricultural fair a century ago. Built to a Spanish-influenced Puerto Rican design, the Cathedral of Our Lady of Guadeloupe dates from 1670, and the Casa Armstrong Poventud, a turn-of-the-century townhouse, has been restored with period furniture and houses a tourist information office. The **Ponce Museum of Art►►**, on the Avenida de las Americas, has an excellent collection of European and Latin American art.

One of the best views of the city is from El Vigia, the enormous cross on the hill, where an earlier version was designed to guide ships to land. **Castillo Serailles►►**, also on the hill, is the extravagant former family home of the distillers of local rum Don Q. Weekend ferries leave the Playa de Ponce for the small and popular offshore island Caja de Muertos (named after the coffin it resembles), which has excellent beaches and coral reefs.

The **Tibes Indian Ceremonial Center►►** is set in forested parkland behind the town. On an Amerindian village site, discovered in the 1970s, thatched houses and *bateyes* have been recreated, and a museum displays bones, weapons, and ceremonial figures found in the area. On Route 10, in the hills above the town, is the **Hacienda Buena Vista►►**, a restored late 19th-century coffee estate, which has a small museum and original machinery, driven by water; when the coffee beans have been mashed, the water is frothed up on a water-slide and dropped into a communal swimming pool (open at weekends by appointment; tel: 722 5882).

Arawak ceremonies
It takes a stretch of the imagination to re-create in your mind the excitement surrounding the games and dancing of the ceremonial parks when Arawak Indians were celebrating. Games were played with shuttlecocks and heavy balls, which had to be kept aloft using a huge belt around the waist. Festivities would continue for two or three days and the participants would spend a lot of time under the influence of a hallucinogenic drug. Having purged himself by vomiting, the chief would make predictions. As well as the Tibes Ceremonial Center, the park at Caguana, near Utuado, set in a lovely forested valley, deserves a visit.

201

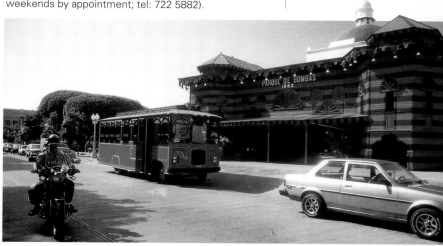

Red and black stripes on the Parque de Bombas

■ **In his book *The Old Man and the Sea*, Ernest Hemingway tells of a poor fisherman in Cuba and his fight to hook an enormous blue marlin. In another of his novels, *Islands in the Stream*, a boy and a marlin are engaged in a desperate struggle. Big game fishing suited Hemingway's macho image, and he was one of the sport's most passionate practitioners, relishing the rich sealife of the Caribbean waters. .....■**

Small and beautiful

One of the most beautiful fish in these waters is the sailfish, a sleek fish with a silver belly, a blue back, and a large, bright blue dorsal fin that looks like a sail. It can grow to about 10 ft. in length and weigh 200 lb. Other, smaller fish include wahoo, a streamlined gray-blue fish with a crescent tail, which grows to nearly 7 ft. and can weigh up to 120 lb. and, about the same size, the tarpon, which is slim and has silvery scales. The dorado (so-called because of its golden color) has red fins and grows to about 3 ft. in length.

Barracuda

Big game fishing was made possible by the invention of the motorized boat at the end of the 19th century, and fishermen soon gathered along the coasts of the Gulf Stream (Cuba, the Florida Keys, and Bimini in the Bahamas), where the biggest fish live, to troll for big game by day and booze and brawl in the bars by night. Today it is possible to fish off most of the Caribbean islands, and the sport is particularly popular off Cuba, Jamaica, and the Cayman Islands.

Deep-sea fishing boats have tall upper decks, from which their pilots can look out, and trail a number of lines from different rods. This is a strenuous, physical sport, and once a fish has been hooked, the fisherman will strap himself into a "fighting chair." Some species are immensely strong, weighing over 1,000 lb., and the fight can last for several hours: line is paid out in order to prevent it from snapping, allowing the fish to dive and move around. The unfortunate catch is then slowly hauled in; most fish are killed in the process.

The Caribbean's principal big game fish are the blue and the white marlin. Both have spears extending from their noses and long dorsal fins. The blue marlin can grow up to 1,500 lb. Other fish include tuna: yellowfin, albacore, and skipjack (the most important commercial fish, which is trawled extensively and processed in Puerto Rico) and, biggest of all, the blue-fin tuna, which can grow to 14 ft. and weigh 1,700 lb.

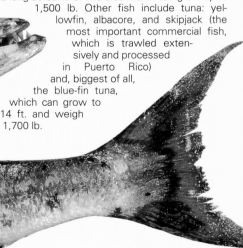

▶▶ San Germán and the Southwest

Puerto Ricans take their vacations in the southwest of the island. Here, the country is hotter and there are good beaches in the area; consequently, a number of small local tourist towns have collected along the coast, and come alive in the summer.

The main road from Ponce to Mayagüez cuts inland and passes close to the town of **San Germán▶▶**, the second on the island to be founded by the Spaniards (in 1573). It remained prominent until the 19th century, despite constant threats from pirates, and now has a university and attractive old townhouses. The **Porta Coeli Church▶▶** (1606) has been restored and now contains a museum of religious art. Contemporary art can be seen at the museum in Bahr House on Acosta Street.

203

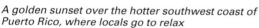

A golden sunset over the hotter southwest coast of Puerto Rico, where locals go to relax

On the coast directly south of San Germán is the town of **Parguera▶▶**, which has a more hedonistic, seaside feel. Local seafood restaurants, cabins on stilts, and small villas overlook the mangroves on the coast, and the beach (not one of the best) is some way out of town. A more worthwhile local attraction is the nearby phosphorescent lake (see panel, page 210).

Perhaps the best town in the area is **Boquerón▶▶**, a small seafront resort on the southwest coast. Backed with huge palm trees, its beach is one of the island's best and gets very lively at weekends. Watersports equipment is for rent and there are several cafés. Other, more isolated beaches lie on the island's southwestern tip.

To the north along the coastline are more resort towns, with *paradores* and restaurants lining the seafront at Playa Joyuda and Playa Laguna. This west-facing coast is excellent for sunset-watching, and offshore there are a number of small islands which are rarely visited, including Desecheo and Mona, a deserted nature reserve with soaring cliffs, which can only be reached by taking a charter plane or fishing boat.

Puerto Rican *paradores*
The *paradores* of Puerto Rico are hotels dotted around the island, judged to be of a certain standard and style by the Tourist Board (from whom a list can be requested). They are usually small, often have great local character and are generally in superb settings. Puerto Ricans themselves use *paradores*, so you are highly likely to meet islanders there. The *mesons gastronomicos* are restaurants chosen according to similar criteria, specializing in local cuisine.

OTHER CARIBBEAN STATES

Pavement cafés in Old San Juan

▶▶▶ San Juan (Old City)

Approached from the sea, Old San Juan looks like a massive fortress. The city is enclosed by over 6 miles of walls, 50 ft. high and 20 ft. thick, and a ring of sentry boxes, or *garitas*. Its formidable appearance was a necessity during the turbulent days when there was continual threat of invasion; both Francis Drake and Jack Hawkins led attacks on the city in the 16th century.

Parts of San Juan date from its foundation in 1520, but most of the colonial city has been restored to its 18th-century style. The streets are laid with blue cobblestones shipped from Spain as ballast, and the wrought-iron streetlamps, balconies, and shuttered windows all add to the rather self-conscious sense of history. Admittedly this is a tourist show-piece, and it can be overrun by visitors from the cruise ships; but Old San Juan is also a city with genuine character and life.

A walk around the city can take in its main features (see **Walk**), but beyond these there is a wealth of museums and galleries to explore. Museums include the Pablo Casals Museum on Calle San Sebastian, where the cellist's instruments are on display; the Museo del Arte de Puerto Rico, on Calle Cristo, which houses a collection of Puerto Rican fine arts; and the Casa del Libro, on the same street, with displays about printing and binding and a library of antiquarian books. When the time comes to rest from the sightseeing, there is ample choice: try La Mallorquina restaurant, on Calle San Justo, or La Bombonera, a noisy café on Calle San Francisco; or sample a daiquiri at La Violata, on Calle Fortaleza. San Juan wakes up after dark and late in the evening Calle de San Sebastian comes alive with promenaders.

The Castillo de San Felipe del Morro

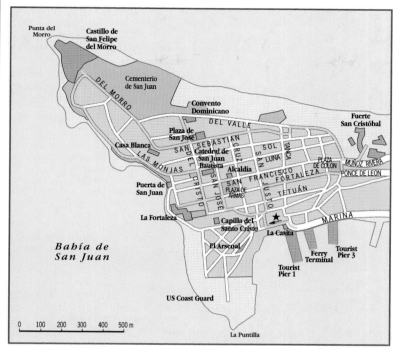

OLD SAN JUAN

Map labels: Punta del Morro; Castillo de San Felipe del Morro; Cementerio de San Juan; DEL MORRO; Convento Dominicano; DEL VALLE; Fuerte San Cristóbal; Plaza de San José; SAN SEBASTIAN; SOL; TANCA; Casa Blanca; Catedral de San Juan Bautista; LUNA; PLAZA DE COLON; MUÑOZ RIVERA; PONCE DE LEON; LAS MONJAS; Alcaldía; SAN FRANCISCO; FORTALEZA; Puerta de San Juan; SAN JOSE; PLAZA DE ARMAS; JUSTO; TETUÁN; La Fortaleza; CRISTO; Capilla del Santo Cristo; La Casita; MARINA; Bahía de San Juan; El Arsenal; Ferry Terminal; Tourist Pier 3; Tourist Pier 1; US Coast Guard; La Puntilla; 0 100 200 300 400 500 m

Walk · Old San Juan

Start at La Casita, a colonial building housing a tourist information center, near the cruise ship port on the inner harbor. Walk uphill, following the city wall to Calle San José. The Plaza de Armas is the city's main square, site of the Alcaldía (City Hall). Calle Fortaleza leads to **La Fortaleza►►**, used as the Governor's Mansion since its construction in 1520 and renovated in 1846 (hourly tours).

At the foot of Calle del Cristo, lined with stores and restaurants, is the tiny **Capilla del Santo Cristo►**, a chapel that marks the spot where a horseman plunged over the city walls during a race around the city. Heading north, you reach the Catedral de San Juan, built in 1540 and altered in the 19th century; Ponce de Léon's bones are entombed there. A stepped alley leads downhill to one of the city gates, and beyond the walls, parkland leads to the vast **Castillo de San Felipe del Morro►►**, San Juan's main defense. Started in 1540, it took over 240 years to complete; its walls rise 138 ft. from the sea, and it has six levels of tunnels and dungeons.

The route back to town brings you to the **Casa Blanca►►**. Built in 1521, this was the ancestral home of the Ponce de Léon family, and now contains a museum of colonial life. On the nearby **Plaza de San José►►**, where youngsters gather at night, is the Ponce de Léon family chapel. From the **Convento Dominicano►**, with its charming inner courtyard, follow the cobbled streets or the northern wall to the city's other defense, **Fuerte San Cristóbal►►**, a 17th-century labyrinth of tunnels and arches. A museum explains its intricate design. Take Calle Fortaleza and turn downhill to return to the dock.

■ **One of the most surprising aspects of the Caribbean landscape is its luxuriant greenery. Some islands are so fertile that you could plant a pencil and expect it to take root. Hundreds of plants grow on these fertile islands, including flowering trees, tropical fruit trees, curious crops and creepers, and the infinite variety of flowers that adorns West Indian gardens. ......■**

Botanical gardens
There are many excellent botanical gardens in the Caribbean. Some of the best are Hope Gardens, Kingston and Castleton in the Blue Mountains in Jamaica; the Jardin Botanico Nacional in Santo Domingo, capital of the Dominican Republic; the Rio Piedras Gardens in the south of San Juan, Puerto Rico; the national gardens in Roseau, Dominica; the Jardin de Balata in Martinique; the botanical garden of St. Vincent; the Flower Forest and Andromeda Gardens on Barbados; and the Emperor Valley Gardens off the Savannah in Port of Spain.

Beaches and swamps Palm trees on the seashore, overhanging the sandy beaches, are a travel brochure cliché nowadays, but they are not the only coastal trees by far—manchineel (see panel opposite), sea grape (with bunches of edible, bitter grapes), and sea almond trees (bearing inedible fruit) all grow near the sea, and around the swamps and coastal lagoons are the mangroves, hardy trees that have adapted to salt water and muddy ground, where they drop a tangle of buttress and aerial roots in order to support themselves. Flowering lilies can often be seen on fresh inland water.

Dry land The drier Caribbean islands, which include low-lying lands such as the Caymans, the Dutch Leewards, and the outer chain of the former British Leewards, are generally covered in green scrub, which turns to yellow as it is bleached by the sun. On Curaçao, where this scrubland is known as *cunucu*, the cactus-like aloe vera produces oil that is used extensively in cosmetics, and the century plant throws out a 30-ft. flowering stem about once every 10 years. In this poor soil the divi-divi tree grows stunted, with branches that bend over in the winds like a head of windblown hair. Cacti cover the arid land, and are used to make fences in many settlements.

Grasses and flowers On the more fertile islands, grassland known as savannah is grazed by cattle, and gardens close to sea level grow a huge variety of flowers. The best known are bougainvillea, which bloom in spiny fingers of purple, pink, and orange, and hibiscus, with around 200 different delicate and brightly colored blooms, each of which lasts only one day. Other species to look out for include white flowering frangipani, allamanda, and plumbago, which has purple blooms; and more exotic garden flowers include heliconia (called "lobster claw" because of its strange shape), red hot cat tail, a fluffy, dangling bright red bloom, and the bird of paradise, with a bird-like form. The ubiquitous anthurium, with its plastic-looking leaf and furry stigma, is used to adorn dinner tables in houses all over the Caribbean.

Left: the evergreen croton shrub

Flowering trees The Caribbean's many dazzling flowering trees include the yellow and pink pouis, African tulip trees, and the immortelle, which is planted to give shade to cocoa beans and makes whole valleys flame in January. The flamboyant, or poinciana, blooms red in June and July, and the ackee produces red pods, whose yellow flesh can be eaten. Other food-bearing trees include the breadfruit and the spiky breadnut; fruit trees are a valuable source of income for many islands (see page 143). The calabash fruit cannot be eaten, but its hard shell was used as a container in years gone by; and the cannon ball tree, despite its delicate flowers, grows fruit like lumps of wood. *Lignum vitae*, or the tree of life, has wood so hard and heavy that it sinks in water; mahogany tree pods release sycamore-like whirling seeds. Beware of the sharp spines on the trunk of the sandbox, so-called because its pods were used to hold sand for ink blotters. The kapok, or silk cotton tree, blooms with white cotton-like buds, once used as stuffing for mattresses.

The Traveler's Tree
The Traveler's Tree, which can be seen at the Andromeda Gardens in Barbados, is sometimes (and incorrectly) called a palm tree. Its leaves grow like a fan, splaying sideways as each new leaf is superseded by another in the middle. Occasionally, a spiky, inedible fruit pokes out and reveals its strange, blue, wax-like material. The tree is so-called because rain collects in the cupped spaces between the leaves, giving travelers a ready supply of drinking water.

Roadside flora in Dominica

Forest flora Higher up the slopes of the larger islands, the vegetation changes and the forests begin. Countless varieties of ferns swirl into an impenetrable, tangled mass; vines use the forest trees as a sort of climbing frame, clambering up the trunks and dropping their lianas into the soil; and "air-plants," orchids and bromeliads thrive on the upper branches of trees and even on telephone wires.

Forbidden fruit
The manchioneel is a bushy evergreen whose small apples are extremely poisonous; one of Columbus's sailors tried his luck, and the fruit quickly became known as the "apple of death."

Skyscraper hotels at Isla Verde

San Juan snacks
Like other Caribbean islanders, the Puerto Ricans adore roadside snacks and there is a grand variety of tasty fillers at *kioskos* in San Juan and around the countryside. *Chicharron* is popular, though perhaps an acquired taste—spiced fried pork rind. *Bacalao* is frittered codfish, and *alca-purrias* are also fritters, either meat or local fish, fried and served on a banana leaf. *Empañadas* are strangely flattened sandwiches, and *picadillas* are meat patties.

► **San Juan (New City)**

Beyond the walls of colonial San Juan there is a real working city with a population of over a million, which has sprawled along the coast and around the lagoons. Hotels and apartment houses crowd the coastline, while further inland, swank commercial buildings and poor shanties highlight the contrasts of Puerto Rican life.

To the east of Columbus Square, at the edge of the colonial city, is **El Capitolio**►►, the seat of the Puerto Rican senate and house of representatives. Built in the 1920s, its style imitates the style of the White House in Washington; in the rotunda, a copy of the 1954 Puerto Rican constitution is on view.

Further along the coast is **Condado**►, one of the town's main tourist strips. Huge hotels, interspersed with stores and conference centers, stand right on the seafront, and behind them are streets full of restaurants, and bars. This line of tall buildings follows the coast solidly for the six or so miles to **Isla Verde**►►, the other main tourist area, crammed with luxury hotels, restaurants, and bars overlooking a large, popular beach.

Inland are the working areas of the capital. Hato Rey, known for its street of glass-fronted skyscrapers, is the commercial heart of San Juan, which is one of the biggest financial markets in the Caribbean. A more traditional Caribbean market operates in Rio Piedras, with tropical fruits and vegetables on sale. To the south, the **Botanical Gardens**► provide a green and welcome retreat from the hustle of the city and its endless traffic. A ferry ride across the bay from Old San Juan takes you to Catano, where the **Bacardi Rum Distillery and Museum**►► provides tours for visitors by cable car.

■ **As tourists have flooded into their resorts and towns, many Caribbean islands have gained reputations for their gambling centers. But beyond the roulette tables, there is a popular tradition of West Indian gambling and bar games, from domino contests to local wrestling matches or even cock fights. ......■**

Caribbean casinos have a predictable line-up of games: *vingt et un*, roulette, craps, and the inevitable slot machines. If casino gambling is an important factor in your vacation choice, the following islands should be on your list: Antigua; Aruba (which has about 10 glitzy gaming rooms with cabaret shows); Bonaire (one small casino at the Flamingo Beach Hotel); the Dominican Republic (casinos in all the main resorts); Guadeloupe and Martinique (two each); Puerto Rico (a host of casinos in Condado and Isla Verde and at a number of hotels around the island); St. Kitts (at the Jack Tar Village), and on the Dutch side of Sint Maarten, where there are nine casinos. Opening hours vary from one casino to the next, but many continue as long as the gamblers do.

Gambling travelers
Cuba was one of the biggest gambling islands, attracting thousands of U.S. visitors to its gaming houses, until 1959, when casinos and all other trappings of capitalism were outlawed by the young Cuban revolutionaries. Since then Puerto Rico (and the Bahamas, which are also close to the States) have taken over as the favorite gambling destinations, especially for American visitors.

209

Fighting cocks in San Juan

Cock-fighting On the French- and Spanish-speaking Caribbean islands, cock-fighting is a major spectator sport. It is a brutal event—the cocks are occasionally killed—staged in a cockpit with steeply banked seats. Cocks are prepared for weeks in advance for a fight, with special diets and grooming. On the day of the fight owners bring their birds into the ring, showing them off to the crowd and brandishing them at one another as the bets are placed. As the fight begins, two cocks lunge at each other, pecking and slashing with their claws, while the audience erupts into screams and shouts of encouragement. In the French Caribbean, a variation on the bloodsport theme is occasionally introduced, when mongeese and snakes are pitted against one another in a contest to the death.

Dominoes
Played in just about every bar throughout the Caribbean, dominoes are even enjoyed by Fidel Castro, the President of Cuba. The pieces are usually laid on the playing board with a grand flourish and a loud slap; in Barbados they are referred to as "cards," and are even "shuffled" in preparation for the game.

Casa del Frances, Vieques

Luminous lake
The phosphorescent lake at Mosquito Bay, Vieques, has an eerie beauty. At night it glows where paddles cut the water; fish leave streaks as they dart away, and in a storm the whole surface is set alight. The cause is bioluminescence; tiny creatures emitting light when agitated.

►► Vieques and Culebra

If you look east from Fajardo, on Puerto Rico's east coast, you will see that the sea is sprinkled with islands and cays as far as the horizon, culminating in the Virgin Islands. About 6 miles from the mainland, Vieques is the largest of the Puerto Rican islands; not far beyond it is Culebra, surrounded by a collection of little satellites. These two islands are dry and low, with rolling hills and some of the best beaches in Puerto Rico. Here the flora and fauna are very different from the mainland—you might see red-billed tropicbirds and turtles, which lay their eggs on the beach—and Culebra is partly given over to a wildlife refuge.

Vieques An hour's ferry ride from the mainland brings you to Vieques' northern shore and its main town, Isabel Segunda, where many of the island's 8,000 inhabitants live. The central square is quiet and pleasant and there is a tourist information office there. A restored 19th-century fort► stands on the hill above the town. In Esperanza►►, on the southern coast, bars and restaurants are strung along the shorefront, a stone's throw from the island's best beaches. Look for the **Casa del Frances►►**, a stylish old plantation house. Much of the island belongs to the U.S. Navy and is used for their exercises (to the resentment of many islanders), but at other times visitors are allowed on to the area's beaches—including Red Beach and Blue Beach.

Puerto Rican license plate

Culebra This tranquil island sits among a small crowd of tiny coral outcrops 25 miles east of the mainland. Only 2,000 islanders live on Culebra, many in the only town of Dewey, better known as Pueblo, where there is a small information office. Culebra was used as a gunnery range by the U.S. Navy for many years, and was subjected to constant shelling, but after a campaign by the islanders the government eventually withdrew in 1975.

▶▶▶ El Yunque Rainforest

The most accessible area of Puerto Rico from the capital is the northeast, with its rich variety of mountains, mangroves and beaches. Perhaps the most popular tour is to El Yunque, an area of rainforest which because of its position in the far northeast of the island enjoys the best of the water-laden Atlantic winds (bringing about 120 billion gallons of rain every year).

El Yunque is approached by Route 3 from town or by following the coast road out of Isla Verde and then heading into the mountains, rampant with tropical foliage, on Route 191. In this 27,000-acre National Park, 240 species of tree grow in three different varieties of forest (rainforest, montane forest, and stunted dwarf forest, near the 3,000-ft. peaks). Trails have been cut into the forest, with explanatory signboards, waterfalls and look-out platforms. There is a visitor's center on Route 191, where information is provided about the plants and animals—such as the coquí tree frog, whose dual note echoes through the greenery—and about the 60 or so species of bird, including the endangered Puerto Rican parrot. As this is rainforest, there are frequent tropical showers, so take a waterproof coat.

Mangrove birdlife
Mangrove swamps harbor lots of crustaceans, providing food for herons, terns, sandpipers, and stilts. The easiest to visit from San Juan are Piñones (from Boca de Cangrejos marina) and Las Cabezas de San Juan. Guanica, in the southwest, is designated a World Biosphere by UNESCO.

211

On the far northeastern tip of the island there is another nature reserve at Las Cabezas de San Juan, where boardwalks lead through the mangroves past the shore and swamp birdlife. A visitor's center is housed in the old Faro (lighthouse), which has superb views towards the Virgin Islands. The route back to town on the north coast road passes Luquillo, site of one of the island's most popular public beaches and a string of excellent roadside snack shops, before reaching Loíza, a poor area known for its costumed *fiesta patronal* (Santiago) on July 25. At Piñones, just before the road comes into Isla Verde, another area of protected mangrove swamps is the habitat of snowy egrets, pelicans, and herons, and provides a home for a rich diversity of other bird and wildlife besides.

Bar at Esperanza

OTHER CARIBBEAN STATES

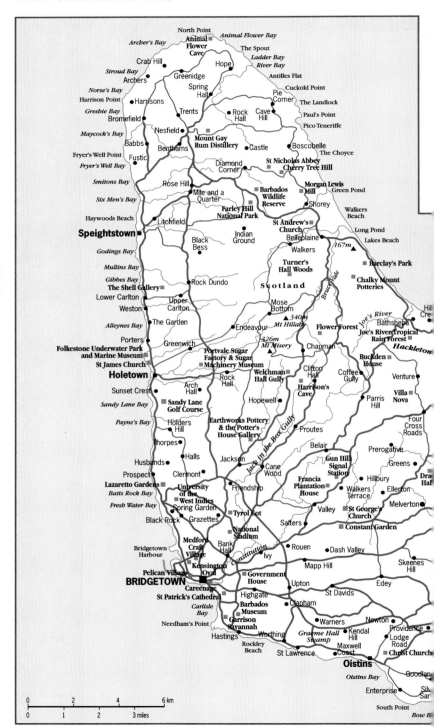

North Point
Archer's Bay
Animal Flower Cave
Animal Flower Bay
The Spout
Ladder Bay
River Bay
Crab Hill
Hope
Greenidge
Antilles Flat
Stroud Bay
Archers
Spring Hall
Cuckold Point
Norse's Bay
Harrisons
Trents
Pie Corner
The Landlock
Harrison Point
Rock Hall
Cave Hill
Paul's Point
Gresbie Bay
Bromefield
Pico Teneriffe
Maycock's Bay
Nesfield
Mount Gay Rum Distillery
Castle
Boscobelle
Babbs
Benthams
The Choyce
Fryer's Well Point
Fustic
Diamond Corner
St Nicholas Abbey
Cherry Tree Hill
Fryer's Well Bay
Smitons Bay
Rose Hill
Barbados Wildlife Reserve
Morgan Lewis Mill
Green Pond
Six Men's Bay
Mile and a Quarter
Shorey
Walkers Beach
Haywoods Beach
Litchfield
Farley Hill National Park
St Andrew's Church
Speightstown
Belleblaine
Long Pond
Lakes Beach
Godings Bay
Black Bess
Indian Ground
Walkers
167m
Mullins Bay
Turner's Hall Woods
Barclay's Park
Gibbes Bay
The Shell Gallery
Rock Dundo
Scotland
Chalky Mount Potteries
Lower Carlton
Weston
Upper Carlton
Mose Bottom
Joe's River
Hil Cre
Alleynes Bay
The Garden
Endeavour
340m Mt Hillaby
Flower Forest
Bathsheba
Joe's River Tropical Rain Forest
Porters
Greenwich
326m Mt Misery
Chapman
Hackleton
Folkestone Underwater Park and Marine Museum
Portvale Sugar Factory & Sugar Machinery Museum
Buckden House
St James Church
Holetown
Rock Hall
Welchman Hall Gully
Clifton Hall
Coffee Gully
Venture
Sunset Crest
Arch Hall
Harrison's Cave
Villa Nova
Sandy Lane Bay
Sandy Lane Golf Course
Hopewell
Parris Hill
Payne's Bay
Holders Hill
Earthworks Pottery & the Potter's House Gallery
Proutes
Four Cross Roads
Thorpes
Halls
Belair
Prerogative
Husbands
Jackson
Greens
Prospect
Clermont
Cane Wood
Gun Hill Signal Station
Hillbury
Dra Hal
Lazaretto Gardens
University of the West Indies Spring Garden
Friendship
Francia Plantation House
Walkers Terrace
Ellerton
Batts Rock Bay
Fresh Water Bay
Grazettes
Valley
St George's Church
Melverton
Black Rock
Tyrol Cot
Salters
Constant Garden
National Stadium
Medford Craft Village
Bank Hall
Rouen
Dash Valley
Skeenes Hill
Bridgetown Harbour
Kensington Oval
Ivy
Mapp Hill
Upton
Edey
Pelican Village
BRIDGETOWN
Careenage
Government House
St Patrick's Cathedral
Highgate
St Davids
Carlisle Bay
Barbados Museum
Clapham
Needham's Point
Garrison Savannah
Warners
Newton
Providence
Hastings
Worthing
Graeme Hall Swamp
Kendal Hill
Lodge Road
Rockley Beach
Maxwell Coast
Christ Church
St Lawrence
Oistins
Goodlan
Oistins Bay
Sil Sar
Enterprise
South Point
Bow B

0   2   4   6 km
0   1   2   3 miles

Barbados

Probably the most British of the Caribbean islands, Barbados has a gentle, undulating interior, ringed by safe and attractive beaches. It is relatively prosperous, relaxed, and welcoming, and has absorbed the tourist industry gradually, without allowing it to overwhelm the life and character of the island. Popular attractions include its famous rum, its lively south coast nightlife and its passion for cricket. Away from the low-key sophistication and luxury hotels of the west (the most developed area), the south coast of the island is known for its up-beat atmosphere, and has simpler accommodation in guesthouses and short-term apartments. In contrast, the east coast is quiet and mostly undeveloped. Because the island has so

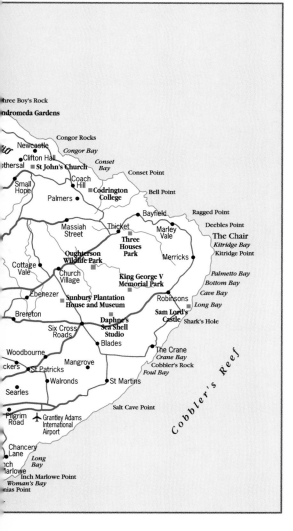

Settling by force
Three centuries ago, to be "Barbadosed" was to be sent forcibly to the West Indies. Settlers were needed on the islands and the courts deported common thieves, prisoners of war, and prostitutes to make up the numbers. They were set to work on the farmland alongside indentured laborers, who sold their labor for five or seven years in return for their passage to the islands, on the understanding that they would be given land to plant at the end of their term. In the late 17th century, African slaves provided a large-scale labor force for the sugar plantations.

Nelson's statue stands in Bridgetown

OTHER CARIBBEAN STATES

Little England
In colonial days, the leading Barbadians were proud of their association with Britain, and of being the only British Caribbean island not to be conquered by another power. They called their island, which was a highly successful colony, Little England, and having been nicknamed "Bims" by their slaves, styled themselves as inhabitants of "Bimshire," as though Barbados were a county of Britain.

King's Beach on the west coast

many hotels and is easily reached on regular flights from Europe and the U.S., good package deals are available to Barbados through tour operators and travel agents.

Barbados is one of the best Caribbean islands for an active beach vacation. By day, watersports are easy to arrange, and there are plenty of beach bars to retire to. Divers come to enjoy the marine life of the coral reefs, and non-divers have access to underwater views from the dry comfort of the **Atlantis Submarine**►► (tel: 436 8929). Barbados has more exploring potential than other islands. The interior, though nowhere near as dramatic or lush as Jamaica or St. Lucia, has pleasant scenery, with mahogany woods, cattle and black-bellied sheep grazing on rough meadows, traditional wooden chattel houses and forests of sugar cane. There are also magnificent plantation houses—some open to the public, some still the homes of "high white" families of the old plantocracy, some the hub of working plantations, and one or two available for rent to visitors. By night there is a wide choice of nightclubs and many good restaurants, serving local and international food. Though not cheap, several of them include magnificent coastal settings in the price.

Shaped like a pear set at a slightly tipsy angle, Barbados is made entirely of coral limestone. It measures 21 miles by 14 miles and lies in the Atlantic Ocean, 100 miles east of the Windward Island of St. Vincent. From the western beaches, gently lapped by the Caribbean Sea, the land rises steadily through the cane fields and cultivated land of the central plains, culminating in the 985-ft. escarpment of Hackleton's Cliff in the east. North of here is the hilly Scotland district, where the island reaches its highest point, Mount Hillaby, at 1,115 ft. Powerful Atlantic waves

Boats at Bridgetown

Little Bristol
In the 17th century, during the early days of colonization, Bristol was the major port on the west coast of England, and many settlers and deportees on Barbados came originally from the West Country. Speightstown's West Country residents earned it the nickname Little Bristol, and their influence can still be heard in the drawled Barbadian vowels.

Rum and exercise
The Sunday walk with the Barbados National Trust (a preservation body, similar to the British National Trust) and the Bajan rum shop are both equally hallowed institutions. On the former, a guide leads walkers through a chosen area of historic interest (perhaps a section of the old railroad, or an abandoned fort) for a couple of hours on Sunday mornings (tel: 426 2421; a small fee is charged). In the rum shops, customers offer informal instruction in such essential pursuits as dominoes and talking politics.

crash constantly against the dramatic eastern shoreline, carving out bizarre rock formations (and eroding the coast steadily year by year).

Island life The island's population of 260,000 is one of the densest in the world, a fact that is clearly visible in the urban sprawl radiating from Bridgetown along the western and southern coasts. Solitude may be hard to find on Barbados, but the island is made special by its people. Bajans, mostly of African descent, are some of the friendliest West Indians; whether at the weekly Sunday National Trust walk▶▶ (see panel) or in a local rum shop for a game of dominoes, the Bajans will give you an amiable welcome and are always ready to fill you in on all the latest island gossip.

A recent recession in the Barbados economy has put pressure on the islanders, and there have been isolated incidents against unwary tourists, but the authorities have reacted quickly and firmly, and although visitors should be careful, the vast majority of Barbadians treat tourism as an important industry and continue to be very friendly to vacationers.

Much is made of Barbados's Englishness, the result of a long-standing colonial connection with Britain. For a time the island was even known as Little England (see panel). While it is true that Barbados has visibly kept more British traits than other islands, in their traditions and manners, the North American influence can also clearly be seen today. Since Independence in 1966, the people have started to take pride in their Afro-Caribbean heritage, and more recently have developed their indigenous Bajan culture.

OTHER CARIBBEAN STATES

▶▶ **Bridgetown**

The capital of Barbados lies on a broad, protected bay in the southwestern corner of the island. Old colonial buildings and modern offices stand side by side in the center of Bridgetown, but over the years the city, which has around 100,000 inhabitants, has spread steadily north and southeast along the coasts.

Bridgetown is the center of island life, where the offices of government and big business stand above lively West Indian street markets. Its traditional heart is the Careenage, a sea inlet where, in the days of seaborne travel, lighters would bring ashore passengers from the ocean-going ships. There is not much nautical activity any more (passengers arriving by sea usually dock at the deep-water harbor), but yachts and fishing boats still use the inlet, and bars such as the Waterfront Café cater to the land-lubbers.

The Careenage
The Careenage takes its name from the system of cleaning or careening the hull of a ship. (A number of harbors in the Windward Islands and the nearby French islands share the same name.) A weight would be attached to the ship's mast in shallow water and the ship would be tilted so that one side of her hull was exposed, to be scrubbed free of barnacles and weeds.

The Careenage, Bridgetown

Nelson
Lord Nelson, "Preserver of the West Indies," arrived in pursuit of the French admiral, Villeneuve, during the Napoleonic Wars and removed the threat of French invasion. Without a column to stand on, the statue in Bridgetown is a lot smaller than that in London, but it has the distinction of being 30 years older. As a legacy of the colonial era Nelson is a somewhat contentious figure, and some islanders would prefer to see a statue of a Barbadian gracing Trafalgar Square—"Put up a Bajan man," sings the Mighty Gabby, calypso star and consciousness-raiser.

On the north side of the Careenage is Trafalgar Square. Though smaller than its namesake in London, this square also has a statue of the Admiral Horatio Nelson, though it has no column to support it. Near him stand the two distinctive colonial Public Buildings, built from local coral rock in the 1870s. Crenellated and with pointed arches, they have red tin roofs and green louvered windows, which keep out the sun but allow ventilation when there is a breeze. The House of Assembly, the seat of the Barbados Parliament, which was founded in 1639, is open to visitors. British monarchs from James I to Victoria are commemorated in stained glass windows in the Parliament chamber.

At the center of Trafalgar Square is a small fountain, its bowls supported on the tails of brightly painted dolphins, which was erected in 1865 to mark the arrival of piped water—an important event in a hot town. From the square leads an important commercial street: Broad Street, where Bridgetown's major stores are housed in old colonial buildings; north of here is Swan Street, a typically Caribbean (weekday) street market where vendors stand

Selling fruit in the capital

Baxter's Road
On the northern outskirts of Bridgetown, Baxter's Road is an ordinary street by day which becomes an open-air barbecue after about 11p.m. Bajans set up small braziers under umbrellas and fry fish, chicken, and vegetables for late evening snacks. There is a safe and comfortable atmosphere, and this is a great place to grab a bite to eat and swap a few stories with the locals.

by their colorful stalls selling anything from oranges to fluorescent shoe laces or mirror shades.

St. Michael's Cathedral, a few blocks east of Trafalgar Square, was built in 1789 and provides a haven from the town's hubbub, showing glimpses of glory and tragedy in the headstones and tablets set into its walls and floor. The restored Synagogue, originally built in the 17th century, off Magazine Lane near the law courts, is worth seeing; in the yard is a gravestone dedicated to Benjamin Messiah, who was renowned as a circumciser, apparently performing with "Great Applause and Dexterity."

Cheapside Market, at the northwest end of Lower Broad Street, is set in a traditional tin market building and sells mainly local food and vegetables, and in the Rasta Mall goods for sale include rastafarian herbal concoctions and leather pendants from Africa. Near by, Pelican Village sells more formal arts and crafts and is worth a quick look.

A couple of miles to the south of the Careenage is the Garrison Savannah, the military district of the colonial era. The old Georgian barrack buildings are still visible, some restored, others in decay, but the 300-acre Savannah itself is now used mainly for sports events, including horse-racing and local cricket matches. The **Barbados Museum▶▶** is at the corner of the Savannah, in the surprisingly successful setting of the island's former prison. Its well-presented displays show aspects of Barbados in Amerindian and colonial times, including the old mobile chattel houses of the former slaves and the ill-fated Barbados Railway (see panel). Rooms here have been fitted using period furniture and a gallery of maps and prints is set in the old cells.

The Barbados Railway
During the 19th century the British built railroads throughout their empire, and despite its small size, even Barbados had one built in the 1880s. The line ran east from Bridgetown through the central sugar cane lands before descending to the Atlantic coast at Bathsheba and continuing to Belleplaine. It was used by workers coming into town in the week and was usually packed for church outings at the weekends. Having suffered financial problems from the start, it finally folded in 1937.

Sandy Lane Hotel, on the west coast

West Coast Beaches
Calm and west-facing, the Caribbean coast is an almost continuous strip of beautiful sands, ideal for early morning walks or for sunset-watching. Though the beaches are never really crowded, you cannot expect to be alone here, because there are so many hotels set along the coast. There are few distinct divisions between the beaches, and in some places you can wade through the shallows to the next beach. All beaches are public and provide a right of way, and hotels provide watersports facilities—non-residents can usually negotiate their use. Paynes Bay, with its easy access and choice of watersports deals, is a good option.

►►► Caribbean Coast

The beach that stretches up the west coast of Barbados is one of the finest in the Caribbean. Its golden sand is washed by the calm Caribbean Sea, and behind the coconut palms and casuarina trees are superb hotels such as the Sandy Lane and the Coral Reef Club, long-renowned havens of luxury which have given Barbados its name for tropical refinement. Interspersed among them are restaurants and cheaper hotels, and there are two golf courses: one at Sandy Lane and the other north of Speightstown at the Heywoods Hotel.

The roads north out of Bridgetown lead to the Spring Garden Highway, which comes alive each year on the first Monday in August with colorful dancing parades during the festival of **Cropover►►►**. North of the town center is the Kensington Oval, the Barbados cricket stadium—a popular venue for Bajans, whose fervor for the game makes attending a cricket match a rousing experience. On the coast near by is the **West India Rum Refinery►►**, where tours include a hearty Bajan lunch, a look at the vats and the distilling process, and, of course, a chance to taste the rum. The history of the sugar-refining process is traced at the **Portvale Sugar Factory►** (inland from the village of Holetown), where copper boilers and steam machinery are on view between February and May.

Holetown itself was the site of the first European settlement on Barbados in 1627, colonized after it was claimed for the British by Captain John Powell in 1625. The small but stately St. James Parish Church is notable for its English style of architecture, but Holetown today mainly consists of open spaces. The **Folkestone Underwater Park►** has a small marine museum and a snorkeling trail through the offshore corals, and inland is **Harrison's Cave►►**, leading to a network of illuminated underground caverns adorned with spectacular stalactites, stalagmites, and waterfalls.

Back on the coast, **Speightstown►** is 7.5 miles north of the capital, a sleepy town with some good bars; beyond it, the countryside opens out to reveal cane fields, small settlements and deserted beaches.

■ **Sports are unifying features of an area made diverse by its geography. Within the former British Caribbean islands, cricket is something of a religion: islanders will drop everything to listen to the commentary of an international match in which the West Indies team is playing. In the Spanish Caribbean the most popular sport is baseball, and life comes to a halt if an important game is being played. ......■**

Cricket The West Indies have had a world-class cricket team for years—a remarkable achievement for an area with so small a pool of players to choose from. Players for the team are drawn from all the British Caribbean islands, but the main centers are the islands where there are international-class (Test Match) grounds (Jamaica, Antigua, Barbados, Trinidad, and Guyana). Barbados has an impressive record, having won the inter-island competition (the Red Stripe Tournament) more often than any other team.

Games of cricket are played on the beaches and in back streets, with a tennis ball and sticks for stumps; tourists are often asked to join in. Success at cricket is a route to fame and wealth, so it is fiercely contested, and the best players attain national hero status. Famous cricketing names from the Caribbean include Viv Richards (from Antigua), Clive Lloyd (from Guyana), and the legendary Gary Sobers, from Barbados.

Other sports
By means of cable TV, the Caribbean is steadily being influenced by sports from America. Basketball is very popular, as is football, though the latter is restricted to the small screen, and is not played on the islands. The major participant sport in the French Caribbean is soccer, but the most popular spectator sport is cockfighting (see page 209), also followed on the Spanish islands, but virtually unknown in the British Caribbean.

219

Baseball This is the national sport in Cuba, the Dominican Republic, and Puerto Rico, and has been played on the U.S. Virgin Islands since the Americans arrived. Just as many West Indian cricketers go to the U.K. to play, so the Dominicans and Puerto Ricans play in American pro leagues—though Cubans are banned because of the U.S.'s tough position on political relations. In the streets the children play a toned-down version of baseball in which they are not allowed to run—and again, any visitors who stop to watch will probably be asked to join in.

The diamond at Charlotte Amalie, St. Thomas

OTHER CARIBBEAN STATES

Gun Hill Signal Station
Now restored, Gun Hill Signal Station stands in the center of the island with impressive views all around. It is one of a string of old military signal posts that could send messages (by mirror-flash or by colored lantern) across the island in minutes, warning the barracks of approaching ships and the merchants of trading vessels. Set far away from the malarial swamps on the coast and bathed in fresh winds, the station was used as a hospital during the later colonial era.

▶▶   **Central Barbados**

Inland from the capital, the land rises steadily through the Bridgetown suburbs (where Bajans grow their ground provisions of sweet potatoes and yams) into open country and cane fields, towards the cliffs that tower above the Atlantic coast. **Francia Plantation▶▶** gives a vivid idea of the privileged lifestyle of the old Barbados planters. Standing on high ground in attractive gardens, Francia is furnished with antique furniture and decorated with maps and prints of old Barbados. **Villa Nova▶▶** is another magnificent plantation house, set in charming gardens. Once owned by the former British Prime Minister Sir Anthony Eden, it was built in the 1830s from bright, pitted coral stone, with louvered shutters on the windows and verandas surrounded by trellises. It is worth taking a quick look at **Codrington College▶**, an imposing religious seminary and school (buildings not open to visitors) that dates from the early 18th century and is approached along an avenue of splendid royal palm trees.

The steep, somewhat remote east coast of Barbados is an unexpected find on an island usually associated with calm seas, gently sloping beaches, and palm trees. From the top of Hackleton's Cliff, the site of **St. John's Parish Church▶**, there is a marvelous view over small country villages and down to the east coast, where Atlantic waves roll in against huge sculpted rocks. The sea here is rough and unpredictable, and signs on the beaches warn of dangerous currents and advise people not to swim. Barbadians tend to do so regardless, but visitors should not follow their example.

The fishing village of Bathsheba

The Atlantis Hotel
In its dramatic setting atop the cliff in Bathsheba, the Atlantis Hotel has a fine view of the Atlantic waves. The hotel is past its best, but it has become famous for its lunch, a traditional West Indian buffet.

Andromeda Gardens▶▶, near Bathsheba, are set out on the hillside, with fiery blooms and flowering trees from throughout the tropical world, including frangipani, orchids, and the Traveler's Tree (see panel, page 207). Bathsheba and Cattlewash are now fishing villages, but attractive seafront villas remain from the time when colonials would come here to escape the Bridgetown heat. The veranda of the Kingsley Club at Cattlewash makes an excellent resting place, where you can have lunch or afternoon tea.

■ **An old rhyme describes the rum punch drunk by planters in colonial days: "One of sour, two of sweet, three of strong and four of weak." The sour is lime, the sweet is cane juice, the strong is rum and the weak is water (more likely to be fruit juice nowadays). Mix these ingredients and sprinkle a little grated nutmeg on top, and you have a genuine Caribbean rum punch. ......■**

Practically every Caribbean island distills its own rum, but the main producers are Cuba and Puerto Rico, where rums are traditionally light in color, and Barbados and Jamaica, where they are darker and fuller in flavor. On the French islands some of the finer rums are aged and then laid down to mellow, to be drunk like a brandy after dinner. Most islands also produce a white rum for local consumption, which is sold in roadside rum shops.

Rum is a by-product of sugar, distilled from the fermented juice of sugar cane or a mix of cane-juice and molasses. Visits can often be arranged to rum distilleries, full of gurgling vats and stills, and the heady, sweet smell of fermentation. All distillations of rum result in a clear liquid; darker rums gain their color from the addition of caramel during the ageing process, and from the oak barrels in which the rum is stored. Barrels of rum were used as currency in colonial times, when rum first became an important export.

Perhaps the most famous rum manufacturer is Bacardi, which was based in Cuba before its revolution but now works mainly from Puerto Rico, where there is a huge factory outside San Juan. In Jamaica the biggest name is Appleton, producing gold rums of different ages and a strong white rum known as John Crow Batty (crow's backside). The Appleton factory can be reached from Montego Bay. From Barbados come Mountgay and Cockspur, as well as white rums such as Alleynes, and producers based on the French islands include Rhum St. James and Trois Rivieres of Martinique (both of which can be visited).

Camerhogne, a mixture of rum, spices and fruit from Grenada

Rum history
Rum first appeared in Barbados in about 1650, when it was known as "kill-devil" and "rumbullion." Pirates would drink an explosive mixture of rum and gunpowder. British sailors were entitled to a daily measure of rum from the 18th century until 1970.

221

The Morgan Lewis Mill

▶▶ Scotland

Scotland is a hilly district in the northeast of Barbados; a series of peaks, including Mount Hillaby, the island's highest, overlook the Atlantic coast. This remote district makes an interesting half-day drive, through isolated settlements where villagers collect water from standpipes.

The Flower Forest▶▶, just off Highway 2, has marked paths lined with trees such as mango and breadfruit, with their green cannonball-sized fruits, and a fine show of tropical blooms such as hibiscus and poinsettia. **Turner's Hall Woods▶** are the last remaining area of the natural woodland that covered Barbados until it was cleared for sugar plantations. Here you can see trees native to the island—fustic, West Indian locust, and sand-box trees—as well as birds and monkeys such as the Lesser Antillean bullfinch and the black Carib grackles.

In the days when it was carpeted with sugar cane, Barbados had about 500 windmills, whose sails turned constantly in the Trade Winds, driving the millstones that crushed the sugar cane to release its juice. The **Morgan Lewis Mill▶** is the last surviving example, and although it does not actually turn, the old crushing gear is on view. Close by, the **Barbados Wildlife Reserve▶▶** is a free-range reserve with paths laid out in a mahogany wood, where agouti, spectacled cayman (which looks like an alligator), and iguanas roam. A café in the grounds sells a range of snacks and Caribbean fruit juices flavored with mango or bitter tamarind.

St. Nicholas Abbey▶▶, in northern Scotland, is not actually an abbey, but a plantation house that was still working until the 1930s. An absorbing film shows shots of turn-of-the-century Barbados, with sugar workers, turning windmills, and "mauby ladies" serving the bitter mauby drink from vats which they carried on their heads.

► South Coast

The south coast of Barbados has a completely different feel from the better known, more sedate west coast. It attracts a younger, livelier crowd and lays a greater emphasis on activity outside the hotels, which are smaller and less expensive (package tourists often end up in this area, and there are also guesthouses here). Visitors tend to spend their days sunning themselves and windsurfing on the beaches; in the evenings they pour into the restaurants and bars, moving on to the clubs in St. Lawrence Gap and Bridgetown, where dancing and live music continue until the early hours. There are places to explore in the southeast, where isolated coves include Foul Bay, Harrismith Beach, and Bottom Bay, but most life centers around the "gaps," the small roads that lead down to the coast off Highway 7.

Highway 7 leads from Bridgetown past the Garrison Savannah and through the seemingly never-ending urbanized sprawl of Hastings, St. Lawrence and Worthing (hotels in this area are the Divi Southwinds Beach Resort, the Casuarina Beach Club, Southern Palms, and Sandy Lane Hotel). Further east, the Crane Beach Hotel sits on a hill-top overlooking the Atlantic. St. Lawrence Gap is set on a small bay where there are watersports facilities and two good restaurants: David's Place and, on the other side of the bay, Pisces. Around the corner is the main area for nightlife, where Bajan bands play to packed crowds. There is usually a friendly atmosphere, but tourists have been robbed here, and you should be careful.

Beyond Maxwell, known for its windsurfing, is Barbados's fourth town, Oistins, a fishing community where the daily catch is sold on the waterfront. Inland, **Sunbury Plantation House and Museum►►** is set in a sugar estate house that dates from the 1660s, when the cultivation of cane on a large scale had just begun. The house has been restored and in the gardens there is a collection of carts and carriages from the 19th century.

Watching the world from a rum shop

Bajan dishes
Whatever it has taken from the British in other respects, Barbados owes little to them in the way of food. Bajan fare depends more on local ingredients, including fish and local vegetables such as yam, plantain, and sweet potato, cooked according to Amerindian and African techniques. Pepperpot is a strong tasting Amerindian stew made with meat and vegetables and served with traditional Caribbean rice and peas, cooked in coconut milk or with pumpkin fritters. Local fish and chicken are usually curried and served in Creole sauces of pepper, tomato, and onion.

223

Sam Lord
Sam Lord's Castle, in Long Bay in the southeast, is now a large hotel, but it has a grim history. It was built in 1820 by Sam Lord, a scoundrel who imprisoned his wife (she eventually escaped), and made a fortune by defrauding and, some say, murdering rich victims. He is also said to have made a pretty penny by plundering ships that he lured onto the rocks by hanging lanterns in the trees at night to fool sailors into thinking they had spotted a harbor. He would then bring his haul along an underground passage to the castle. The tale may be fanciful—the underground passage is fictitious—but Sam Lord and his crooked ways were real enough.

Trinidad and Tobago

Curfew parties
The Trinidadian tradition of partying is not confined to Carnival. In 1990 Abu Bakr and a group of Muslim activists stormed the Parliament building, in an attempt to stage a coup. A night curfew was imposed, and the islanders promptly introduced the "curfew party," for which people would lock themselves overnight into each other's houses. Eventually these had to be stopped, due to the high incidence of accidents caused by drunk drivers on their way home in the morning.

This two-island nation offers a vivid contrast between bustling, cosmopolitan Trinidad and peaceful, rural Tobago. Trinidad is loud, lively, and full of ethnic and cultural diversity; Tobago is less developed and more traditionally Caribbean, with its pretty beaches and rolling countryside. Port of Spain attracts hundreds of thousands of spectators to its exhilarating carnival, while Tobago is a better option for those looking for a quieter dose of sand and sun.

This southernmost nation of the Caribbean lies off the coast of South America. Trinidad was still joined to the continent 10,000 years ago and in some places its mountains (the Southern, Northern, and Central ranges), fertile plains, and mangrove swamps are separated from Venezuela by only 10 miles of water. Its spectacular flora and fauna are similar to the mainland's; there are hundreds of species of butterflies and birds (more than can be found on any other Caribbean

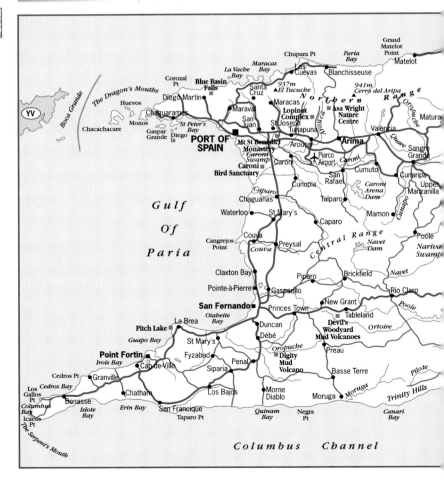

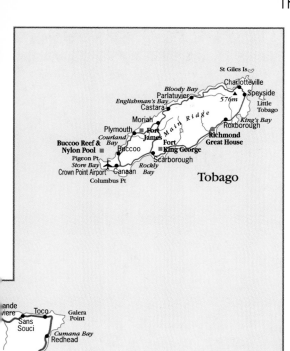

St Giles Is
Charlotteville
Bloody Bay
Parlatuvier
Englishman's Bay
Castara
Speyside
576m
Little Tobago
Moriah
Main Ridge
King's Bay
Plymouth
Courland Bay
Fort James
Roxborough
Buccoo Reef &
Nylon Pool
Buccoo
Richmond Great House
Fort King George
Pigeon Pt
Store Bay
Scarborough
Crown Point Airport
Canaan
Rockly Bay
Columbus Pt
Tobago

ande
viere
Toco
Galera Point
Sans Souci
Cumana Bay
Redhead
Rampanalgas
alybia
Balandra Bay
Saline Bay
Matura Bay
Lower Manzanilla
Manzanilla Bay
Cocos Bay
Trinidad
Guatuaro Pt
Pierreville
Mayaro Bay
Guayaguayare
Galeota Point
ran Cayo Pt

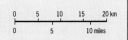

| 0 | 5 | 10 | 15 | 20 km |
| 0 | | 5 | | 10 miles |

225

Festivals
Divali is celebrated in Trinidad during October or November and honors Lakshmi, the Hindu goddess of light. During the festival, followers go from one open house to the next, drinking and feasting, and hundreds of coconut oil lamps are lit in small clay pots, illuminating whole valleys. Phagwa is celebrated in the streets in March with huge paper floats and bottles of red food dye, which is thrown over spectators, and Hosay (dates vary) commemorates the martyrdom of Hussein and features a parade of his tomb, accompanied by dancers and drummers.

island), including 15 varieties of hummingbird and the scarlet ibis—the national bird—which can be seen flying in to roost in the Caroni Swamp (situated just south of Port of Spain) during the evening.

Tobago broke off from the continent in an earlier geological age and lies 22 miles northeast of Trinidad. Its spine of volcanic mountains, the Main Ridge, is mantled with rainforest, which descends to a plain in the southwest. Much of the coastline is gouged with steep-sided bays and the underwater slopes are clad with corals, but in the gentler western end of the island there are some fine white sand beaches that are well worth seekng out.

History Christopher Columbus landed on Trinidad in 1498, during his third voyage to the Americas, and named it in honor of the Holy Trinity. During the 16th century, the island was used as a Spanish staging post in the search for El Dorado, the Golden One, whose kingdom was thought to be on the mainland near here. Tobago was probably not seen by Columbus, but after Europeans had settled there in the mid-17th century, there followed fierce battles for its possession, and the island changed hands more times than any other island in the Caribbean before it was eventually taken into British ownership in 1814.

Trinidad and Tobago were politically linked in 1888 and remained a British colony until 1962, so they retain similarities to other English-speaking islands in the area—but theirs is a far more complex heritage. Spanish names can still be found, and there are strong traces of French Creole, a legacy of the Royalist settlers who fled from France during the Revolution. The locals joke that when the British took over, Trinidad became a Caribbean island with a French population, governed by the British according to Spanish laws.

A house in Buccoo, Tobago

Island life The British added new strains to Trinidad's already potent mix of peoples, shipping in African slaves to work the sugar plantations and, later, after emancipation, turning to Asian "East" Indian, Chinese, and Middle Eastern immigrants, who worked as indentured laborers. The result is that Trinidad has a cosmopolitan population, of which nearly half is made up of descendents of Indian immigrants. Hindi, Spanish, and French are spoken as well as English; parish churches stand side by side with Islamic minarets; Indian and Chinese restaurants operate alongside tropical fruit stalls; and Hindu and Muslim festivals such as Divali and Hosay are celebrated as well as the Caribbean Carnival.

Tobago was also a plantation island and most of its population is of African descent, but for the traveler and the tourist, the two islands offer radically different experiences. Trinidad has a vibrant cultural life—theaters, a concert hall and festivals—while Tobago is altogether quieter (Trinidadians tend to go there for a rest), with secluded sandy coves. Trinidad is the place to experience hectic Caribbean bustle. Its mini-buses, or "maxi-taxis," are the liveliest and loudest in the area, thumping and pulsing to the local sound, soca, a racing rhythm with a double beat. A visit to a calypso evening, or a "Tent" at Carnival time, is an essential Trinidadian experience (even though the language and repartee are hard to follow); the songs, which deal with island gossip and current affairs, are performed with great gusto by popular calypsonians, especially in the days leading up to the ultimate Trinidadian experience—**Carnival▶▶▶** (see pages 234–5). After a week of steel bands (which were invented here) and calypso shows, Carnival culminates on Mardi Gras with a two-day pageant around the streets of Port of Spain, with hundreds of thousands of costumed revelers dancing in the streets.

Bamboo cannon
Loud explosions resounding through a Trinidadian valley (or elsewhere in the Caribbean) may indicate that someone has been given a bamboo cannon, a popular child's toy that is still used at Caribbean festivities. The cannon is made by hollowing out a length of bamboo, leaving only the bottom section untouched. A small hole is then cut about 6 in. from the end and kerosene is poured inside and warmed so that it turns into gas, which is lit with touchpaper, causing a heart-stopping bang.

Trinidad

Miguel Street is an imaginary setting, created by Trinidadian writer V.S. Naipaul in his novel of the same name, but it has all the characters and life of a typical West Indian town. It could speak for many places in the Caribbean, but Naipaul, perhaps the Caribbean's best-known writer, was born in Trinidad and set his story in Port of Spain, the island's capital.

Port of Spain is a large, active, modern city of about 300,000 people, lying on the Gulf of Paria in the northwest. In style it's a typical Caribbean mix, with modern glass-fronted high-rises and traditional Creole wooden houses overlooking the bustling streets, where vendors sell wares from their carefully arranged stalls. The heart of the town (or at least its traffic system) is Independence Square, a wide avenue a couple of blocks in from the waterfront. Perpendicular to the Square is one of the city's main shopping areas, Frederick Street. A walk up this street (driving is down only) brings you to Woodford Square, named after Governor Woodford, who had the town re-built in 1813 after its destruction by fire five years earlier. On the square's western side is the **Red House►►**, Trinidad's parliament building, a massive Victorian pile whose two chambers can be visited, and diagonally opposite is the Anglican Cathedral of the Holy Trinity. The center of the square, tree-shaded and surrounded by very British-looking iron railings, is a gathering place where people gossip and chat about politics and less weighty topics. This was the spot where Dr. Eric Williams, the leader of Trinidad for many years before and after Independence, held his political rallies.

Further along Frederick Street, beyond the Tourist Information Office (Nos. 134–8) is the **National Museum and Art Gallery►►**, where displays of

Trinidadian dishes
Trinidad's food is as varied as its racial heritage, and includes Indian, Chinese, and French as well as Caribbean cuisine. Probably the finest local fare can be bought at Veni Mange, at 13 Lucknow Street, St. James, where two sisters prepare meals for lunch only. The breakfast sheds on the waterfront in downtown Port of Spain sell rice and peas or callaloo at good prices, and street stalls sell snacks such as *rotis* (crêpe-like envelopes filled with chicken, beef, shrimp, or potato stew) or doubles (unleavened bread doubled over with a filling of split peas). Another local delicacy is the mangrove oyster, which is picked off the aerial roots of mangrove trees and eaten raw with a squeeze of lime.

King George III's cypher on the cannon that once protected Trinidad from rival European powers

Beer advertisement, Trinidad

Trinidad historical and cultural life include the latest Carnival costumes. There is also an exhibition of the paintings of Trinidadian artist Michel Cazabon.

Just north of Frederick Street, Port of Spain's vast central park, the 200-acre **Savannah►►**, is where Trinidadians go to walk, jog, play cricket, hockey and football, go to the races, and buy their chilled coconuts and evening snacks. Look for the spectacularly extravagant houses on the park's western side.

Among the plants displayed in the **Botanic Gardens►►**, north of the Savannah, are the red blossoms of the Trinidad national flower, the chaconia, a wild poinsettia that takes its name from the last Spanish Governor, and an orchid collection. Local animals such as the jaguar-like, buff-brown ocelot are kept in the **Emperor Valley Zoo►**, next door to the grounds of the Presidential House.

Outside Port of Spain Beyond **Fort George►**, an old defensive bastion with a line of cannons covering the approaches to Port of Spain, the Western Main Road passes through some of the city's prosperous suburbs and continues to the northwestern Chaguaramas peninsula. During World War II this was an American base and in the 1950s it was hoped that it would house the parliament building for the ill-fated Federation of the West Indies, in which the islands of the British Caribbean would come together in one political unit. (Trinidad and Tobago left the Federation to seek full independence after the secession of Jamaica.) A golf course is laid out near by, and the Anchorage is a popular swimming area, though the beach itself is not very attractive. There are caves on Gaspard Grande Island, in the channel, and at the end of the peninsula is the Dragons' Mouths, the short channel that separates Trinidad from the Venezuelan coast.

Views of the past
C.L.R. James and Eric Williams were two Trinidadian historians who between them overturned the conventional colonial view of British Caribbean history. James, who lived in London until his death in 1989, was a Marxist historian, best known for his account of the Haitian Revolution, *The Black Jacobins*. Williams, whose works include *From Columbus to Castro* and *A History of the Peoples of Trinidad and Tobago*, was Prime Minister of Trinidad for many years until his death in 1981.

■   **When Europeans first arrived in the Caribbean, turtles provided a reliable source of food because they could be kept alive on their backs on board ship. Today, numbers have dwindled drastically, and some species of turtle are endangered. Their eggs (highly prized by some as an aphrodisiac) are often stolen and the turtles themselves are particularly vulnerable since they lay their eggs on the beach. .....■**

Turtles are seaborne reptiles with hard shells and flippers, which have remained basically unchanged for 250 million years. Five species of turtle live in the Caribbean: the loggerhead, the hawksbill, the ridley, the green turtle (once the most common, but now endangered), and, largest of all, the leatherback (also endangered), which can dive to 5,000 ft., weigh up to 1,550 lb. and live to 150. Caribbean leatherbacks have been known to cross the Atlantic and swim as far north as Newfoundland.

The most fascinating part of a turtle's life-cycle is the way the young are hatched. The female leatherback nests between April and June, arriving at night (often returning

Helping the hatchlings
Earthwatch (U.S. tel. 617 926 8200, U.K. tel. 0865 311600) sponsors a project to protect leatherback turtles in St. Croix (the largest population of leatherbacks in the U.S.). Volunteers can take part in nightly patrols to collect data on nesting females (measuring and tagging the turtles, counting eggs, and relocating nests in erosion zones). They also help hatchlings that are disoriented by the lights of Frederiksted, and keep predators away while they reach the sea.

He or she
The sex of a turtle, like that of alligators and crocodiles, is determined by the temperature of the nest; the warmer the weather, the more females are hatched. Hatchlings tend to be male early in the season (the beginning of the year) and females later on, when the temperatures warm up.

to the beach from which she originally came) and crawling laboriously up onto the beach to a point above the high water mark. For two hours she digs a hole with her hind flippers, to a depth of about 18 in., and lays up to 200 eggs, each the size of a billiard ball. Then she covers them with sand and crawls back into the sea. The process is repeated perhaps 10 times during the season.

Over the next eight weeks the eggs incubate, and eventually the 4-in. hatchlings dig their way to the surface and set off for the sea, running the gauntlet of predators; apart from humans, herons and crabs lie in wait, and mongeese will actually dig them out of their nests. There is safety only in numbers.

Several Caribbean hotels can arrange special trips to watch turtles nesting, and at the turtle farm on Grand Cayman, in the Cayman Islands, visitors see turtles at different stages of their development.

Whitehall, Port of Spain

The beaches nearest to Port of Spain are on the north coast, beyond the mountains of the Northern Range, which tower above the city. The best route, and the most spectacular drive, is through the Maraval Valley. Maracas Bay, 1 mile wide, is flanked by massive headlands, thrown off by El Tucuche, Trinidad's highest peak. Here, the water is occasionally rough; it is calmer at Las Cuevas, a few miles beyond it, where there are beach facilities. From the north coast fishing village of Blanchisseuse a road leads southwards across the Northern Range, providing another long, twisting, and visually stunning drive.

The Eastern Main Road leads from just behind the waterfront in downtown Port of Spain towards St. Joseph, the original Spanish capital of the island. It then passes between the Northern Range and the northern edge of the **Caroni Swamp▶▶▶**, which harbors about half of the island's bird species, including the scarlet ibis, which flies in during the evening. It is said that up to 12,000 ibises can be roosting here at a time, and tours (with a guide) start at around 4:30p.m. Angostura Bitters is produced in a factory in St. Joseph which is open to visitors (see panel), and high above the town is the **Mount St. Benedict Monastery▶**, a peaceful spot with a fine view over the central plain.

A few miles up the Arouca river the **Lopinot Complex▶▶** is an old cocoa estate cut into the huge valley early in the 19th century by the Comte de Lopinot, a refugee from turbulent Saint Domingue (Haiti). Part of the original estate house survives, set in pleasant gardens where Trinidadians picnic at the weekends. Early in the year the immortelle trees that were planted to shade the cocoa plants burst into a blaze of orange blooms. Several Amerindian descendants live in this area, where many locals speak French patois.

Angostura Bitters
Trinidad is the home of the world-famous aromatic Angostura Bitters, often added to cocktails. The business was started by the Venezuelan Siegert family in the 19th century, and the recipe is a secret, but involves a mixture of roots, barks, dried leaves, and spices with alcohol, boiled to give the dark bitters. The Angostura factory, on the main road to St. Joseph, is open to visitors (tel: 623 1841).

V.S. Naipaul
Vidiadhar Surajprasad
Naipaul was born of a
Brahmin family in Trinidad
in 1932 and educated at
Queen's Royal College,
Port of Spain, and
University College, Oxford.
Many of his novels express
pessimistic and critical
views of his native culture.
A House for Mr Biswas
(1961), whose hero is
based on Naipaul's father,
describes the collapse of
the Caribbean way of life,
and his earliest books, *The
Mystic Masseur* (1957),
The Suffrage of Elvira
(1958), and *Miguel Street*
(1959) all satirize life and
politics in Trinidad.

In the Arima Valley is another delightful retreat, the
Asa Wright Nature Centre▶▶▶, a balconied estate
house looking out onto a vast, green valley. Here you
can hear the strange "boing, boing" call of bell-birds
and see the colorful flash of a toucan or an oro pendula
in flight. Guided walks are offered in the grounds.

Beyond Valencia, southeast of the nature center, the
strip of urban development gives way to forested and
cultivated land. The road forks here and heads south
towards the Atlantic coast at Manzanilla or north via
Balandra to Toco, where there are good beaches.

To reach the south of the country from Port of Spain,
turn right on the Uriah Butler Highway, just out of town,
which skirts the Caroni Swamp and then heads out into
the cane fields. The first major town is Chaguanas; V.S.
Naipaul lived here and the house described in *A House
for Mr Biswas* stands on Main Street. The road continues to San Fernando, Trinidad's second city; en route, it
passes the Pointe-à-Pierre oil refinery, a reminder that
oil was at one time the island's chief export, funding its
highways and development during the boom years
before oil prices fell.

Trinidadians refer to the wilder country beyond San
Fernando as the Deep South. At the town of La Brea,
about 10 miles along the coast from San Fernando, is
one of Trinidad's oddest attractions, the **Pitch Lake▶▶**,
a 100-acre cauldron of natural asphalt, fed by tar from
beneath and forever turning; occasionally branches,
ancient artifacts, and even bones are pushed up to the
surface. It is worked as a mine and the pitch has been
used in roads all over the world.

Maracus Bay, Trinidad

Tobago

A steel band performer making music on Tobago

With few large hotels and no crowds, this little island (only 20 miles by 6 miles) still has a tranquil charm. Tourism has gravitated around the southwestern tip of the island, where the best beaches are to be found, but elsewhere there are deserted coves set in the sinuous coastline, and quiet West Indian villages.

Most people arrive on Tobago at Crown Point Airport, on the far southwestern tip of the island. From here it is a short walk to most of the guesthouses and small hotels and to **Store Bay►►**, one of the island's liveliest beaches, where breakfast sheds have been set up selling such local dishes as "bakes" or "Johnny Cakes," served with salt fish buljol.

Just north of Store Bay is the island's most popular beach, **Pigeon Point►►**, where there are palm-thatch bars and watersports. An entry charge has to be paid, but some people avoid it by walking in below the high-

Carnival

■ Trinidad's annual carnival is the Caribbean's largest, liveliest, and most flamboyant party. For two days before Lent, hundreds of thousands of revelers flood onto the streets of Port of Spain, clad in bright lycra, sequins, and feathered head-dresses, and dance in "bands" of a thousand or more, all shuffling and strutting in rhythm. Mas, as it is familiarly known, has been adopted by other islands all over the Caribbean, but the Trinidadians still claim to do it better than anyone else. .....■

Mas has its roots in Catholic pre-Lenten festivities of two centuries ago, in which the Trinidadian French Creoles would visit one another's houses for masked balls. After emancipation in the 1830s, ex-slaves adopted the masquerade, turning it into a drum-driven street-party. Suppressed by the authorities many times, it has grown since World War II into a massive, exuberant celebration.

Carnival begins to warm up soon after Christmas, when the calypsonians (see page 238) release their songs and the steel band preliminaries are held. "Mas Camps" are busily sewing the costumes to be worn by the carnival players—including the huge King and Queen costumes—which can be designed up to a year in advance, and depict themes such as birdlife or pirates.

The real action begins during the weekend before the beginning of Lent. On the Friday night, a competition is held to select the winning King and Queen of the Bands—magnificent centerpiece figures which can be up to 35 ft. tall and are lavishly constructed.

These pirates—in carnival mood—sport sunglasses and wristwatches

Carnival

On Saturday the children take their turn in Kiddies Carnival, and in the evening Panorama, the finals of the steel band competition (see pages 80–1), features the last eight steel bands, many 60 players strong, competing for the year's top title.

The Calypso Competition finals are held on Sunday night, with calypsonians vying for the year's most prestigious singing title, the Calypso Monarch. During the evening the winners of the King and Queen of the Band competitions put in an appearance.

On Monday the dancing begins and the revelers are out on the streets by 4 a.m. for jouvert (from the French Créole *jour ouvert*, but pronounced "jouvay"), with music provided exclusively by steel bands. Leading the parade are impish "djab-djabs" (from the French *diable*) and "moko-jumbies" who walk on stilts. Many dancers cover themselves in axle grease and mud (snazzily dressed onlookers are liable to be hugged). Jouvert comes to an end at about 9 a.m., and is followed by more music and dancing by the Carnival Bands.

Tuesday, Mardi Gras, is the day of the main procession and judging day for the Carnival Bands. These assemble early in the morning and begin their procession around the streets, passing the three main judging areas—Independence Square, Adam Smith Square in Woodbrook, and the Savannah. Each Band, which may have as many as two or three thousand players, is divided into sections, with players dressed in different costumes. At the rear of each Band are the King and Queen. Music is provided by trucks interspersed among the sections, and the noise is deafening. In the full heat of the Trinidadian sun, dancing is especially exhausting work, and the players usually employ someone to wheel a portable bar around. By dusk carnival is finished and the players can finally retire to bed.

Although most Caribbean carnivals are held on Mardi Gras and run along similar lines, some islands stage them in the summer, to celebrate the end of the cane-cutting season. In Barbados, Cropover is on the first Monday in August, and in Cuba, the Zafra celebrations are at the end of July. Perhaps the most enjoyable feature of Caribbean carnivals is that, unlike those of Rio or New Orleans, they are open to anyone to join in and dance.

Carnival dances

Dances go in and out of vogue year by year, but the traditional step is the "chip," in which players drag their feet and swing their knees and hips, occasionally throwing their arms up in the air. Wining and grinding are dances in which players move their hips with their legs wide apart, sometimes alone, sometimes pushing up against another dancer (or in a conga). Groins and backsides feature prominently in the dance and partners perform in all imaginable combinations (back to back, back to front, etc).

Carnival designers

Carnival costume design is very big business in Trinidad. Peter Minshall is perhaps the best known of the carnival designers and his very elaborate creations, such as "Carnival is Colour" and "Jungle Fever," have won the Band of the Year prize several times. Other winning designers include Wayne Berkeley, an international stage set-designer who has been a leading competitor for over 20 years, and Raoul Garib.

235

water mark (as in most of the Caribbean, the sand below the high-water mark is not private).

Offshore are two Tobagonian landmarks: **Buccoo Reef►►**, which you can visit by glass-bottom boat, and the **Nylon Pool►►**, a waist-deep area of warm water with a silky, sandy bottom and colorful coral and fish. On the other side of the bay is the village of **Buccoo►►**, where fishing boats with brightly painted diamond patterns lie on the sands. Hendrix bar in Buccoo is the site of a weekly jump-up known as **Sunday School►►**.

Past Mount Irvine Bay, the site of Tobago's 18-hole golf course, and Stonehaven Bay (both good beaches), is Courland Bay. The name Courland has a strange origin: it comes from a principality in what is now Latvia, from which a number of settlements of Tobago were attempted in the 17th century. At the head of Courland Bay is **Plymouth►**, Tobago's second town, where there are just a couple of streets and Fort James, on the point overlooking the bay. **Back Bay►►**, on the other side of Plymouth, is an attractive stretch of sand.

Drinks-shack-cum-vegetable stall, Tobago

Beaching a boat on the Tobago shore

Beyond Plymouth, the road winds into Tobago's countryside, through hillside villages such as Les Coteaux and Moriah, before descending to the coast and a series of sandy, palm-backed bays: **Castara▶▶**, **Englishman's Bay▶▶▶**, and **Parlatuvier▶▶**. From Bloody Bay the main road leads up into the **Tobago Forest Reserve▶▶**, a rainforest with walking trails, reaching the south coast at Roxborough.

Scarborough▶ is the capital of Tobago, a quiet and undistinguished town set over the hills above Rockly Bay on the south coast. About 10,000 of the island's 55,000 inhabitants live here. At the top of the hill is the town's old defense, **Fort King George▶**, where there is a museum of Tobago history and a small gallery of paintings; and on the other side of town are the **Botanical Gardens▶**.

The road to the eastern end of the island winds its way along the palm-backed south coast, in and out of huge bays and through small Tobagonian settlements. **Richmond Great House▶** is an old wooden estate house, now restored, recalling Tobago's days as a plantation island. A 15-minute walk from Roxborough, near the junction of the inland and coastal roads, is the **Argyle Waterfall▶▶**, a three-stepped cascade where you can take a swim after the walk. There is another waterfall at **King's Bay▶**, to the east of Roxborough.

After climbing an impossibly steep hill the road reaches Speyside and then Charlotteville (lying at the island's eastern tip), two quiet Tobagonian towns with guesthouses, in the island's best scuba diving area.

The frigatebird
The magnificent frigatebird, or Man-o'-War bird, nests on Tobago's northeastern cliffs. With its dark plumage, scissor-shaped tail, and a wingspan of over 3 ft., this is an impressive but aggressive bird which attacks other species for their food. It swoops from above or behind, shaking the victim until it disgorges its meal. Tours of Tobago's wildlife are arranged by David Rooks (tel: 639 9408).

■ **Calypso is a flamboyant and witty singing tradition that originated in Trinidad. Styles range from rap to serenade, and lyrics touch on life, the universe, and everything. Some have a socially conscious edge; some are political; some are gossipy, and others are just plain "slack" (raunchy). But all calypsos entertain, and they jam the airwaves during the run-up to Carnival every year. .....■**

Calypso stars

Most calypsonians adopt colorful singing names. The most popular prefixes are "The Mighty" and "Lord," and past winners include The Mighty Sniper and Lord Pretender. The two biggest names in the world of calypso are The Mighty Sparrow (alias Slinger Francisco), who first won the Calypso King title in 1956 and who, because of his saucy lyrics, has been crowned seven times since, and Lord Kitchener (Aldwyn Roberts), who is known for composing steel band songs and has won the Roadmarch title 11 times. Other names include Watchman (a policeman) and The Mighty Chalkdust (a schoolteacher). Calypsos are sung fast, in local dialect, so to get the best out of a calypso evening visitors should find out about the songs before hearing them performed.

Calypso is a legacy of Trinidad's dual African and French heritage. The first known calypsonian or "shantwell" was Gros Jean, who sang for a French planter 200 years ago. Since the beginning of this century calypsos have been sung in English, the language of Trinidad, and as their popularity has increased, other English-speaking Caribbean islands have adopted the tradition.

Calypsos are the major musical force behind Carnival, at the beginning of Lent each year (see pages 234–5). There are three main calypso competitions. The Roadmarch competition judges the year's best dancing tune in the parties (fêtes) and in the Carnival parade. The title is won by the calypsonian whose song is played most as the Carnival bands cross the judging stages.

In Ex-tempo, two calypsonians compete in quickfire singing, alternating verse by verse. A topic written on a piece of paper is handed to the singers, who are given 30 seconds to prepare a calypso. Teasing the opponent is more important than rhyme or meter, and the winner is usually the person who gets the biggest laugh.

The most coveted and fiercely contested title is the Calypso Monarch (changed from Calypso King when women entered the field). Calypsonians release their songs in January, so that they become well known on the radio. Then they perform in calypso "tents," acting the songs out in an attempt to be selected for further rounds. Calypso Monarch finals are held on the Sunday before Lent—a cross between a variety show and a comedy evening. Calypsonians perform to huge audiences, making digs at the other singers and adding topical comments to their songs to provoke a response from the crowd.

TRAVEL FACTS

GENERAL INFORMATION

Arriving

The best way of getting to the Caribbean is to put yourself in the hands of experienced tour operators, who nearly always command the best rates from airlines. Airlines with regular scheduled services from the United States include Delta, American Airlines, British Airways, BWIA International, Virgin Atlantic, KLM, Lufthansa, Iberia and Air France. In addition there are numerous charter flights to the more popular destinations, mainly during the winter season (December to April). It is possible to buy three types of Liat Air Pass, which enable island-hopping: the Liat Caribbean Explorer (valid up to 21 days, maximum three stopovers), the Liat Eastern Caribbean Air Pass (maximum 21 days, minimum three stopovers, maximum six) and the Liat Super Caribbean Explorer (linking the Caribbean with Guyana and Venezuela, maximum stay 30 days, unlimited stopovers).

BWIA International (tel: 071 839 9333) also offers an Air Pass: unlimited travel for 30 days, though backtracking not allowed.

Departure tax is payable from most islands; this varies and there may be exemptions for children.

Cruising is another popular way of seeing a little of a lot of places. Cruise lines offering trips to the Caribbean include: Carnival; Celebrity; Costa; Cunard; Dolphin; Fantasy; Holland America; Norwegian; Premier; Princess; Regency; Seabourn; Seawind; and Windstar.

Camping and student/youth travel

In general camping is discouraged, particularly on the beaches. Few islands have designated campsites, and there are very few youth hostels. In Barbados, the Girl Guides (Girl Scouts), Boy Scouts and Cadet Corps conduct organized camping for their worldwide counterparts.

The Caribbean is not known for budget accommodations, but there are inexpensive guesthouses and diving lodges on many islands, which

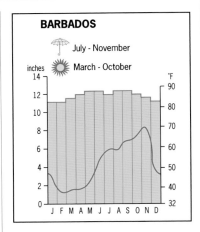

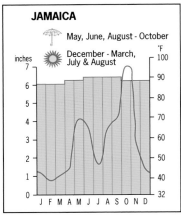

usually do not appear in tourist brochures. Write to tourist offices for a list.

Car rental

See individual island entries.

Climate

Broadly speaking, temperatures average 78°F–85°F but are lower the greater the altitude. October and November are the wettest months (June in Trinidad and Tobago); December to May is the driest period.

Crime

Attacks and robberies are rare; the most hassle you are likely to encounter is from persistent souvenirs salespersons. There is a good deal of poverty, which brings with it the temptation to petty theft.

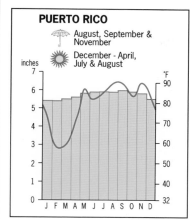

PUERTO RICO

☂ August, September & November

☀ December - April, July & August

Keep doors locked, take care of your valuables and watch where you walk after dark. Don't take too much money out with you and don't make too conspicuous a display of wealth by wearing expensive jewelry or producing large wads of money. Most hotels have safes, either in the rooms or at the reception desk. Report lost property first to the hotel or apartment manager, and then to the police and/or the tourist board.

Dialing codes
Numbers given in the text below do not include the international dialing code, so they should be prefaced with the relevant numbers if you are calling from abroad or from an island with a different code.

0101 809 for Jamaica, the Cayman Islands, Dominican Republic, Puerto Rico, U.S. Virgin Islands, Anguilla, Antigua and Barbuda, Montserrat, Nevis, St. Kitts, Dominica, Grenada, St. Vincent and the Grenadines, St. Lucia, Barbados, Trinidad and Tobago. 010 599 followed by: Bonaire (7), Curaçao (9), Sint Maarten (5), Saba (4) and Sint Eustatius (3).
0101 809 49 for the British Virgin Islands.
010 2978 for Aruba.
010 590 for Guadeloupe, St. Barts, Saint-Martin.
010 596 for Martinique.

Travelers with Disabilities
The Caribbean is not particularly well-equipped to handle the needs of travelers with disabilities. Many hotels are built on hillsides, which makes wheelchair access difficult. The Jamaica Tourist Board does have a list of hotels with facilities for the handicapped; Trinidad and Tobago do, too, but you'd be well advised to check exactly what the facilities are before booking. Individual island tourist boards can certainly find out more details about specific properties that might be suitable.

Emergency telephone numbers
These telephone numbers are in the process of being standardized. Make sure you check the relevant numbers on arrival.
Anguilla Police and ambulance: 911
Antigua and Barbuda Police and ambulance 999
Aruba Police: 100; ambulance: 115
Barbados Police: 112; ambulance: 115
Bonaire Police: 11; ambulance: 14
Curaçao Police: 114; ambulance: 112
Cayman Islands Police: 911; ambulance: 555/911
Dominica Police and ambulance: 999
Dominican Republic Police and ambulance: 711
Grenada Police: 911; ambulance: 434
Guadeloupe Police: 17; ambulance: 82 89 33
Jamaica Police: 119; ambulance: 110
Martinique Police: 17; ambulance: 71 59 48
Montserrat Police: 999; ambulance: 911
Puerto Rico Police: 343 2020; ambulance: 343 2500
Saba Police: 63237; ambulance: 63288
St. Barts Police: 27 66 66; ambulance: 27 60 85
St. Eustatius Police: 82333; ambulance: 82211
St. Kitts and Nevis Police and ambulance: 911
St. Lucia Police and ambulance: 999
Saint-Martin Police: 17; ambulance: 18
Sint Maarten Police: 22222; ambulance: 22111
St. Vincent Police and ambulance: 999
Trinidad and Tobago Police: 999; ambulance: 990

241

Virgin Islands (British) Police and ambulance: 999
Virgin Islands (U.S.) Police: 915; ambulance: 922.

Health

Immunization against yellow fever may be required if you are arriving from an infected area. Otherwise immunization is not generally required, but typhoid, polio and tetanus shots are often recommended, as well as hepatitis A for those staying outside tourist areas. Consult your doctor before leaving.

Health insurance should be taken out before you travel, and those on regular medication should take supplies with them in case they are not sold on the island. Tapwater is not always safe to drink. Check your destination on arrival.

Money

On islands where the official currency is the Eastern Caribbean dollar (EC$), the exchange rate is fixed to the U.S. dollar and U.S. currency is widely accepted: **Anguilla; Antigua; Dominica; Grenada; Montserrat; Nevis; St. Kitts; St. Lucia; St. Vincent.**

Other currencies:
Aruba Aruban florin (AFI) (U.S. dollars accepted); **Barbados** Barbados dollar (BDS$) (U.S. dollars accepted); **Bonaire** Netherlands Antilles florin/guilder (NAf); **Cayman Islands** Caymanian dollar (C.I.$) (U.S. dollars accepted); **Curaçao** Netherlands Antilles florin/guilder (NAf); **Dominican Republic** Dominican peso (RD$); **Guadeloupe** French franc (FF); **Jamaica** Jamaican dollar (J$); **Martinique** French franc (FF); **Puerto Rico** U.S. dollar; **Saba** Netherlands Antilles florin/guilder (NAf) (U.S. dollars accepted); **St. Barts** French franc (FF); **St. Eustatius** Netherlands Antilles florin/guilder (NAf) (U.S. dollars accepted); **Saint-Martin** French franc (FF); **Sint Maarten** Netherlands Antilles guilder/florin (NAf) (U.S. dollars accepted); **Trinidad and Tobago** Trinidad and Tobago dollar (TT$); **Virgin Islands (British)** U.S. dollar; **Virgin Islands (U.S.)** U.S. dollar.

Public restrooms

There are not many of these, though some islands have basic beach facilities (not great), usually in conjunction with a rustic beach bar. Stick to hotels and restaurants.

Travel insurance

This should cover accident, health, baggage and possessions, cancellation, etc. If you are taken ill or have an accident, you will nearly always be expected to pay, and health care is generally not cheap in the Caribbean. Medicaments, if not already on the island, are usually flown in from the United States, and there are plenty of pharmacies for over-the-counter medicines. Make sure your insurance policy covers you in the event of a watersports accident—read the small print.

THE WINDWARD ISLANDS

DOMINICA

Car rental and driving

A local driver's license is required, obtainable from the airports or the Traffic Department, High Street, Roseau (Monday to Friday). You must be 25–65 and have had at least two years' driving experience and a valid driver's license.

Rental companies include **Anselm's** (tel: 448 2730), **Budget** (tel: 449 2080), **Fiesta Car Rentals** (tel: 448 3221), **Jerry's Car Rentals** (tel: 448 2559), **Pierro Auto Rental & Nature Safari** (tel: 448 5826), **STL Rent-a-Car** (tel: 448 2340); **Sag Motors** (tel: 449 1093), **Tropical Jeep Rentals** (tel: 448 4821), **Valley Rent-a-Car** (Roseau 448 3233; Portsmouth 445 5252), **Wide Range Car Rentals** (tel: 448 2198), good for four-wheel drive vehicles.

Driving is on the left. The main roads are well maintained; others are hazardous, with potholes and hairpin bends and a distinct lack of road signs. The speed limit is 20mph (32kph) in populated areas. Petrol is paid for in cash. Seatbelts are not mandatory, but recommended. Drunk-driving laws are enforced. Get an Ordnance Survey map from the Tourism Office in the Old Market, Roseau.

TRAVEL FACTS

Getting around
By air Nature Island Express (tel: 449 2309/448 4210) operates a daily service between Barbados, Dominica, St. Lucia and Sint Maarten. **Liat** (tel: 448 2421/2 or 449 1421 or 445 7242) links with Antigua, St. Lucia, and Sint Maarten. Air Guadeloupe and Air Martinique are represented by **Whitchurch Travel Agency** (tel: 448 2181): flights to Sint Maarten, Guadeloupe, and Martinique. **Air Caraibes** (tel: 449 2998) connects with Sint Maarten and Antigua and does short hops between Dominica's two airports. **Air Anguilla** (tel: 497 2643) connects with Puerto Rico via Anguilla. **BWIA** (Antigua tel: 462 0262) also flies in.
By boat Caribbean Express, a scheduled ferry service, offers connections between the port of Roseau, Dominica, and Guadeloupe and Martinique. Dominica agent: **Whitchurch & Co** (tel: 448 2181).
By road Taxis, minibuses and rental vehicles are denoted by license plates with H as the last letter. Taxi rates are fixed and quoted in EC$ and US$: make sure you know which the driver is quoting you. They are displayed at the airport and tourist office. In Roseau, try **Mally's Taxi Service** (tel: 448 3360). Not many taxis work after 6 p.m., so prearrange your ride if you go out in the evening.

Bus fares are cheaper than taxi fares; flag them down on the road by the airport. The tourist office will provide information on other routes.

Motorcycles can be rented from **DEA's Rent-a-Bike** (tel: 448 5075); bicycles from **Den's** (tel: 448 5095).
Sightseeing Tours, planned and tailor-made, including hiking and photo safaris, are offered by: **Antours Dominica** (tel: 448 6460), **Dominica Tours** (tel: 448 2638), **Emerald Safaris** (tel: 448 4545), **Ken's Hinterland Adventure Tours** (tel: 448 4850), **Mally's Tour & Taxi Service** (tel: 448 3114), **Nature Island Taxi & Tour Service** (tel: 448 3397), **Nature Tours of Dominica** (tel: 448 3706), **Paradise Tours** (tel: 448 5999), **Pierro Nature Tours** (tel: 448 5826), **Rainbow Rover Tours** (tel: 448 8650), **Roxy's Tours** (tel: 448 4845), **Wide Range** (tel: 448

2198), **Whitchurch Travel Agency** (tel: 448 2181). You need an experienced guide for tours in the Morne Trois Pitons National Park. **Dive Dominica** (tel: 448 2188) has a wide range of diving packages.

Tourist information
Dominica Division of Tourism, PO Box 73, Roseau, Commonwealth of Dominica (tel: 448 2045). There is a Tourist Information Bureau on the Old Market Plaza, Roseau (tel: 448 2186) and offices at the airports. **Dominica Hotel Association**, PO Box 384, Roseau, Commonwealth of Dominica, W.I. (tel: 448 6565).

GRENADA
Car rental and driving
A local driving permit can be purchased from most rental companies or the Fire Station on the Carenage; you need to show an international driver's license.

Car-rental companies include: **Avis** (tel: 440 3936); **Budget** (tel: 444 1620); **Coyaba Car Rentals** (tel: 444 4129); **David's Car Rentals** (tel: 440 2399); **Jerry's Auto Service** (tel: 440 1730); **Kayam's Auto Rentals** (tel: 440 2312); **Maffiken Car Rentals** (tel: 444 4255); **Maitland's Motor Rentals** (tel: 444 4022); **McIntyre Bros** (tel: 440 2044); **MCR** (tel: 440 5398); **Ride Grenada** (tel: 444 1157); **SR Car Rentals** (tel: 444 3222); **C Thomas** (tel: 444 4384); **Thrift Rent-a-Car** (tel: 444 4984); **Y&R Car Rentals** (tel: 444 4448); **Zamba's Car Rentals** (tel: 444 2237). **Carriacou: Barba's Rentals** (tel: 443 7454).

Driving is on the left. Seatbelts are recommended but not mandatory. Gas has to be paid for in cash.

Getting around
By air Airlines that link Grenada with the Grenadines, the rest of the Caribbean and Venezuela, with their local reservation numbers, are **Aereotuy/Aeropostal** (tel: 444 4732); **Airlines of Carriacou** (tel: 444 2898); **American Airlines** (tel: 444 2222); **British Airways** (tel: 440 2796); **BWIA International** (tel: 440 3818); **Helenair** (tel: 444 4101 ext 290); **Liat** (tel: 440 2796). Helenair/Fun Tours provides day trips around the Gren-

243

adines with private charter flights.
By boat Ferries operate from St.
George's quayside to Carriacou and
Petit Martinique. Reservations not
necessary. There are numerous yacht
charter companies (see list of local
tour operators).
By road Any rental vehicle has a
license plate with the latter H. Taxi
rates are set by the government and
quoted in U.S. dollars.

Buses leave from Market Square,
St. George's. More comfortable minibuses ply some of the shorter routes,
and fares are low. There are bus
stops, even on country roads, but
you can flag buses down in between.

Motorcycles can be rented from
hotels or car-rental firms; inquire at
your hotel about bicycles.
Sightseeing Taxis can be rented as
guides for a day of sightseeing. Local
tour operators: for excursions around
Grenada, trips to Carriacou, Petit
Martinique and the Grenadines, hik-
ing tours, boat trips, yacht charter,
car rental and taxi service. St.
George's: **Arnold's Tours** (tel: 440
0531); **Dovetail Leisure Services**
(tel: 444 2550); **Fun Tours** (tel: 444
3167); **Grenada Hotels Taxi
Association** (tel: 444 4882); **National
Taxi Association** (tel: 440 6850);
Sunsation Tours (tel: 444 1656)
Otways Tours (tel: 440 2558);
Henry's Safari Tours (tel: 444 5313);
Sea Spice Vacations (tel: 440 5180).
In Grand Anse: **Carib Tours/Carin
Travel** (tel: 444 4363); **New Trends
Tours** (tel: 444 1236); **Sunshine
Tours** (tel: 444 4296). At Point
Salines airport: **Windward Islands
Travel & Regattas** (tel: 444 4732).

Tourist information
Grenada Board of Tourism, The
Carenage, St. George's (tel: 440
2001); **Grenada Hotel Association**,
Ross Point Inn, Lagoon Road, St.
George's (tel: 444 1353); Cruise Ship
Office (tel: 440 2872).

ST. LUCIA
Car rental and driving
A St. Lucia temporary driver's license
must be purchased, on presentation
of your current driver's license, at the
airport, the police station in Castries
or the car-rental office. Companies

include **Avis** (tel: 45 22700), **Budget**
(tel: 45 20233), **Courtesy Rent-a-Car**
(tel: 45 28140), **CTL Rent-a-Car** (tel:
45 20732), **Inter Island Car Rental**
(tel: 45 22780), **National Car Rental**
(tel: 45 28028), **St. Lucia Yacht
Service Car Rental** (tel: 45 25057).
Some companies insist on a minimum
number of years' driving experience,
and a minimum age.

Driving is on the left and seatbelts
are recommended but not compulsory. Speed limits are 48kph (30mph),
and there are penalties for drunk driving and illegal parking. Gas must be
paid for in cash.

Getting around
By air Vigie airport, just outside
Castries, is used for inter-island traffic,
and is served by **Liat** (tel: 45 23051/3),
Air Martinique (tel: 45 22463),
American Eagle (tel: 45 21900), and
Helenair (tel: 45 27196). Helicopter
transfers are available from
Hewanorra International Airport to
Castries, and Windjammer Landing
has a helipad. There are helipads at
Pointe Seraphine and Rodney Bay. **St.
Lucia Helicopters** tel: 45 36950.
By boat A new ferry service,
Caribbean Express (tel: 22211/2/3),
operates between St. Lucia and
Martinique, Guadeloupe, and
Dominica. A service runs between
Soufrière and Castries. Contact one of
the local tour operators (list below) for
reservations and to check the cost. A
few hotels have their own boats:
Jalousie, Windjammer, and Sandals
(private yachts), and Anse Chastanet
(motor boat). Yacht charter companies
include: **The Moorings**, Marigot Bay
(tel: 45 34357); **Sunsail**, Stevens
Yachts, Rodney Bay (tel: 45 28648);
Trade Winds Yachts, Rodney Bay
Marina (tel: 45 28424).
By road The north around Castries
and Gros Islet are served very well by
buses and private minibuses, which
run until about 10 p.m. (longer on
Friday night from the weekly dance at
Gros Islet). The last bus from Soufrière
to Castries leaves at noon, but there is
no scheduled bus timetable.

Taxis or minibuses are easily available. A recommended list of local taxi
fares is available from any taxi company (who will also organize tours):

244

Courtesy Taxi (tel: 45 21733), **Vigie Taxi** (tel: 45 21599), **All Generations Taxi Service** (tel: 45 26077), **Boulevard Taxi** (tel: 45 21531). Agree on the fare in advance with the driver and determine whether the quote is in EC$ or US$.

Sightseeing Tours are usually organized through the hotel or your tour company's local representative. Most tours include a stop for swimming and snorkeling. Local tour operators (for sightseeing on land or sea) include: **Barefoot Holidays** (tel: 45 20507), **Barnards Travel** (tel: 45 21615), **Carib Touring** (tel: 45 26791), **Carib Travel Agency** (tel: 45 22151), **Cox & Co** (tel: 45 22211), **Fletcher's Touring Service** (tel: 45 22516), **Minvielle & Chastanet** (tel: 45 22811), **Pitons Travel Agency** (tel: 45 21227), **Spice Travel** (tel: 45 23219), **St. Lucia Representative Services** (tel: 45 23762), **Sunlink International** (tel: 45 28232).

Tourist information

St. Lucia Tourist Board, Pointe Seraphine, PO Box 221, Castries, St. Lucia (tel: 45 25968/30053/24094). There is also a tourist information office in Jeremie Street, Castries, and in Soufriere, along the main street in front of the beach.

ST. VINCENT AND THE GRENADINES

Car rental and driving

A local driver's license must be purchased at the airport or at the police station in Bay Street or the Licensing Authority in Halifax Street, on presentation of your normal or international driver's license. The minimum age for driving is only 17, but some companies may insist on you being older to sign a rental agreement. Rental companies on St. Vincent include: **Avis** (tel: 456 5610); **David's Auto Clinic** (tel: 457 1116); **Johnson's U-Drive** (tel: 458 4864); **Kim's Rentals** (tel: 456 1884); **Lucky Car Rental** (tel: 457 1913); **Star Garage** (tel: 457 1169); **Sunshine Auto Rentals** (tel: 456 5380); **Unico** (tel: 456 5744).

Driving is on the left. Seatbelt laws do exist, and speed limits are 32kph (20mph) everywhere (24kph/15 mph for buses and trucks); neither restric-

tion is very rigidly enforced. Gas must be paid for in cash.

Getting around

By air St. Vincent is linked with Barbados, St. Lucia, Martinique, Trinidad and Grenada by BWIA, British Airways, Air Canada, American Airlines, Air France. **Air Martinique** (St. Vincent tel: 458 4528; Union Island tel: 458 8328) links St. Vincent with St. Lucia, Barbados, Mustique, Union Island, Canouan and points north. **Liat** (Kingstown tel: 457 1821; ET Joshua Airport tel: 458 4841; Union Island airport tel: 458 8230) links St. Vincent with Martinique, Barbados, St. Lucia and the other Grenadines. **Mustique Airways** (tel: 458 4380) and **SVG Air** (tel: 456 5610) offer charters; Mustique Airways waits for your international arrival.

By boat Ferries leave St. Vincent every day to Bequia and three times a week to the Grenadines (Canouan, Mayreau, and Union): they depart from Grenadines dock in Kingstown harbor and arrive at Port Elizabeth in Bequia between 70 and 90 minutes later. The ferries in operation are the MV *Admiral* (tel: 458 3348) and *Sand Island* (tel: 458 3472); check before traveling the times of ferries and current prices. The MV *Snapper* mailboat travels south on Mondays and Thursdays at 10 a.m., stopping at Bequia, Canouan, Mayreau, and Union, returning on Tuesdays and Fridays. You can reserve a clean but simple cabin for early departures; no electricity after 8 p.m. The island schooner *Friendship Rose* leaves St. Vincent about noon on weekdays. Yacht charter companies, for sailing around the Grenadines, include, on St. Vincent: **Barefoot Yacht Charters**, Blue Lagoon (tel: 456 9526); **Lagoon Marina & Hotel** (tel: 458 4308). Bequia: **Frangipani Yacht Services** (tel: 458 3244); Union: **Anchorage Yacht Club** (tel: 458 8221).

Boat trips to inaccessible beaches and places of interest: **Dive St. Vincent** (tel: 457 4714); **Dennis Hideaway** (tel: 458 8594); **Grand View Beach Hotel** (tel: 458 4811); **Sea Breeze** (tel: 458 4969); **Dive**

Canouan (tel: 458 8648); **Anchorage Yacht Club** (Union tel: 458 8221); **Grenadines Dive** (Union tel: 458 8138).

By road All parts of St. Vincent and Bequia are accessible by bus and taxi. Taxi and minibus rates are fixed by the government and a list is available at the Department of Tourism offices or at the airport. To pre-arrange a taxi tour, ask in your hotel or contact the **Taxi Drivers' Association** (tel: 457 1807); or **Sam's Taxi Tours and Yacht Assistance Service** (island tours, plus laundry, telephone services, etc. for yachts: 456 4338; Bequia: 458 3686).

Minibuses depart from Market Square in Kingstown. You can hail them anywhere along the route, and their route direction is indicated on the windshield. Smaller islands have taxi-vans and pick-up trucks with benches in the back and tarpaulin covers in case it rains.

Water taxis are available from docks. Arne Hansen and his catamaran *Toien* can be contacted through **Frangipani Hotel** (tel: 458 3255).

Bicycles can be rented from **Lighthouse**, Bequia (tel: 458 3084), bicycles and motorscooters from **Sailors Cycle Centre**, St. Vincent (tel: 457 1712), motorscooters from **JG Agencies**, St. Vincent (tel: 456 1409).

Sightseeing Tours by air, sea or land throughout the islands, as well as flights and other travel arrangements, can be organized on St. Vincent through **WJ Abbott & Sons**, Upper Bay Street, Kingstown (tel: 456 1511): **Barefoot Holidays**, Blue Lagoon (tel: 456 9334); **Caribbean International Travel Services**, Granby Street, Kingstown (tel: 457 1841); **Corea & Co.**, Halifax Street, Kingstown (tel: 456 1201); **Emerald Travel & Tours**, Halifax Street (tel: 457 1996); **Global Travel Service**, White Chapel, Kingstown (tel: 456 1601); **Grenadine Travel Co.**, Arnos Vale (tel: 458 4818); **Kim's Rental**, Grenville Street, Kingstown (tel: 456 1884); **Paradise Tours**, PO Box 280, Kingstown (tel: 458 5417); **Travel World**, Bay Street, Kingstown (tel: 456 2600). On Bequia: **Grenadine**

246

Travel Co., Port Elizabeth (tel: 458 3795). On Union: **Eagles Travel**, Clifton (tel: 458 8179).

Tourist information
St. Vincent and the Grenadines Department of Tourism, PO Box 834, St. Vincent (tel: 457 1502). A tourist information office is on the first floor of the Department of Tourism building, in Bay Street, Kingstown; there is also tourist information at ET Joshua Airport. Bequia's **Tourism Bureau** is on the main dock, Port Elizabeth (tel: 458 3286); **Union Island Tourist Information** tel: 458 8350.

THE LEEWARD ISLANDS

ANGUILLA
Car rental and driving
You have to produce a valid driver's license to obtain a temporary license, which can be purchased from rental companies or from the police station in The Valley. The minimum age for renting a car is 18; some companies prefer 21, others even 25. Prices do not include personal accident insurance or collision damage waiver. Car-rental companies include **Apex** (tel: 2065); **Avis** (tel: 6221); **Budget** (tel: 2217); **Connors** (tel: 6433); **Paradise Car Rentals** (tel: 2168); **Triple K Car Rental** (tel: 2934).

Driving is on the left. The speed limit is 48kph (30mph). Seatbelts are not required by law, but you're better off wearing one. Gas can be paid for by cash or credit card at the larger stations, but smaller ones prefer cash.

Getting around
By air Local airlines linking Anguilla with the rest of the Caribbean include **Winair** (tel: 2748/3748), **Air Anguilla** (tel: 2643/2725), **Tyden Air** (tel: 2719), **Liat** (tel: 5000/1/2), **American Eagle** (tel: 3131/2).

By boat Ferries between Blowing Point and Marigot Bay, Saint-Martin, leave every 30 minutes from 7:30 a.m. on, and you can also take day trips to St. Barts. Boat trips can be booked through your hotel or through **Enchanted Island Cruises** (tel: 3111) or **Princess Soya Catamaran Cruises**.

By road Taxis or rental cars are just about the only motorized way of getting around the island: official taxi rates are set by the government (there are no meters). There are no buses or maxi taxis: for larger groups, car-rental companies and taxi companies do have minibuses. Motorbikes are not available for rental, but bicycles are through one of the travel agents (see below).

Sightseeing Tours and off-shore trips to the smaller islands and cays are usually organized through your hotel or villa manager, but you can go direct to a travel agent (see list below). Taxi drivers will also arrange tours; their fees are negotiable. Local tour operators include: **Bennie's Travel & Tours**, Box 254, The Valley (tel: 2788/2360) and **Malliouhana Travel & Tours**, Box 237, The Quarter (tel: 2431/2348).

Tourist information
Anguilla Tourist Office, The Valley (tel: 2759).

ANTIGUA AND BARBUDA
Car rental and driving
You need to purchase a provisional license, issued on presentation of a valid driver's license. Some companies set a minimum age for renting a car (21 or 25), and you have to be 18 to drive. Some companies include "extras" in their quoted prices; others do not. Companies include **Budget** (tel: 462 3009), **National** (tel: 462 2113), **Carib Car Rentals** (tel: 462 2062) and **Avis** (tel: 462 2840).

It is virtually impossible to rent a car during Carnival, so if you're going to need one then, book ahead. If you want to rent a car in Barbuda, it's best to arrange it before leaving Antigua.

Driving is on the left, but most roads are unmarked, so it's not difficult to keep to the 64kph (40mph) speed limit. Seatbelts are not mandatory but recommended; and there are no drunk-driving laws as such. Gas stations usually ask you to pay in cash.

Getting around
By air Liat (tel: 462 0700) operates a regular service to Barbuda and to most other Caribbean islands. Various charter airlines also stop in at Antigua.

By boat There are no ferries between Antigua and Barbuda, but you can hop aboard catamarans run by a number of companies for a day trip with picnic and rum punches, swimming and snorkeling, etc., to Barbuda and Bird Island. Try the *Falcon* (tel: 462 4792), **Wadadli Watersports** (tel: 462 2890), *Paradise I* (tel: 462 4158) or *The Jolly Roger* "pirate" ship (tel: 462 2064). If you prefer to do it yourself, try **Nicholson Yacht Charters** (tel: 662 6066) or ask the tourist office for a list of other boat charter companies.

By road Taxis are not metered but official rates are displayed at the airport and drivers should have a rate card with them. Check whether they are quoting the fare in U.S. or EC dollars. All taxi drivers double as guides, and hotels usually have a team of three or four who take turns doing the tours. Alternatively contact **Capital Car Rental** (tel: 462 0863).

A private bus system operates in Antigua, with no timetables and few stops, but it is certainly the cheapest way of getting around the island. Ask in your hotel for the nearest bus stop. There are no buses in Barbuda: the best way of getting around is to rent a jeep in advance.

Bicycles can be rented from **Sun Cycles** in Antigua (tel: 461 0324).

Sightseeing As well as taxi tours, local tour operators will fix island and inter-island excursions. The major local operators are **Antours**, Thames and Long Streets, St. John's (tel: 462 4788), **Alexander Parrish**, St. Mary's Street, St. John's (tel: 462 0187/0387/4458) and **Bryson's Travel** (tel: 462 0223), which also does cruises and deep-sea fishing trips.

Tourist information
The Antigua and Barbuda Department of Tourism, Thames and Long Streets, St. John's (tel: 462 0480). There is also a tourist information desk at the airport. Try also **Antigua Hotels Association**, Long Street, St. John's (tel: 462 3702).

247

MONTSERRAT
Car rental and driving
In Montserrat it is not possible to step straight off an international flight and rent a car; the earliest it can be delivered is the following morning. A temporary Montserrat driving permit must be purchased on presentation of a valid driver's licence from the car-rental company or through your hotel. Car-rental companies include: **Pauline's Car Rental** (tel: 2345); **Neville Bradshaw Agencies** (tel: 5270); **Jefferson's Car Rental** (tel: 2126); **Taxi Stand, Plymouth** (tel: 2261); **Budget** (tel: 6065); **Montserrat Enterprises** (tel: 2431); **Rent-a-Car Montserrat** (tel: 2626); **Reliable Car Rentals** (tel: 6990); **Ethelyine's Car Rentals** (tel: 2855); **Sales & Services** (tel: 3402). Driving is on the left and the speed limit is 48kph (30mph). Seatbelts are optional, and gas can be paid for by credit card at the large stations: smaller stations prefer cash.

Getting around
By air You can charter **Montserrat Airways** (tel: 5342), **Carib Aviation** or **Air St. Kitts/Nevis** to get to other islands, and **Liat** (tel: 2533/2362) runs scheduled services.
By boat Round-island catamaran cruises can be booked through a travel agent (see below) or your hotel, or directly with **Captain Martin Haxby** (tel: 5738).
By road There are no buses or maxi-taxis, so rental cars and private taxis are the only motorized way of moving. Taxi fares between principal destinations are set by the government; check whether the fare you are being quoted is in U.S. or EC dollars.
Bicycles can be rented from **Island Bikes** (tel: 4696); some travel agents (see below) rent motorbikes.
Sightseeing Local tour operators in Plymouth include **Carib World Travel** (tel: 2014); **Jus Looking** (tel: 4076); **Runaway Travel** (tel: 2776).
Tourist information
The Department of Tourism, PO Box 7, Plymouth (tel: 491 2230).

ST. KITTS AND NEVIS
Car rental and driving
A local temporary driver's license must be purchased from the Police Traffic Department, at Police Headquarters, Cayon Street, Basseterre (tel: 465 2241) or the Nevis Police Headquarters in Charlestown (tel: 465 5391), issued on presentation of a national or international driver's license. Most companies insist on a minimum age of 25 to rent a car. A government tax of 5 percent is added to rates.
On St. Kitts, cars can be rented from: **Avis** (tel: 465 6507), **Caines' Rent-a-Car** (tel: 465 2366), **Choice Car Rental** (tel: 465 4422); **Delisle Walwyn** (tel: 465 8449; **Huggins Car Rental** (tel: 465 8080); **Island Car Rental** (tel: 465 3000); **Kitts Car Rental** (tel: 465 1665); **Sunshine Car Rental** (tel: 465 2193), **TDC Rentals** (tel: 465 2991—also has a courtesy telephone at the airport).
In Nevis, cars can be rented from: **D&R Rent-a-Car** (tel: 469 1922); **Gajor's Car Rental** (tel: 469 5367); **Nisbett Rentals** (tel: 469 9211); **Noel's Car Rental** (tel: 469 5199); **Parry's Car Rentals** (tel: 469 5917); **Skeete's Car Rental** (tel: 469 9458); **Stanley's Car Rental** (tel: 469 1597); **Striker's Car Rental** (tel: 469 2654), **TDC Rentals** (tel: 469 5960, or at Four Seasons tel: 469 1111).
Driving is on the left on both islands. Beware the potholes and wandering livestock in Nevis. There are no seatbelt laws.

Getting around
By air From St. Kitts and Nevis to the rest of the Caribbean: there are no ferries, but regular air services—scheduled and charter—link St. Kitts and Nevis with other Caribbean islands, including: **Liat and BWIA** (tel: 465 2286), **American Eagle** (tel: 465 8490), **Winair** (tel: 465 2186), **Air St. Kitts-Nevis Charters**, at Golden Rock Airport (tel: 465 8571) and Newcastle Airport (tel: 469 9241) and **Carib Aviation**, Circus (tel: 465 3054), Golden Rock Airport (tel: 465 3055) and Newcastle Airport (tel: 469 9295).
Between St. Kitts and Nevis: **Liat** (tel: 465 2286) runs several flights a day.
By boat There is a regular 45-minute passenger ferry service between Basseterre (St. Kitts) and Charlestown (Nevis) with several sailings a

day. For information on times of sailings, contact General Manager, St. Kitts and Nevis Port Authority, Basseterre, St. Kitts (tel: 465 9621). You can also obtain information and reservations from **Nevis Cruise Lines** (tel: 469 9373). The Four Seasons Hotel, Nevis, also operates a powerful passenger launch between the hotel's jetty and the quay in Basseterre, taking just 20 minutes. Even if you are not a guest, it's worth inquiring whether there's space on board. Sea taxi services are also operated by dive instructor **Kenneth Samuel** (tel: 465 2670) and by **Pro-Divers** (tel: 465 2754).

Also on the water: **Leeward Islands Charters** (tel: 465 7474) operates the Spirit of St. Kitts and the Caona catamarans, for day sails to Nevis with snorkeling, barbecue etc. **Tropical Tours** (tel: 465 4167) does night-time cruises; **Tropical Dreamer** (tel: 465 8224) is another catamaran for rent for day and evening cruises; **Blue Frontier** (tel: 465 4945) runs a two-man submarine.

By road On St. Kitts there are privately run minibus services making regular but unscheduled runs between villages. The Nevis bus system is vague, to say the least. Taxis have set rates between principal destinations (no meters), usually quoted in EC dollars, but check before traveling in case you are being quoted U.S. dollars. Nevis taxis are very expensive—virtually twice the price of those on St. Kitts. On St. Kitts add 25 percent to the fares between 11p.m. and 6 a.m.; on Nevis add 50 percent. Most hotels have lists of the rates, and they are also displayed at the airports and in *Traveller* magazine (from the tourist office), but on Nevis it's almost certainly cheaper to rent a car to do your sightseeing.

Motorscooters can be rented on St. Kitts from **Economy Car/Delisle Walwyn** (tel: 465 8449).

Sightseeing Most operators are based at Basseterre in St. Kitts but handle everything on Nevis too, including transfers, car/motorscooter rental, boat charter, sightseeing tours, scuba diving, airline reservations: **Kantours** (tel: 465 2098); **St. Kitts Taxi Association** (Basseterre tel: 465 4253, airport tel: 465 8487); **Tropical Tours** (tel: 465 4039); **Delisle Walwyn Travel Agency** (tel: 465 2631); **Kisco Travel** (tel: 465 4167); **Scarborough Tours/Stars Rental** (tel: 465 5429); **TDC Airlines** (tel: 465 2286); **Travel World** (tel: 465 4085); **Sunshine Travel & Tours** at Jack Tar Village (tel: 465 2193). Specialists in touring the rainforest and volcano, caves and plantations on St. Kitts: **Kriss Tours**, New Street, Basseterre (tel: 465 4042; tours include lunch and drinks); **Greg's Safaris** (tel: 465 4121). Diving specialist: **Kenneth's Dive Centre**, Bay Road and Timothy Beach, St. Kitts (tel: 465 2670).

Jan's Travel Agency has offices both in Fort Street, Basseterre (tel: 465 4383) and Main Street, Charlestown (tel: 469 5426); other operators based on Nevis, which organize tours of both islands, flight reservations etc., include: **All Season Tours**, Bath Estate (tel: 469 5705); **Evelyn's Travel Agency**, Main Street, Charlestown (tel: 469 5238; no credit cards); **Nevisian Travel**, Main Street, Charlestown (agents for Windward Island Airways tel: 469 5423); **Travel World**, Main Street, Charlestown (tel: 469 1460). Taxi tours of St. Kitts take about four hours. Ask for Rosie and Jim, both of whom drive snazzy little minibuses.

Tourist information
St. Kitts and Nevis Department of Tourism, Pelican Mall, Bay Road, PO Box 132, Basseterre, St. Kitts (tel: 465 2620/4040). **St. Kitts-Nevis Hotel Association**, PO Box 438, Basseterre, St. Kitts (tel: 465 5304). **Nevis Tourist Office**, Main Street, Charlestown, Nevis (tel: 469 5521).

THE VIRGIN ISLANDS

BRITISH VIRGIN ISLANDS
Car rental and driving
A temporary BVI license must be purchased, issued on presentation of a current foreign license (rental companies can provide these). The minimum age for renting a car is 25. Cars can be rented in Road Town, Tortola, from: **Anytime Car Rental** (tel: 42875); **Alphonso Car Rentals** (tel:

43137); **Avis** (tel: 42193); **Budget** (tel: 42639); **Caribbean Car Rental** (tel: 42595); **Island Suzuki Rentals** (tel: 43666); **International Car Rentals** (tel: 42516). In Virgin Gorda: **Speedy's Car Rentals** (tel: 55235).

Driving is on the left and the speed limit is 30mph. In residential areas the limit is 16–24kph (10–15mph). Most cars are left-hand drive, and it's recommended that you rent a four-wheel drive vehicle. Gas stations take credit cards. Seatbelts are compulsory.

Getting around
By air Sunaire Express (tel: 52480) and **American Eagle** (tel: 52559) operate various services between Beef Island (Tortola), Virgin Gorda, St. Thomas, St. Croix, and Puerto Rico. Antigua, St. Kitts, Sint Maarten, and Dominica are also linked to Beef Island by **Liat**.
By boat There are daily passenger launches between Tortola, Virgin Gorda, Jost Van Dyke, St. Thomas, and St. John. Ferries from Tortola to St. Thomas and St. John are operated by **Native Son** (tel: 54617), **Smith's Ferry Services** (tel: 44430), **Inter Island Boat Services** (tel: 776 6597); from Tortola to Peter Island: **Peter Island Boat** (tel: 42561); from Tortola to Virgin Gorda: **Speedy's Fantasy** (tel: 55240); **Smith's Ferry Services** (see above) and **North South Express** (tel: 42746). From Virgin Gorda to St. Thomas, **Speedy's Fantasy** (see above) and **Native Son** (see above). From Tortola to Jost Van Dyke: **Reel World** (tel: 59277) or the **Jost Van Dyke Ferry Service** (tel: 52775). Yacht charter is one of the major industries: bareboats can be rented for cruises, local boats for special tours, and ferry services arranged, given notice. Road Town tour operator **Travel Plan** (tel: 42872) looks after cruise ships and organizes day-sails either in bareboats or crewed yachts. You can also take the Bomba Charger hydrofoil between Tortola and Virgin Gorda or St. Thomas.
By road The BVI Taxi Association (tel: 42875) operates a range of standard journeys at fixed rates; all drivers are capable tour guides. Also on Tortola, guided taxi tours are

offered by **Style's Taxi Service** (tel: 42260) and **Travel Plan Tours** (tel: 42872). Taxis can also be rented on hourly or daily basis. On Virgin Gorda: **Andy's Taxi and Jeep Rental** (tel: 99911); **Mahogany Taxi Service** (tel: 55542) does island tours for a minimum of two people. **Scato's Bus Service** (tel: 42365)—more of a large taxi service really, since there is no public bus service—operates around Tortola. Scooter rentals: **D.J's Scooter Rentals**, Road Town, Tortola (tel: 45071); **Honda Scooter Rentals**, The Valley, Virgin Gorda (tel: 55212).

Tourist information
BVI Tourist Board, Social Security Building, Waterfront Street, PO Box 134, Road Town, Tortola (tel: 43134).

THE U.S. VIRGIN ISLANDS

ST. CROIX
Car rental and driving
The minimum age is 18, but some companies won't rent a car to anyone under 25; a full driver's license will suffice.

Car-rental companies include: **Avis** (tel: 778 9355), **Budget** (tel: 778 9636), **Caribbean Jeep & Car** (tel: 773 4399), **Charlie's** (tel: 778 8200), **Hertz** (tel: 778 1402), **Olympic** (tel: 773 2208), **Thrifty** (tel: 773 7200).

Driving is on the left. The speed limit is 88kph (55mph). Drunk-driving and seatbelt laws are strictly enforced. Gas is cheap; credit cards are accepted.

Getting around
By air Sunaire (tel: 776 9322), **Delta** (tel: 777 4177), **Air Anguilla** (tel: 776 5789) and **American Eagle** (tel: 774 6464) fly between St. Thomas and St. Croix.
By boat There are no ferries servicing St. Croix, but yacht charter, short cruises, and day-sails are all possible: Try **Mile-Mark Charters** in Christiansted (tel: 773 2628), **St. Croix Yacht Club** (tel: 773 9531), **St. Croix Marine** (tel: 773 0289). Contact **Paradise Parasailing** (tel: 773 7060) or **Big Beard's Adventure Tours** (tel: 773 4482) for catamaran trips around the island.
By road Taxi vans can be called from

your hotel or found in Christiansted, at the airport and, when cruise ships are in, at the pier in Frederiksted. Rates are set, and displayed at the airport. The **St. Croix Taxi Association** (tel: 778 1088) runs taxi vans throughout the main roads from Christiansted to Frederiksted; try also the **Cruzan Taxi Association** (tel: 773 6388) in Christiansted and the **Frederiksted Taxi and Tour Service** (tel: 772 4775).

There is no public bus system, but island bus tours are offered by the following: **St. Croix Transit Tours** (tel: 772 3333); The **Traveller's Tours** (tel: 778 1636/773 9799); **St. Croix Safari Tours** (tel: 773 6700), in a 25-seater open-air bus. Horseback tours of rainforest and hills are run by **Paul and Jill's Equestrian Stable** (tel: 772 2880).

Tourist information
The **U.S. Virgin Islands Division of Tourism** has an office at Box 4538, Christiansted, St. Croix (tel: 773 0495) and on the pier, Strand Street, Frederiksted (tel: 772 0357). There is a visitor center at the Old Scale House at the waterfront in Christiansted, opposite Fort Christiansvaern. **St. Croix Hotel and Tourism Association**, PO Box 2438, Gallows Bay, St. Croix U.S.V.I. (tel: 773 7117).

ST. THOMAS AND ST. JOHN
Car rental and driving
You need a valid driver's license, and the minimum age for drivers is 18, but car-rental companies in general prefer you to be at least 25.

On St. Thomas: **ABC Rentals** (tel: 776 1222); **Anchorage E-Z Car** (tel: 775 6255); **Avis** (tel: 774 1468); **Budget** (tel: 776 5774); **Cowpet Auto Rental** (tel: 775 7376); **Dependable** (tel: 774 2253); **Discount** (tel: 776 4858); **Hertz** (tel: 774 1879); **Sea Breeze** (tel: 774 7200); **Sun Island** (tel: 774 3333); **Thrifty** (tel: 775 7282).

On St. John: **Avis** (tel: 776 6374); **Cool Breeze** (tel: 776 6588); **Delbert Hills Rentals** (tel: 776 6637); **O'Connor Car Rental** (tel: 776 6343); **Spencer's Jeep** (tel: 776 7784); **St. John Car Rental** (tel: 776 6103).

Driving is on the left. Seatbelts are compulsory, and the drunk-driving laws are strictly enforced. The speed limit in St. Thomas and St. John is 56kph (35mph). Gas is very cheap; credit cards are accepted; pay before filling up.

Getting around
By air St. Thomas is linked to St. Croix by regular services operated by **Air Anguilla** (tel: 776 5789), **American Eagle** (tel: 774 6464), **Delta** (tel: 777 4177) and **Sunaire** (tel: 776 9322). The U.S.V.I. are linked with the rest of the Caribbean by **Air Anguilla** (to St. Kitts), **Sunaire** (to Puerto Rico and other islands), **Delta** (to Puerto Rico), **American Eagle** (to Puerto Rico and Trinidad), **Windward Island Airways** (tel: 775 0183, to Sint Maarten, St. Kitts, Nevis, Anguilla, Saba, and Guadeloupe), **Liat** (tel: 778 9930, to Antigua and Trinidad) and **Virgin Air** (tel: 776 2722, to Puerto Rico and Virgin Gorda).

There are two companies offering helicopter travel: **Air Center Helicopters** (tel: 775 7335) and **Antilles Helicopters** (tel: 776 7880). You can also take a seaplane between St. John and St. Croix: **Seaborne Seaplane Adventures** (tel: 777 4491).

By boat There are two ferry routes between St. Thomas and St. John: Charlotte Amalie to Cruz Bay (six a day each way) and Red Hook to Cruz Bay (daily, every hour). For more information contact **Transportation Services** (tel: 776 6282) or **Varlack Ventures** (tel: 776 6412).

Ferries link St. Thomas and the British Virgin Islands (Tortola, Virgin Gorda, and Jost Van Dyke); proof of citizenship is required to embark here. Ferries from Red Hook (St. Thomas) to Jost Van Dyke, stopping en route at Cruz Bay (St. John) take an hour. To check times and to book, contact **Inter Island Boat Services** (tel: 776 6597). Ferries from Charlotte Amalie (St. Thomas) to Tortola take 45 minutes to the West End or an hour-and-a-half to Road Town; contact **Native Son** (tel: 774 8685) or **Smith's Ferry** (tel: 775 7292). There are also ferries from Red Hook (St.

Thomas) to West End (Tortola), 30 minutes (contact Native Son or Smith's Ferry) and from Cruz Bay (St. John) to West End (Tortola), 30 minutes (contact Inter Island Boat Services).

Ferries also leave from Charlotte Amalie and Red Hook (St. Thomas) for Virgin Gorda. From Charlotte Amalie, two hours; contact Native Son, Smith's Ferry, or **Speedy's** (tel: 1 495 5235); from Red Hook, stopping at Cruz Bay, St. John, one-and-three-quarter hours; infrequent, so best to book with Transportation Services.

Yachts can be chartered with or without crew, usually through a broker. Check that the vessel you are booking is a member of the V.I. Charter-yacht League, the local professional association of crewed charter boats. A full list of brokers is available from the tourist office.

Powerboats with or without captains can be rented from numerous companies—ask the tourist board for the full list. A small powerboat to see the islands can be rented from **Calypso Boats** (tel: 775 2628 on St. Thomas, 776 6922 on St. John).

You can also book day-sails, submarine rides or short fishing excursions with **Red Hook Charter** (tel: 775 9333), **Coconut Cruises** (tel: 775 5959) on St. Thomas, or **Connections** (tel: 776 6922) on St. John.

By road On St. Thomas, taxis are usually found at the ferry, the airport, shopping and resort areas, opposite Emancipation Gardens (behind the post office) and along the waterfront in Charlotte Amalie. In St. John they cluster around Cruz Bay Dock, but you can hail them anywhere along the road.

Taxi fares are fixed (no meters) and published at the airport and hotels. St. Thomas taxis are usually station wagons or minivans that take five or six passengers to drop off at different stops; on St. John open-air safari buses double as taxis.

Public buses on St. Thomas are minimal and irregular, though there are some big new buses operating from the east and west of the island into Charlotte Amalie (but no service

north yet). Bus service begins at 5:35 a.m. from the bus depot and the last one leaves at 8:30 p.m. Open-air safari buses operated by the V.I. Taxi Commission travel between Charlotte Amalie and Red Hook and Charlotte Amalie and Havensight Mall: Monday to Friday 12:15–5:15 p.m., every 15 minutes.

One-speed bicycles can be rented on St. Thomas at Admiral's Inn, Frenchtown (tel: 774 1376).

Sightseeing St. Thomas: tours are mainly conducted in minivans or safari buses. The **Virgin Islands Taxi Association City-Island Tour** (tel: 774 4550) and **Destination V.I.** (tel: 776 2424) offer a variety of island tours; **Tropic Tours** (tel: 774 1855) does half-day tours, including shopping and sightseeing, by bus; **St. Thomas Historical Trust** (tel: 775 7843) offers walking tours and excursions with a historical bent. Contact the **Virgin Islands Conservation Society**, Box 3839, St. Croix 00822 (tel: 773 1989) for details of when to see the hawksbill turtles lay their eggs; also bird and whale-watching.

St. John: the **St. John National Park Visitor Center**, Cruz Bay (tel: 776 6201) does guided tours on and offshore; a **St. John Taxi Association** (tel: 776 6060) island tour covers Cruz Bay, Annaberg Plantation and the north coast beaches. You could also try **Miss Lucy** (tel: 776 6804) for a tour with an extra measure of local culture.

Tourist information
The **U.S.V.I. Division of Tourism** can be contacted at PO Box 6400, Charlotte Amalie (tel: 774 8784, ext. 250) and at PO Box 200, Cruz Bay, St. John (tel: 776 6450). There are two Visitor Centers in Charlotte Amalie, one opposite Emancipation Square and the other at Havensight Mall. The National Park Service has visitor centers at the ferry areas on St. Thomas (Red Hook) and St. John (Cruz Bay).

FRENCH ANTILLES

GUADELOUPE
Car rental and driving
Your normal driver's license is valid

here for up to 20 days, after which you need an international one. The minimum driving age is 18; car-rental companies vary on their minimum driving age policy. Cars can be rented from: **Avis** (airport 82 33 47); **Budget** (tel: 82 95 58); **Hertz** (airport 82 00 14); **Thrifty** (tel: 91 55 66), **Europcar** (airport 82 50 51), **Nad'incar** (tel: 88 32 45), **Carpentier** (airport 82 35 11), **Guadeloupe Car** (tel: 83 22 88). Car-rental companies also have desks at hotels and in Pointe-à-Pitre and Basse-Terre.

Driving is on the right. Seatbelt and drunk-driving laws are enforced. Gas can be paid for by credit card at most stations.

Getting around
By air Airlines serving Guadeloupe from the rest of the Caribbean include **Liat** (tel: 82 12 26—between Pointe-à-Pitre and Antigua, Barbados, Grenada, Montserrat, St. Kitts, St. Lucia, St. Vincent, and Trinidad); **Air Guadeloupe** (tel: 82 28 35—to Marie-Galante, Désirade, Les Saintes, Saint-Martin, St. Barts, Dominica, St. Lucia, St. Thomas, Puerto Rico); **Air St. Barts** (tel: 27 71 90—to St. Barts), **Air Saint-Martin** (tel: 82 96 63—to Saint-Martin); **Air France** (tel: 82 61 61—to Martinique, Saint-Martin, Puerto Rico, Dominican Republic); and **Air Caraibes** (charter 82 12 25). Helicopter tours are offered by **Heli Inter** (tel: 91 45 00); **Caraibe Air Tourisme** (tel: 91 61 24) and **Safari Tours** (tel: 84 06 74).
By boat Ferries to and from Marie-Galante, Les Saintes, and La Désirade are operated by **Trans Antilles Express** (ATE) (tel: 83 12 45/91 13 43) and **Transport Maritime Brudey Frères** (tel: 90 04 48).

To Marie-Galante: Ferries leave three times a day from the pier at Pointe-à-Pitre, 35-minute journey; and from St-François on Tuesdays and Thursdays, 45 minutes. To Les Saintes: daily ferries from Pointe-à-Pitre at 8 a.m., returning from Terre-de-Haut at 4 p.m., 45 minutes; twice a week from St-François, via Marie-Galante, one hour 20 minutes; and daily from Trois Rivières (one-and-a-half hours from Pointe-à-Pitre), 30

CONVERSION CHARTS

FROM	TO	MULTIPLY BY
Inches	Centimeters	2.54
Centimeters	Inches	0.3937
Feet	Meters	0.3048
Meters	Feet	3.2810
Yards	Meters	0.9144
Meters	Yards	1.0940
Miles	Kilometers	1.6090
Kilometers	Miles	0.6214
Acres	Hectares	0.4047
Hectares	Acres	2.4710
U.S. Gallons	Liters	3.7854
Liters	U.S. Gallons	0.2642
Ounces	Grams	28.35
Grams	Ounces	0.0353
Pounds	Grams	453.6
Grams	Pounds	0.0022
Pounds	Kilograms	0.4536
Kilograms	Pounds	2.205
U.S. Tons	Tonnes	).9072
Tonnes	U.S. Tons	1.1023

253

MEN'S SUITS

U.K.	36	38	40	42	44	46	48
Rest of Europe	46	48	50	52	54	56	58
U.S.	36	38	40	42	44	46	48

DRESS SIZES

U.K.	8	10	12	14	16	18
France	36	38	40	42	44	46
Italy	38	40	42	44	46	48
Rest of Europe	34	36	38	40	42	44
U.S.	6	8	10	12	14	16

MEN'S SHIRTS

U.K.	14	14.5	15	15.5	16	16.5	17
Rest of Europe	36	37	38	39/40	41	42	43
U.S.	14	14.5	15	15.5	16	16.5	17

MEN'S SHOES

U.K.	7	7.5	8.5	9.5	10.5	11
Rest of Europe	41	42	43	44	45	46
U.S.	8	8.5	9.5	10.5	11.5	12

WOMEN'S SHOES

U.K.	4.5	5	5.5	6	6.5	7
Rest of Europe	38	38	39	39	40	41
U.S.	6	6.5	7	7.5	8	8.5

minutes. To La Désirade: daily ferry from St-François (different times each day).

The **Caribbean Express** (tel: 83 04 43) services link Pointe-à-Pitre with Martinique, Dominica, and St. Lucia (in conjunction with ATE). All times and prices are subject to change, so check before traveling. There are no ferries to St. Barts or Saint-Martin.

Multi Marine Charter (tel: 83 32 67) does one-day excursions from St-François to Marie-Galante, and from St-François to Les Saintes, with or without lunch.

Safe anchorages and marinas, for ferries and yachts, are at Marina du Bas-du-Fort, Gosier; Marina de St-François (in the heart of town); Marina de Rivière Sens, Basse-Terre. Numerous companies around the Bas-du-Fort marina rent out bareboat or crewed yachts and motorboats, including: **Locaraibes** (tel: 90 82 80), **Vacances Yachting Antilles** (tel: 90 82 95), **Soleil et Voile** (tel: 90 81 81).

By road Taxi fares are set by the government and posted at the airport, taxi stands, and major hotels. Taxi stands in Pointe-à-Pitre are on Blvd. Faidherbe et Chanzy, rue Achille René Boisneuf, rue Alexandre Isaac, in front of the tourist office. In Basse-Terre: Cours Nolivos. Radio cabs (you'll need to speak French) can be contacted on 82 15 09/83 64 27/84 37 65.

Taxi tours have set fares to various points, and the tourist office or your hotel can arrange for an English-speaking driver.

A public bus service operates around the island, 5 a.m.–6 p.m., stopping anywhere along the road—just give the driver a wave—or at stops marked *arretbus*. The fare is paid when getting off. There are three bus stations in Pointe-à-Pitre, serving different parts of the island: La Darse, Mortenol, and Bergevin stations; fares to all regions are posted in the stations.

Vespas can be rented through: **Dingo Location** (tel: 83 81 19); **Easy Rent** (tel: 88 76 27); **MM** (tel: 88 59 12); **Vespa Sun** (tel: 91 30 36); **Location de Motos**, Meridien Hotel, St-François (tel: 88 51 00). Bicycles: **Velo-Vert**, Pointe-à-Pitre (tel: 83 15

74); **Le Relais du Moulin**, Ste-Anne (tel: 88 23 96); **Cyclo-Tours**, Gosier (tel: 84 11 34); **Le Flamboyant**, St-François (tel: 84 45 51); **Rent-a-Bike**, Meridien Hotel (tel: 88 51 00); **VTT Evasion**, Ste-Rose (tel: 28 85 60—18-speed mountain bikes).

Sightseeing Ask the tourist office to help find English-speaking guides. Pick-ups at the hotel, lunch and guide services are usually included in the price. Sea excursions, particularly to the mangrove reserve, can be organized by companies around Bas-du-Fort Marina. **Organization des Guides de Montagne de la Caraibe** (80 05 79) provide guides for hiking tours in the mountains. It is also possible to arrange trips to neighboring islands. Local operators in Basse-Terre include: **Agence Gerville Reache**, rue du Dr Pitat (tel: 81 10 00); **Agence Penchard**, 1 bis rue de la République (tel: 81 27 12). In Pointe-à-Pitre: **Agence Havas**, corner rues Frébault and Delgres (tel: 90 27 27); **Agence Marie-Gabrielle**, 21 rue Alexandre Isaac (tel: 82 05 38); **Agence Petrelluzzi**, 2 rue Jean-Jaures (tel: 82 82 30); **Agence R Poirier et Fils**, 16 rue François Arago (tel: 82 00 46); **Guadeloupe Voyages**, 40 bis rue de Noziere (tel: 82 22 89); **International Voyages** (Pravaz), corner rue A R Boisneuf and Quai Foulon (tel: 82 00 51); **Navitour**, 10 rue de Nozières (tel: 83 49 50); **Nouvelles Frontières**, 28 rue Delgres (tel: 90 36 36); **Riverain Tour**, Galeries du Port (tel: 91 72 10). At Le Raizet airport: **Carib Jet** (tel: 82 26 44).

Tourist information
Office Départemental du Tourisme de la Guadeloupe, 5 Square de la Banque, 97181 Pointe-à-Pitre Cédex (Guadeloupe) (tel: 82 09 30). **Office du Tourisme de Basse-Terre**, Maison du Port, 97100 Basse-Terre (tel: 81 24 83); **Office du Tourisme de St-François**, Avenue de l'Europe, 97118 St-François (tel: 88 48 74). There is also a tourist information booth at the airport.

MARTINIQUE
Car rental and driving
Drivers must be at least 21 and hold

a driver's license; after 20 days you'll need an International Driver's Permit. Companies include **Agence Martiniquaise de Location** (tel: 63 01 64); **Antilles Location** (tel: 63 33 05); **Avis** (airport 51 26 86, **Fort-de-France** 70 11 60), **Budget** (airport 51 22 88, Fort-de-France 70 22 75); **Carib Rent-a-Car** (tel: 51 50 76); **Europcar** (tel: 51 20 33); **Euro Rent** (tel: 60 43 62), **Garage Grabin** (tel: 71 51 61); **Hertz** (airport 51 28 22, **Fort-de-France** 60 64 64); **Lam/Citer** (airport 51 65 75, Fort-de-France 72 66 48); **Locanord Worrel** (tel: 56 34 46); **Madinina Rent-a-Car** (tel: 71 64 58); **Parking Rent-a-Car** (tel: 60 00 83); **Pop's Car** (tel: 51 02 72); **Safari Car** (tel: 66 06 26); **Thrifty** (tel: 66 09 59).

The speed limits are 100kph (62mph) on the highway and 50kph (31mph) in town. Seatbelts are mandatory; drunk-driving is strictly penalized.

Getting around

By air: Air France (tel: 55 33 33) connects with Puerto Rico, Haiti, and Guadeloupe; **Air Martinique** (tel: 51 08 09) connects with Dominica, Guadeloupe, Antigua, Montserrat, St. Kitts, Saint-Martin, St. Croix, St. Thomas, St. Lucia, Barbados, St. Vincent, Grenada, Trinidad, Mustique, and Union Island; **Liat** (tel: 51 21 11) connects with St. Lucia, Barbados, St. Vincent, Dominica, Antigua, and Trinidad; **American Eagle** (tel: 51 12 29) links with Puerto Rico. Day charters can be arranged through **Air Caraibe** (tel: 51 17 27) or **Martinique Air Service** (tel: 51 51 51). You can also take a sightseeing flight with **ULM Caraibes** (tel: 54 60 79) or with **Helicaraibes** (tel: 73 30 03) by helicopter.

By boat Caribbean Express is a power-catamaran linking Martinique with Guadeloupe and Dominica. Information and reservations at all travel agents or tel: 60 12 38. A ferry service between Fort-de-France and Pointe du Bout leaves from Quai Desnambuc on the sea front in Fort-de-France several times a day, returning from the Marina at Pointe du Bout—late returns on Sunday and Monday—takes 20 minutes. There is also a service from Fort-de-France to Anse Mitan and Anse à l'Ane, several times a day. For information about timetables call **Somatour** (tel: 63 06 46) or **Madinina** (tel: 63 06 46). Numerous companies rent boats for day-sails or longer, with or without skipper: names from the tourist office.

By road Taxis can be found mainly at the airport, in Fort-de-France, and at major hotels; radio taxis may be contacted on 63 63 62. Fares are regulated by the government (list from the airport tourist office). These are expensive, especially if you arrive at night, when a 40 percent surcharge is added to taxi fares. There are private taxi stands at the Savane, along Blvd. General de Gaulle and Place Clemenceau in Fort-de-France.

You can also travel by bus or shared taxi: The main terminal is at Pointe-Simon, on the sea front in Fort-de-France, and they can also be found around Blvd. General de Gaulle. Buses are run privately, from 5 a.m. to 8 p.m., and leave when they're full. Shout *arret* to flag a driver down. There is also an inter-urban bus network. Shared taxis (*taxi collectif* or *Taxicos*) start early and run until 6 p.m. with regular fixed routes. Most start at Pointe Simon and serve all the *communes*.

Motorscooters and bicycles can be rented from **Discount** of Trois-Ilets (tel: 66 05 34); **Funny** (Fort-de-France 63 33 05, Ste-Anne 76 92 16); **T S Auto** (tel: 63 42 82); **Vespa** (tel: 71 60 03). **VTTilt** (tel: 66 01 01) offers Velo Tout Terrain 18-speed mountain bikes. The **Parc Naturel Regional de la Martinique** (tel: 73 19 30) has designated biking routes off the beaten track, and organizes island tours by bike, as well as walking tours in the best beauty spots.

Sightseeing The following local agents will find you guided sightseeing tours by car or bus, trips on sailing boats and cruise ships, excursions in glass-bottom boats, trips to Dominica, St. Lucia, and the Grenadines: **Laroc Voyages** (tel: 63 66 66), **Richard Flechon Voyages** (tel: 73 35 35), **SMCR** (tel: 63 44 54), **STT Voyages** (tel: 71 68 12), **Jet Tours Jumbo Carib Jet** (tel: 66 05

07), **Roger Albert Voyages** (tel: 71 71 71); **Havas Voyages** (tel: 63 55 55), **Caribtours** (tel: 66 02 56), **Madinina Tours** (tel: 70 65 25). Bus excursions to out-of-the-way places are offered by **Sapran** (tel: 78 59 49).

Tourist information
Office Départemental du Tourisme de la Martinique, rue Ernest Deproge, Bord de Mer, BP 520-97206 Fort-de-France Cédex (tel: 63 79 60). Local information can be obtained from **Office Municipal de Tourisme**, Mairie de Fort-de-France (town hall): 59 60 00. There is also a tourist information desk at the airport (tel: 51 28 55). There are Syndicats d'Initiative (local information bureaus) in all main towns and villages.

ST. BARTHÉLEMY
Car rental and driving
Cars can be rented next to/at the airport, though in peak season there may be a three-day minimum. You need a driver's license. Some hotels have their own car fleets, and many offer 24-hour emergency road service, which rental companies do not. Companies include: **Avis** (tel: 27 71 43); **Budget** (tel: 27 67 43); **Europcar** (tel: 27 73 33); **Mathew Aubin** (tel: 27 73 03). There are two gas stations, one near the airport and the other in Lorient (closed Thursday, Saturday afternoon, and Sunday). The one near the airport has credit card–operated self-service pumps, open around the clock, but closed Sunday.

Getting around
By air Air St. Barts (tel: 27 71 90) links with Guadeloupe, Puerto Rico, Sint Maarten/Juliana and Saint-Martin/L'Espérance, Antigua, and St. Kitts; **Virgin Air** (tel: 27 71 76) links with St. Thomas and Puerto Rico; **Air Guadeloupe** (tel: 27 61 90/27 64 44) links with Puerto Rico, Guadeloupe, Saint-Martin, and Antigua; **Winair** (tel: 27 61 01) links with Saint-Martin. Helicopter tours can be arranged with **Heli St-Barts** (tel: 27 81 11); **Heli Inter** (tel: 27 71 14).
By boat St. Barts Express (tel: 27 77 24), an engine-driven, 12-seat power catamaran, links St. Barts with Sint

Maarten (Philipsburg) and Saint-Martin (Marigot, also bookable through the **Yacht Charter Agency**, 27 62 38). **The Pearl Express Line** (tel: 27 77 38) also runs ferries between St. Barts and Saint-Martin, under 45 minutes, on the *Galatea*. Catamarans between Philipsburg (Sint Maarten) and Gustavia make one-day excusions; reservations at Bobby's Marina, **Philipsburg** (tel: 599 5-23170). **Marine Service** (tel: 27 70 34) does day trips around St. Barts and cruises to Saint-Martin, Anguilla, Saba, and the Virgin Islands on its four-cabin catamaran; also rents out powerboats; **La Calèche Yacht Charter Agency** (tel: 27 62 38) sails to Colombier Bay and Fourchue island, all-day, half-day, or sunset cruises; **La Maison de la Mer** (tel: 27 81 00) runs day trips to Fourchue and Colombier Bay, with snorkeling and scuba-diving possibilities, as well as cruises to Anguilla, Saba, and St. Kitts. **Stardust** (tel: 27 79 81) offers day charters and week cruises around St. Barts and Saint-Martin, and day tours by boat from Gustavia to Colombier beach.
By road There are two taxi stands, one at the airport and one in Gustavia on rue de la République (tel: 27 66 31). Cabs are unmetered, so you may be charged more if you stop on the way—check ahead. Minibuses and taxis do island tours. Radio cabs can be called on 27 66 31, 27 60 59, or 27 63 12. Fares are 50 percent higher after 8 p.m.

Motorcycles can be rented near the airport and in Gustavia (helmet compulsory). Try **Ouanalao Motos**, at airport (tel: 27 88 74), **Denis Dufau**, Gustavia (tel: 27 70 59), **Topolino's** (tel: 27 70 92), **Rent Some Fun** (tel: 27 70 59).
Sightseeing Tours can be arranged through your hotel, the tourist office or any of the taxi operators including **Hugo Cagan** (tel: 27 61 28), **Florian La Place** (tel: 27 63 58). Local operators include **Agence Mast'air**, St-Jean (tel: 27 77 43); **St. Barth Voyages**, Gustavia (tel: 27 79 79).

Tourist information
The **Office du Tourisme** is in the Mairie de St. Barthélemy (town hall),

rue Auguste Nyman, Gustavia (tel: 27 60 08).

SAINT-MARTIN/SINT MAARTEN
Car rental and driving

Your own driver's license is sufficient to rent a car on both sides: you must be at least 25. Cars can be rented at Juliana Airport, but you have to take a taxi to the rental parking lots (Hertz is the nearest). Companies include: **Avis** (tel: 87 50 60 or 42322); **Budget** (tel: 87 38 22 or 54274); **Cannegie Car Rental** (tel: 22397); **Concordia Rental** (tel: 87 94 18); **Continental** (tel: 87 77 64); **Dollar** (tel: 22698); **Esperance** (tel: 87 51 09); **Express** (tel: 87 70 98); **Fantastic** (tel: 87 96 98); **Hertz** (tel: 54314 or 87 73 01); **Hibiscus** (tel: 87 74 53); **Island Trans** (tel: 87 91 32); **National** (tel: 44268); **Risdon's** (tel: 22579); **SandyG Rent-a-Car** (tel: 53 335 or 87 88 25); **Sunset** (tel: 87 51 46); **Triple A** (tel: 87 37 17).

Driving is on the right, and road signs are international. Speed limits are 80kph (50mph) outside the towns, 30kph (19mph) in towns; drunk-driving carries fines, as do illegal parking, speeding, and running traffic lights; seatbelts should be worn and gas is paid for in cash.

Getting around

By air Saint-Martin/Sint Maarten is linked to many other Caribbean islands on regional and international carriers (lighter aircraft use L'Esperance Airport on the French side): by **Air Guadeloupe** (tel: 54212) to Dominica, Guadeloupe, Les Saintes, Marie Galante, Martinique, Puerto Rico, St. Barts, St. Thomas; by **Air Martinique** (tel: 53599) to Guadeloupe, Martinique, St. Lucia, St. Vincent; by **Air Saint-Barthélemy** (tel: 53152) to St. Barts; by **ALM** (tel: 54230) to Aruba, Bonaire, Curaçao, and the Dominican Republic; by **American Eagle** to Puerto Rico; by **BWIA** to Antigua, Jamaica, Puerto Rico, Trinidad; by **Liat** (tel: 54203) to Anguilla, Antigua, Barbados, Dominica, Grenada, Guadeloupe, Martinique, Montserrat, Puerto Rico, St. Croix, St. Kitts/Nevis, St. Lucia, St. Vincent, Trinidad and Tobago; by

Winair (the local airline tel: 44230) to Anguilla, Dominica, Montserrat, Saba, St. Barts, St. Eustatius, St. Kitts/Nevis, St. Thomas, Tortola. **Saint-Martin Helicopters** (Dutch side tel: 54287) and **Heli-Inter Caraibes** (French side tel: 87 37 37) run sightseeing excursions and act as taxis or as emergency services.

By boat There are anchorages around the island, and you can get to any of the neighboring islands of Anguilla, Saba, St. Eustatius, and St. Barts by boat. The St. Barts Express leaves St. Barts every morning (except Sunday), stopping at Philipsburg and the deep-water harbor at Marigot (French side), returning via the same route later in the day.

Ferries between Marigot and Anguilla leave from both every half hour between 8 a.m. and 5:30 p.m., and there are two late-evening crossings. It takes 20 minutes. You need your passport or some other form of identification with photograph, and there is a departure tax.

A catamaran service (tel: 22167) links Philipsburg (Bobby's Marina) with Saba four times a week. Day-trips by sail or motorboat can be arranged, for example from Marina Port La Royale, Marigot (tel: 87 20 43), or from Port Longvilliers, Anse Marcel (tel: 87 31 94). Companies chartering boats, with or without skipper, include: **Sun Yacht-Charters** (tel: 800 772 3500) in Oyster Pond; **The Moorings** (tel: 87 32 55), also in Oyster Pond; **Dynasty**, Port La Royale Marina (tel: 87 85 21). Picnics to nearby islands or coves, including Anguilla, are organized from the Dutch side aboard *Gabrielle* (tel: 23170); *Pretty Penny* (tel: 52167); *Bluebeard II* (tel: 42801); *White Octopus* (tel: 23170—also does day trips to St. Barts from Bobby's Marina, Philipsburg). From the French side, sailing excursions are organized through **Pat Turner Watersports**, Le Galion (tel: 87 51 77); **Papagayo**, Club Orient (tel: 87 33 85); **L'Habitation** (tel: 87 33 33); **La Belle Créole** (tel: 87 58 66); **La Samanna** (tel: 87 51 22).

By road Taxi rates across the island are fixed and standardized—you can get a list from the tourist offices, and rates are posted at the airport. Taxis can be called at 87 56 54 (Marigot) or 54317 (Juliana Airport); also at 23362/23366 (Dutch side). Authorized taxis display stickers of the Sint Maarten Taxi Association.

Buses run frequently between 7 a.m. and 7 p.m. from Philipsburg through Cole Bay to Marigot.

Sightseeing Various companies offer tours, including **Dutch Tours**, Welgelegen (tel: 23316), minimum 10 people; **Fantasy Tours & Services**, Philipsburg (tel: 23201); **Paradise Vacation Tours**, Philipsburg (tel: 22230); **Rep Tourism**, Marigot (tel: 87 03 79); **Sint Maarten Sightseeing Tours**, Philipsburg (tel: 22753); **Saint-Martin Evasion**, Galisbay (tel: 87 73 01); **Services Touristiques**, Laguna Beach (tel: 87 89 96). **Sint Maarten Limousine Services** (tel: 24698 or 22698) will ferry up to six people, with stereo, bar, etc., minimum three hours.

Tourist information

Dutch side: **Sint Maarten Tourist Bureau**, Walter Nisbeth Road #23, Philipsburg, Sint Maarten (tel: 22337). There is a tourist information bureau on Cyrus Wathey Square, Philipsburg, at the cruise ship pier (tel: 22337). French side: **Office du Tourisme de Saint-Martin**, Port de Marigot, 97150 Saint-Martin (tel: 87 53 26). Tourist information office on the water front in Marigot: 87 57 21/23.

NETHERLANDS ANTILLES

ARUBA
Car rental and driving

You need a valid national or international license; each car-rental company specifies an age range for rental (min. 21, or 25–65, or 23–70, for example). All companies include unlimited mileage, but not insurance. Try **Airways** (tel: 21845); **Avis** (tel: 28787; airport 25496); **Budget** (tel: 28600; airport 25423); **Dollar** (tel: 22783; airport 25651); **Five Star** (tel: 27600); **Hertz, De Palm** (tel: 24545; airport 24886); **Marco's** (tel: 25295); **National** (tel: 21967; airport 25451); **Ricardos** (tel: 21161); **Thrifty** (tel:

35335); **Toyota Rent-a-Car** (tel: 34832; airport 34902).

Main roads are in good condition, but most of the major sites worth seeing are down dirt roads, and traveling by car is the only way to get there. Four-wheel drive vehicles are recommended. Driving is on the right, and traffic from the right has right of way; watch out for aggressive local drivers and goat herds. Road signs are international. The speed limit in towns is 40kph (25mph), 60kph (37mph) out of town.

Getting around

By air Call the airport (tel: 24800) for information on **KLM**, **ALM** or **BWIA** flights. ALM links Aruba to Bonaire, Curaçao, Sint Maarten and other islands. Ask about its Visit Caribbean Pass. **American Eagle** (tel: 22700) links with Puerto Rico. BWIA flies to Trinidad and Tobago. **Air Aruba** (tel: 36600) links with the Dominican Republic (Santo Domingo), Sint Maarten, Bonaire, and Curaçao.

By boat There is a ferry linking Aruba with Curaçao and Venezuela (cars carried), but it is not recommended for tourists—more of a cargo boat. Bookings are made through **Rufo U Winterdaal** (tel: 21533/21156). There is also a fruit boat running between Oranjestad and Punto Fijo, Venezuela (contact **Agencia Maritima La Confianza**: 23814).

Atlantis Submarine (tel: 36090) visits Barcadera Reef, 50 minutes. Sailing cruises around the island, or moonlight, catamaran or dinner cruises, with stops for swimming and snorkelling, can be arranged through **De Palm Tours** (tel: 24400), **Mi Dushi** (tel: 26034), **Red Sail Sports** (tel: 31603), **Pelican Watersports** (tel: 24739), **Wave Dancer** (tel: 25520), **Topaz** (tel: 24401). Classic yachts for island hopping, day-sails etc: *Tranquilo* (contact Mike, its captain, 47533) and *Wyvern II* (tel: 36184).

The tourist office has a list of boats available for day or half-day charter for deep-sea fishing.

By road Taxi rates are fixed—make sure you agree on the price before setting off; prices go up in the evening and overnight. Taxis can be

258

flagged down, or called at 22116 (main dispatch office, Oranjestad), or 45160 in San Nicolas. Taxi drivers should all have Tourism Guide Certificates and speak English.

Buses run between Oranjestad and the southeast of the island, and to the beach hotels, and between Oranjestad and the airport. Oranjestad bus station is on Zoutmanstraat. A free, colorful shopping tour bus, the Let's Go Town bus, departs every hour from 9:15 a.m. to 3:15 p.m. from the Holiday Inn, stopping at all major hotels (you have to make your own way back). There are also jitney cars that operate like shared taxis. A jitney or bus from Oranjestad to San Nicolas will drop you off at the airport. Buses stick to their timetables—available from the tourist offices—and run one or two an hour.

Motorcycles, scooters, and mopeds can be rented from **Donazine Cycle Car Rental** (tel: 27014); **George Cycle Center** (tel: 25975); **Ron's Motorcycle Rental** (tel: 32090); **K&M Scooter Rental** (tel: 32671); **Nelson Motorcycle Rental** (tel: 26801); **Semver Cycle Rental** (tel: 26851).

Sightseeing The major local operator is **De Palm Tours** (tel: 24400/24545), which has offices in most hotels. It offers a large choice of excursions, including a three-hour tour of Aruba's highlights, and a day-tour to Curaçao and to Caracas, Venezuela. Archeological/ geological tours, with day-long field trips, plus architectural, bird-watching, and botanical tours, are best arranged through **Corvalou Tours** (tel: 21149).

Other operators for island tours by bus, watersports, boating, transfers, trips to Caracas, etc.: **Pelican Tours** (tel: 23888/31228); **ECO Destination Management** (tel: 26034); **Aruba Taxi Transfer & Tours** (tel: 22116); **General Travel Bureau** (tel: 26609); **Tiny Tours** (tel: 47449); **Friendly Tours** (tel: 25800); **Pacer Survival Tour** (tel: 36791; morning tour by 18-speed bikes); **Marlin Booster Tracking Inc** (tel: 45086/41513, six-hour historical and wildlife tour with archeologists); **Private Safaris Educational Tours** (tel: 34869, land

cruisers into the interior).

Hiking: three-hour guided trip to spots only accessible on foot, minimum four people, through **De Palm Tours** (tel: 24545).

Tourist information
Aruba Tourism Authority, LG Smith Blvd. 172, Box 1019, Oranjestad (tel: 23777) for brochures and guides. There are also tourist information centers at the harbor in Oranjestad and at the airport.

BONAIRE
Car rental and driving
A national or international license is required, and most of the 10 or so companies stipulate a minimum age. Try **ABC** (tel: 8980); **Avis** (tel: 5795); **Budget** (tel: 8300; airport 8315); **Camel Rent-a-Car** (tel: 5120); **Dollar** (tel: 5600); **Erkar** (tel: 8536); **Flamingo Car Rental** (tel: 8313); **Sunray Car Rental** (tel: 5600); **Trupial Car Rental** (tel: 8487).

Driving is on the right. The speed limit in built-up areas is 33kph (20mph), and outside towns 60kph (37mph) unless otherwise specified. There are no traffic lights, and the main roads are good, but there are 20 miles of unpaved roads that get very muddy during the rainy season. Roads are apt to become one-way halfway along. Beware of potholes, lizards, and herds of goats. There are very few watering holes: On island trips take food and drink supplies.

There are gas stations in Kralendijk, Antrejol, and Rincon, these being open Monday to Saturday 7 a.m.–9 p.m.; Kralendijk also open Sunday 9 a.m.–3:30 p.m.

Getting around
By air ALM provides links with Curaçao, Aruba, Sint Maarten and other Caribbean islands via Curaçao. **Air Aruba** links with Aruba. Both also connect with South America. ALM/KLM/Air Aruba can be contacted on 8300, ext. 220, 221, 222 or, out of normal office hours, on 8500. Ask about an ALM Visit Caribbean Pass for inter-island travel.
By boat More people come to Bonaire to dive than to sail or putter around in boats (ask hotels about

259

their diving packages). Klein Bonaire is reached by diving boats: hitch a lift if you do not plan to dive, and don't miss the return. Snorkeling, picnicking, and sunset cruises are offered by the *Samur* (tel: 5252), the *Iltshi* (tel: 5252), the *Woodwind* (tel: 8285) and the *Oscarina* (tel: 8290).

By road Taxis are not metered, but prices are fixed, and should be agreed with the driver before setting off. Taxis meet flights, or can be ordered through hotels or from a central dispatch office (tel: 8100); they do not drive around looking for fares. Any taxi driver will take you on an island tour.

Motorbikes and scooters can be rented from **Happy Chappy Rentals** (tel: 8761) and **Bonaire Trading Company** (tel: 8300); bicycles from **Divi Flamingo Beach Hotel** (tel: 8285), **Sand Dollar Grocery** (tel: 5490); **Captain Don's Habitat** (tel: 8290).

Sightseeing Ask in the tourist office about guided visits to the two Flamingo nesting sites. **Bonaire Sightseeing Tours** (tel: 8300) does four island tours and day trips to Curaçao.

Tourist information
Bonaire Tourist Board, Kaya Simon Bolivar 12, Kralendijk (tel: 8322/8649) can provide a small amount of tourist information and leaflets but no maps. **Bonhata**, the Bonaire Hotel and Tourist Association, can be contacted at 5134.

CURAÇAO
Car rental and driving
Your own national or an international driver's license must be presented. Many of the car-rental companies have airport offices, allowing you to compare prices. **Avis** (tel: 681163); **Budget** (tel: 683466); **Caribe Rentals** (tel: 613089); **Dollar** (tel: 690262); **Love Car Rental** (tel: 379044); **National Inter-rent** (tel: 683489/636182); **Pro Rent a Car** (tel: 691489); **Romart Car Rental** (tel: 627688); **Ruiz Rent a Car** (tel: 373184); **Star Rent a Car** (tel: 627444); **24 Hours Car Rental** (tel: 617568). Take a jeep for driving in the country or through Christoffel

Park (Buggy Rental Madeirense 73333).

Driving is on the right, and international signs are used. The speed limit in built-up areas is 40kph (25mph), and out of town 60kph (37mph) unless specified. Traffic from the right has right of way.

The north coast is worth seeing by car but much of it is down dusty lanes.

Getting around
By air ALM (tel: 613033), which uses Curaçao as its hub, provides links with Miami, Trinidad, Aruba, Bonaire, Sint Maarten, Puerto Rico, Jamaica, Dominican Republic, and South America. **Air Aruba** (tel: 683777/683659) operates between Curaçao and Miami, Aruba, Bonaire, and Sint Maarten. **American Airlines** flies to Puerto Rico. Flights from Curaçao to Aruba or Bonaire take 15–20 minutes. KLM information: 613033; BWIA 687835/613033. Helicopter flights can be booked with **Pelican Air** (tel: 628155).

By boat A cargo/ferryboat runs between Aruba, Curaçao, and Venezuela (see Aruba section). Contact **Sail Curaçao** (tel: 676003) for boat trips, sailing school, or yacht charter.

By road Taxis have TX on their licenses. Fares are fixed, and should be agreed upon first. Meters are soon to be installed. There are taxi stands at the airport and hotels and Plaza Jojo Correa, downtown Willemstad. Fares go up by 25 percent after 11 p.m., and there may be a charge for excess baggage. Central taxi office: 690747/52. Tipping is not obligatory. Some hotels provide free transportation to and from the city center.

Yellow public buses (known locally as convoys) or private vans or cars with BUS on their license plates, take 6–14 passengers and are an inexpensive way of getting around. There are regularly scheduled bus routes between important sights, hotels, beaches, airport. Most leave from Punda Bus Terminal (market place) or the Otrabanda Bus Terminal, Rif Fort. For prices and schedules contact **ABC** (tel: 684733).

Sightseeing It is worth taking a tour if you are going beyond Willemstad. Try

Casper Tours (tel: 653010); **Taber Tours** (tel: 376637); **Harbour Tours** (tel: 611257); **Daltino Tours** (tel: 614888); **Old City Tours** (tel: 613554). Hourly tours of the Hato Caves are given by local guides, reservations and information 680379. Christoffel Park (640363) offers bird-watching and guided jeep trips—take the Westpunt bus from Otrobanda bus terminal, every two hours from 7 a.m.

Tourist information
There are three offices of the **Curaçao Tourism Development Board**: a booth at the airport (tel: 686789), the main office on Pietermaai 19, PO Box 3266, Willemstad (tel: 616000), an office in the Waterfort Arches, Punda (tel: 613397). There are also various visitor information kiosks, one at the Cruise Terminal in Otrobanda, another at Wilhelminaplein in Punda. **Curaçao Hotel and Tourism Association**, International Trade Center, Piscadera Bay (tel: 636260).

SABA
Car rental and driving
Cars can be rented (produce your own driver's license), including a full tank of gas and unlimited mileage, from **Avis** (tel: 62279); **Doc's Car Rentals** (tel: 62271); **Scout's Place** (tel: 62205); or **Juliana's** (tel: 62269), all in Windwardside.

Driving is on the right, along the island's only road, The Road. In the event of a breakdown, call the only gas station (Fort Bay) on 63272.

Getting around
By air Winair (local: 62255; Sint Maarten 5 42255/44237) flies several times a day between Saba and Sint Maarten and also to St. Eustatius. Reconfirm flights in advance.
By boat An open-air, 50-passenger ferry, *Style* (Sint Maarten 5 22167), plies between Saba (Fort Bay) and Sint Maarten (Great Bay Marina, Philipsburg) between Tuesday and Saturday, leaving Great Bay at 9 a.m. and returning from Saba at 5 p.m. The journey takes 60 minutes.

The three dive operators on Saba, **Saba Deep** (tel: 63347/62201), **Sea Saba** (tel: 62246), and **Wilson's Dive**

Shop at Fort Bay Pier have boats available for round-island trips, deep-sea fishing, trips to nearby islands or other parts of Saba; the latter has two boats you can stay on for week-long diving vacations.
By road There are about 10 taxi drivers on Saba, all of whom do guided tours. Taxi drivers can also arrange diving or nature walks; some double as guest house owners. It is also safe to hitchhike, and there are key places to wait for a lift: the wall opposite the Anglican Church in The Bottom; the wall opposite Saba Deep in Fort Bay. There are no buses.
Hiking Saba has 18 nature trails through the rain forest and up Mount Scenery. For a guided walk, try **Bernard Johnson** (tel: 62209) or **Anna Keene** for botanical tours (through the tourist office); or ask in the tourist office.

Tourist information
Saba Tourist Office, Windwardside (tel: 4 62231).

ST. EUSTATIUS
Car rental and driving
You need a valid driver's license from your own country or an international driver's license. There is an **Avis** desk at the airport (tel: 82421); or try **Lady Ama's Services** (tel: 82451); **Rainbow Car Rental** (tel: 82586). Cars are reliable, but the roads are not: Watch out for potholes. Driving is on the right, but some roads are very narrow and liable to be frequented by cows, goats, and sheep. Road signs are in Dutch and English.

Getting around
By air Liat (tel: 82398) links with St. Kitts (15 mins); **Windward Island Airways** (tel: 82362/82381) flies to and from Sint Maarten several times a day, and to St. Kitts, Saba (10 minutes), Nevis (35 mins). Liat flies once a week from Antigua via St. Kitts or Nevis.
By boat A boat runs between Statia and Marigot, Saint-Martin, once a week; it will sometimes takes passengers.
By road On round-the-island taxi tours the driver will give the guided

261

tour or play a tape. You can also get this from the **Historical Foundation** in Doncker/de Graaff House, 12 Van Tonningenweg (tel: 22288). Most places are within walking distance: the Historical Foundation has a brochure detailing a one-and-a-half-hour walking tour of the Upper and Lower Towns; there is also an information booth in the Lower Town.

Moped rental can be arranged through your hotel, the tourist office, or the Avis desk at the airport. Hiking: there are 12 nature trails, detailed on a leaflet available from the tourist office. Or take a two-and-a-half-hour guided trek into tropical rainforest on the Quill volcano, organized through the tourist office.

Tourist information
There are three tourist offices: at the airport, in Lower Town (Oranjestad) opposite Roro Pier (St. Eustatius Historical Society), and the main **St. Eustatius Tourist Bureau**, at the entrance to Fort Oranje, 3 Fort Oranjestraat, Oranjestad, St. Eustatius, Netherlands Antilles (tel: 3 82433/82209).

OTHER CARIBBEAN STATES

JAMAICA
Car rental and driving
Most major international companies are represented and there are many local ones; a list of the Jamica U-Drive Association members is obtainable from Jamaica Tourist Board, address below. A valid driver's license is required, and you must usually be at least 23, if not 25. A 10 percent government tax is added; accident and health insurance and collision damage waiver optional.

Some gas stations are closed on Sundays, and gas must be paid for in cash. The speed limit is 48kph (30mph) in towns and 80kph (50mph) on the highway. Driving is on the left.

Getting around
By air There are two main domestic carriers: **Airways International** and **Trans-Jamaican** (booking in Kingston tel: 923 8680/9098; in Montego Bay 952 5401/2/3; in Negril 957 4251; in Ocho Rios 979 3254), serving airports across the island (Negril, Ocho Rios, Port Antonio, Tinson Pen). You need to book at least a day in advance with Trans Jamaican Airlines.

Helitours (tel: 974 2265) runs sightseeing trips, with pick-ups at most local airports. Helicopters can also be chartered.

By boat Ask at your hotel or nearest tourist information center about private charters for deep-sea fishing, scuba diving, and sailing.

By road Buses are by far the cheapest way to get around. Minibuses run all over the island and can be flagged down at bus stops and in between. Bicycles and motorbikes can be rented at most resorts or through the following companies: **Montego Bike Rentals** (tel: 952 4984); **Western Bike Rental**, Montego Bay (tel: 952 0185); **Motor Trails**, Ocho Rios (tel: 974 5058); **Negril Bike Rentals** (tel: 957 4357); **Rhodes Hall Plantation** (tel: 957 4232).

Taxis are in all resort areas but are not often metered; prices between destinations are usually fixed, so ask the price for the journey before starting, or be prepared to bargain with the driver. Look out for red P.P.V. plates (Public Passenger Vehicle).

By train Jamaica Railway Corporation used to operate two daily services from Montego Bay to Kingston and back through mountains. It is not currently in service, but may be again in the future. Call 922 6620 (Kingston), or 952 4842 (Montego Bay) to check.

Sightseeing Get the Tourist Board leaflet *Things to know before you go*, updated annually, which lists prices of main excursions and attractions, together with hours and days of operation. These might include: Boonoonoonoos Beach Party (reggae, dinner, floor show); guided half-day tour of Croydon in the Mountains (working plantation in Catadupa); Evening on the Great River (canoe trip, dinner); full-day guided tour of Hilton High plantation;

one-hour rafting trip on The Great River with hayride and plantation tour, etc. Contact the **Touring Society of Jamaica** (tel: 954 2383) for information on bird-watching tours. Your hotel will be able to organize any tour, which may be in a taxi with driver-guide or minibus and include any admission price in the cost.

Local tour operators for organizing your own island tour and inter-island travel: **Blue Danube Tours** (tel: 490 1890); **Caribic Vacations** (tel: 952 5013); **CS Tours Jamaica** (tel: 952 6260); **Forsythe Tours** (tel: 952 0797); **Glamour Tours** (tel: 952 0640); **Grace Tours** (tel: 929 7860); **Greenlight Tours** (tel: 952 2636); **Jamaica Tours** (tel: 952 2887); **JUTA Jamaica** (tel: 952 0813); **Martin's Vacations** (tel: 594 4561); **Pleasure Tours** (tel: 952 5383); **Sun Holiday Tours** (tel: 952 5629); **Tourmarks** (tel: 929 5078); **Tourwise** (tel: 952 4943); **Travel International Tours** (tel: 952 9362); **Tropical Tours** (tel: 952 1110); **Xaymaca Tours** (tel: 952 3274); **Vacations Tours** (tel: 952 0728).

Tourist information
Jamaica Tourist Board, 1 High Street, Black River (tel: 965 2076); Tourism Centre, 21 Dominica Drive, Kingston (tel: 929 9200); 21 Ward Avenue, Mandeville (tel: 962 1072); Cornwall Beach, Montego Bay (tel: 952 4425); Shop #9, Adrija Plaza, Negril (tel: 957 4243); Ocean Village Shopping Centre, Ocho Rios (tel: 974 2582); City Centre Plaza, Port Antonio (tel: 993 3051).

CAYMAN ISLANDS
Car rental and driving
A valid driver's license must first be produced and a Cayman driving permit produced. Different companies specify different minimum ages for renting cars, ranging between 18 and 25. The main companies represented are: **Ace Hertz** (tel: 949 2280); **Andy's Rent-a-Car** (tel: 949 8111); **Budget** (tel: 949 5605); **CICO-Avis** (tel: 947 4044); **Coconut Car Rentals** (tel: 947 4377); **Economy Car Rental** (tel: 949 9550); **Holiday Payless** (tel:

949 7074); **National Car Rental** (tel: 949 4790). Gas is sold in imperial (160-oz.) gallons.

Driving is on the left, and some rental vehicles have left-hand drive, but not many; drunk-driving laws are strictly observed; seatbelts are recommended.

Getting around
By air Between the three islands of Grand Cayman, Cayman Brac, and Little Cayman, **Cayman Airways** (tel: 949 2311) and **Island Air** (book through Cayman Airways) fly regular scheduled services.

By road There is no public transportation on Grand Cayman but plenty of cars, motorscooters, bicycles, and other vehicles to rent and taxis to hire. Taxi rates to and from principal destinations are determined by the government and published in CI$, so ask the driver how much the trip will cost before you start.

Motorcycles and bicycles can be rented from: **Cayman Cycle Rentals** (tel: 947 4021); **Honda Rentals/Caribbean Motors** (tel: 949 7386); **Soto Scooters** (tel: 947 4652).

A private bus service runs between West Bay and George Town at irregular intervals. It can be caught from the Kirk Freeport Centre or Kirk Plaza Supermarket in George Town.

By sea Boat excursions can be organized through **Red Sail Sports** (tel: 949 7965).

Sightseeing Numerous local travel agents (see those listed below) offer land and water-based excursions and tours; all can be booked on arrival in Grand Cayman. Local tour operators are mostly in Grand Cayman: **Evco Tours** (tel: 949 2118); **Majestic Tours** (tel: 949 7773); **Reid's Premier Tours** (tel: 949 6531); **Rudy's Travellers** (tel: 949 3208); **Tropicana Tours** (tel: 949 0944).

Tourist information
Department of Tourism 4th floor, Harbour Centre, North Church Street, George Town (tel: 949 8989).

DOMINICAN REPUBLIC
Car rental and driving

Your own driver's license, or an international license, allows you to drive in the Dominican Republic for 90 days. The minimum age for renting a car is 25. The following companies all have offices in Santo Domingo: **Avis** (tel: 532 2969); **Budget** (tel: 567 0177); **Dollar** (tel: 689 5329); **Nelly** (tel: 532 7346); **Hertz** (tel: 685 1251/1216/0454); **Honda Rent-a-Car** (tel: 567 1015); **National** (tel: 562 1444); **Patsy** (tel: 686 4333); **Rentauto** (tel: 567 5545); **Thrifty** (tel: 800 367 2277). Rental is expensive because of high tariffs on vehicles; credit cards are accepted and a large deposit taken, usually twice the weekly rental fee.

Driving is on the right, but local drivers can be erratic; watch out also for motorcyclists in towns. Tolls of a few cents are levied on all principal roads out of the capital. Speed limits are 80kph (50mph) on highways, 60kph (37mph) in suburban areas; 40kph (25mph) in cities unless otherwise specified. Gas stations are few and far between in country areas and generally close at about 6 p.m. Avoid night driving as narrow mountain roads are dark and treacherous. Cars driven by tourists are often stopped by police at the entrance to and exit from towns—this is nothing to worry about.

Getting around
By air Several regional carriers serve neighboring islands, including **ALM** (tel: 687 4569, to Sint Maarten and Curaçao); **American Eagle** (tel: 542 5151, to Puerto Rico from La Romana airport); **Air France** (tel: 686 8419, to Martinique, Guadeloupe and Haiti); **Air Aruba** (tel: 567 3072, to Aruba and Sint Maarten); **Aeropostal** (tel: 541 4232, to Curaçao); **Dominicana** (tel: 532 1146, to Puerto Rico). **Columbus Air** (tel: 571 2711) organizes tours by plane to Haiti or the Turks and Caicos Islands, and domestic flights between Santo Domingo, Puerto Plata, and Samana. **Agencia Portillo** (tel: 565 0832) offers air taxi services from Santo Domingo (Herrera airport) to Puerto Plata and Punta Cana. Other domes-

tic flights (linking Santo Domingo, Puerto Plata, Santiago, Samana, Barahona, Portillo, and La Romana) are operated by **Servicio Aereo Dominicano** (tel: 541 2667) and **Aeronaves Dominicanas** (tel: 567 7195).

By boat Leisure craft go to offshore islands, such as Cayo Levantado, from the dock at Samana and from Los Cacaos.

By road Taxis are unmetered. Although fares are government-regulated, they are negotiable assuming you and the driver speak the same language. Fares to destinations outside the city are posted in hotels and the airport.

Telephone-dispatched taxi services are another option: 24-hour service with rates agreed over the telephone, roughly depending on distances covered (but you usually need to speak Spanish). Taxi firms include **Centro Taxi** (tel: 687 6128), **Taxi la Paloma** (tel: 562 3460) and **Taxi Raffi** (tel: 689 5468).

Publicos, blue-and-white or blue-and-red cars that run regular routes stopping to let passengers on and off, are much cheaper; rates are fixed between cities. The cars are often crowded and uncomfortable.

Private buses—*conchos* or *colectivos*—are the colorful way to get around. Most leave from around Parque Independencia in Santo Domingo; exact change required.

Private air-conditioned buses make regular trips from Santo Domingo to Santiago, Puerto Plata, etc. To reserve a seat call **Metro Buses** (tel: 566 6590 in Santo Domingo, 586 6063 in Puerto Plata, 583 9111 in Santiago, 584 2259 in Nagua) or **Caribe Tours** (tel: 687 3171/586 4544), whose prices tend to be cheaper.

Motoconchos—motorbike taxis—are found on the streets of Puerto Plata, Sosua, and Jarabacoa: Flag them down on the road and in town and negotiate the fare.

Motorcycles are rented out around Puerto Plata and Playa Dorada; be sure to use the lock, as there is no insurance on motorcycle theft. Bicycles can be rented from **Villas Doradas**, Puerto Plata (tel: 586

3000), **Dorado Naco**, Dorado Beach (tel: 586 2019), **Jack Tar Village**, Puerto Plata (tel: 586 3800) and **Cofresi Beach Hotel**, Puerto Plata (tel: 586 2898).
Sightseeing Prieto Tours (tel: 685 0102) offers half-day bus tours of Santo Domingo, beach tours, tours to Cibao Valley and the Amber Coast, and others. **Turinter** (tel: 685 4020) does a full-day tour of Samana, and specialty tours (museums, shopping, fishing, casino visits). **Apolo Tours** (tel: 586 5329) offers a full-day tour covering Playa Grande, Santiago, and Sosua. **Ecoturisa** (tel: 221 4104) does wildlife tours of the western end of the country; **Maritissant** (tel: 685 7910) also specializes in tours to the national parks. **Museo de Historia y Geografia** (tel: 686 6668) does archeological and historical bus tours of the east of the country.

Tourist information
There is a Secretary of Tourism, opposite the Obelisk, in Av. George Washington, Box 497, Santo Domingo (tel: 682 8181); and in Puerto Plata, at Malecon 20 (tel: 586 3676). Tourist information can be obtained in most local town halls, and there are offices at Las Americas International Airport, La Union Airport, in Ayntamiento, Santiago (tel: 582 5885), in Jimani, Samana, and Boca Chica.

PUERTO RICO
Car rental and driving
Your national driver's license is preferred by rental companies to an international license. There are about 13 rental agencies including **Avis** (tel: 721 4499), **Hertz** (tel: 791 0840), **National** (tel: 791 1805), and **Budget** (tel: 791 3676).

Driving is on the right, with maximum speed on the expressway 88kph (55mph). Take a Spanish phrasebook if you are heading off the beaten track.

Getting around
By air American Airlines operate domestic flights every hour between San Juan and Ponce. Several local airlines operate services within Puerto Rico and between Puerto Rico and the rest of the Caribbean, including BWIA, Liat, Antilles Air Boats, Air Jamaica, Dominicana Airline, Sunaire Express, Virgin Islands Seaplane, Caribair, Prinair, Air Best, Culebra Aviation, Crownair, Air Indies, Aero Virgin Islands. All have offices at the Luis Munoz Marin International Airport (tel: 462 3147). **Vieques Air Link** (tel: 722 3736) flies from Isla Grande Airport to Vieques, about $28 one-way, and **Flamenco Airways** (tel: 725 7707) to Culebra.
By boat Passenger ferries run by the Fajardo Port Authority (tel: 863 0705) ply between Fajardo Beach and Vieques twice daily, taking 80 minutes. From Fajardo to Culebra there are daily ferries; from Vieques to Culebra, ferries go three times a week.
By road All taxis are metered but can be hired unmetered for sightseeing, etc. Shared taxis (*publicos*) have yellow license plates with P or PD at the end and operate all over the island, stopping in each town's main plaza. They take up to 17 passengers, and their routes and fares are fixed by the Public Service Commission (tel: 751 5050). Main terminals are at the airport and Plaza Colon in Old San Juan. **Airport Limousine Service** (tel: 791 4745) provides a minibus or shared-taxi service from the airport to hotels in Isla Verde, Condado, and Old San Juan. **Dorado Transport Service** (tel: 796 1214) serves hotels and villas in the Dorado area.

The city buses in San Juan (*guaguas*) are operated by the Metropolitan Bus Authority (tel: 767 7979) and travel on a special route against the traffic flow. Bus stops, which are yellow posts, are marked *Parada de Guaguas*. City buses are not frequent: 30–45 minutes apart, and not after 10 p.m. The main terminals are Intermodal Terminal on Calles Marina and Harding in Old San Juan and Capetille terminal in Rio Piedras, next to the Central Business District.

Elsewhere on the island, **Puerto Rico Motor Coach Co** (tel: 725 2460) has daily scheduled service between San Juan, Arecibo, and Mayaguez through Caguas and Cayey or Salinas. Bus T1 goes between the airport and

Plaza Colon in San Juan; people take precedence over luggage if the bus is full. Open-air trolleys also rattle around Old San Juan, leaving from La Puntilla and the marina; you can board anywhere, and there is no charge.

Bicycles can be rented at Boqueron Balnearios (beaches), and from Hyatt hotels (tel: 796 1234).

Sightseeing Tours of San Juan, the Bacardi Rum plant, the beaches, and the rainforest, etc., can be arranged through: **Borinquen Tours** (tel: 725 4990); **Gray Line of Puerto Rico** (tel: 727 8080); **Normandie Tours** (tel: 725 6990); **Rich Sunshine Tours** (tel: 729 2929); **Rico Suntours** (tel: 722 2080); **United Tour Guides** (tel: 725 7605); **Cordero Caribbean Tours** (tel: 799 6002).

Tourist information
Puerto Rico Tourist Bureau, PO Box 4435, San Juan 00905. There are tourist information offices at the international airport (tel: 791 1014/2551), at Convention Center Condado (tel: 723 3135), at La Casita, near Pier 1, Old San Juan (tel: 722 1709), and also in Ponce at Casa Armstrong-Poventud, Plaza, Las Delicias (tel: 840 5695). Town halls throughout the country will have information desks. The government-sponsored **Puerto Rico Tourism Company** (tel: 721 2400) is good for maps, brochures, etc., and *Que Pasa*, the official visitors guide.

BARBADOS
Car rental and driving
A visitor's driver's license must be purchased from car-rental companies, the airport, or Oistins, Hastings, Worthing, Holetown, District E, or Speightstown Police Stations; drivers must have held a full license for at least two years and be over 24. There are car-rental companies in every district (the tourist board has the complete list), including: **Regency** (tel: 427 5663), **National** (tel: 426 0603), **Dear's Garage** (tel: 429 9277), **Sunny Isle** (tel: 435 7979), **Sunset Crest Rentals** (tel: 432 1482), **P&S Car Rentals** (tel: 424 2052).

Driving is on the left, and speed limits are 59kph (37mph) in the country, 34kph (21mph) in towns and 96kph (60mph) or 128kph (80mph) on the highway. Seatbelts are not mandatory, and there are no drunk-driving laws as such, though police could stop you for bad driving. Gas generally has to be bought in cash.

Getting around
By air Airlines linking Barbados with St. Vincent and the Grenadines, St. Lucia, Trinidad, and the rest of the Caribbean on scheduled services include **British Airways** (local booking tel: 436 6413), **BWIA** (tel: 426 2111), **Liat** (tel: 436 6224), **Air St. Vincent/Air Mustique** (tel: 456 4176).

Helicopter tours, a stomach-lurching way of seeing the island, are offered by **Bajan Helicopters** (tel: 431 0069).

By boat There are no ferries linking Barbados with other islands. The *Jolly Roger* "pirate" ship (tel: 436 6424) is the rum-and-lunch way of seeing the island from the water; or try more low-key cruises on the *Wind Warrior* (tel: 425 5800) or the *Secret Love* (tel: 425 5800). Yacht charter companies include: **Blue Jay Charters** (tel: 422 2098 for deep-sea fishing), **Sailing Charter Tiami Cruises** (tel: 425 5800), and **Carie-Dee** (tel: 422 2319).

By road Bright yellow minibuses with blue stripes, run by the Barbados Transport Board, provide a regular service around the island, with destinations usually displayed at the bottom left-hand corner of the windshield. There are three terminals in Bridgetown, plus Speightstown Terminal in the north providing a service to Bridgetown along the west coast, to eastern areas, and a bypass service from Speightstown to the south coast. For information on routes call the Transport Board Headquarters (tel: 436 6820).

A number of privately-owned maxi-taxis (minibuses) and route taxis also operate (not color-coded). These can be picked up at normal bus stops.

Taxi fares between principal destinations are set in Bds dollars—check before traveling.

Sightseeing Tours can be organized through hotels or through companies such as: **LE Williams Tour Co** (tel: 427 1043); **United Taxi Owners' Association** (tel: 426 1496); **Barbados Transport Cooperative Society** (tel: 428 6565); **VIP Tour Services** (tel: 429 4617), which runs private air-conditioned cars with driver/guides.

Bike Barbados (tel: 422 2858) arranges cycling tours and rents bicycles. Motor scooters and bicycles also available from **Fun Seekers Inc** (tel: 435 8206).

Hike Barbados (tel: 426 2421) organizes guided Sunday walks. For visits to the Grenadines, St. Lucia, Grenada, Tobago, and Angel Falls by sea and air: **Islands à la Carte** (tel: 427 5100); **St. James Travel & Tours** (tel: 432 0774); **Chantours** (tel: 432 5591); **Grenadine Tours** (tel: 435 8451).

Tourist information
Barbados Tourism Authority, PO Box 242, Harbour Road, Bridgetown, Barbados (tel: 427 2623/4). **Barbados Hotel Association** (tel: 426 5041).

TRINIDAD AND TOBAGO
Car rental and driving
To rent a car you must have a valid driver's license from your own country and be at least 21. For a comprehensive list of car-rental companies in Port of Spain, Piarco Airport, San Fernando, and the south of Trinidad, and Tobago, ask for the *Discover Trinidad and Tobago* booklet from the tourist office. Beware: In Trinidad it can sometimes take an entire morning for a satisfactory rental car to be delivered. On Tobago it is more economical to rent a jeep than take a taxi, although there are some great taxi driver/guides. Try **Sweet Jeeps** (tel: 639 8533) or **Tobago Travel** (tel: 639 8778).

Driving is on the left, and the roads are good in cities and towns, but check with the locals before venturing elsewhere, particularly in Tobago; you might be halfway down one side of the island only to find the road impassable.

All gas stations are owned by National Petroleum, and all should accept credit cards. There is no seat-belt law, but drunk-driving laws are strictly enforced (fining or detention). Speed limits are 80kph (50mph) on the highways, 40–60kph (25–37mph) on minor roads and 30kph (18mph) in residential areas.

Getting around
By air Regular 15-minute flights on BWIA (Trinidad tel: 625 5866; Tobago 627 2942) and **Liat** (tel: 623 4480/ 1837/8) link Trinidad and Tobago (up to 10 a day), so you can hop from one to the other for a day. Liat also links Trinidad and Tobago with the rest of the Caribbean. Aircraft may be chartered in Trinidad from **Sun Island Aviation** (tel: 623 1301); **Briko Air Services** (tel: 664 3915); **Diamond Air** (tel: 624 4555); **Ibis Air Services** (tel: 638 3808); **Light Aeroplane Club** (tel: 669 1845); **Nealco Air Services** (tel: 664 5416); or through **Trinidad & Tobago Sightseeing Tours** (tel: 628 1051).

By sea A car ferry/passenger service from Port of Spain to Tobago (Scarborough) leaves twice a day, taking between five and six hours, with food and drink on board; you can return by plane if you prefer. You can rent a cabin if you take the evening sail. Timetables and reservations can be obtained through the tourist board (see below); tickets are sold at ferry offices in Port of Spain (tel: 625 4906) and Scarborough (tel: 639 2181).

For scuba diving and snorkeling, try **Dive Tobago** (tel: 639 0202), **Sean Robinson** (tel: 639 1279), **Tobago Marine Sports** (tel: 639 0291), **Tobago Scuba** (tel: 660 4327), **Tobago Dive Experience** (tel: 639 0191).

By road There are two types of taxis: rental and route, identifiable by their H license plates. Rental taxis are private, carrying you where you want. They do not have meters and although their rates are theoretically fixed, they tend to be negotiable (especially during Carnival) if you have the energy to haggle. An official list of rates for some routes, quoted in TT dollars (though some taxi drivers will accept U.S. dollars), is posted at the airport or obtainable from the Tourist Board. Drivers do tours also: Prices depend on how many passengers, how far you are traveling, how long you want the driver to wait: Take the official rate as the basis for your negotiations.

Less expensive are route taxis, which operate like buses on prescribed routes, picking up as many passengers as can fit. They tend to start and finish around Independence Square, Port of Spain, and come in two forms: Cars taking four or five passengers (some with small signs on their dashboards denoting the route—otherwise you have to spot the H license plate, flag one down and ask where it's going), and maxi-taxis. These are color-coded, 11- or 25-seat minibuses—complete with blaring stereos—that ply particular routes according to their color (you can hail them anywhere also). Yellow ones operate around Port of Spain, red in eastern Trinidad, green for south Trinidad, black for Princes Town, brown for San Fernando, and blue in Tobago. Both kinds of taxi will honk their horns as they go, to let you know they have space on board.

Public buses run by the Public Transport Service Corporation (PTSC) are either very old (the blue ones) or spanking new and air-conditioned (red, white, and black ones). They follow special bus lanes from Port of Spain to San Fernando, to Arima, and to Chaguanas. Check with your hotel or the tourist board for rates and pick-up points for all modes of transportation.

On Tobago, motor scooters can be rented from **Banana Rentals** at Kariwak Village next to Crown Point (tel: 639 8441).

Sightseeing On Trinidad two of the most popular excursions are to the Caroni Swamp during the flight of the scarlet ibis, and to the Asa Wright Centre in the rainforest. Tours of the Caroni Bird Sanctuary are run by naturalists **Winston Nanan** (tel: 645 1305) and **David Ramsahai** (tel: 663 2207). Try **KPE Nature Tours** (637 9664) for advice on these and other nature-based outings, such as Humming Bird Orchid Farm, Point-à-Pierre Wild Fowl Trust.

Other tour companies in Port of Spain include: **Bacchus Taxi and Car Rentals** (tel: 622 5588); **Bayshore**

Charters (tel: 637 8711); **Classic Tours** (tel: 628 7053); **Eastman's Tours and Camps** (tel: 625 3232); **Hub Travel,** Hilton Hotel Lobby (tel: 625 3155) or Piarco Airport (tel: 664 4359); **Legacy Tours** (tel: 623 0150); **Loving Tours in T&T** (tel: 623 2446); **St. Christopher Taxi Service,** Hilton Hotel (tel: 624 3560); **The Travel Centre** (tel: 623 5096); **Travel Trinidad & Tobago** (tel: 625 2201); **Trinidad & Tobago Sightseeing Tours** (tel: 628 1051; also in Tobago: 639 7422); **Tropical Tours** (tel: 623 8020); **Twin Island Tours** (tel: 622 5245; also on Tobago: 639 7491). For operators outside Port of Spain, look in the *Discover Trinidad & Tobago* booklet from tourist office. On Tobago, trips to the rainforest, to Bon Accord swamp, and to Little Tobago, as well as car rental, can be fixed up through **Twin Island Tours** (tel: 639 7491). David Rooks of **Nature Tours** offers guided walks and trips to offshore bird colonies (tel: 639 4276). Other companies in the sightseeing business include **Ansyl Tours** (tel: 639 3865); **Bruce Ying Tours** (tel: 639 1009); **Educatours** (tel: 639 7422); **Geo Tours** (tel: 639 4032); **Hew's Tours** (tel: 639 7984); **Pioneer Journeys** (tel: 660 4327); **Rainbow Tours** (tel: 639 2863); **Star Tour** (tel: 639 7826); **Tobago Travel** (tel: 639 8778); **Trinidad & Tobago Sightseeing Tours** (tel: 639 7422); and **TUI Tours** (639 8493).

Tourist information
Trinidad and Tobago Tourism Development Authority, 134–8 Frederick Street, Port of Spain (tel: 623 1932). **Tobago Tourist Bureau,** Jerningham Street, Scarborough (tel: 639 2125). The TDA is also at Piarco Airport (tel: 664 5196) and Crown Point Airport (tel: 639 0509). **Trinidad and Tobago Hotel and Tourism Association,** The Travel Centre, Uptown Mall, 44–58 Edward Street, Port of Spain (tel: 624 3928). **Bed and Breakfast Association of Trinidad and Tobago,** PO Box 3231, Diego Martin (tel: 637 9329); **Tobago Bed and Breakfast Association** (tel: 639 3926).

HOTELS AND RESTAURANTS

ACCOMMODATION

Styles and standards of Caribbean accommodation vary enormously, as shown by the differences in price. There are very sophisticated beach clubs where individual cabins have ocean views, but most hotel rooms are in large resort complexes. In every recommendation except the very cheapest, rooms have their own bathrooms. A number of villas and short-term apartments are mentioned below. For independent travelers there are a few guesthouses and local business hotels on each island. Most hotels are set on the beach; if not, this is indicated. Most also have swimming pools.

There is no standardized system of classification in the Caribbean, but all hotels booked through tour operators and travel agents will be registered with the tourist board on the island and checked by the operators.

Prices, highest from January to April, are reduced by 20–25 percent during the rest of the year. Each island has a different system, with supplementary room rates. A service charge of 10–15 percent is often levied.

Hotels are divided into four price categories, based on the rate for a double room in *high season*:

budget ($): a double room for less than U.S.$75
moderate ($$): a double room for between U.S.$75 and $200
expensive ($$$): expect to pay between U.S.$200 and $400
very expensive ($$$$): expect to pay more than U.S.$400

THE WINDWARD ISLANDS
Dominica
Hotels on Dominica levy a 5 percent goverment tax on all bills.
Layou Valley Inn ($) (tel: 449 6203). Charming setting in the mountainous foothills of the Dominican Forest Reserve. Just 10 rooms, with a warm welcome and French food. Plenty of walking.

Papillote Wilderness Retreat ($) (tel: 448 2287). Ten rooms set in a grand tropical garden fed by the Trafalgar Falls above Roseau. A home away from home; good walking.
Picard Beach Cottage Resort ($$) (tel: 445 5131). Eight beach cabins, very comfortable Caribbean colonial style, to the south of Portsmouth.
Reigate Hall Hotel ($$) (tel: 448 4031). Elegant and reclusive hotel built in local stone and timber, on the mountainside above Roseau. Good restaurant, superb views.

Grenada
Hotels on Grenada levy an 8 percent government tax on all bills.
Coyaba ($$) (tel: 444 4129). Friendly beach resort with 40 rooms in Grand Anse. Comfortable rooms in large buildings in a neat tropical garden. Entertainment in the bar and thatch-roof restaurant; sports facilities on the beach.
Ramada ($$) (tel: 444 4371). Large active resort on Grand Anse Beach, air-conditioned rooms in apartment buildings in neat gardens. Pool, sports, beauty salon, stores, entertainment.
Secret Harbour ($$–$$$) (tel: 444 4548). Quiet, secluded, sophisticated retreat (no children) in Spanish style, tucked away in the south of the island. Rooms elegant with fine views, but the beach is not the best.
Spice Island Inn ($$$) (tel: 444 4258). High luxury on Grand Anse beach. The 56 rooms are large and air-conditioned, and some stand directly behind the palms and sand. Entertainment in the beachfront restaurant and bar.

The Grenadines
Hotels on Carriacou charge 8 percent government tax; the rest charge 5 percent.
The Caribbee Inn ($$) Carriacou (tel: 443 7380). Charming old colonial-style inn set on a hillside a short walk from the extremely fine cove, Anse la Roche. Intimate and friendly; home-cooked Caribbean cuisine.
Cotton House Hotel ($$$$) Mustique (tel: 456 4777). Set in the ancient stone estate building of a former cotton plantation; sumptuous beds and furnishings. Pool and fantastic views to go with superb food.
Dennis's Hideaway ($) Mayreau (tel: 458 8594). Six rooms with a restaurant and bar near by; modern but made special by Dennis himself, who plays the guitar and sings to the guests.
Frangipani ($$) Bequia (tel: 458 3255). Set in an old family vacation villa on the Port Elizabeth waterfront. Antique gentility and personable West Indian style.
Plantation House ($$$) Bequia (tel: 458 3425). Very pretty mock-colonial cottages set in a seafront palm garden. Lively, with evening entertainment.

St. Lucia
All hotels on St. Lucia levy an 8 percent government room charge.
Anse Chastanet ($$) Soufrière (tel: 459 7000). Forty-eight rooms and villas scattered on the hillside above the gray sands of secluded Chastanet bay; good diving and seclusion.
Islander Hotel ($$) Rodney Bay (tel: 452 8757). Not that luxurious, and not on Reduit beach itself, but the Islander puts you right among the restuarants and bars of St. Lucia's main tourist area. Pool and restaurant.
Jalousie Plantation ($$$) (tel: U.S. 305 856 7083). The height of St. Lucian luxury and sophistication, in a setting to beat them all, between the Pitons. Sumptuous rooms in cottages around neat gardens. All-inclusive plan.
Le Sport ($$$) Cap Estate (tel: 450 8551). A large and busy resort built in celebration of the body. Windsurfing, seaweed wraps, massages, and saunas all available. In manicured, Moorish surroundings. Entertainment, pools, sports, boutiques.
Marigot Bay Resort ($$) (tel: 451 4357). In the wonderful setting of Marigot Bay, a narrow, steep-sided inlet festooned with graceful palms.

Villas and cottages; charming and laid-back.
Royal St. Lucian ($$$) Reduit Beach (tel: 450 9999). A grand and luxurious hotel, with central atrium and wings, commanding the beach. Every modern convenience in the huge rooms. Very fine cuisine.

St. Vincent
All hotels on St. Vincent levy a 5 percent government room tax.
Petit Byahaut ($–$$) (tel: 457 7008). Cabins and tents above the secluded beach of Petit Byahaut bay, which can be reached only by boat. Stylishly rustic, but has hot running water.
Umbrella Beach Hotel ($) (tel: 458 4651). Set in lively strip of restaurants and bars at Villa. Small and simple.
Young Island ($$$$) (tel: 458 4651). A Caribbean gem—cottages scattered around the tropical garden of Young Island, 20 yds. off St. Vincent's southern coast. Pool, bar, restaurant, and sports, even hammocks for two.

THE LEEWARD ISLANDS
Anguilla
Hotels on Anguilla add a government tax of 8 percent.
Cap Juluca ($$$$) (tel: 497 6666). A mile-long line of bright, white Moorish domes rising out of the Anguillian scrub along the stretch of Maunday's Bay in the southeast. High luxury with sunken baths and Oriental rugs.
Coccoloba ($$$) (tel: 497 6871). A beach resort with a sporting feel. Beneath the large main house on the cliff there are gingerbread cottages spread along the waterfront of the beautiful Barnes Bay.
La Sirena ($$) (tel: 497 6827). A small and friendly hotel perched above Mead's Bay, at an affordable price on an island of heavyweights. Some entertainment.
Malliouhana ($$$–$$$$) (tel: 497 6111). On a cliff overlooking the superb Mead's Bay, Maillouhana has a mix of styles; terra-cotta tiles, slender columns and arches,

touched with colorful Haitian prints. Smoothly run hotel, luxurious, with a very fine dining room.

Antigua
Hotels on Antigua add a government tax of 7 percent.
Admiral's Inn ($$) (tel: 463 1027). Within the historic walls of English Harbour; rooms quite simple. A lively crowd of sailors collects at the bar.
Copper and Lumber Store ($$–$$$) (tel: 463 1058). A small hotel set in the grounds of English Harbour; functional brick walls covered with tropical plants and urgent naval air turned into a retreat of historic laziness.
Curtain Bluff ($$$$) (tel: 462 8400). Once again the height of Antiguan elegance since its renovation. Main house on the bluff, between two excellent beaches. Trusty and quiet, lavish in the dining room and wine cellar.
Jumby Bay ($$$$) (tel: 462 6000). Exclusive and extremely expensive, but a reliable refuge on an island just off the Antiguan coast. Lavish all-inclusive package, in villas set above the four beaches. Drinks left in coolers at strategic points under the palm trees.

Montserrat
Hotels on Montserrat add a government tax of 7 percent.
Montserrat Springs Hotel ($$) (tel: 491 2482). Plush modern rooms with white tiles and pastel colors stand in buildings looking down to the sea. Generally quiet and comfortable.
Vue Point Hotel ($$) (tel: 491 5210). Friendly hotel with cabins ranged on the hillside above Old Road Bay. Beach bar down below; a crowd gathers some evenings.

Nevis
Hotels on Nevis add a government tax of 7 percent.
Four Seasons ($$$$) (tel: 469 1111). A reliable beach vacation spot, with watersports, golf, massage parlor, and the never-ending strip of Pinney's Beach. Elegantly decorated and luxurious

rooms. "Olde Worlde" decor in the main house and tropical profusion in the garden.
Hermitage ($$$) (tel: 463 3477). A gem of the Caribbean, set in one of its most ancient wooden houses. Rooms modern, in cottages embellished with gingerbread pointing, each with a hammock with a view.
Nisbet ($$$) (tel: 469 9325). In Nevis's best plantation-estate tradition, but with the advantage of a beach. Very comfortable rooms with screened terraces scattered around a lawned garden with huge palms.
Oualie Beach Club ($$) (tel: 469 9735). Twelve comfortable rooms on the calm Oualie Beach in the north of the island, overlooking St. Kitts. Low-key but fun.

St. Kitts
Hotels on St. Kitts add a government tax of 7 percent.
Ocean Terrace Inn ($$–$$$) (tel: 465 2754). Set behind a wall in town like a secret garden, OTI has 52 rooms that attract an easy-going crowd, locals, and businesspeople as well as stopover travelers.
Rawlins Plantation ($$$) (tel: 465 6221). The closest you can come to the lavish grandeur of plantation life. Ten luxurious rooms scattered around the estate grounds; fine, home-cooked West Indian cuisine and rum punch with a view from the 18th-century great house.
Timothy Beach Resort ($$) (tel: 465 8597). Good value suites on the fine strip of sand in Frigate Bay. Beach hotel, but pretty quiet.

THE VIRGIN ISLANDS
THE BRITISH VIRGIN ISLANDS
Hotels in the B.V.I. add a government tax of 7 percent to all bills.
Anegada, Jost van Dyke and Necker Island
Necker Island ($$$) (tel: U.S. 800 926 0636, U.K. 081 741 9980). You and a crowd of friends (up to 20) can rent the island. Huge Indonesian-style villa with split-level pools and all the trimmings of Caribbean luxury.

HOTELS AND RESTAURANTS

Peter Island $$$$ (tel: 494 2561). The best of the 50 rooms are the elegant suites on the fantastic sand of Dead Man's Bay. A sophisticated beach vacation—genteel and low-key, fine dining.

Tortola
Cane Garden Bay Beach Hotel ($–$$) (tel: 495 4639). A lively hangout on Tortola's busiest beach. Rooms air-conditioned and simple, but plenty of activity all around.
Long Bay Hotel ($$$) (tel: 495 4252). Delightful collection of rooms and villas in Long Bay in Tortola's northwest. Some on stilts above the beach, others nestled in the profusion of the tropical gardens. Quiet but classy.

Virgin Gorda

Biras Creek Hotel ($$$$) (tel: 494 3555). Very elegant retreat in the North Sound; 34 rooms in stone cottages looking out to the Atlantic Ocean. Very fine dining in the hilltop gazebo.
Bitter End Yacht Club ($$$–$$$$) (tel: 494 2746). Lively resort for watersports fans—sailing school, wind-surfing, short hops to nearby beach bars. Some entertainment, but also hideaway hillside cabins of high luxury.
Little Dix Bay ($$$$) (tel: 495 5555). Low-key high luxury. Cottages in spacious and neatly tended grounds, looking down onto an excellent strip of sand. Very quiet, but activity if you want it.
Olde Yard Inn ($$) (tel: 495 5544). Quiet and charming retreat where guests are as likely to be relaxing in the well-stocked library as on the beach (a short drive/ride off). Attractive open-terrace restaurant.

THE U.S. VIRGIN ISLANDS
St. Croix
Hotels in the U.S.V.I. add a government tax of 7.5 percent.
Club Comanche ($$) (tel: 773 0210). Old colonial townhouse in Christiansted that has sprouted terraces, wings, and verandas, all connected by walkways. Cozy and hip, piano enter-

tainment in the bar in the evenings.
Cormorant Beach Club ($$$) (tel: 548 4460). Low-key beach hotel—very attractive rooms with terraces or balconies overlooking the palms and sea. Quiet and refined with an excellent restaurant.
St. Croix by the Sea ($$) (tel: 778 8600). Friendly beach resort near Christiansted. Comfortable rooms and hammocks slung between palm trees. Entertainment nightly.
Villa Madeleine ($$$–$$$$) (tel: 773 8141). Set on a hillside in the east of St. Croix, each of the suites of the Villa Madeleine has its own pool and is charmingly decorated. New and very plush.

St. John
Caneel Bay Resort ($$$–$$$$) (tel: 776 6111). A very elegant resort on St. John's north shore, where rooms are set in beautifully tended gardens around a great house. Watersports on the resort's seven beaches, otherwise reliable relaxation.
Cinnamon Bay Camp Ground ($–$$) (tel: 776 6330). Permanent tents and bare sites in the forest behind Cinnamon Bay—very popular. Barbecues, entertainment and forest orienteering.
Hyatt Regency ($$$–$$$$) (tel: 776 7171). A large resort set in attractive grounds—perfect for a pampered Caribbean beach vacation: watersports galore, kids' programs, three restaurants, entertainment.
Raintree Inn ($–$$) (tel: 776 7449). In the heart of Cruz Bay, a small and friendly hotel with 11 rooms set in an oddly alpine timber house. Seafood restaurant attached.

St. Thomas
Bolongo Bay Beach Club ($$$) (tel: 775 1800). Lively sporting resort—watersports, scuba, tennis—on a charming sandy bay on the south of the island. Sports by day, entertainment by night.
Grand Palazzo ($$$–$$$$) (tel: 775 3333). The newest in St. Thomas: super-luxury, a large suite-hotel set around a bay on the east coast.

Watersports (excellent windsurfing) and gourmet dining.
Mark St. Thomas ($$–$$$) (tel: 774 5511). This guesthouse basks in Charlotte Amalie's delightful antique grandeur. A charming townhouse with wooden floors and metal balconies. Quiet, sophisticated air, dinner to a piano accompaniment.
Sapphire Beach Resort ($$$) (tel: 775 6100). Large resort hotel right on Sapphire Beach where there are good snorkeling and watersports. All the Caribbean comforts in the rooms; lively beach party each Sunday.

THE FRENCH ANTILLES
Guadeloupe
Some hotels on Guadeloupe add a room tax of a few dollars.
Auberge de la Vieille Tour ($$$) Montauban (tel: 84 23 23). Large but genteel resort, rooms ranged in dwellings on the hillside around an old windmill tower. Dining room above the private hotel beach.
Auberge des Petits Saints ($$) Terre de Haut, Les Saintes (tel: 99 50 99). A charming bungalow in the main town of Terre de Haut. Just 11 well-decorated rooms; fine French cuisine.
La Toubana ($$–$$$) Ste-Anne (tel: 88 25 78). The main house of this laid-back hotel stands high on a clifftop above Ste.-Anne beach; 32 very comfortable rooms spread in bungalows around the valley beneath.
Le Hamak ($$$–$$$$) St.-François (tel: 88 59 99). Rarified relaxation in private bungalows, tucked away in a profuse Guadeloupean garden on the seafront. As the name suggests, each bungalow has its own hammock.
Les Flamboyants ($–$$), Gosier (tel: 84 14 11). On a hilltop just outside town, an old family villa with neat and simple rooms. A walk from the beach; pool and kitchen, only breakfast served.

Martinique
Some hotels on Martinique add a room tax of a few dollars.

Auberge de l'Anse Mitan ($–$$) (tel: 66 03 19). A friendly hotel, still with some old West Indian charm; tucked away at the end of Anse Mitan beach, but not far from the action of the town.

Club Med ($$$) Ste.-Anne (tel: 76 72 72). Usual Club Med facilities, entertainment and standards on the Ste.-Anne peninsula. Comfortable rooms in a huge palm garden, fine beach.

Hotel Diamant les Bains ($$) Diamant (tel: 76 40 14). Quiet and very friendly hotel; 24 rooms overlooking a pretty garden; views of Diamond Rock. An ideal retreat.

Hotel Meridien ($$$) Trois-llets (tel: 66 00 00). Huge, humming hotel with activities at all hours. High luxury, bars and restaurants a short walk away. Casino.

La Bonne Auberge ($) Trois-llets (tel: 66 01 55). Small and friendly hotel, with simple rooms set in modern buildings in the heart of the tourist town of Trois-llets. Nice tropical dining room.

Plantation de Leyritz ($$) Basse Pointe (tel: 78 53 92). Isolated in Martinique's agricultural northeast, set around an old sugar estate. Rooms in the old slave cabins (more comfortable now), dining in the splendor of an old colonial setting.

Saint-Barthélemy
Some hotels on St. Barts add a room tax of a few dollars.

Club la Banane ($$$) (tel: 27 68 25). Amusing crowd in the bar; rooms decorated with traditional Caribbean flourishes, lost in a tropical garden that overhangs an inviting pool. Short walk to the beach.

Hotel Manapany ($$$$) (tel: 27 66 55). The finest luxury on a luxurious island; 52 rooms in sumptuous suites and cottages, ranged by a good beach. Watersports and fine cuisine, room service to the veranda.

Ile de France ($$$$) (tel: 27 61 81). On the superb sand of the Baie des Flamands, a variety of rooms decorated with antique furniture.

Sophisticated beach resort; sports room and fine dining.
La Petite Anse ($$) (tel: 26 64 60). Above Anse des Flamands beach, this hotel has 16 relatively inexpensive rooms (for St. Barts), with kitchens if you wish to cook for yourself.

Saint-Martin
Some hotels on Saint-Martin add a room tax to your bill.
Captain Oliver's ($$$) (tel: 87 40 26). Small east coast hotel on Oyster Pond lagoon, from where many of the guests, a friendly crowd, take to the seas to sail. Short water-taxi ride to the beach.

Esmeralda Resort ($$$–$$$$) (tel: 87 36 36). A new resort that has taken traditional gingerbread style and added to its luxurious cottages, each of which has its own pool. Sports and restaurants.

Grand Case Beach Hotel ($) (tel: 87 50 90). A cheaper option in Grand Case town. Simple rooms but clean and comfortable.

La Samanna ($$$$) (tel: 87 51 22). Extremely chic and stylish, standing above the excellent sand of Long Beach. Built in a curious mix of styles, with vast rooms, fine views, extreme luxury, and extreme prices.

THE NETHERLANDS ANTILLES
Aruba
Hotels on Aruba add a government tax of 5 percent to all bills.
Americana Aruba Hotel ($$$) (tel: 24500). High-rise and large, plush and brightly painted, on excellent Palm Beach. Watersports. Glitzy feel in the evenings, with floor shows and a casino.

Bushiri Beach Resort ($$) (tel: 25216). Relaxed resort on Eagle Beach, comfortable and luxurious rooms set in dwellings above the sand; plenty of beach activity on the vast expanse of sand.

Divi divi Beach Resort ($$$–$$$$) (tel: 23300). Low-rise hotel in the land of high-rises; excellent beachfront setting, rooms set in complexes in attractive gardens. Pools, bars, and watersports.

Bonaire
Hotels on Bonaire add a government tax of 5 percent to all bills.
Captain Don's Habitat ($$–$$$) (tel: 8290). Has grown from a small diving resort to a very comfortable and laid-back hotel, now with cottages and villas as well as rooms. Still concentrating on diving.

Carib Inn ($–$$) (tel: 8819). Excellent choice for relative comfort and price. Nine simple rooms, good diving. No restaurant, but kitchenettes; within walking distance from town restaurants.

Harbour Village Hotel ($$$) (tel: 7500). The most comfortable hotel on Bonaire, with plush and brightly painted suites in villas dotted around a sandy garden and pool. Beach resort sports by day; casino for the evening.

Curaçao
Hotels on Curaçao add a government tax of 5 percent to all bills.
Avila Beach Hotel ($$–$$$) (tel: 614377). The most elegant and traditional of Curaçao's hotels, now modernized. On edge of town with a small beach and a dining room under awnings open to the breezes.

Lion's Dive Hotel ($$) (tel: 618100). A lively resort hotel with a young crowd of divers. Friendly atmosphere; rooms colorful but simple and small.

Princess Beach Hotel ($$) (tel: 614944). A large resort with rooms in buildings spread out along the seafront, where a beach has been built. Active with sports by day and gambling by night.

Saba
Hotels on Saba add a government tax of 5 percent to all bills.
Captain's Quarters ($$) (tel: 62201). Set in a lovely old Saban house at the foot of the hill in Windwardside; antique furniture and ambience, but a lively bar when the crowds gather.

Queen's Garden Resort ($$) (tel: 62236). Saba's newest hotel stands high above The

273

HOTELS AND RESTAURANTS

Bottom—a series of modern dwellings with comfortable rooms that retain Saba's old style in the colored window frames and roofs.
Scout's Place ($–$$) (tel: 62205). Intriguing spot on the hillside in Windwardside. You can escape to the comfortable rooms, but you might also want to join the activity in the bar.

St. Eustatius
Hotels on St. Eustatius add a government tax of 7 percent to all bills.
The Kingswell Inn $, Upper Town. Just a few apartments and a small, lively restaurant.
The Old Gin House ($–$$) (tel: 82319). A Caribbean gem, built of Statia's historic red and yellow bricks (from the former trading warehouses). Elegant, with a charming bar and restaurant.

Sint Maarten
Hotels on Sint Maarten add a government tax of 5 percent to all bills.
Dawn Beach ($$–$$$) (tel: 22929). Quiet and relaxed beach resort on the east coast, away from the hubbub of town, seemingly smaller than its 155 rooms because of the profuse gardens. Set on a fine beach.
Mary's Boon ($$) (tel: 54235). One of a number of small hotels with character on Simpson Bay. Refined air about the 12 rooms with their colonial furniture and the bar, complete with library, which overlooks the sea.
Passangrahan ($$) (tel: 23588). Old colonial air in the louvered lobby and some of the rooms; a welcome oasis of quiet in the shopping turmoil of Front Street. Thirty rooms, a restaurant, and bar.

OTHER CARIBBEAN STATES

JAMAICA
Hotels in Jamaica add a general consumption tax of 10 percent to all bills.
Black River, Blue Mountains
Ivor Guest House ($–$$) Jack's Hill (tel: 977 0033). Beautifully restored wooden

colonial home perched on the mountains above Kingston. Just three bedrooms, dining room, and terrace with a magnificent view of the capital.
South Sea View Guest House ($–$$) Whitehouse (no phone). Modern villa with eight rooms, above its own rocky but swimmable bay.

Kingston
Terra Nova Hotel ($$) New Kingston (tel: 926 9334). A grand old uptown house in lawned gardens. Elegant and relaxed; 33 attractive rooms, pool, and a good dining room.
Wyndham Hotel ($$) New Kingston (tel: 926 5430). Modern, high-rise hotel, in the business area. Restaurants, pool, and health club. Business facilities.

Mandeville
Astra Hotel ($–$$) (tel: 962 3265). Set in a modern building just outside the town, 40 rooms. Family-run and friendly. Tours arranged to surrounding countryside.

Montego Bay
Coral Cliff Hotel ($) (tel: 952 2147). On Gloucester Avenue near town center; a graceful old villa. Some rooms in the modern buildings behind. Pool, beach within walking distance.
Half Moon Club ($$$–$$$$) (tel: 953 2211). Simply the classiest in Jamaican high luxury, just east of the town, on a fine beach. Very large and elegant rooms decorated in black and white; 19 pools, tennis, golf, riding, health club, and very fine dining.
Richmond Hill Inn ($$) (tel: 952 3859). On the hilltop above the Montego Bay, an elegant townhouse, now with rooms added. Pool and dining with a view, short ride to the beach.
Round Hill ($$$) (tel: 952 5150). Another enclave of sophisticated super-luxury, to the west of the town. Impeccably presented villas scattered over the hillside above a stunning bay. Tennis, riding, watersports, dining on the waterfront.

Negril
Charela Inn ($$) (tel: 957 4277). Beach hotel, with an intimate feel; 39 rooms, watersports, and a fine French restaurant.
Grand Lido ($$$$) (tel: 957 4010). On the fine sand of Bloody Bay, a top-grade all-inclusive hotel—champagne on command, jackets for dinner (*à la carte*). Sumptuous rooms, stunning sea views.
Hedonism II ($$$) (tel: 952 4200). The name says it all—all the requisites for Caribbean pleasure here. Beach, scuba, sailing, trapeze lessons, toga parties, disco until very late, all-inclusive package for singles.
Rock House ($$) (tel: 957 4373). On the cliffs in the south of the town, simple cabins with palm thatch roofs and a fine sunset view.

Ocho Rios
Boscobel Beach ($$–$$$) (tel: 974 3331). All-inclusive resort on a fine beach, designed especially for families with children. Finger-painting instruction through to kiddies' disco lessons to occupy them while you indulge in watersports and sunning.
Couples ($$$) (tel: 974 4271). The original fun-packed, all-inclusive resort, on its own beach east of the town. Everything comes in couples here, even the deckchairs. Endless entertainment, day and night.
Hibiscus Lodge Hotel ($–$$) (tel: 974 2813). Simple but comfortable rooms on the clifftops, near the action. Garden, good restaurants, watersports, short walk to the beach.
Jamaica Inn ($$$) (tel: 974 2514). An enclave of super-luxury. Impeccably decorated rooms set above a charming cove, one of Jamaica's prettiest beaches. Low-key and very sophisticated.

Port Antonio
De Montevin Lodge ($) (tel: 993 2604). A throwback to a century ago: a classic townhouse of gingerbread and brick. Rooms simple, some with balconies.

Trident Villas ($$$–$$$$) (tel: 993 2602). An enclave of supreme elegance, stunningly presented main house and rooms in manicured gardens. On a ledge of coral reef, so no real beach, but a fine pool. Very fine dining.

THE CAYMAN ISLANDS

Hotels on the Cayman Islands add 6 percent government tax to all bills.

Divi Tiara Beach Hotel ($$) Cayman Brac (tel: 948 7553). In the southwest, right on the seashore, behind the beach and palms. Diving is the primary activity, but rooms very comfortable.

Hyatt Regency ($$–$$$$) (tel: 949 1234). The most luxurious accommodation in Cayman, just across the road from Seven-Mile Beach. Modern building, but with attractive old-colonial flourishes. Three restaurants, golf course, dip-and-sip pool bar, watersports on the beach.

Sunset House ($$) (tel: 949 7111). South of George Town, a small and friendly hotel dedicated to diving by day, but with a lively bar in the evenings. Near beach.

Villa Caribe Inn ($$) (tel: 947 9636). On the north coast away from the main action. Small and friendly, rooms neat and clean, good local restaurant.

CUBA
Havana

Havana Libre ($$) (tel: 305011). Tall building at the head of La Rampa, built as the Havana Hilton in the 1950s and renamed the Havana Libre by the young revolutionaries. Busy town hotel with excellent views from the top floor bar. Taxi ride to the colonial city.

Hotel Victoria ($$) (tel: 326531). Plush modern conversion in Vedado district, ideal for business travelers (some business services), but also swimming pool.

Inglaterra ($) (tel: 618351). On the Parque Central at the edge of the colonial city. Pleasant bar in the elaborate foyer. Rooms comfortable, short walk to the sights.

Plaza ($$) (tel: 622006) A fine, colonnaded building on the Parque Central, grand breezy interior with palms and pillars. Rooms newly decorated, very comfortable.

Outside Havana

Casa Granda ($) Santiago de Cuba. In the center of town, on Parque Cespedes, in a large old townhouse. Foyer always busy, rooms small, but convenient for the sights.

Hotel Colony ($–$$) Isla de Juventud (tel: 98282). In the southwest of island; lively resort hotel with good diving and watersports by day, bar and club by night.

Las Americas ($) Santiago de Cuba (tel: 8040). Short drive from the town center, simple rooms, pool, and bar.

Los Delfines ($) Varadero (tel: 63815). Small, friendly hotel in a pretty coral rock house right on the beach.

Motel Los Jazmines ($) Viñales (tel: 93205). Not a motel at all, but an old villa standing high above the Viñales valley, fine views.

Paradiso ($) Varadero (tel: 63917). One of Cuba's new resorts. Luxury rooms in beach villas; good Caribbean beach vacation with watersports by day, bars and clubs for the evening.

HAITI

Some hotels in Haiti add an energy tax of a few dollars.

Mont Joli Hotel ($$) Cap-Haïtien (tel: 620300). A small, elegant hotel on the hill above the town, very comfortable rooms, good restaurant. Driving distance to the beach and the sights.

Moulin sur Mer ($–$$) Montrouis (tel: 221844). Modern rooms set around a restored sugar mill on a fantastic beach. Watersports.

Oloffson Hotel ($) Port-au-Prince (tel: 234000). Set in wonderful gingerbread building, former presidential palace. Amusing and lively bar full of travelers and passing journalists.

El Rancho ($–$$) Pétionville (tel: 572080). Grandest of the hotels built before Haiti's present troubles. Spanish revival decor, lavish rooms, antique furniture. Pool.

Villa Créole ($–$$) Pétionville (tel: 571570). Charming and elegant hotel in a quiet street. Attractive rooms, tennis, pool with a view.

THE DOMINICAN REPUBLIC

Hotels in the Dominican Republic add a government tax of 6 percent.

Altos de Chavon and the Southeast, Cordillera Central

Bavaro Beach Hotel ($$) Higuey (tel: 682 2161). Behind the superb palm-fringed beach are four hotels, with a strong resort feel. Comfortable air-conditioned rooms, plenty of restaurants and bars, every watersport, golf, and tennis.

Casa de Campo ($$$–$$$$) (tel: 523 3333). A top resort complex with some of the Caribbean's most chic villas and hotel rooms—polo, golf, beach sports, nine restaurants in beautifully land-scaped and tended grounds.

Puerto Plata and the Amber Coast

Auberge du Roi Tropicale ($–$$) Cabarete (tel: 571 0770). A wind-surfing hotel on the beach, sponsored by world champion Mickey Bouwmeester. Rooms simple, pool under palms, restaurant on the sand.

Hostal Jimesson ($) John F. Kennedy 41, Puerto Plata (tel: 586 2177). A good stopover in center of town with 22 neat rooms behind a charming antique foyer.

Princess Resort ($$–$$$) Playa Dorada (tel: 586 5350). Snazzy, elegant modern hotel in the grounds of Playa Dorada—golf, tennis, gyms, health clubs, discos, and a very fine beach. Lavish suites with balconies, dip-and-sip pool bar.

Tropix Hotel ($) Sosua (tel: 571 2291). A charming, guesthouse, beloved of travelers. Friendly atmosphere, honor bar, home cooking. A walk from the beaches and downtown restaurants.

Samana

El Portillo Beach Club ($$) Las Terrenas (tel: 589 9546).

275

HOTELS AND RESTAURANTS

All-inclusive resort just out of the town, on a superb beach. Rooms and villas in a sandy palm garden. Sports galore. **Hotel Tropic Banana** ($) Las Terrenas (tel: 566 5941). One of the best and most amusing travelers' haunts in the Caribbean. A lively crowd gathers for music at the poolside afternoon and evening; 30 rooms in a spacious palm garden near the beach.

Santo Domingo
Boca Chica Resort ($$) (tel: 567 9575). The closest beach resort to the capital (about 30 minutes). All-inclusive plan, but sophisticated ambience. Elegant rooms.
Don Juan Beach Resort ($$) (tel: 687 9157). Also in Boca Chica, on the busy beach itself. Lively crowd gathers around the pool and bar, rooms in complexes, not elaborate. Plenty of nightlife.
Hostal Nicolas Nader ($) Calle Luperon (tel: 687 6674). Charming guest house set in the ancient stone of one of the city's oldest buildings. Rooms surround a courtyard, with palms and a parrot.
Hostal Nicolas de Ovando ($–$$) Calle de las Damas (tel: 687 3101). The historic grandeur of the colonial city continues into the hotel, in the flagstones, courtyards, and corridors. Ideal for exploration of sights, but some rooms noisy at night.
Jaragua ($$–$$$) Avenida Independencia (tel: 686 2222). Reliable luxury in a large and glitzy hotel right on the Malecon. Four restaurants, club with entertainers, casino. Tours arranged.

PUERTO RICO
Hotels in Puerto Rico add a government tax of 7 percent (9 percent in hotels with a casino).

Cordillera Central
Hacienda Gripinas ($) Jayuya (tel: 828 1717). A gem of the Caribbean: a quiet, charming timber-framed coffee estate house. Not elaborate, but wonderful old-time Caribbean feel on the balcony and in upstairs rooms.
Horned Dorset Primavera ($$$) (tel: 823 4030).

Luxurious rooms that overlook the hotel garden or the sunset out to sea. Elegant central area with a library for afternoon tea and cocktails. **Parador Casa Grande** ($) Utuado (tel: 894 3939). Set in a mountain valley; 20 rooms in cabins along a hillside. The main house has a restaurant and pool. An ideal retreat.

Ponce
Hotel Melia ($) (tel: 842 0260). Just off the central square in Ponce, the Melia has pleasant foyer with tiles and stained wood. The rooms are modern and air-conditioned.

San German and the South West
Parador Boquemar ($) Boqueron (tel: 851 2158). A modern building near Boqueron beach. Comfortable rooms; pool and restaurant.
Villa Parguera ($–$$) Parguera (tel: 899 3975). Welcoming resort hotel on the waterfront, set in a tropical garden. Pool and good local restaurant on the bay.

San Juan: New City
Casa Mathieson ($–$$) Calle Uno 14 (tel: 762 8662). Clean, simple rooms within a short walk of Isla Verde beach. Air-conditioning, restaurant.
Hotel Condado Beach ($$) Condado (tel: 721 6090). The Vanderbilt family home, built in 1919, now converted but still with many of its original features—antique furniture, marble floors and graceful curved staircases in the foyer. Large resort hotel.
El Prado Inn ($–$$) 1350 Calle Luchetti (tel: 728 5925). Set in a neat family villa, between Condado and Isla Verde; walls festooned with tropical blooms. El Prado has 10 simple rooms and a pool.
El San Juan Hotel and Casino ($$$) (tel: 791 1000). A huge and humming resort hotel on the excellent beach at Isla Verde. Foyer and casino paneled and low-lit with gas lamps. Rooms luxurious, pool in tropical garden, seven restaurants and snack bars.

San Juan: Old City
Gallery Inn ($$) (tel: 722

1808). Restored townhouse with circular staircases, courtyards and terraces: bohemian feel; art gallery downstairs. **Gran Hotel El Convento** ($$–$$$) (tel: 723 9020). A magnificent old building in the colonial city—checkerboard tiles, stained paneling, and tapestries hung on the walls. Once a convent, retains a calm and cloistered air.

Vieques
Casa del Frances $$ (tel: 741 3751). A charming old estate house, with checkerboard tiles and a cool courtyard, owned by a Hemingway-like character, always amusing. Pool, home-cooked food.

BARBADOS
Hotels on Barbados add a 5 percent government tax to all bills.

South Coast
Barbados Windsurfing Club ($) Maxwell (tel: 428 9095). On the Maxwell shoreline, a windsurfing hotel as the name suggests; 15 rooms and a lively bar.
Crane Beach Hotel ($$–$$$) (tel: 423 6220). In a superb setting on the south coast cliffs, where the pool and restaurant, high above the pretty cove 100 ft. below, have magificent views. Eighteen rooms in a small apartment building and in a coral stone castle.
Divi Southwinds Beach Resort ($$$) St. Lawrence Gap (tel: 367 3484). Large, relaxed resort; some of the 166 rooms overlook the superb south coast beach. Watersports with scuba, central pool with a swim-up bar.

West Coast
Cobbler's Cove ($$$$) (tel: 422 2291). South of Speightstown, Cobbler's Cove has 38 beautifully decorated suites set above a fine strip of sand.
Royal Pavilion ($$$$) (tel: 422 5555). Classical columns and arches form a theme throughout the hotel. Almost all 75 luxurious suites have an oceanfront setting. Two restaurants above the beach.
Sandy Lane Hotel ($$$$) (tel: 432 1311). A legend in Carib-

bean elegance and hospitality, it was refitted for its 30th birthday in 1992. Rooms in coral-stone wings overlook the beach. The mock-classical central area has restaurants and bars.

TRINIDAD AND TOBAGO

All hotels in Trinidad and Tobago add VAT of 15 percent to published prices.

Trinidad

Asa Wright Nature Centre ($$) Arima (tel: 667 4655). Grand colonial estate house with a huge screened veranda, lost in the forests of the northern range. Ideal for bird-watching and relaxation.
Hilton ($$) central Port of Spain (tel: 624 3211). Busy center for those passing through capital, also quite well organized for tourists. The rooms have a superb view over the Savannah.
Hotel Normandie ($–$$) St. Ann's (tel: 624 1181). Quiet hotel built in a mix of architectural styles, tucked away in a valley that has now been swallowed up by the town. Fine French fare.

Tobago

Arnos Vale ($$) (tel: 639 2881) In its own steep-sided valley festooned with tropical blooms, the Arnos Vale has 30 rooms in a complex and in a central estate house. Beach bar, pool, boutique.
Blue Waters Inn ($$) Speyside (tel: 660 4341). Twenty-nine rooms of rustic simplicity in a secluded cove at the isolated eastern end of the island. Beach, scuba, restaurant and bar.
Cocrico Inn ($) Plymouth (tel: 639 2961). Friendly and pleasant small hotel in a modern building in the lazy streets of Plymouth. Pool and restaurant, near beach.

RESTAURANTS, BARS AND NIGHTCLUBS

The restaurants listed below are divided into the following categories:

budget ($)
moderate ($$)
expensive ($$$)

THE WINDWARD ISLANDS

Dominica

Castaways ($) Mero Beach. A good lunchtime stop on the black-sand beach at Mero, particularly popular on Sundays.
Guiyave ($$) Roseau. Pretty balcony setting above the street for a hearty local lunch (no dinner).
La Robe Créole ($$$) Roseau. Charming old colonial setting, waitresses in traditional costume, local ingredients in delicious combinations.
The Orchard ($$) Roseau. Pleasant dining room indoors or in a courtyard, traditional West Indian fare, friendly atmosphere.
Reigate Hall ($$$). Subdued candle-lit dining room high above the town, the best in local cuisine.

Grenada

The Boatyard ($$) L'Anse aux Epines. Bar and restaurant in marina, simple fare, bar livens up at the weekend, some entertainment.
Canboulay ($$$) Grand Anse. Charming, bright dining room set high above the bay, innovative and delicious West Indian fare.
Coconuts ($$$) Grand Anse. Classic Caribbean beach setting, tables inside the pretty house or just above the sand. Also known as the French restaurant; fine French cuisine.
La Belle Créole ($$$) Grande Anse. The terrace dining room of the Blue Horizons hotel, *nouvelle cuisine* with a West Indian lilt.
Mama's ($$) Lagoon Road. A legendary haunt for its local fare. Set menu with a striking variety of dishes that never seem to stop coming.
Nutmeg ($$) Carenage. A view of the Carenage from the first floor; local fare and international dishes.

The Grenadines

On the small Grenadine islands you will be dependent on your hotel.
Basil's Bar ($$) Mustique. In a charmed setting on stilts on a magnificent bay; the

favorite haunt of island visitors and passing yachtsmen. Entertainment Monday and Wednesday.
Callaloo ($$) Carriacou. Very pretty restaurant in a Hillsborough house, excellent Creole food.
Dawn's Creole Tea Garden ($$) Bequia. Tucked away in Lower Bay, a tiny terrace restaurant lost in tropical greenery, serving superb West Indian food.
Dennis' Hideaway ($$) Mayreau. Bar and dining room on a terrace on the hillside, good local fare. Dennis himself sings occasionally.
Lambi's ($$) Union Island. Very local dining room covered in shells; local food.
Mac's Pizzeria ($$) Bequia. Wooden deck above a tropical garden, excellent pizzas.

St. Lucia

Capone's ($$$) Rodney Bay. Mock gangster world decor, but good cocktails and well-prepared international food. Lively restaurant.
Jimmie's ($$) Vigie Bay. Veranda with colored lights tucked away in Vigie Harbour, seafood and fish restaurant.
The Lime ($$) Rodney Bay. Very popular restaurant and bar, burgers and salads, and some local dishes. Look out for happy hours.
Naked Virgin ($$) Castries. The finest in St. Lucian fare, in a simple dining room tucked away in a Castries suburb.
Rain ($$$) Castries. Magnificent timber-frame townhouse. Cocktails on the veranda followed by snacks or the famous five-course dinner from a century ago.
San Antoine ($$$) Morne Fortune. Top Caribbean cuisine in the setting of a beautiful old stone house, magnificent view across the north coast.

St. Vincent

Aggie's ($$) Grenville Street. Upstairs dining room and bar popular with the locals, good local fare.
Basil's Bar ($$$) downstairs from the Cobblestone Inn. In the old stone setting of a

277

HOTELS AND RESTAURANTS

trading warehouse; international and local fare.

French Restaurant ($$$) Villa. Neat veranda setting above the water, delicious French cuisine with local additions.

Lime N' Pub ($$) Villa. Video bar and terrace for meals overlooking Young Island on the Villa strip. Can get lively.

THE LEEWARD ISLANDS
Anguilla

Hibernia ($$$) Island Harbour. In a modern house with tables indoors and on the balcony, dishes from the Far East and France.

Lucy's Harbour View ($$) above Sandy Ground. Tables on a large veranda with a view. Classic West Indian fare, chicken or fish with ground provisions.

Mango's ($$$) Barnes Bay (tel: 6479). Above the beach on a breezy veranda, well prepared new American cuisine, intimate feel. Reserve.

Smuggler's Restaurant ($$) Forest Bay (tel: 3278). On a wooden deck above the waves on the isolated south coast. Menu French, with the best Caribbean seafood.

Antigua

La Perruche ($$$) English Harbour. Pleasant terrace and tropical garden, menu French and West Indian, intimate evening out.

Lemon Tree ($$) Long Street, St. John's. Lively dining room in town with entertainment. Local and international food.

Miller's Dickenson Bay. Riotous beach bar at the center of the action, often a live band.

Nations ($$) Easy-going spot just outside the dockyard for local fish, local vegetables, and tropical fruit juices.

Shirley Heights Lookout ($$). High above English Harbour, a veranda with a view. Burgers and salads or West Indian dishes, best known for riotous Sunday afternoon assembly.

Montserrat

Belham Valley ($$$) (tel: 491 5553). Intimate dining on a veranda festooned with greenery. West Indian and Continental dishes. Reserve.

Blue Dolphin ($$) Parsons. Local feel, slightly chaotic dining room with cable TV, but good local fish and ground provisions.

Emerald Café ($$) Wapping. Easy-going spot set in a courtyard lost in palms and other tropical plants. Food Continental and West Indian.

Mrs Morgan's ($) St. John's. A long way to go, right to the north of the island, but reputedly the best goat water (Montserrat stew) on the island.

Nevis

Hermitage Plantation ($$$) (tel: 469 3477). Elegant, candle-lit veranda in the main house of the hotel, adventurous and delightful West Indian cuisine. Reserve.

Nisbet Plantation ($$$) (tel: 469 9325). In the charming old colonial setting of the main house, often dinner with piano accompaniment. Continental and Caribbean dishes. Reserve.

Oualie Beach Club ($$). Easy-going beachside haunt on a terrace on the north coast, looking out to St. Kitts. Salads and burgers or local fish.

Prinderella's ($$) (tel: 469 9291). Views across the Channel to St. Kitts from a pretty tropical garden veranda, local and international food.

Unella's ($$) Charlestown. An upstairs terrace above the waterfront, good local fare as well as Continental dishes.

St. Kitts

Ballahoo ($$) Basseterre. On a balcony right above the Circus in town center. Salads, snacks and bigger meals.

Golden Lemon ($$$). Exquisite local and Continental fare in the delightfully restored historic surroundings. Fine lunchtime stop, but even better at dinner.

Lighthouse ($$) On a cliff just south of town, dining with a view, sometimes dancing. Menu Caribbean and Continental.

The Patio ($$$) Frigate Bay (tel: 465 8666). Elegant restaurant set in modern villa. Continental cuisine with Caribbean dishes too.

Reserve.

Rawlins Plantation ($$$). Some of the best West Indian food in the islands, served in the charming setting of an 18th-century plantation house. Good lunchtime stop, dinner also available.

Turtle Beach Bar ($). On a beach on the southeast peninsula, overlooking Nevis. Simple salads and burgers and some local fish dishes. Good day out.

THE VIRGIN ISLANDS
THE BRITISH VIRGIN ISLANDS

Cooper Island Beach Club ($$) (VHF Channel 16). The only bar on the island, a rustic affair right above the sand where you can catch a grill and a salad with a passing sailing crowd.

Foxy's Jost van Dyke. The liveliest of a string of beach bars on Great Bay. Beer, cocktails, and simple food. Foxy occasionally sings.

Peter Island ($$$) (tel: 494 2561). Worth the short ride from Roadtown to Peter Island for top Caribbean and international cuisine after a day out on the island.

Tortola

Brandywine Bay ($$$) (tel: 495 2301). With a magnificent view of the Channel from the breezy terrace, fine Italian cuisine. Reserve.

Jolly Roger West End. Lively bar with light snacks, a short walk from customs.

Mrs. Scatliffe ($$) Cane Garden Bay (tel: 495 4556). Delectable local fare, pumpkin soup and curry goat followed by tropical fruit ice-creams.

Pusser's Store and Pub Road Town. Lively haunt, located near the ferry terminal; decorated with burnished brass and paneled walls.

Sugar Mill Restaurant ($$$) Apple Bay (tel: 495 4355). In the charming setting of a candle-lit stone building from old colonial times; extremely fine West Indian cuisine. Reserve.

Virgin Gorda

Chez Michelle ($$$) The Valley. An intimate meal, French cuisine with some

local ingredients, in a candle-lit setting.
Drake's Anchorage ($$$)
Prickly Pear Cay (tel: 494 2254). Restaurant with view, from a wicker chair, across the North Sound. Seafood and international fare.
Pirate's Pub Saba Rock, North Sound. Riotous bar on a tiny blip of rock. Popular with passing sailors. Instruments at hand for those who want to play them.
Teacher Alma ($$) The Valley. Best in local Caribbean food, modern setting.

THE U.S. VIRGIN ISLANDS
St. Croix
Blue Moon ($$$)
Frederiksted (tel: 772 2222). Deep and dark setting under the arches in an old Front Street trading building. Jazz and cajun fare, gets busy.
Dino's ($$$) Christiansted (tel: 775 8005). Cozy and welcoming restaurant with tables inside and out, on the road south out of town. Italian dishes with home-made pastas. Reserve.
Kendrick's ($$$) King Street, Christiansted (tel: 773 9199). Upstairs in the rooms of an old townhouse with wooden floors and ceilings, top international fare with *nouvelle* presentation.
Top Hat ($$$) Company Street, Christiansted (tel: 773 2346). Very pleasant restaurant in an old townhouse, menu international, notable for its Danish dishes.

St. John
Fish Trap ($$$) Cruz Bay. Fish and seafood restaurant on wooden terraces hidden by palms and banana trees.
Garden of Luscious Licks Cruz Bay. Delicious health foods and ice-creams to go.
Old Gallery ($$) Cruz Bay. Fine West Indian fare in a charming old wooden house where you can sit on the gallery (veranda).
Paradiso Restaurant ($$$) Cruz Bay. Decor worthy of a Manhattan nightclub, cocktail bar and quiet music, Italian dishes.
Shipwreck Landing ($) Coral Bay. Set above the sea surrounded by a tropical gar-

den. Simple local and international dishes.

St. Thomas
Café Normandie ($$$) Frenchtown (tel: 774 1622). Classic old Caribbean townhouse setting, intimate atmosphere, very fine French fare. Reserve.
East Coast ($$) Red Hook. Breezy wooden terrace looking out onto a tropical garden, serves ribs, wings and burgers.
Eunice's ($$$) Smith Bay. Charming setting on veranda with wicker chairs, excellent West Indian cuisine.
Fiddle leaf ($$$) Charlotte Amalie. Rarified ambience on a veranda overlooking town. *Nouvelle cuisine* with West Indian ingredients.
For the Birds ($$) Compass Point. Very lively bar (particularly on Saturdays, womens' night), set above the beach, some light food.
Virgilio's ($$$) Back Street, Charlotte Amalie (tel: 776 4920). Intimate mock-antique dining room; Italian cuisine, some tropical dishes, exotic coffees to follow. Reserve.

THE FRENCH ANTILLES
Guadeloupe
Château de Feuilles ($$$) Grande-Terre (tel: 22 19 10). Worth a trip to the far northeast of Grande-Terre, where you dine on a terrace in a profuse garden. Excellent French and local fare, followed by fruit-flavored rums. Reserve.
Chez Clara ($$) Basse-Terre (tel: 28 72 99). Pretty setting in the village of Sainte-Rose, where Clara herself serves the best in French Caribbean food. Very popular, reserve.
Chez deux Gros ($$$) Grande-Terre (tel: 84 16 20). Hidden in overgrown garden beyond Gosier. Easy-going dining room in an antique store, jazz music, menu innovative, cuisine local.
La Canne à Sucre ($$$) on the cruise-ship dock in Point-à-Pitre (tel: 82 10 19). Sumptuous dining room above the port, with some of the finest French cuisine and most inventive dishes on the island. Reserve.

La Louisiane ($$$) St-François (tel: 88 44 34). A family-run restaurant in a house swamped by tropical growth. Traditional French and French Caribbean cuisine. Reserve.
La Plantation ($$$) Bas du Fort Marina (tel: 90 84 83). Chi-chi and neat in pink, elaborately prepared French cuisine. Reserve.
Le Filibustier ($$$) outside Ste-Anne. Faintly riotous setting, decorated like a pirate lookout, which the hill may well have been. Reliable French fare—imported steaks and local fish.
Le Rocher de Malendure ($$) overlooking Pigeon Island. Covered terraces on the hillside. Fish and seafood on the menu, with the best of Caribbean vegetables. Good stop for lunch.
Victoria. One of a row of lively bars and discos in the town of Bas du Fort.

Martinique
L'Arbre à Pain ($$$) Ste-Anne (tel: 76 72 93). Townhouse with tables downstairs looking out onto the garden. Delectable French dishes with tropical additions.
La Biguine ($$$) route de la Folie, Fort-de-France (tel: 71 47 75). Set in a townhouse; dinner by candlelight upstairs, where you will find the finest French and Creole cuisine. Reserve, jacket required for dinner.
La Fontane ($$$) route de Balata, Fort-de-France (tel: 64 28 70). In the charming setting of a gingerbread house. Top French cuisine. Reserve, jacket and tie required.
Le Colibri ($$) Morne des Esses (tel: 69 91 95). A veranda with a fantastic view and some of the most adventurous French Creole food in the island, all prepared by Clothilde Palladino.
Le Lafayette ($$$) rue de la Liberté, Fort-de-France (tel: 63 24 09). Upstairs in the Lafayette hotel; pretty, intimate setting and excellent French and Creole fare.
Poi et Virginie ($$) Ste-Anne (tel: 76 76 86). Charming rus-

279

tic balcony above the waves, seafood menu with exotic variations.

Villa Créole ($$$) Anse Mitan (tel: 66 05 53). Terrace restaurant hung with plants. French Creole fare, entertainment by the host himself, who will serenade you with his guitar. Very popular; reserve.

Saint-Barthélemy

Chez Francine ($$) St-Jean. Right off the beach onto the terrace for lunch (only), which is grilled meat with salads and fries.

Cote Jardin ($$) Gustavia. On hillside in the town, Italian menu; pizzas a specialty.

Le Flamboyant ($$$) Grand Cul de Sac. Dinner on a veranda with a view, top Continental cuisine.

Le Patio ($$) St-Jean. Above the busy bay, friendly restaurant with a mixed menu, including salads and grills.

Le Pelican St-Jean. Charming tropical courtyard where you can grab a cocktail to the sound of jazz and the waves.

Marius et Fanny ($$) Gustavia. Low-key bistro just over from the waterfront. Provençal menu with local catch and vegetables.

Saint-Martin

Bar de la Mer. Cocktail bar just off the waterfront in Marigot, open all day for snacks and drinks.

Bistrot Nu ($$) on an alley in Marigot. A tiny but charming Creole house; some of the best Creole food in the island.

La Fiesta. Charmingly decorated cocktail bar in town. Live music some nights and a lively crowd.

Le Poisson d'Or ($$$) Marigot waterfront. Rarified atmosphere in an age-old stone building, with paintings for sale on the walls, delectable French cuisine.

Le Tastevin ($$$) Grand Case. On a tropical terrace, above the waves. Classic French cuisine and service.

Les Lolos ($) Grand Case. Very cheap barbecued food and beer from the roadside in the middle of town. Worth a lunchtime stop.

Maison sur le Port ($$$) Marigot waterfront. Very

pretty veranda with gingerbread trimmings, delectable French cuisine making best use of the local ingredients.

THE NETHERLANDS ANTILLES
Aruba

Bon Appetit ($$$) Palm Beach (tel: 25241). Brightly decorated dining room to go with Continental and Dutch Antillean dishes. Reserve.

Gasparito ($$) Gasparito 3 (tel: 37044). The best in Dutch Antillean food in a traditional old Aruban country house, behind Palm Beach.

Old Cunucu House ($$$). Just behind Palm Beach, a traditional Aruban house where you can dine on seafood and local dishes as well as Continental fare.

Papiamento ($$$) Washington 61 (tel: 24544). The best Aruban cuisine in the best setting, a country house where tables are inside or by the pool. A delightful experience. Reserve.

Bonaire

Bistro des Amis ($$$) (tel: 78003). Top-class but also adventurous French cuisine in an air-conditioned dining room in town.

Raffles Kralendijk waterfront. Friendly bar, at the upturned boat hull, and restaurant serving fish and seafood.

Rendez-vous ($$$) (tel: 8454). Charming restaurant set in a modern townhouse, where you dine on the veranda or inside. Continental dishes, with some local cuisine.

Richard's ($$$). Easy-going but pleasant spot on a seafront terrace in the south of the town. Locals stop over at the bar after work. Fine local cuisine.

Curaçao

Chez Suzenne ($$) (tel: 688545). Excellent local cuisine cooked by Suzenne herslf in her low-lit dining room.

De Taveerne ($$$) Salinja (tel: 370669). Intimate atmosphere in the low-lit cellar of an old estate house. Menu Continental, using the best of local fish and vegetables.

Fort Nassau ($$$) near Juliana Bridge (tel: 613086).

Stupendous setting above the lights of Willemstad (and the refinery). New World cuisine, delectably prepared.

Fort Waakzamheid ($$) off highway, Otrobanda (tel: 623633). Open-air setting in an old fortress high on a hill in the west of Willemstad. Cocktails or a beer and grilled food.

Golden Star ($$) Dr. Maalweg (tel: 612746). Low lit, cold and over-decorated dining room, but the finest West Indian food in town.

Plaza Biejo ($) next to the market building in town. A refectory for the workers of Willemstad. Vats of *sopi, toetoe, funchi*. Simply point at something that looks good. Lunchtime only.

Rum Runners ($$) St. Annabaai waterfront, Otrabanda side. Hip, lively cocktail bar and restaurant.

Saba

Brigadoon ($$) Windwardside. Local and some Chinese dishes in one of Saba's fine old buildings.

Chinese Restaurant ($$) Windwardside. Modern house high on the hill with a long list of Chinese dishes to eat in or take out.

Guido's Pizzeria ($) Windwardside. Pizzas and pasta at the top of the hill.

Scout's Place ($$) Windwardside. Drinks with a view, wholesome and hearty portions of Caribbean food, and some entertainment.

St. Eustatius

Kingswell Inn ($) between Upper and Lower Town. Breezy veranda on the hillside, Austrian and steaks.

La Maison sur la Plage ($$) Zeelandia Bay. Fine French fare, using the best local ingredients, set in a bamboo-covered courtyard on the eastern side of the island.

Mooshay Publick House ($$$). Historic setting in the bar and dining room of the Old Gin House hotel. Excellent Continental menu.

Stone Oven ($). Good Caribbean food—curry goat and fried fish—in a small townhouse with neat wooden tables.

Sint Maarten

Antoine's ($$$) Front St. (tel: 22964). On terrace above the waves of Great Bay, candle-lit tables, international menu with delicious French dishes.
Da Livio ($$$) Front St. (tel: 22960). Delectable Italian fare on a waterfront terrace in Philipsburg. Very popular.
Le Perroquet ($$$) Simpson Bay (tel: 44339). In a pretty house overlooking a tropical garden, menu French with some very exotic extras like lion and ostrich.
Spartaco ($$$) Cole Bay (tel: 45379). In an old estate house, with guardian lions, very fine Italian cuisine, many of the ingredients brought from there.
Wajang Doll ($$$) Front Street. Set in a charming and neat old townhouse and garden, Indonesian food.

OTHER CARIBBEAN STATES

JAMAICA

Restaurants add a General Consumption tax of 10 percent to all bills.

Black River, Blue Mountains

Bill Laurie's Steak House ($$) Mandeville. Steaks and local fare in a classic old Jamaican house, bar crowded with car license plates.
Blue Mountain Inn ($$$) Gordon Town (tel: 927 7400). Old plantation house setting, very fine fare of Creole dishes as well as international classics. Reserve.
Ivor Lodge ($$) Jack's Hill (tel: 977 0033). Wonderful view over Kingston and West Indian cuisine in a restored country house. Intimate; reserve.
The Restaurant ($$$) Temple Hall (tel: 942 4430). Exotic Jamaican *nouvelle cuisine* in a splendid old colonial setting in the mountains. Good wine list. Reserve.

Kingston

Chelsea Jerk Centre ($) Chelsea Avenue. Very local; pork and chicken jerked meat; watch the hot pepper sauce.
Grog Shoppe ($$) Devon House. Cocktails and Caribbean dishes under a mango tree in the historic grounds of Devon House.
Heather's ($$) Haining Road. Courtyard pub with chairs and tables under a mango tree, popular with expats.
Indies Pub ($$) Holborn Road. Popular pub with garden in New Kingston with a crowd of locals and visitors.
Minnie's Herbal Healthfood Restaurant ($) Hope Road. Exotic Ethiopian and Jamaican recipes in a wooden and palm thatch cabin.
Norma's ($$$) 8 Belmont Road (tel: 929 4966). Top cuisine in veranda setting. Innovative menu using local ingredients. Lunch daily, dinner Thursday and Friday; reserve.
Pepper's ($) Upper Waterloo Road. Cool hangout, popular with young Kingstonians. Snacks and music.

Montego Bay

Georgian House ($$$) Orange Street (tel: 952 0632). Old colonial ambience in a magnificent restored townhouse. Continental fare; reserve.
Glistening Waters ($$) Rock (east of town). Fish and other local and international dishes on a terrace above the lagoon, where the phosphorescent waters glisten.
Marguerite's ($$) Gloucester Avenue. Terrace on the sea and under the stars, for cocktails and light meals.
Norma's ($$$) Reading (tel: 979 2745). Stunning waterfront setting opposite the town, very fine Caribbean cuisine. Reserve.
Pork Pit ($) Gloucester Avenue. Take-out or sit at the garden benches, pork, chicken, fish, and spare ribs with coconut milk or beer.
Town House ($$$) Church Street (tel: 952 2660). Refined old colonial ambience to go with international and local dishes. Reserve.

Negril

Cosmo's ($$) on the beach. Local seafood dishes with bammy and local juices or beer. Great setting, well placed for an after-lunch dip.
Hungry Lion ($$) on the cliffs. Great garden setting for natural foods and juices. Hip, popular spot; get there early or be prepared to wait.
Paradise Yard ($) inland from the rotary. Classic rustic setting on a terrace under palms, local Jamaican fare.
Rick's ($$) on the cliffs. Ever popular and over-crowded, when the masses pour in to watch the sunset and jump off into the sea.

Ocho Rios

Almond Tree ($$$) Hibiscus Lodge Hotel. Fine setting on the cliffs with floodlit greenery around; local cuisine.
Carib Inn ($$$) on Main Street. Elegant seafood restaurant, dining on a veranda looking onto a floodlit tropical garden.
Double V Jerk Centre ($) Main Street heading east. A wooden cabin in a tropical garden, good stopover for jerk and a Red Stripe.
Evita's ($$$) Eden Bower Rd (tel: 974 2333). Fantastic old Caribbean gingerbread setting on the hillside. Adventurous local dishes, plus plenty of pasta. Reserve.
The Mug ($$) Runaway Bay. Waterfront bar west of town, popular with locals, some light meals.
The Ruins ($$) da Costa Drive (tel: 974 2442). Boardwalk setting beneath pretty floodlit waterfall. International dishes; gets crowded.

Port Antonio

Admiralty Club ($$$) Navy Island. Charming setting on a comfortable wooden terrace standing above the bay. International and local fare.
Boston Bay ($). A few miles east of the town, the home of jerk, where pork, chicken, sausages, and even fish are jerked. Best between noon and 3 p.m.
Daddy D's ($) West St. Best local fare, chicken and fish, in a typical West Indian setting.
Trident Villas ($$$) (tel: 993 2602). Very elegant setting of a colonial-style veranda, top local cuisine. Reserve.

THE CAYMAN ISLANDS

Almond Tree ($$$) (tel: 459 2893). South Sea decor in a floodlit tropical garden.

281

HOTELS AND RESTAURANTS

Strong on seafood. Reserve.
Apollo 11 North Sound. Very cool waterfront bar in an old shed. Live music and plenty of drinking.
Cook Rum ($$$) (tel: 949 8670). Pretty West Indian house and reliable West Indian fare—lobster, conch, turtle, and pepperpot.
Cracked Conch ($$) Selkirk Plaza. Very lively bar and restaurant, where conch is served cracked (beaten to tenderness) along with other fish. Live music.
Crows Nest ($$). Right on the waterfront just north of George Town, great sunset views and superb local fare.
Grand Old House ($$$) Church Street (tel: 949 9333). In a charming old colonial house, Chef Tell of TV fame serves his excellent Continental dishes as well as few local ones. Reserve.
Periwinkle ($$$) West Bay Road (tel: 947 5181). Pink decor, intimate air, and European menu, with local fish and vegetables.
Ristorante Pappagallo ($$$) Spanish Cove (tel: 949 1119). Huge palm-thatched, air-conditoned cabana set on an isolated lagoon. Northern Italian menu. Reserve.

CUBA
Havana
Bodeguita del Medio ($$) Calle Empredado, colonial city. Bohemian hangout with quick service, simple Cuban dishes. They will lend you a pen to add to the graffiti.
Coppelia, La Rampa, Vedado. Havana's ice-cream parlor. Long lines, but worth it.
Don Giovanni ($$) Calle Tacon, colonial city. Pizzas and simple Italian dishes in an old colonial house.
El Patio ($$) Cathedral Square, colonial city. Charming setting under the arches. Café downstairs on the cobbles, meals upstairs.
Floridita ($$$) Calle Montserrate. A favorite of Hemingway's, famed for its daiquiris (worth going just for them). Elegant if ritzy dining room, fine cuisine.
Hemingway Marina, west of the city. Restaurant and marina complex, popular with

foreigners, particularly for the lively disco.
La Cecilia ($$$) 5th Avenue, Miramar. Top Cuban cuisine in an attractive townhouse.
La Divina Pastora ($$$) Morro castle in Casablanca. Just beneath the Havana lighthouse; seafood menu.
Tropicana, southwest Havana (tel: 66224). Once world-famous nightclub still stages mesmeric cabarets. Reserve.
Turquino Bar, Havana Libre, Vedado. Bar with a superb view all over town, excellent at sunset.
1830 ($$$) Malecon, Vedado. Set in a pretty colonial palace on the waterfront with tables inside and on the veranda. International cuisine.

Outside Havana
El Meson de Quijote ($$) Varadero. Set in open grounds far down the peninsula; Spanish menu.
Las Americas ($$$) Varadero. Once a private home on the waterfront, now serving international dishes; fine views.
Los Jazmines ($) Viñales. Magnificent setting high in an old villa above the valley. Local Cuban cuisine.
Mi Casita ($) Varadero (tel: 3787). Charming coral stone house just behind the beach. Fine Caribbean fare.
Taberna de Dolores ($$) Calle Aguilera, Santiago de Cuba (tel: 23913). Lively restaurant with local dishes such as rice and peas Cuban style.
1900 ($$) Calle San Basilio, Santiago de Cuba (tel: 23507). Charming old town-house; local Cuban food.

HAITI
Ananda ($) Place d'Italie, Port-au-Prince. Lunch only; soup, salad, and fresh fruit juices.
Champs de Mars ($) Port-au-Prince. Stalls selling barbecued chicken and beer.
Chez Gerard ($$$) Pétionville (tel: 571949). Charming tropical garden setting, very fine French and kreyol cuisine.
La Belle Epoque ($$) rue Gregoire, Pétionville. Covered veranda and courtyard setting, menu French and kreyol.

THE DOMINICAN REPUBLIC
Altos de Chavon
Café del Sol ($$). Pizzas, pasta, and salads on an open-air terrace lost in tropical greenery.
Casa de Rio ($$$). Fantastic setting above floodlit river, a mix of Caribbean and international dishes, exquisitely prepared and presented.

Puerto Plata and the Amber Coast
Café Atlantico ($$) Sosua. Superb, breezy setting above Sosua bay, excellent seafood combinations; catch of the day and paella specialties.
De Armando ($$$) Calle Separacion, Puerto Plata (tel: 586 3418). Very neat, air-conditioned townhouse dressed up in pink for an intimate meal. Fine international and Dominican cuisine. Reserve.
Kao Ba Cabarete. The coolest tropical garden bar on the island.
Leandros ($) Cabarete. Local dishes in a lively palm-thatch dining room.
Lucimar ($$) Cabarete. Excellent beachfront setting under palms, seafood menu.
Pavillon ($$) Sosua. Lively haunt in an imitation Arawak thatched *bohio*. Simple menu with steaks and seafood.
Valther's ($$) Calle Hermanas Mirabal. Dinner on the veranda of a charming wooden Caribbean house, lost in greenery; international menu with Caribbean ingredients.

Samana
Chez François ($$). Mock-colonial setting just off the beach, Caribbean cuisine.
El Rincon ($$). Great bar with wooden floors and thatched roof above the waves. French menu.
Jikaco ($$). Fine French menu and Caribbean ingredients in delightful Dominican garden lit by flaming torches.

Santo Domingo
Don Pepe ($$$) Calle Santiago (tel: 689 7612). Very plush setting in a suburban house. Huge menu, Spanish and Dominican dishes.
Drake's Pub, La Atarazana. Rumbustious bar in walls of

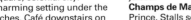

the city's oldest area.
El Conuco ($$) Calle Casimiro de Moya. Riotous restaurant with decorations from the *conuco* (country). Waiters who sing to you periodically. Country food too, but made easy for the urban palate.
Independencia ($) just off Parque Independencia. Some of the best local food around, slightly chaotic service but a good Dominican experience all in all.
Vesuvio ($$$) on the Malecon (tel: 221 3333). Big, very popular restaurant. Top Italian and Dominican fare, using the best of the seafood and local vegetables.

PUERTO RICO
San German and the Southwest
El Bohio ($$) Playa Joyuda. A seafood restaurant on a breezy deck above the waves. Unpretentious but the best of local fish.
Perichi's ($$) Playa Joyuda. A *meson gastronomico*, fine local and international food in an air-conditioned lounge.
Ruicof ($$) Boqueron. A waterfront deck in sight of the famous beach, simple but tasty local fish and some Dominican dishes.

Ponce
El Ancla ($$$) Playa de Ponce. Out of the city center, an air-conditioned lounge, menu mainly seafood with copious local vegetables.

San Juan
Amadeus ($$) Calle San Sebastian. Stylish restaurant serving Italian food, near the lively bars of Plaza San Jose.
La Bombonera ($$) Calle San Francisco. Very local, very lively snack bar and simple restaurant in the heart of the city. Just a drink with the newspaper or a full meal.
La Casita Blanca ($$) eastern outskirts of the city. Small but very lively restaurant specializing in Puerto Rican food, and lots of it. Charming setting, amusing waiters.
La Mallorquina ($$$) Calle San Justo. Set in a century-old house, still with its antique furnishings. Brisk

service, good local food.
Torreblanca ($$$) Calle Magdalena, Condado. Plush Spanish-style villa, mainly Spanish cuisine but with some Caribbean dishes.
Zaragozana ($$$) Calle San Francisco. Elegant old-colonial setting with antique furniture and paneled walls, top Caribbean and international cuisine.

BARBADOS
Atlantis ($$) Bathsheba. The hotel itself is clearly past its prime, but the setting on the clifftops and the food, a West Indian buffet, is still superb.
Bagatelle Great House ($$$) (tel: 421 6767). Colonial elegance on gallery of old plantation house in the country, fine Continental fare. Jacket and tie required; reserve.
Baxter's Rd ($). Open all night. Battered fish, a beer and a chat.
Carambola ($$$) (tel: 432 0832). Superb setting on the cliffs on the west coast, delectable Caribbean and Continental cuisine.
David's Place ($$) Main Road, Worthing (tel: 435 6550). Breezy setting above pretty St. Lawrence Bay, excellent Bajan food, followed by delicious desserts.
Fathoms ($$) Payne's Bay (tel: 432 2568). Fine position on the cliffs for candle-lit dinner, good seafood and fish.
Ile de France ($$$) Hastings (tel: 435 6869). A lively crowd collects here for the pleasant atmosphere and the classical French cuisine.
La Cage aux Folles ($$$) (tel: 424 2424). A charming townhouse with louvered windows and wooden floors, exquisite dishes from around the world. Jacket and tie required, reserve.
Pisces ($$) (tel: 435 6564). Charming setting on a trellis-lined veranda above St. Lawrence Bay. Mainly seafood and fish, some other dishes.
Ship Inn St. Lawrence Gap. One of a number of very lively bars in St. Lawrence Gap.
Shirleys ($$) Speightstown. Terrace setting above the waves, the best in local food cooked by Shirley herself, formerly of the Sandy Lane.

TRINIDAD AND TOBAGO
Trinidad
The Breakfast Shed ($) Waterfront, Port of Spain. Refectory-style dining room with vast pots and pans bubbling away, fine local fare.
Il Giardino ($$$) Nook Avenue, St. Ann's. Overgrown tropical garden of a dining room, Italian menu, pasta specialties.
Moon Over Bourbon Street ($$) West Mall. A delightful cocktail bar and rooftop restaurant out of town, decked up like a transatlantic liner. Some entertainment.
Pelican Pub St. Ann's. Busy bar below Hilton Hotel, lively on Thursday and Sunday.
Rafters ($$) Warner Street. Hip video bar and restaurant in an old warehouse.
Seabelle ($$$) Mucurapo Road (tel: 622 3594). Hidden away in a modern house in a western suburb; fine seafood restaurant. Small, so reserve.
Tiki Village ($$) Kapok Hotel (622 6441). Brisk and busy restaurant on top floor, Polynesian and Chinese menu.
Veni Mange ($$) 13 Lucknow Street, St. James. Very popular lunchtime (only) haunt. Delicious, innovative West Indian cuisine.
Wazo Deyzeel ($$) Carib Way, St. Ann's. Hip local bar and restaurant above the town, parrot mobiles, lively crowd, Caribbean music.

Tobago
Black Rock Café ($$$). Veranda painted pink with white louvers, Creole dishes with salads and steaks.
Blue Crab ($$) Scarborough. Simple townhouse veranda with tropical plants; the best in local food, catch of the day and Caribbean vegetables.
Old Donkey Cart House ($$$) just out of Scarborough. Charming floodlit garden and pretty house, good local and international fare.
Rouselle's ($$) Scarborough. Upstairs lounge bar with tables where you get good local food.
Store Bay ($). Local take-out meals, curry goat, crab and dumpling, and local fruit juices.

283

Index

INDEX

INDEX

Picture credits

The Automobile Association would like to thank the following for their assistance in the preparation of this book:
ALLSPORT UK LTD: 219a Cricket. **BRIDGEMAN ART LIBRARY**: 178–9 *Voodoo Dance* by Jean Pierre; 178 *Voodoo ceremony around a tree* by Valcin. **S CAMPBELL**: 162 Sunrise at Brac Reef; 163 Totem pole; 164 Swimming with stingrays; 165 Straw-weaver. **MARY EVANS PICTURE LIBRARY**: 25 Raiding cattle ranches; 28–9a Columbus's fleet 1492; 28 Columbus lands San Salvador; 29 Columbus; 30–1 Drake attacks Spanish; 30 Pirates; 31 Buccaneer; 32–3a Slaves working; 32 Slaves dancing; 33 Slave in chains; 34–5 Treadmill; 35 Sugar mill; 36–7 Emancipation parade; 36 Emancipation; 37 Burke in House of Commons; 43b Spaniards and Caribs; 100b Blackbeard; 101 Spaniards loading ship. **J HENDERSON**: 9 Barbados; 10a St. Vincent; 12–13 Children; 15b Oranjestad, Aruba; 16–17a Church, Trinidad; 18–9a Poster; 27 Arawak carvings; 40 Calabas Hotel; 49 St. Georges; 50a Market, St. Georges; 52 Maurice Bishop, St. Georges; 53 Admiralty Harbour; 68 Man; 70 Boat; 76 Barbuda; 83 Nevis; 83 Old windmill; 91b Bombas, Tortola; 96 Jost van Dyke; 98 Frederiksted, St. Croix; 103 Legislature, Charlotte Amalie; 112a Guadaloupe cemetery; 113a Boats; 113b Deshaires; 120 Islands; 121a Airport, St. Barts; 121b Club La Banane; 124a Aruba; 124b Bolatabla, Curaçao; 125–6 Sailing ship; 125 Saba; 126 Craft stall; 128–9 Oranjestad, Aruba; 129a Windmill; 129b Jet ski; 130, 131 Salt stacks, Bonaire; 134–5 Handelsgade, Willemstad; 134a b Floating market; 135 Fisherman; 136 House; 137a Windwardside, Saba; 137b Flags; 137c sign; 138 Sint Eustatius; 139a Sign; 139b Children; 140 Car; 141a St. Georges; 143c Breadfruit; 166 Car; 167 Main Square, Trinidad, Cuba; 168 Poster; 169a Santa Clara; 169b House, Cuba; 170a Old Havana; 170b Cathedral, Old Havana; 173 Cien Fuegos; 175 Port-au-Prince; 176 Tap-tap; 177 Fishermen; 180–1 Dessalines barracks; 181a Sans-Souci Palace; 181b Man; 183 Carvings; 186 Windsurfers; 187 Hotel Sousa; 189 Palm fronds; 190 Boats; 191 Sugar mill; 192 Children; 193a Columbus lighthouse; 193b Columbus Palace; 197b Festival of the Innocents; 198 Hacienda Gripinas; 210 Fire station, Ponce; 203 Sunset, Puerto Rico; 206 Croton; 210a Casa del Frances, Vieques; 211 Limers Bar, Esperanza; 215a Bridgetown Harbour; 215b Sombaero; 219b Baseball; 228 Canon, Trinidad; 234b Carnival, St. Lucia; 236 Shack; 238b Calypso singer. **IMAGES COLOUR LIBRARY**: 179 Mask. **IMAGES DES ANTILLES**: 109 Course de Yoles; 155 Images des Antilles. **INTERNATIONAL PHOTOBANK**: 20a Ocho Rios market; 24 drinks; 45b Dunn's River Falls; 47, 50b St. George's Saturday Market; 58b Woman and bananas; 80–1 Steel band; 155 Straw market, Montego Bay; 159 Beach, Ocho Rios; 160 Port Antonio; 206–7 Royal Poinciana tree; 233 Tobago steel band. **NATURE PHOTOGRAPHERS LTD**: 74–5 Orange clown fish, Queen Angel fish (S C Bisserot); 116a Scarlet Ibis (P R Sterry); 117 Iguana (E A Janes); 230a Green turtle (D A Smith); 230b Loggerhead turtle (J Sutherland). **PARIA PUBLISHING CO LTD**: 61a The Soucouyant; 61b Mama Dio; 61c Pappa Bois. **PICTURES COLOUR LIBRARY LTD**: Cover Carnival, Port of Spain, Trinidad. **REX FEATURES LTD**: 152a,c Shabba Ranks; 152b Shaggy; 156a,b Bob Marley. **ROYAL GEOGRAPHICAL SOCIETY**: 25 Map. **SPECTRUM COLOUR LIBRARY**: 6 Bequia; 22–3a Buffet; 38 Nightlife; 81 Musician; 95a Faune Sous Marine; 111 Rainforest; 131 Kralendick Town, Bonaire; 133 Curaçao; 162 Drinks; 171 Tropicana cabaret, Havana; 184 Mexican night; 188 Restaurant, Puerto Rico; 189 Palm-fringed beach; 200 Shell; 234–5 Carnival; 238a Nightlife. **THE MANSELL COLLECTION LTD**: 26 Indians sowing maize. **ZEFA PICTURE LIBRARY (UK) LTD**: 200a Coral.

All remaining pictures are held in the Association's own library (**AA PHOTO LIBRARY**) with contributions from:
P BAKER: Spine; 3; 4; 7; 11; 13b; 14–5; 16b; 19; 20b; 21; 41; 42; 43a; 44; 48a,b; 51; 54a,b; 55; 56; 57; 58a; 59; 60; 62–3a; 62b; 63; 64; 65; 66; 67; 68–9; 71; 72; 73; 77; 78a,b; 79; 80; 84; 85a,b; 86; 87a,b; 90; 91a; 92a,b; 93; 94a,b; 96–7; 99; 102; 105; 106a,b; 107; 108; 109a,b; 110a,b; 111b,c; 112b; 114; 115a,b; 118; 119a,b; 122; 123a,b,c; 140; 141a,b; 142a,b; 143a,b; 144–5; 161a,b; 191a; 194; 196; 197a; 199a,b; 202; 204a,b; 207; 208; 209b; 210b; 213; 214; 216; 217; 218; 220; 221a; 222; 23; 226a,b; 227; 229; 231; 232; 269. **R HOLMES**: 100–1. **S & O MATHEWS**: 77. **A SOUTER**: 209a. **R VICTOR**: 5a,b; 10b; 12; 23b; 45a; 88; 95b; 116b; 146; 149a,b; 150; 151a,b; 153; 154; 157; 158; 161c; 239.

Acknowledgments

The Automobile Association would also like to thank the Sandridge Beach Hotel, Barbados, and the Ocean View Hotel, Barbados for their assistance in the making of this book.

Contributors

Series advisor: Ingrid Morgan   **Designer**: celsius design
Joint series editor: Susi Bailey   **Indexer**: Marie Lorimer
Copy editor: Nia Williams